INTERNATIONAL LAW STUDIES

Volume 82

The Law of War in the 21st Century: Weaponry and the Use of Force

Anthony M. Helm
Editor

Naval War College
Newport, Rhode Island
2006

INTERNATIONAL LAW STUDIES

Volume 82

Library of Congress Cataloging-in-Publication Data

The law of war in the 21st century : weaponry and the use of force / Anthony M. Helm, editor.

p. cm. -- (International law studies ; v. 82)

Includes index.

ISBN-13: 978-1-884733-40-6 (hard cover)

ISBN-10: 1-884733-40-9 (hard cover)

1. War (International law) I. Helm, Anthony M.

KZ6385.L385 2006

341.6--dc22

2006102080

Table of Contents

The Law of War in the 21st Century: Weaponry and the Use of Force

Foreword

The International Law Studies (the "Blue Book") series was inaugurated by the Naval War College in 1901 as a forum for essays, treatises, and articles that promote a broader understanding of international law. The eighty-second volume of this historic series, *The Law of War in the 21st Century: Weaponry and the Use of Force*, is a compilation of scholarly papers derived from the proceedings of a June 2005 colloquium hosted by the Naval War College.

The purpose of this colloquium was to examine international legal standards applicable to the use of force, as well as the development and employment of weapons systems in the 21st century. Participants came to Newport from more than 20 countries and included government officials, military commanders, representatives of nongovernmental organizations, esteemed international law scholars, and military and civilian lawyers. During the course of events, attendees grappled with vexing issues such as the suitability of principles developed for inter-State conflict to a global threat environment increasingly influenced by non-State actors. Undoubtedly, the ideas generated during the summer colloquium and revisited in this Blue Book volume will contribute substantially to the ongoing examination of the major legal challenges accompanying 21st-century armed conflict.

On behalf of the Secretary of the Navy, the Chief of Naval Operations, and the Commandant of the Marine Corps, I extend a warm thank you to Professor Charles Garraway, the 2004–2005 Stockton Professor of International Law, and Major Richard Jaques, USMC, under whose leadership this colloquium was organized. I also wish to thank the authors and editors for their invaluable contributions and for engendering a greater understanding of international law. Thanks also to the Lieber Society of the American Society of International Law and Roger Williams University's Ralph R. Papitto School of Law, gracious cosponsors of this colloquium. And, finally, a very special note of gratitude goes to the Naval War College Foundation and Israel Yearbook on Human Rights, whose tremendous support made this conference and, particularly, this "Blue Book" possible.

JACOB L. SHUFORD
Rear Admiral, U.S. Navy
President, Naval War College

Introduction

The Naval War College hosts an annual conference to examine international law issues and developments that affect military operations, both in peacetime and during armed conflict. The 2001 conference examined the *Legal and Ethical Lessons of NATO's Kosovo Campaign*. In 2002, following the tragic events of 9/11, we looked at *International Law and the War on Terror*. In 2003, a broad spectrum of issues were analyzed in *Current Issues in International Law and Military Operations*, including, of course, a discussion of the initial events of Operation Iraqi Freedom, which had begun on March 20th of that year. In 2004 the work of the 2002 conference was continued in *Homeland Security & Combating Terrorism*.

By 2005, we determined that it was time to examine the manner in which rapid advances in the types and capabilities of weapons and the methods of warfare were changing how warfare will be conducted in the future, and the implications of that change for the law of armed conflict. The conference began with a discussion of the International Committee of the Red Cross's then just published *Customary International Humanitarian Law* study (hereinafter the Study). We were fortunate enough to have Jean-Marie Henckaerts, one of the authors, present an overview of the Study, which purports to be a "restatement of contemporary customary international law." A panel of equally distinguished scholars and government and military lawyers questioned both the methodology of the Study and certain of its conclusions, while acknowledging it was an indispensable resource. The scholarly articles contributed to this volume by Mr. Henckaerts and the panelists provide valuable insight into the Study.

Another important development is that participation by the United States in future conflicts is likely to be as one member of a coalition of nations, as was the case in Operations Allied Force, Desert Storm, Enduring Freedom, and Iraqi Freedom. The panel on coalition warfare addressed the implications and challenges of bringing together warfighters whose nations may have differing views on the content of customary law and are parties to different treaties.

Immediately following the conclusion of the conference, a Conference Summary was prepared and distributed to the participants. This excellent review summarized the remarks of the speakers and the discussion that followed. It has been incorporated into the Preface. I encourage you to read it.

The conference was cosponsored by the Lieber Society on the Law of Armed Conflict of the American Society of International Law and was organized under the leadership of Professor Charles Garraway, the Naval War College's Charles H. Stockton Professor of International Law, and Major Richard Jaques, US Marine Corps, of the International Law Department. It was made possible with the support of the Naval War College Foundation and the Israel Yearbook on Human Rights. Without the dedicated efforts and support and assistance of these individuals and organizations, neither the conference nor this volume would have been possible.

I would particularly like to recognize and express my appreciation to Rear Admiral Joseph Strasser, Executive Director of the Naval War College Foundation, for the continuing contributions of the Foundation to our annual conferences and the publication of the "Blue Book" series that reflect the proceedings of those conferences. On the eve of Admiral Strasser's retirement as Executive Director of the Foundation, we extend to him our profound thanks, both for the Foundation's contributions and his own personal support of the International Law Department.

I also would like to extend my sincere thanks and gratitude to editors *extraordinaire*, Captains Jack Grunawalt and Ralph Thomas, USN JAGC (Ret.). Responsible for the "nuts and bolts" editing of these outstanding papers, Jack and Ralph devoted myriad hours to this project, assuring painstakingly and skillfully that this work would be the best-ever *International Law Studies* volume. Colonel Tony Helm, JAGC, US Army, Deputy Chairman, International Law Department, served as managing editor of this volume. His dedication and perseverance in communicating with contributing authors throughout the world, marshaling authors' papers, packaging the volume, and overseeing the complex publishing and distribution process also are deserving of special thanks. In short, this Department is truly indebted to these three professionals who worked so diligently to bring this Blue Book to its readers.

For over one hundred years the United States Naval War College has committed itself to combining a scholarly understanding of the laws of war with an appreciation for and insight into the perspective of the warfighter—the one who must apply those laws in the crucible of conflict on land, at sea and in the air. This conference and this "Blue Book" continue that tradition.

DENNIS L. MANDSAGER
Professor of Law & Chairman
International Law Department

Preface

While planning this volume of the International Law Studies series, we concluded that an excellent conference summary prepared painstakingly by Captains Timothy Flynn and Stephen Sarnoski, both reserve officers in the Navy Judge Advocate General's Corps, would be a fitting preface for this book. Major Richard Jaques, USMC, who was the 2005 conference coordinator for the International Law Department, also played a key role in this compilation.

Thus, we offer the following edited summary as both a snapshot of the 2005 International Law Conference and an appropriate retrospective context from which the works in this volume flow. Of course, at the first mention of editing, it is fitting to thank and praise those who breathed life into this volume—Professor Emeritus and Captain Jack Grunawalt and Captain Ralph Thomas, both retired Navy Judge Advocates and long-time supporters of the International Law Department. Indeed, they made tidying up the text and scouring the footnotes of the authors' papers look easy, and it was plain to us from the start that they love their work just as much as we truly enjoy and love having them work side-by-side with us in the Department. I can think of no one else I'd rather entrust my own writings to than Jack and Ralph. They know the law, understand the dynamics of the annual conference, and have internalized the protocols and nuances of the legal writer's bible we refer to respectfully as "the other Bluebook." Indeed, but for their genuine sense of modesty, their names unquestionably should grace the spine of this volume of the *International Law Studies* series. Gentlemen . . . Bravo Zulu—well done. A hearty thank-you is also in order for several key members of the Naval War College Desktop Publishing Office. As Jack and Ralph brought this volume to life, Ms. Susan Meyer was personally responsible for its care and feeding—formatting, providing "camera-ready" copy, and otherwise completely packaging the volume for publication. It would be hard to find a more responsive, thorough, and dedicated professional than Ms. Meyer. Likewise, Ms. Meyer's boss, Mr. Jeremiah Lenihan, was instrumental in resolving ticklish formatting matters, and two superb proofreaders, Ms. Susan Farley and Ms. Angela Daughtry, whose eagle eyes caught every figurative uncrossed "t" and undotted "i," also were indispensable Blue Book contributors. Again, thanks to all at Desktop Publishing for helping deliver such a quality project to our distinguished readers.

Introduction

As alluded to above, as time passed and the dust of conference past settled, we believed it would be useful to recount salient themes and highlights—not just for historic value but as a basis for understanding and appreciating the fine works of this volume's contributors. For example, during the 2005 Conference, *The Law of War in the 21st Century: Weaponry and the Use of Force*, participants debated energetically the measure of importance and authority to be accorded the recently published International Committee of the Red Cross (ICRC) *Customary International Humanitarian Law* study. Attendees and panelists also pointed out the need for careful and timely legal review of weapons development programs to ensure their by-products ultimately would pass legal muster under international law. Another recurring general theme—undoubtedly a truism—was that the realities of today's substantially asymmetrical conflicts raise unique international law issues that demand serious examination. Participants also emphasized the importance of coalitions and stressed the need for a common methodology for conducting combined operations, particularly with regard to rules of engagement (ROE) and detainee treatment. Finally, the colloquium wrestled with an array of challenges emanating from technological advances that will affect future navies and require careful discussion and analysis today.

Keynote Address

In his keynote address, Professor David Kennedy observed initially that the aspirations of international humanitarian law proponents and the goals of those who practice the military arts are inextricably intertwined. He observed that evolving principles of the law of armed conflict have engendered an alliance between military and civilian practitioners and between warriors and their lawyers. Recognizing that conflict presents more than a set of easily recognizable legal problems, Professor Kennedy addressed the future of international humanitarian law by challenging the colloquium to answer several incisive questions. Do law of war principles differ depending upon the nature of a conflict? Does it matter whether the survival of a nation is at stake or a coalition of nations is simply enforcing a United Nations mandate to preserve or restore peace following a low-intensity conflict? If conflict presents something more than a complex set of legal problems resolved by application of a discrete set of principles and procedures, does application of the modern law of armed conflict also require moral judgments using a broader interpretive framework? Professor Kennedy concluded by inviting the conference attendees to answer these and other questions, recognizing that "[l]aw doesn't provide the answers . . . we do."

Conference Panel I—Defining Customary International Humanitarian Law

Following Dr. Kennedy's presentation, Conference Panel I opened with a stimulating debate about the efficacy of the ICRC *Customary International Humanitarian Law* study. Mr. Jean-Marie Henckaerts, ICRC legal adviser and co-author of the study, explained that the study was commissioned in 1995 by the 26th International Conference of the Red Cross and the Red Crescent in Geneva, Switzerland. During the course of the study, members consulted extensively with 35 law of armed conflict experts, reviewed the practices of 47 States, and delved into ICRC archives covering more than 40 international and non-international armed conflicts. Study members adopted an inductive reasoning process, reviewing State practices and producing 161 rules, most of which address both international and non-international conflicts. Mr. Henckaerts also explained the principal reasons for embarking on a study aimed at defining principles reflective of customary international law: international humanitarian law treaties bind only those States that ratify them, and parties to the same conflict may be bound by different treaty obligations; treaties governing non-international armed conflict are not always well developed; and characterizing a conflict is required before determining which treaties or protocols apply. In fact, Mr. Henckaerts emphasized that while certain aspects of international humanitarian law exist in treaties, not all States are parties to such treaties and not all elements of international humanitarian law are codified in such treaties. Likewise, according to Mr. Henckaerts, not all current treaties reflect a normative framework for non-international conflicts.

Professor Tim McCormack, the Australian Red Cross Professor of International Humanitarian Law at Melbourne University and the Director of the Asia-Pacific Centre for Military Law in Australia, characterized the ICRC study as an invaluable primary source of information on the practice of States in international humanitarian law. He asserted, however, that criticism of the study was inevitable because any attempt to identify the content of customary international law is invariably controversial and because the authors of the study have relied on official documents which in some cases were drafted and tabled with no thought to their status as examples of State practice.

Mr. Joshua Dorosin, Assistant Legal Adviser for Political-Military Affairs in the U.S. State Department Office of the Legal Adviser, noted the ICRC study is an indispensable resource, but he also expressed concern over the methodology of formulating the rules in the study. In his view, the rules are not adequately analyzed and do not reflect a separate consideration of State practice versus opinio juris. Indeed, in some parts of the study, there are very few references to State practice.

Former Charles H. Stockton Professor of International Law, Professor Yoram Dinstein from Tel Aviv University expressed grave concern over the ICRC study's reliance on numerous statements that have no bearing on the practice of States, which is the bedrock of customary international law. As examples, he referred to various reports submitted by rapporteurs to United Nations bodies and to comments made by persons not representing States. Professor Dinstein also observed that, although military Manuals are indeed a primary source of customary international law, at least two of the so-called manuals referred to in the study are not real manuals. He also highlighted a number of inconsistencies and errors in both the black-letter rules and commentary of the study.

In an afternoon session, Mr. Henckaerts noted that the ICRC study was not intended to be the last word on customary international humanitarian law. Instead, the study is where enlightened discussion about further development and clarification of the subject must begin. During ensuing general discussion, conference attendees emphasized that there is a clear distinction between State practice, as such, and customary international law. Likewise, Professor Dinstein stressed the need to distinguish between State practice and *opinio juris*, a distinction that, in his view, was not made adequately in the study. He also challenged the leap from treaty law to customary law and emphasized that, although treaties may stimulate custom, the evidence must be found in the practice of or vis-à-vis non-contracting Parties. Others also noted that the ICRC study cannot be viewed as evidence of a substantive body of customary international law merely because States have signed Additional Protocol I to the 1949 Geneva Conventions. In this regard, it was widely agreed that evidence of any State practice in support of the existence of customary international law must be formulated independently of the voluntarily assumed treaty obligations of signatory States.

Conference Panel II—Disseminating International Humanitarian Law

Conference Panel II focused on the public awareness of and appreciation for international humanitarian law. Commentators emphasized that the Red Cross and Red Crescent Societies (RCRC) were founded and operate on the fundamental principles of humanity, neutrality, and impartiality. In particular, Dr. Mohammed Al-Hadid, President, Jordanian National Red Crescent Society, emphasized that there is no religious connotation associated with either the Red Cross or the Red Crescent emblems. Both are meant to be purely humanitarian symbols. Dr. Hadid also voiced his support for the creation of a third additional protocol to the 1949

Geneva Conventions that would adopt a new emblem—the Red Crystal—to enhance the protection of victims and the status of humanitarian assistance, especially during armed conflict, where in recent years respect for protective emblems has eroded. This third protocol also would promote the universality of the ICRC movement and help overcome the objection of certain States to the use of the two traditional symbols.

Ms. Lucy Brown, Senior Adviser, International Humanitarian Law, American National Red Cross Society, emphasized the need to increase public awareness of and support for the principles of international humanitarian law, particularly among school age children and youth. Ms. Brown introduced the "Exploring Humanitarian Law" curriculum to the conference and noted that it is being piloted or implemented in the United States and 94 other countries. Ms. Brown observed that a necessary by-product of dissemination is the reinforcement of principles of peaceful coexistence and facilitation of a return to peace in the event of an armed conflict.

Mr. David Lloyd Roberts, MBE, and formerly of the ICRC addressed the efforts of the ICRC to bring international humanitarian law training to the armed forces. He cited the importance of the supporting role played by the ICRC and urged conference participants to ensure training is completed during peacetime because "[o]nce the fighting has started, it's too late." Mr. Roberts outlined certain potential obstacles to successful implementation of international humanitarian law training and noted the lack of support for international humanitarian law principles among some senior military personnel, skepticism concerning the effectiveness of training, and the difficulty of adapting such training to the realities and pressures of combat.

Conference Panel III—Modern Weaponry and Warfare

On a completely different tack and heading, Conference Panel III addressed issues associated with modern weaponry and warfare. Mr. Ed Cummings, Assistant Legal Adviser for Arms Control, Office of the Legal Adviser, US State Department, began by recounting the substantial development of conventional weapons principles over the past 100 years. Reminding the audience that weapons treaty negotiations necessarily occur in a political context, he reinforced the fact that the United States always seeks treaty consensus with an overriding goal of reducing human suffering during armed conflict. Mr. Cummings noted that the rules focused originally on the effect of weapons on combatants but that rules tend now to concentrate on effects on civilians. Mr. Cummings also explained that States are reluctant to be too technical when negotiating agreements because rapid technological advances may make definitions and descriptions of weapons obsolete shortly after agreements are executed. On the other hand, he observed that advances in technology can improve the reliability of weapons and reduce casualty rates. Indeed, the US Department of Defense has directed that at least 99 percent of its submunitions produced detonate properly and has proposed an amendment to the treaty covering anti-vehicle mines that calls for inclusion of detection devices for such weapons.

Doctor Marie Jacobsson, Principal Legal Adviser on International Law to the Swedish Ministry for Foreign Affairs, discussed Sweden's compliance with Article 36 of Additional Protocol I to the Geneva Conventions. This article requires that a State party determine whether employment of a new weapon would be prohibited by Protocol I or any other rule of international law applicable to that State party. She averred that very few States complete weapons studies and that ICRC representatives have been discussing what the parameters for such studies should be. In 1974, it established a delegation to review conventional weapons, which factors humanitarian, human rights, and disarmament laws into its Article 36 studies. The delegation may set conditions on the development of weapons relating to primary, secondary, and indiscriminate effects, and occasionally it proposes alternative designs or limits the use of a weapon in military or law enforcement applications. In 2003, Sweden pledged to review whether international humanitarian law also should be considered when evaluating weapons for export. Dr. Jacobsson commented further that weapons reviews occasionally are stymied by the absence of a clear distinction between interstate armed conflict and operations such as peacekeeping.

Colonel Ken Watkin, Canadian Defense Forces Deputy Judge Advocate General/ Operations, offered his views on whether certain legal principles developed for international armed conflict should apply equally to asymmetric warfare between States and non-State actors. Colonel Watkin framed the issue with two weapons in mind—chemical agents and expanding bullets. A large body of well-developed treaty law bars the use of chemical weapons in armed conflict, but not for law enforcement purposes. Colonel Watkin, however, argues that it may be more humane to use prohibited riot control agents to clear a cave in combat than to use a flame thrower or grenade for the same purpose. Certain chemical agents, such as malodorants, calmatives, and darts, though prohibited by treaty law, may offer non-lethal alternatives to deadly force in armed conflict. Colonel Watkin observed that expanding bullets were banned by the 1899 Hague Declaration. He queried, however, whether their use should be prohibited in all aspects of non-international armed conflict particularly where the military forces are executing a law enforcement function. If use by police in a domestic law enforcement context is considered humane, how is it inhumane to use such bullets for similar purposes in armed conflict?

Professor Mike Schmitt from the George C. Marshall European Center for Security Studies, Garmisch, Germany, opined that law and conflict are in a mutually affective relationship and mused how future military technology may affect the existence, application, and interpretation of the law of armed conflict. Professor Schmitt noted further that while a substantial number of treaties govern specific means and methods of warfare, future agreements may cover depleted uranium shells, computer network attacks, and space-based offensive operations. Indeed, in February 2005, the US Defense Advanced Research Projects Agency (DARPA) published a report listing likely future developments in US military technology and means, including detection and destruction of elusive surface targets, robust tactical networks, networked manned and unmanned systems, detection of underground structures, assured use of space, cognitive computing, and the biorevolution. According to Professor Schmitt, developments of this nature will increase weapon precision, enhance command and control, render the battlespace more transparent, and promote use of autonomous unmanned attack platforms. In the context of the law of armed conflict, these developments also will increase the asymmetry between technologically advantaged and disadvantaged combatants. Professor Schmitt commented further that asymmetry disrupts the balance between military necessity and humanitarian concerns because the law does not operate equally for both sides. Thus, the disadvantaged combatant may resort to tactics prohibited under the law of armed conflict as a way to survive or prevail in battle, because legally permissible tactics likely will be futile. Such tactics may include fighting in civilian clothes, use of human shields and protected places, perfidy, marking mustering points with protected symbols of the ICRC, and resort to suicide bombers. Even if a technologically disadvantaged combatant does not disregard the law of armed conflict, the combatant may instead compensate for its disadvantage by defining military objectives broadly while undervaluing collateral damage. A technologically advantaged combatant may engage in effects-based operations rather than a serial destruction of the enemy's military force. During the question and answer session, Professor Schmitt asserted that many critics are "captured by technology" and have proposed that a State should reduce the asymmetry in armed conflict by foregoing use of advanced weapons.

Conference Panel IV—Coalition Warfare

Conference Panel IV tackled the timely and highly relevant topic of coalition warfare. Discussion began with comments by Brigadier General Charles Dunlap, Jr., USAF, Staff Judge Advocate, Headquarters, Air Combat Command, Langley Air Force Base, Virginia. General Dunlap noted that 21st century warfare has become increasingly legalistic and complex, and that coalition warfare is no exception. He identified a number of challenges facing coalition partners, including differences in treaty obligations between and among coalition partners, disagreement over what constitutes customary international law, and differences in domestic implementing legislation. General Dunlap emphasized the importance of developing ROE for all coalition forces, but noted the obvious difficulty in achieving this goal, particularly with regard to the definition of self-defense and the meaning of hostile intent. He also cautioned that legal hurdles facing coalition forces, e.g., the inability of US forces to provide logistic support to its coalition partners absent an international agreement concerning reimbursement for costs, have important operational effects that cannot be ignored by military commanders. General Dunlap commented that creating a formal judge advocate general corps among coalition partners would be a positive initiative. He observed that when coalition partners deploy JAGs with their operational forces, coordination is facilitated and synergies result. The General emphasized, however, that military commanders must understand and internalize the proper role of their military legal advisers, instructing that "JAGs provide advice; commanders make decisions." General Dunlap concluded by warning conferees about the development of the phenomenon of "lawfare," which he described as the use of legal principles such as those applicable to the law of armed conflict to mischaracterize and undermine a State's actions. The General emphasized the importance of recognizing the practice of "lawfare," and encouraged the US and its coalition partners to meet lawfare activity head-on by actively and publicly providing their own legal analysis and justification for their actions.

Commander (CMDR) Dale Stephens of the Royal Australian Navy and liaison officer to the International Law Department, US Naval War College, echoed General Dunlap's comments concerning the importance of harmonizing ROE among coalition partners, and briefly summarized the process through which such ROE might be developed. CMDR Stephens warned against a purely formalistic approach to the development of coalition ROE, however, emphasizing that a more realistic approach is necessary. Among considerations pertinent to the development of coalition ROE, CMDR Stephens mentioned the importance of exercising "calibrated discretion on key operational law concepts," the value of the socializing experience achieved by participation in international coalition operations, and the need to globalize the training of military officers. Commander Stephens also identified a number of challenges to the effective development of common coalition ROE, including difficulties associated with translating the principles of the law of armed conflict into a State's domestic law and the pressing need to reinforce a commonality of language between international military lawyers and internal government agencies. He capped his presentation with a quote from renowned author and Professor Louis Henkin, who once stated, "Almost all nations observe almost all principles of international law and almost all of their obligations almost all of the time."

Professor Charles Garraway, the 2004–2005 Charles H. Stockton Professor of International Law, US Naval War College, observed that in order for a multi-national coalition to work, the principles underlying the reason for coming together in the first place must be internally and externally consistent. Professor Garraway wisely commented that "[i]f there is no coalescing, there is no coalition." Professor Garraway instructed that the distinctiveness of each coalition partner need not be sacrificed in order achieve the goals of a successful coalition. Rather, he noted, the secret is to work around those distinctions. Professor Garraway also voiced concern about the apparent uncertainty regarding the US position on which principles of the law of armed conflict codified in Additional Protocol I are considered by the United States to reflect customary international law. Professor Garraway noted that the only existing US viewpoint, articulated in 1987 by Michael J. Matheson in *The United States Position on the Relation of Customary International Law to the 1977 Protocols Additional to the 1949 Geneva Conventions*, is no longer considered authoritative. Professor Garraway concluded his presentation by questioning whether the principles of human rights law, codified, for example, in the International Covenant of Civil and Political Rights, coexist with or are replaced by law of armed conflict principles during times of armed conflict. He asserted that the language of the various human rights conventions made it clear that the two legal regimes were intended to co-exist, despite the former being considered *lex generalis* and the latter *lex specialis*. Professor Garraway again noted a lack of clarity in the US stance on this matter and called for the United States to articulate its position more clearly.

Leslie Green, Professor Emeritus, University of Alberta, Canada, and former Charles H. Stockton Professor of International Law, picked up where Professor Garraway left off. He opined that the law of armed conflict prevails in situations of armed conflict where its principles deviate from those embraced by human rights law. Professor Green agreed with previous commentators, however, in calling for the development of common ROE and a mutual understanding of detainee operations. Professor Green also commented that it was time for a new treaty to replace the current NATO treaty. In his view, NATO has become an international organization that has transcended its original mandate. Professor Green argued that a new treaty would reflect more accurately NATO's current goals and aspirations and would be more representative of its current membership.

Conference Panel V—Future Navies

The penultimate conference panel generally considered the shape, methods, and means of future navies. RADM Robert Cox, Associate Director, Assessment Division, Office of the Chief of Naval Operations, tracked the progression of operational concepts in the ongoing transformation of the US Navy. In short, the Navy has evolved from the 1950s task group with specific missions, to the platform centric motif of the 1970s sporting multi-mission battle groups, to today's network centric force focused on defeating anti-access capabilities. According to RADM Cox, the future Navy must be joint, distributed, netted, persistent, surge-based, and surge-ready at home. Planning now occurs in minutes and hours rather than in days. Naval forces must be fully netted with required kinetic and non-kinetic capability, employable when directed by the Combatant Commander. In this context, sea basing does not consist only of technology. Sound doctrine is required to support the best use of forces in an effects-based environment. A move from a platform centric to a network centric environment has spawned legal challenges concerning employment of unmanned aerial vehicles, civilian mariners, frequency spectrum management, and the maritime commons while the United States strives to maintain a global naval presence through doctrinal and technological transformation.

Rear Admiral Raydon Gates of the Royal Australian Navy spoke of a future navy from the perspective of an operator in a mid-sized sea service. The trend for the future is projection of naval power at home and offshore, wherever Australia's interests are at stake. Australia's participation in coalition operations may reflect its national interests in the endeavor rather than common interests with other participants. Different national objectives reflect different national priorities, and military commanders must manage and harmonize these varied interests. Joint application of power is another trend. According to Admiral Gates, national military forces must not only operate jointly, but must work with other instruments of national power to assure a concerted defense effort. There will be a maritime element to future security undertakings, particularly in the littoral environment and primarily involving ROE development and targeting principles. Technological developments in weapons systems also will breed legal issues related, in particular, to the employment of missiles with artificial intelligence and development of corresponding ROE. Australian forces also will be required to balance the implementation of network centric warfare with existing technology and fiscal considerations. The Royal Australian Navy of the future will be smaller with no corresponding decrease in operational tempo, while its operating budget likely will not increase. On the other hand, future ships will feature more automation and be staffed with fewer sailors. Greater use of contractors to support naval forces also will raise questions about whether to characterize contractor employees as combatants and appropriate methods of command and discipline.

Captain Jane Dalton, Assistant Judge Advocate General (Civil Law) and Commanding Officer, Naval Civil Law Support Activity, identified several aspects of future navies that require timely consideration by military lawyers. For example, employment of civilian mariners aboard naval ships in billets historically held by military members grows out of the Chief of Naval Operations' effort to move sailors from non-war fighting jobs to positions in direct support of fleet and combat operations. Likewise, the proposed Maritime Prepositioning Force cargo ship is a key part of the sea basing concept and will serve as a floating logistics center. Use of this ship in an "assault echelon" with combat forces and aircraft aboard raises the question of whether civilian mariners lawfully may manage engineering, navigation, and deck functions. Under international law, a warship must be "manned by a crew which is under regular armed forces discipline." Yet this phrase is undefined and calls into question whether the civilian crew must be subject to the same system of discipline as the military members. Whether civilian mariners could be considered unlawful combatants depends upon whether they take a direct or active part in hostilities. Would manning a weapons system or navigating a ship constitute direct activity? The Navy has developed a legislative proposal that includes Navy Reserve affiliation as a requirement for detailing civilian mariners to a warship. Unmanned airborne and undersea vehicles are already engaged in combat operations. Should they be treated like their manned counterparts? Is an unmanned undersea vehicle a "vessel" under international rules to prevent collisions at sea and are they required to comply with the innocent and transit passages regimes under the UN Convention on the Law of the Sea? Captain Dalton also noted unanswered questions related to hospital ships, which, while protected by law from capture or intentional attack, may not utilize encrypted communications. Changes in technology, domestic laws on privacy, and national communications policy, however, have prompted the Navy to insist that its two hospital ships deploy with secure communications systems in order to complete their humanitarian missions and comply with domestic law. Captain Dalton also observed that the Law of the Sea Convention supports Sea Power 21 and the Proliferation Security Initiative, and does not affect US intelligence-gathering activity. She would contend further that reference in the Convention to use of the high seas for other internationally lawful uses permits the United States to stage forward-deployed sea bases in the exclusive economic zones of coastal States. In any event, US sea basing will comport with the law, whether the operation involves humanitarian relief, UN sanctions enforcement, or international armed conflict.

Professor Doctor Wolff Heintschel von Heinegg of the University of Frankfurt-Oder and University of Augsburg, Germany, also a former Charles H. Stockton Professor of International Law at the US Naval War College, reviewed the current state of the law of naval warfare and its future challenges. Professor Heintschel von Heinegg noted first that current provisions regarding signal encryption and arming of hospital ships have been questioned and may be somewhat anachronistic. He noted further that deception rules and principles must be adjusted to reflect developments in the electronic environment. Similarly, according to Professor Heintschel von Heinegg, the concept of blockade remains settled, but must be distinguished from other methods of naval warfare, such as maritime interception, zones, and control of enemy commerce and operations under a UN Security Council resolution. Professor Heintschel von Heinegg asserted, as well, that maritime zones must be analyzed carefully to determine whether they are intended to be unlawful free fire zones or legal ruses of war. In short, a zone must have a legitimate purpose and must limit the area of naval warfare, protect neutral and innocent shipping, and subject neutral shipping and aviation to extensive control measures. In Professor Heintschel von Heinegg's view, future challenges to the law of naval warfare include excessive maritime claims to well-defined geographical areas, different interpretations of basic legal concepts, confusion about political aims and legal targets, and the impact of human rights law. Additionally, challenges regarding asymmetric actors are based on the increasing multitude of terrorists and non-State actors and other difficult questions have arisen as well from the indefatigable trend toward civilianizing positions within the armed forces. The technology gap in naval warfare also has raised the technological inferiority argument which has engendered a decreasing willingness to accept legal regulation of armed conflict. So, too, has the illusion of "clean warfare" been fostered by today's precision weaponry generated by advances in technology. According to Professor Heintschel von Heinegg, however, these various challenges to the law of naval warfare do not justify the various demands for new rules.

Conclusion

The foregoing, in a nutshell, was an overview of the 2005 International Law Department conference and a glimpse of the scintillating views, discussion, and opinions cloaked by the pages of this the 82d volume of the *International Law Studies* series. And if this conference and volume have taught us anything, it is that, as this world entered the Age of Aquarius, it changed in ways only the most forward thinkers could have imagined—speed-of-light communication available to the masses; transnational enemies who rely on this capability, as well as the ready means to flit about the globe with relative ease; enemies who have waged with impunity a type of asymmetrical conflict that endures without regard for even the most basic tenets of international humanitarian law; the "lawfare" phenomenon that thrives on the Internet and other mass media and is used by our enemies daily to contest the legitimacy of well-intentioned acts or highlight isolated failings; prolific use of unmanned vehicles and precision weaponry; basing a fighting force at sea where coastal access is curtailed; and attempts to over-define ("codify" indirectly?) specific principles of customary international humanitarian law; and the growing practice of employing civilians in positions traditionally held by members of the military, to name a few. In the wake of these changes, those entrusted with the defense of their nations have struggled to adapt both technologically and operationally. It is perhaps for these reasons and in the face of other such challenges that Professor Kennedy recognized so poignantly that a firm and durable alliance has been struck between warriors and their lawyers.

In closing, then, it is our sincere desire that the following works of the preeminent authors who contributed so graciously to this volume will assist those seeking answers to today's hard questions and propagate thoughts and action that shape the future.

PART I

KEYNOTE ADDRESS

I

War and International Law: Distinguishing Military and Humanitarian Professions

David Kennedy*

Introduction: a Common Profession

I would like to begin by thanking Admiral Shuford, Professor Dennis Mandsager and Professor Charles Garraway, as well as Major Richard Jaques and Commander Dale Stephens, who have given me—and my students—a warm welcome at the Naval War College. I appreciate their generous hospitality and good counsel.

For civilian students and academics like me, who have never served in uniform, the military profession can seem to be a different universe. But how different are we, professionals within and outside the armed services? How different are the professions of war and peace?

When I was a young man, they could not have seemed more different. I registered as a conscientious objector after the Christmas bombings of Hanoi in 1972, and eventually became an international lawyer. I hoped I would find work promoting peace, economic development, humanitarian and progressive values on the global stage. Nothing seemed as different as the humanitarian and military

* Manley O. Hudson Professor of Law, Harvard Law School. The viewpoints expressed in this article are the author's alone.

professions—the one made war, the other sought to limit war's incidence and moderate war's violence.

Indeed, the military seemed to me then all that international law was not—violence and aggression in contradiction to our reason and restraint. It was only later that I learned how many international lawyers serve with the military—and how readily humanitarians have rushed to legitimate the use of force.

War and peace. I studied history and political science. War, we learned, "broke out" when "disputes" could not be resolved peacefully, when cosmopolitan reason gave way to nationalist passion, when the normal "balance of power" was upset by abnormal statesmen. These bad guy statesmen pursued outmoded projects of aggrandizement, domination, aggression or imperialism. They were in cahoots with what we called "the military industrial complex"; not knowing we were quoting Eisenhower.

Realpolitik was the disease; the softer wisdom of international law and international relations was the cure. The key to peace was wise statecraft and conflict management. We put our faith in negotiations among the disputing parties—which we hoped to facilitate. We were sure that reasonable aspirations for peaceful change should—and would—be accommodated by wise leaders, for whom we would serve as advisors. Leaders who would act for the common good, in a global humanitarian and cosmopolitan spirit. Leaders like that would address the roots of war in poverty, cultural backwardness, nationalist isolation, or ideological fervor. They would need—and want—help from the institutional machinery of the international community.

More than anything else, management for peace would require procedures—good practices, good offices, a steady and imaginative institutional framework and a cadre of dedicated humanitarian policy experts who could express and implement the world's general interest in peace. The United Nations, the non-governmental organizations (NGOs), and civil society, the peacemakers and peacekeepers, needed to succeed so that the military would never again be needed.

How did we imagine the military? Our knowledge was limited, our imagery vague. All that ceremony and hierarchy, training to kill. They were hot, passionate; we were cooler heads prevailing. We were dry, focused, pragmatic and managerial. I think we imagined war as it is depicted in films of the ancient world. The troops mass at the border, a command is given and everyone rushes forward helter-skelter, applying lethal force as fast and furiously as possible.

But of course it is not like this at all. Scoundrels do rule—often there simply is no wise and benevolent ruler waiting for our advice about the general good.

More importantly, military and civilian professionals, although certainly different, are no longer oil and water. War must also be managed by experts. The more I have known military officers and military lawyers, the more obvious the parallels between our professions have become. The more I've come to see us all as managers. And the more I've seen that when we differ, it is often the military that are the cooler heads.

Some years ago, before the current war in Iraq, I spent some days on board the *USS Independence* in the Persian Gulf. Nothing was as striking about the military culture I encountered there as its intensely regulated feel. Five thousand sailors, thousands of miles from base, managing complex technologies and weaponry, constant turnover and flux. It was absolutely clear that even if you could afford to buy an aircraft carrier, you couldn't operate it. The carrier, like the military, is a social system, requiring a complex and entrenched culture of standard practices and shared experiences, rules and discipline.

The carrier is also a small town. I remember the eager salesman in a crowded mess hall selling Chevrolets for delivery when the crew next hit shore. I came away completely ready to believe that, at least in principle, no ship moves, no weapon is fired, no target selected without review for compliance with regulation, not because the military has gone soft, but because there was simply no other way to make modern warfare work. Warfare has become rule and regulation.

In a way, of course, the routinization of law—humanitarian law—in the military professions is a terrific achievement. Military professionalism affirms civilian control. But more, our military and humanitarian professions have merged, yielding a humanitarian military and a realistic, pragmatic humanitarianism.

But I worry. Was there nothing valuable in the separation of military and humanitarian professions? As our professions merge, what happens to the virtues of standing outside, speaking humanist truth to military power? And what happens to the real political necessity for the military to break some eggs when the going gets tough? What, moreover, happens to the legal "principle of distinction?"—the principle that military and civilian professions must be distinguished.

My project this morning is to retrace the laws about warfare to illuminate, as best I can, the ways in which the military and legal professions have marked and unmarked the boundary between war and peace, and some of the virtues and vices of strengthening and weakening our sense that humanitarian and military professionals march to different drummers.

Looking back, the legal mind has sometimes sharply distinguished war and peace, and sometimes blurred them together. The modern laws of war inherit both traditions—and now offer us a confusing mix of distinctions that can melt into air when we press on them too firmly. A law of firm rules and loose exceptions, of foundational principles—and counter principles. This complex professional language can certainly limit our vision. For the legal professional—whether serving in the military or the humanitarian world—the challenge is to engage this slippery body of material strategically as a partner in, rather than a substitute for, political leadership and command responsibility.

The narrative line in this very complex historical story is actually quite simple—the rise and fall of a distinction between war and peace. For the early 19th-century jurist, war and peace were far less distinct than they came to seem in the half century before the First World War. After that war, 20th-century international lawyers sought to bridge the gap that had opened between war and peace, to routinize humanitarianism in the military profession and pragmatism among humanitarians.

Although they were quite successful—our professions have merged—the potential to distinguish has not been eliminated. Instead, the relationship between war and peace has become, for the humanitarian lawyer and military professional, itself something to be managed. We now have the rhetorical and doctrinal tools to make and unmake the distinction between war and peace. And we do so as a tactic in both war and peace. The result is less a difference between the outside of humanitarian virtue and the inside of military violence than a common profession whose practitioners manage the relationship between war and peace within a common language; all the while working in the shadow of a new outside, the world we think of as "politics."

Historical Backdrop: the Rise of "Modern War"

Our laws of war were forged in the shadow of a new "modern" conception of warfare. In the late 18th and early 19th centuries, what had been an aristocratic endeavor of the old regime became the general project of a nation—an extension of public policy, an act of the whole.

This is the development crystallized by Clausewitz as a continuity between war and peace. We have come to treat his formulation as classic:

> We know, certainly, that War is only called forth through the political intercourse of Governments and Nations; but in general it is supposed that such intercourse is broken off by War, and that a totally different state of things ensues, subject to no laws but its own. We maintain, on the contrary, that War is nothing but a continuation of political intercourse, with a mixture of other means.[1]

The new attitude Clausewitz proposes had been building for a generation. But the revolutionary break with the *ancien regime*—and the Napoleonic wars that followed—drove it home. The transformation of war from the interpersonal, dynastic and religious struggles of an aristocracy to the public struggles of a nation—a citizens' army, the *levee en masse*, the army "of the republic"—made war visible as an extension of national policy, as a project of the whole society.

War became continuous with the political intercourse of peacetime as it became the public affair of a nation—an instrument of national policy, an expression of national sovereignty, a sign of national honor. The ancient marks of military distinctiveness, the uniform, the profession, the codes of honor, became synonymous not with aristocratic status, but with public life—and often with submission to civilian leadership.

Latent in the merger of war and public policy lay a distinction between the old war and the new—wars of chivalry, honor and passion, versus wars of reason, calculation and policy.

It took some time for this new vision to take hold. In 1838, a few years after Clausewitz wrote, and long before he would became a wartime president, Abraham Lincoln spoke of the abolitionist cause in these terms: "Passion has helped us, but can do so no more. It will in future be our enemy. Reason, cold, calculating, unimpassioned reason, must furnish all the materials for our future support and defense."[2]

In saying this, Lincoln was understood to set himself against war—the just cause would need the calm determination of cooler peacetime heads. Two and a half decades later, however, Lincoln would be embroiled in a war that would confound this easy opposition of passionate war and reasoned peace.

Our Civil War—birthplace for so much of the law in war—is often remembered as the first "modern" war. In part, this is winner's history—a war of the modern North against the antebellum South, a war of industrial power and the Federal Nation, against the old military order of chivalry and the old sectarianism of region. A culture of commerce defeating a culture of honor, cold Northern reason slowly quenching the hot passions of the South in the name of a National Whole.

But the Civil War's modernity lay not only in the Northern victory. For both sides, this was a war pitting the full economic and spiritual powers of their imagined community against another in a struggle for national identity. Modern war conducted as total war, war of the whole, war for the whole. In this sense, Lincoln's unimpassioned reason would not forestall war; it would become war. But neither would it remain split from passion, as Lincoln's inspired vocabulary of sacrifice, sanctification—"we cannot dedicate, we cannot consecrate, we cannot hallow this ground"[3]—would attest.

More than anything, the modernity of the Civil War lay in the strange brew of reason and passion through which the struggle was understood by both sides. The Northern cause was also a crusade, the Southern military also a redoubt of professional skill, thought, and art, against an often brutal Northern campaign. The rhetorical tools for distinguishing war and peace, new wars and old wars, were there, but they were redirected to define the relations between the warring parties.

This mix of passion, reason and national expression on both sides conjured up a war of singular ferocity. In a sense, the Clausewitzian vision had been realized—war had become continuous, in reason *and* passion, with the great political struggles of the nation.

Legal War: Modern War Encounters Modern Law

On the one hand, 19th-century legal developments contributed to this emerging vision of warfare. The private modes of warfare associated with the old regime, now thought incompatible with a unitary public sovereign monopoly of force, were progressively eliminated. The 1856 Paris Declaration,[4] for example, eliminated "privateering," a complex legal institution through which "letters of marque" authorized private vessels to carry out belligerent acts. Henceforth there would be one sovereign, one military.

At the same time, however, late 19th century changes in legal consciousness transformed what it meant for war to be the exclusive act of a public sovereign. Most crucially, by the end of the 19th century, it no longer meant that war was continuous with peace, or a project of the *whole*—more the opposite.

The emergence of a sharp distinction between public and private brought with it the image of a transnational commercial space that should be kept free from contamination by public force. Private armies, mercenaries, privateers; all these were outmoded, not only because they were part of an aristocratic past, but because they did not fit with the new, exclusively *public* nature of sovereign war powers.

The public realm had become one sphere of power among many, marked off from the private realm of the market and the family. Public warfare that had seemed general, continuous with the whole society, now seemed, in legal terms, specific—the project of the *government*, not the society.

Law's Allies: Humanitarians Speaking Virtue to Violence

Humanitarian voices supported the legal separation of war from the domain of peace. Broad pacifist campaigns arose from diverse sources: church leaders, proponents of woman's suffrage, heirs to the abolition movement, as well as political activists of all types—anarchists, socialists, populists, progressives, Catholics.

These diverse voices marked the distinction between war and peace in various ways—as ethics against politics, as faith against the cruel logic of commerce, as calm reason against fanaticism, modern logic against the primitive culture of honor. In fact, the terms with which they marked the line from peace to war parallel those by which both sides distinguished North and South.

All these voices spoke to war, to the statesmen and military who made war, from outside—in the name of an alternative ethical vision, sometimes national, more often universal. War and peace were separate—Clausewitz was now the problem. We might now say they pled for peace by speaking truth to power. The point was to shrink the domain of war through moral suasion, agitation, shaming, and proselytizing. In their view, blurring war with peace was both dangerous and immoral.

This conviction lent an ethical urgency to the emergence of a sharp legal distinction between war and peace. Each was now a legal status, separated by a declaration. Combatants and noncombatants, neutrals and belligerents have different bundles of legal rights and privileges. The battlefield, the territory of belligerency, was legally demarcated. The legal treatises of the period began to place the law of peace and the law of war in separate volumes. In part, these distinctions aimed to limit the carnage of war by expanding the privileges of civilians and limiting the military privilege to kill.

These distinctions were also part of a broader reorganization of legal thought, sharpening the distinction between the public and the private sphere, hardening private rights and limiting public powers to their respective spheres.

For all, peace and war were to be legally separated, for example, private rights were increasingly thought to be continuous across the boundary. It is here that we began to see the logic of thinking that when the dust settles after a war claiming the lives of millions, destroying empires, and remaking the political and economic landscape of the planet, people might reasonably feel they are still entitled to get their property back.

In short, the late 19th century developed an alliance between two rather different sets of ideas. A moral conviction that the forces of peace stand outside war, demanding that swords be beaten into ploughshares, and a legal project to sharpen the distinction between public powers and private rights.

The result was a legal conception of war as a public project limited to its sphere. The legal distinctiveness of war reinforced the idea that war was itself a discrete and limited phenomenon—over there, the domain of combat. It seemed reasonable to expect that warriors stay over there—and that protected persons, even women soldiers, stay outside the domain of combat.

This alliance of ethics and legal form has continued across the 20th century and is with us still. We see it in the effort to restrain war by emphasizing its moral and legal distinctiveness—by walling it off from peace and shrinking its domain. We see its echo in the many varieties of 20th-century pacifism, in efforts to revive "just war" theory as an exogenous truth that can limit military power, and in the struggle to bring the language of human rights to bear on the military, that is, to judge the effects of war by a different and higher ethical standard. But we also see it in efforts to treat combat and "police action" as fundamentally—ethically, legally—different; the one the domain of human rights, the other the proper domain of the law of armed conflict.

I have a great deal of sympathy for this outsider approach. It is where my own professional and ethical journey began; in a moral world for which the Clausewitzian perspective was precisely the problem. To think war and peace continuous was to think the unthinkable. And to embrace a cynical, *realpolitik* point of view which, because it could think war, would also find itself making war, was similarly unthinkable. If you can't tell the difference between war and peace, how can we even have a conversation about limiting war's violence? In this view, our only hope is to bring an external reason to bear on the violence of war—and an external ethical passion to the cold calculation that war might sometimes make sense.

The Dark Sides of Outsider Virtue: Limits to the Alliance

Nevertheless, the dark sides of this outsider's perspective are now familiar. There is, and I will come back to this, the uneasy feeling that war simply is no longer as distinct as all that. Even assuming war might be conducted "over there," in its own domain, it has always been difficult to keep one's ethical distance from warfare in modern discussions of international affairs.

There is the nagging problem that force also has humanitarian uses in a wicked world. Moreover, war can strengthen our moral determination. We know that great moral claims often become stronger when men and women kill and die in their name. There is some kind of feedback loop between our ethical convictions and our use of force. Moreover, we know how easily moral clarity calls forth violence and justifies warfare. It is a rare military campaign today that is not launched for some humanitarian purpose.

Looking back, this was a great lesson of the Civil War—both parties experienced their project and excoriated their opponents as both cool reason and hot crusade. Both battled in the name of the National Whole. Everyone was speaking truth to power as they went at one another tooth and nail.

In the years since, we have learned how easily ethical denunciation and outrage—triggering intervention in Kosovo, Afghanistan, even Iraq—can get us into circumstances where we are not able to follow through and cause the making of humanitarian promises which war cannot deliver. The universal claims of human rights can seem to promise the existence of an "international community" which is simply not available to back them up.

Indeed, the discourse of ethical denunciation often has a tip of the iceberg problem. Take Abu Ghraib. Sexually humiliating, even torturing and killing prisoners is probably not, ethically speaking, the worst or most shocking thing our Coalition has done in Iraq. We should worry that our outrage at the photos may also be a way of not thinking about other injuries, deaths and mutilations our government has wrought.

Outrage can distract us from the hard questions. Was the problem in Abu Ghraib a legal violation—or a failure of leadership? Was the failure one of human dignity—or tactics? The whole episode was clearly a military defeat. But we are left with the nagging question. If it could be kept secret, if it could be done pursuant to a warrant, perhaps sexual humiliation can help win the war; might, on balance, reduce the suffering of civilians and combatants alike.

We know, moreover, that following absolute ethical precepts in wartime—as any other time—can become its own idolatry. Is it sensible to clear the cave with a firebomb because pepper spray, lawful when policing, is unlawful in "combat"? Absolute rules lead us to imagine we know what violence is just and what is unjust, always and for everyone. But justice is not like that, it must be imagined, built by people, struggled for, and redefined, in each conflict in new ways. Justice requires leadership—on the battlefield and off.

Of course, for all these difficulties, much can sometimes be achieved by bringing humanitarian reason to bear on cultures of violence and by opposing the cruel calculations of cynical statesmen with ethical commitment.

Still, an external moral discourse may not be able to stay all that external. Often, the trouble begins when it hits the problem of exceptions. What if it were Hitler, what if there were genocide, what if they were raping your mother? What about self-defense? What about deterrence? These classic questions take us straight to the doctrinal world of flexible standards, balancing conflicting considerations, assessing proportionality that is familiar to the professional weighing costs to achieve gains. To figure out when and how much self-defense is "just," we need technical, professional military expertise.

Some commentators reacted to the 1996 International Court of Justice opinion on the *Legality of the Threat or Use of Nuclear Weapons*[5]—a fabric of legal equivocations—by shaming the Court for speaking with nuance about an apocalypse; for parsing the "slaughter of the innocents" into the awkward categories of Article 38; for worrying more about the validity of norms than the future of humanity.

The horrors of warfare, the dead and mangled bodies, the lives and families ripped apart, the intense anxiety and suffering on and off the battlefield, the pain of a single wounded child crying out, it seems obscene to speak of these things in any language but that of moral clarity, regret and outrage.

But is there, in fact, an alternative mode of discussion on which to ground this sensibility? Once we set out to speak of nuclear war as "slaughtering the innocents," we would soon enough need a definition for innocent. We would need to account not merely for the horrors of Hiroshima and Nagasaki, but also for their singularity. How can the dangers of nuclear proliferation, nuclear error, nuclear first use best be prevented? Serious, difficult questions. What about deterrence, does it work? When? And, of course, what about torture? When does it work?

Moreover, presuming we speak about the slaughter of the innocents in order to reduce the likelihood of nuclear war—rather than merely to bear witness, we will need to assess ethical denunciation itself in tactical terms. What are the costs and benefits of denunciation? When should we trim our sails a bit, hold back, even flatter those whose fingers are on the button, in the name of an effective pacifism? Of course, if we hold our rhetorical fire this time people may die. People whose death we might have prevented, in whose torture we acquiesce, whom we sacrifice for the larger ethical objective of a stronger law in war, or a more legitimate International Committee of the Red Cross (ICRC).

Strategy Switching: Humanitarian Pragmatism and Antiformalism

Over the last century, these difficulties and ambiguities have eroded confidence in the outsider strategy; an erosion sped by the fate of the legal consciousness with which this strategy had been allied. The first half of the 20th century saw a widespread loss of faith in the formal distinctions of classical legal thought; in the wisdom, as well as the plausibility, of separating law sharply from politics, or private right sharply from public power.

This loss of faith has had consequences for efforts to limit the violence of warfare through law; both undermining classic distinctions, between belligerent and neutral, for example, and opening new strategies for moving more fluidly between military and humanitarian professional vocabularies.

As a result, the strategy of external denunciation—naming and shaming—has never had the grip in the law of force that it has had, say, in the field of human rights. Indeed, the modern law of force represents a triumph for grasping the nettle of costs and benefits and infiltrating the background decision-making of those whom it would bend to humanitarian ends.

The result was a new, modern law in war. This is the law known to the ICRC and much of the European international law establishment as "humanitarian law," and to the US military as the "law of armed conflict." They are speaking about the same thing. I prefer the classic term "laws in war" or *jus in bello.*

As early as the Civil War, the humanitarian project sought less to distinguish war from peace, or just war from unjust war, or good guys from bad guys, than to limit the violence of all sides through an insider strategy of professionalization. It is not surprisingly that Francis Lieber, author of an early code of conduct for battle[6] had relatives on both sides in our Civil War. The law in war we have inherited eloquently illustrates the strengths and weaknesses of this professionalization strategy.

The "law in war"—associated most prominently with the International Committee of the Red Cross—has always prided itself on its pragmatic relationship with military professionals. It is not unusual to hear military lawyers speak of the ICRC lawyers as their "partners" in codification—and compliance—and vice versa. They attend the same conferences, and speak the same language, even when they differ on this or that detail.

Developing a common insider vocabulary did not mean jettisoning rules; it meant first of all placing the rules on a firmer footing in the militarily plausible. Rules are not external expressions of virtue, but internal expressions of professional discipline.

Already in the 19th century, many humanitarians thought the best way to proceed was to work with the military to codify detailed rules they can respect—no exploding bullets, respect for ambulances and medical personnel, and so forth. To this day, the most significant codifications have indeed been negotiated among diplomatic and military authorities.

In this, the codified 19th-century law in war was something of an exception to the prevailing spirit of classical legal thought—and a precursor for what would follow in the 20th century. Rather than elaborating private rights against public powers, it harnessed the authority of public sovereignty to the articulation of limits; foreshadowing an international legal positivism that would be theorized only in the early decades of the 20th century as a repudiation of 19th-century efforts to ground law outside sovereign consent.

Of course, this reliance on military acquiescence limited what could be achieved—military leaders outlaw weapons which they no longer need, which they feel will be potent tools only for their adversaries, or against which defense would be too expensive or difficult. Narrowly drawn rules permit a great deal—and legitimate what is permitted.

Recognition of these costs is one reason the pragmatism of the law in war has always meant more than positivism; more than deference to sovereign consent; more than legal clarity; more than realism about the power of nation States. Pragmatism has also meant antiformalism—principles and standards replacing rules.

As you all know, since at least 1945, a vocabulary of principles has grown up alongside tough-minded military bargains over weaponry. The detailed rules of

The Hague or Geneva law have morphed into standards—simple ideas which can be printed on a wallet-sized card and taught easily to soldiers in the field. "The means of war are not unlimited," "each use of force must be necessary" and "proportional." These have become ethical baselines for a universal modern civilization.

Humanitarians have sought to turn rules into principles to render the narrow achievements of negotiation in more general terms; transforming narrow treaties into broad custom. Military professionals have done the same for different reasons—to ease training through simplification, to emphasize the importance of judgment by soldiers and commanders operating under the rules, or simply to cover situations not included under the formal rules with a consistent practice. Apparently, for example, a standard Canadian military manual instructs that the "spirit and principles"[7] of the international law of armed conflict apply to non-international conflicts not covered by the terms of the agreed rules.

It is not just that rules have become principles—we as often find the reverse. Military lawyers turn broad principles and nuanced judgments into simple bright line rules of engagement for soldiers in combat. Humanitarians comb military handbooks and government statements of principle promulgated for all sorts of purposes, to distill "rules" of customary international law. The ICRC's recent three volume restatement of the customary law of armed conflict is a monumental work of advocacy of just this type.

In the modern law in war, both rules and standards are simultaneously understood in the quite different registers of "validity" and "persuasion." In the world of validity, the law is the law—you should follow it because it is valid. If your battlefield acts do not fall under a valid prohibition, you remain privileged to kill. Full stop. On the other hand, however, as a tool of persuasion, the law in war overflows these banks. It will be hard to argue—particularly to persistent opposers—that many of the purportedly customary rules in the ICRC restatement are, strictly speaking, "valid." But there is no gainsaying their likely persuasiveness in many contexts and to many audiences.

We are used to working with the law of armed conflict in the key of validity. We make rules by careful negotiation. We influence customary rules by intentioned and public behavior. We send ships through straits or close to shorelines both to assert and to strengthen rights.

But we will need to become more adept at operations in the law of persuasion. The domain in which the image of a single dead civilian can make a persuasive case for a law of armed conflict violation trumps the most ponderous technical legal defense.

The law in war of persuasion is not only the product of overreaching humanitarian outsiders, of course. The military also interprets, advocates, seeks to persuade. This reinterpretation of rules and principles has brought humanitarian law inside the vocabulary of the military profession and brought complex considerations of strategy to the humanitarian professions. As a framework for debate and judgment, this new law in war embraced the unavoidability of trade-offs, of balancing harms, of accepting costs to achieve benefit—an experience common to both military strategists and humanitarians.

Take civilian casualties. Of course, civilians will be killed in war. Limiting civilian death had become a pragmatic commitment—no unnecessary damage, not one more civilian than necessary. In the vernacular of humanitarian law, this becomes no "superfluous injury" and no "unnecessary suffering." The range of complex strategic calculations opened up by this idea, for those inside and outside the military, is broad indeed.

We might say that the old distinction between combatants and civilians has been relativized. What, in any event, can it mean for the distinction between military and civilian to have itself become a principle? The "principle of distinction"—there is something oxymoronic here—either it is a distinction, or it is a principle.

Of course, it is but a short step from here to "effects-based targeting," and the elimination of the doctrinal firewall between civilian and military, belligerent and neutral. But, thinking in humanitarian terms, why shouldn't military operations be judged by their effects, rather than by their adherence to narrow rules that might well have all manner of perverse and unpredictable outcomes?

I was struck during the NATO bombardment of Belgrade—justified by the international community's humanitarian objectives in Kosovo—by the public discussions among military strategists and humanitarian international lawyers of the appropriateness of targeting the civilian elites most strongly supporting the Milosevic regime. If bombing the bourgeoisie would have been more effective than a long march inland toward the capital, would it have been proportional, necessary, indeed humanitarian to place the war's burden on young draftees in the field rather than upon the civilian population who sent them there? Some argued that targeting civilians supporting an outlaw, if democratic, regime would also extend the Nuremberg principle of individual responsibility. Others disagreed, of course. But the terms of their disagreement were provided by shared principles.

The law in war today offers the basis for both external denunciation of military action and internal calculation of its necessity or proportionality. Although they do not lie easily with one another, our thinking fades easily from one to the other. Take the Abu Ghraib photos. The law in war offers us two quite different vocabularies for reacting to the photographs, neither of which is satisfactory. First, moral outrage. We have repeatedly heard it said that the administration, like so many others, was "shocked by the photos." They may have been—but I wonder. If Rumsfeld was indeed shocked, might he not be just a bit too naïve to be entrusted with taking the country to war? He was shocked in part, as we all were, because the violence was gratuitous, unnecessary, not instrumentally justified, and, of course, because it was photographed. But was it really not necessary? How does sleep or sensory deprivation compare to humiliation, or to chills, or to intense fear? Which is more humane? Which more effective? Can we still distinguish the two questions?

Asymmetry—Severing the Laws of Validity and Persuasion

There is something else about this new vocabulary that is disturbing. You may remember Major General James Mattis, poised to invade Falluja, concluding his demand that the insurgents stand down with these words: "We will always be humanitarian in all our efforts. We will fight the enemy on our terms. May God help them when we're done with them."[8] I know I shivered at his juxtaposition of humanitarian claims and blunt threats.

It is troubling, of course, that this so often has been a vocabulary for judgment of the center against the periphery. When the Iraqi insurgent quoted on the same page of the *New York Times* as Mattis threatened to decapitate civilian hostages if the coalition forces did not withdraw, he was also threatening innocent civilian death—less of it actually—but without the humanitarian promise. And he also made me shiver.

It is no secret that technological advances have heightened the asymmetry of warfare. In the framework of validity, it is clear that all are bound by the same rules. But as persuasion, this assumption is coming undone. When the poor deviate from the best military practices of the rich, it is tempting to treat their entire campaign as illegitimate. But before we jump to the legitimacy of their cause, how should we evaluate the strategic use of perfidy by every outgunned insurgency battling a modern occupation army? From an effects-based perspective, perfidious attacks on our military—from mosques, by insurgents dressing as civilians or using human shields—may have more humanitarian consequences than any number of alternative tactics. And they are very likely to be interpreted by many as reasonable, "fair" responses by an outgunned, but legitimate force.

There is no question that technological asymmetry erodes the persuasiveness of the "all bound by the same rules" idea. It should not be surprising that forces with vastly superior arms and intelligence capacity are held to a higher standard in the court of world public opinion than their adversaries. As persuasion, the law in force has indeed become a sliding scale.

Persuasion and the CNN Effect

In 1996, I traveled to Senegal as a civilian instructor with the Naval Justice School from here in Newport to train members of the Senegalese military in the laws of war and human rights. At the time, the training program was operating in 53 countries, from Albania to Zimbabwe. As I recall it, our training message was clear: humanitarian law is not a way of being nice. By internalizing human rights and humanitarian law, you will make your force interoperable with international coalitions, suitable for international peacekeeping missions. To use our sophisticated weapons, your military culture must have parallel rules of operation and engagement to our own. Most importantly, we insisted, humanitarian law will make your military more effective—will make your use of force something you can sustain and proudly stand behind.

I was struck when we broke into small groups for simulated exercises, by a regional commander who kept asking the hard questions—when you capture some guerrillas, isn't it better to place a guy's head on a stake for deterrence? Well, no, we would patiently explain, this will strengthen the hostility of villagers to your troops, and imagine what would happen if CNN were nearby. They would all laugh, of course, and respond "we must be sure the press stays away."

Ah, but this is no longer possible, we said, if you want to play on the international stage, you need to be ready to have CNN constantly by your side. You must place an imaginary CNN webcam on your helmet, or, better, just over your shoulder. Not because force must be limited and not because CNN might show up, but because only force which can imagine itself being seen can be enduring. An act of violence one can disclose and be proud of is ultimately stronger, more legitimate.

Our lesson was written completely in the key of persuasion, not validity. It was a lesson apparently lost on those who considered the interrogation of "high value targets" in our own war on terror. Nevertheless, the Senegalese had learned, as Secretary Rumsfeld now seems to be learning, what was required for a culture of violence to be something one could proudly stand behind. What was required, in a word, for warfare to be civilized. The more I thought about that, however, the more it made me shiver as well.

Comparative Law: the International Law of Armed Conflict and Military Discipline

I have been speaking about the law in war as if we could rather easily identify its terms. But what law governs the battlefield? If you ask an international commercial lawyer, what law governs the transaction, the answer will be anything but straightforward. Treaty law on the subject—even the World Trade Organization agreements—would only be the beginning. There would be international private law, of course. But far more importantly, national regulation with transnational effects, and the national private law built into the transaction through private ordering. Assessing the significance of these various bodies of law requires not only inquiry into their formal jurisdictional validity, but also their sociological effect. Who will want to regulate the transaction? Who will be able to do so? What rules will influence the transaction even absent enforcement?

The answer for warfare is no simpler, particularly for coalition operations, or for campaigns that stretch the "battlespace" across numerous jurisdictions. Who will try to apply what rules, who will succeed? When the Italians decide to prosecute CIA operatives for their alleged participation in a black operation of kidnapping and rendition, the law of the battlefield has shifted. The practice of military law today requires complex and shifting predictions of fact and law. Whose interpretation will prevail and before what audience?

This kind of analysis will require sophisticated comparative law, for there are more than one laws of armed conflict. The rules simply look different if you anticipate battle against a technologically superior foe, or live in a Palestinian refugee camp in Gaza. Moreover, although a national military may translate the words of the international law of armed conflict directly into its operations manual, the interpretation and intent may well be different. More often, different nations, even in the same coalition, will have implemented and interpreted the shared rules and principles quite differently. Humanitarians looking at the same rules might lean toward restrictive interpretations, adopting the perspective of the potential "victim," while the military might lean towards greater freedom of maneuver. Although we might disagree with one another's interpretation, we must recognize that our professional materials are elastic enough to enable quite diverse interpretations. Military law is comparative law.

As humanitarians, when we compare international rules with the military's rules of engagement, we might well be surprised: the military rules might well be the stricter. The strength and significance of the military's own culture of discipline can be difficult for civilians to grasp. I have tried to explain it to civilian audiences by saying it is bureaucratic necessity, central to the effectiveness of the mission and to the safety of colleagues. But my sense is that military discipline is as much passion as reason; instrumentalism wrapped in honor and integrity in a culture set off from civilian life—a higher calling.

As a social production, military discipline is also of course, and perhaps more importantly, a work on the self. The United States Army runs recruitment commercials which implore "see your recruiter, become an Army of One." The promise is power, to be sure. But also discipline—self-discipline. If you join, you will be transformed inside—you will become an army, coordinated, disciplined, your own commanding officer, your own platoon, embodying within yourself the force of hundreds because of the work you will do, and we will do, on you.

Of course, there is opportunity for individual judgment—and error. Soldiers who run amok. We remember the pilots who flew beneath the Italian ski lift slicing the cables. And the precision guided missile fired in Kosovo with the tail fins put on backwards, spinning ever further from its programmed target until it exploded in a crowded civilian marketplace. We remember the American pilots who bombed their Canadian allies. Or, for that matter, My Lai, the abuse of prisoners in Baghdad, and all the other tales of atrocity in war.

It can be particularly hard for civilians to grasp that when soldiers are tried for breach of military discipline, their defense is often stronger under the vague standards of international humanitarian law than under national criminal or military law. Or that international law provides the framework less for disciplining the force than for unleashing the spear at its tip.

Indeed, the international legal standards of self-defense, proportionality and necessity are so broad that they are routinely invoked to refer to the zone of discretion rather than limitation. I have spoken to numerous Navy pilots who describe briefings filled with technical rules of engagement and military law. After the military lawyer leaves, the commanding officer summarizes in the empowering language of international law—"just don't do anything you don't feel is necessary" and "defend yourself; don't get killed out there." The fighter pilot heads out on a leash of rules, assembled in a package coordinated by a complex transnational array of operating procedures. Only at the last moment, in contact with the enemy, is he released to the discretion framed by the law of armed conflict, that is, necessity, and self-defense.

What are we to make of the widespread sense that military professionals are the most disturbed by the current administration's efforts to shrink or skirt humanitarian standards in their war on terror? Has the military gone soft? Become less willing than their civilian masters to condone harsh tactics? Or is the scandal that the JAG Corps has been more courageous in their opposition to harsh tactics than those civilian humanists who stand outside, wringing their hands, but uncertain whether they are in fact qualified to judge? Perhaps the scandal is our sense that to torture or not to torture has become a professional judgment in the first place, unavoidably linked to the question of whether harsh treatment will work. Again, how effective, in fact, is sexual humiliation, or isolation, or torture?

After the Gulf War, it was widely acknowledged that the decision to take down the electrical grid by striking the generators had left power out for far longer than necessary, contributing to unsanitary water supply and the unnecessary death of many thousands from cholera. Military planners involved have admitted this was a mistake, and they have reportedly revised their procedures accordingly. In Kosovo and Iraq, such a devastating blow to the electrical grid was not struck.

But in reviewing the Gulf War experience, they will not say that taking out the generators lacked proportionality or necessity, or that it was excessive given what they knew then and what they were trying to achieve. These legal standards remain the solid ground on which their acts, and, ultimately the deaths of many thousands, can remain legitimated

Weighing and Balancing—What Exactly?

The transformation of the law in war into a vocabulary of persuasion about legitimacy is not the end of the matter. We still need to figure out, for a given purpose, a given argument, just what is, in fact, necessary or proportional. And of course, it is in this spirit that targets in the recent Iraq conflict were pored over by lawyers. But even in the best of times, the promise of weighing and balancing is rarely met.

I have learned that if you ask a military professional precisely how many civilians can you kill to offset how much risk to one of your own men, you won't receive a straight answer. When the Senegalese asked us, we'd say "it's a judgment call." Indeed, at least so far as I have been able to ascertain, there is no background exchange rate for civilian life. What you find instead are rules kicking the decision up the chain of command as the number of civilians increases, until the decision moves offstage from military professionals to politicians.

In the early days of the Iraq war, coalition forces were certainly frustrated by Iraqi soldiers who advanced in the company of civilians. A Corporal Mikael McIntosh reported that he and a colleague had declined several times to shoot soldiers in fear of harming civilians. "It's a judgment call," he said, "if the risks outweigh the losses, then you don't take the shot." He offered an example: "There was one Iraqi soldier, and 25 women and children, I didn't take the shot." His colleague, Sergeant Eric Schrumpf chipped in to describe facing one soldier among two or three civilians, opening fire, and killing civilians: "We dropped a few civilians, but what do you do. I'm sorry, but the chick was in the way."[9]

There is no avoidance of decisions of this type in warfare. The difficulty arises when humanitarian law transforms decisions about whom to kill into judgments. When it encourages us to think the chick's death resulted not from an exercise of human freedom, for which a moral being is responsible, but rather from the abstract operation of professional principles.

We know there are clear cases both ways—destroying the village to save it, or minor accidental damage en route to victory—but we also know that the principles are most significant in the great run of situations that fall in between. What does it mean to pretend these decisions are principled judgments? How should we evaluate the irreducibly imaginary quality of the promise that costs and benefits will be weighed, that warfare will be proportional, its violence necessary?

I was struck that Iraq war reporting was filled with anecdotes about soldiers overcome by remorse at having slaughtered civilians, and being counseled back to duty by their officers, their chaplains, and their mental health professionals, who explained that what they had done was necessary, proportional, and therefore just.

Of course, if you ask leading humanitarian law experts how many civilians you can kill for this or that, you will also not get an answer. Rather than saying "it's a judgment call," however, they are likely to say something like "you just can't target civilians," thereby refusing to engage in the pragmatic assessments necessary to make that rule applicable in combat; defaulting, if you will, to the external strategy of denunciation abandoned a century ago by humanitarian law.

In psychological terms, it is hard to avoid interpreting this pragmatism-promised-but-not-delivered as a form of denial; a collaborative denial—by humanitarians and military lawyers—of their participation in the machinery of war.

In the military vernacular, it might be more accurate to sense a collaborative avoidance of command responsibility and leadership; a willingness to push responsibility up to the domain of politics or down to the domain of rules. The tendency to blame the civilian leadership—or the lawyers—is well known. But we also know lawyers, whether inside or outside the military, who make that easy by pretending the law is more decisive—or more open—than it is.

The Law in War Comes Unstuck

In this audience, I do not need to emphasize the extent to which the traditional law in war is becoming unstuck; questioned from every angle.

In part this is a matter of blurring boundaries—new technologies and new modes of warfare pressing a doctrinal world imagined in the wake of wars that seemed "modern" in the 1860s. The language has proliferated—self-defense, war, hostilities, the use of force, resort to arms, police action, peace enforcement, peacemaking, peacekeeping. Who can align them confidently, like "chop," "whip," "blend" on the Cuisinart? They are all technical terms in military parlance and legal doctrine, but also in ethical and political discourse.

Earlier this month I participated in a lengthy discussion at the Council on Foreign Relations on "post-conflict" reconstruction. All agreed we were far from 19th-century warfare. Who was the enemy and where was the battlefield? The old days of industrial warfare are over; you're not trying to blow stuff up on the battlefield until the political leadership surrenders. It's asymmetric, it's chaotic, it's not linear. The battlespace is at once global and intensely local; there are no front lines. Here at home, we hardly seem at war—the enemy, the conflict, the political goal, all have become slippery.

For the military, everything important and difficult seems to happen in a kind of grey area between war and peace. The idea of a boundary between law enforcement, limited by human rights law, and military action, limited by the laws of armed conflict, seems ever less tenable. In the same city troops are at once engaging in conflict, stabilizing a neighborhood after conflict, and performing humanitarian, nation-building tasks.

I heard military men with experience in Bosnia, Kosovo, and Iraq all stress the continuities of the transition from war to peace; they insisted the term "post-conflict" was a misnomer. In principle, planning and training for the post-conflict phase should begin before the conflict, even if it seems hard to imagine identifying "spare" troops in the preparation phase who might be saved for later tasks. In any event, restoring water or eliminating sewage after the conflict are part of winning the war. To paraphrase Clausewitz, post-conflict action is the continuation of conflict by other means. Anyway, they wondered, when did the war start—on 9/11? In 1991? In 2003?

The boundaries are blurry. Everywhere we find public/private partnerships, outsourcing, insurgents who melt into the mosque, armed soldiers who turn out to work for private contractors. There are civilians all over the battlefield, not only insurgents dressed as refugees, but special forces operatives dressing like natives, private contractors dressing like Arnold Schwarzenegger, and all the civilians running the complex technology and logistical chains "behind" modern warfare.

The rules of engagement are no longer just those of humanitarian law or military discipline, there is also private law, contract, environmental regulation. Apparently at one point the Swiss company backing up life insurance contracts for private convoy drivers in Iraq imposed a requirement of additional armed guards if they were to pay on any claim, slowing the whole operation.

There is no question that all this generates enormously difficult doctrinal problems; we will deal with many of them over the next days. Why should weapons permissible in domestic riot control and policing—non-penetrating bullets, certain gases—not be available on the battlefield if combat blurs easily with stabilization and law enforcement? In close quarters on board a ship interdicted during a blockade should seamen be issued weaponry appropriate for combat or law enforcement? To what extent does law shape or limit this decision?

In this new environment, we hear that humanitarian law will have to be rethought. But this is more than simply a more complex legal situation requiring more sophisticated analysis. Adjusting the law in war to post-modern warfare will require more than doctrinal ingenuity. It will require a new way of thinking about the role of law—and warfare.

Indeed, it might be more accurate to say that the fluid modern vocabulary of clear rules and sharp distinctions, broad principles and vague calculations of proportionality and necessity was designed precisely for this. It is a professional vocabulary for making distinctions and eroding them, for applying principles and simply invoking them. What will be required is a new understanding of the work of law—and of the responsibilities of command.

Sophisticated analyses of necessity and proportionality, no less than the external vocabulary of distinction and denunciation, seem ever less convincing. Each has, in its own way, become a vocabulary of warfare. More importantly, we are increasingly likely to interpret whatever military or humanitarian professionals say about the use of force in strategic terms, that is as things said for a reason, things said for tactical advantage. As professionals, civilian or military, we know how to make—and unmake—the distinctions between war and peace, between civilian and combatant.

Brigadier General Charles Dunlap gave me the arresting term "lawfare," using law as a weapon, offensively and defensively, to legally condition the battlefield. Partly this is public relations; shaping expectations about what will happen and what will be legitimate. Getting the word out that we will—and we may—kill some civilians.

Take the difficult question, when does war end? The answer is not to be found in law or fact, but in strategy. Declaring the end of hostilities might be a matter of election theater or military assessment. Just like announcing that there remains "a long way to go," or that the "insurgency is in its final throes." These appear as factual or legal assessments, but we should understand them as arguments—messages but also weapons. Communicating the war is fighting the war.

The old distinctions have not disappeared. Indeed, we sometimes want to insist upon a bright line. For the military, after all, defining the battlefield defines the privilege to kill in the same way that aid agencies want the guys digging the wells to be seen as humanitarians, not post-conflict combatants. Defining the not-battlefield opens a "space" for humanitarian action. For both professions, distinguishing, like balancing, has become at once a mode of warfare and of pacifism.

Ending conflict, calling it occupation; ending occupation, calling it sovereignty; then opening hostilities, calling it a police action; suspending the judicial requirements of policing, declaring a state of emergence, a zone of insurgency. All these things are also tactics in the conflict. We are occupying, but Falluja, for a few weeks, is again a combat zone, and so on. Defining the battlefield is both a matter of deployed force and a rhetorical claim. This is a war, this is an occupation, this is a police action, this is a security zone. These are insurgents, those are criminals, these are illegal combatants, and so on. And these are all claims with audiences. The old legal issues are there—the claim must have a plausible validity; we must understand its persuasive potential.

Audience reaction matters. For detainees at Guantanamo the "war" may never end. What war, which war? The war on terror? The war on poverty? Al Qaida? In Iraq? The Taliban? Afghanistan? The war for security, for oil, for . . . ? What is, precisely, the objective that once achieved will end their war? What limits our ability to extend the war for which they are held indefinitely—doctrines of the law of armed conflict? Hardly, the CNN effect gets closer to the mark. When publics with power to impede our ability to achieve our strategic objectives find our argument that the war for those prisoners has not ended so unpersuasive that they exercise that power, we will need to change course.

We have heard that police and combat operations now go side-by-side; the zone of combat abuts, overlaps the zones of occupation and military action. Must we therefore conclude that human rights law and the law of armed conflict operate concurrently, across the battlespace? Yes and no. The assertion that human rights limits action in combat will seem persuasive to some audiences in some situations; as will the assertion that the activities are distinct, the laws separate. Lawfare—managing law and war together—requires a strategic assessment of both claims and both responses, and an active strategy by military and humanitarian actors to frame the situation in one or the other.

In these strategic assessments, the legal questions become these: who, understanding the law in what way, will be able to do what to affect our ongoing efforts? How, using what mix of behavior and assertion, can we transform the strategic situation to our advantage? This is not a question of validity, not even of persuasion. This requires a social analysis of the dynamic interaction between ideas about the law and strategic objectives.

As humanitarian and military professionals work with the law of armed conflict, they change it. Of course the law that pre-exists a conflict constrains its course—conditioning expectations, establishing habits of mind and standard procedures of operation. Humanitarians and military professionals are used to thinking about influencing the law in peacetime through careful negotiations, through codification, through advocacy, and through assertions of right. It can be hard, in combat, to see that the law is, if anything, more open to change. When humanitarian voices seize on vivid images of civilian casualties to raise expectations about the required accuracy of military targeting, they are changing the legal fabric.

In the Kosovo campaign, news reports of collateral damage often noted that coalition pilots could have improved their technical accuracy by flying lower, although this would have exposed their planes and pilots to more risk. The law of armed conflict does not require you to fly low or take more risk to avoid collateral damage; it requires you to avoid superfluous injury and unnecessary suffering. But these news reports changed the legal context—flying high to reduce risk seemed "unfair." Humanitarians seized the moment, developing various theories to demand "feasible compliance" that would hold the military to technically achievable levels of care. In conference after conference, negotiation after negotiation, representatives of the US military have argued that this is simply not "the law." Perhaps not, but the effect of the legal claim is hard to deny.

Of course, the military also seeks to affect the legal context through its public affairs activity and through its action on the battlefield. Asserting a right to attack a given objective may induce defenders to tie up assets in its defense, regardless of whether you intend to attack it or not. Attacking—or not attacking—a mosque is as much a message, as a tactic on the ground.

Military action has become legal action, just as legal acts have become weapons. When the United States uses the United Nations Security Council to certify lists of terrorists to force seizure of their assets abroad, we might say that they have weaponized the law since they could, presumably, have immobilized those assets using other technologies. Similarly when they use contracts to buy up access to commercially available satellite images of the battlefield, they could presumably have denied their adversary access to those images using other weapons. The legal and military professions have indeed merged.

None of this would have surprised Clausewitz. He continued his famous paragraph on war as a continuation of policy with a striking turn to language:

> [T]he chief lines on which the events of the War progress, and to which they are attached, are only the general features of policy which run all through the War until peace takes place. And how can we conceive it to be otherwise? Does the cessation of diplomatic notes stop the political relations between different Nations and Governments? Is not War merely another kind of writing and language for political thoughts? It has certainly a grammar of its own, but its logic is not peculiar to itself.[10]

Clausewitz might well be surprised, however, by the extent to which the turn to language has revitalized the distinction between warfare and the political. In my experience, military and humanitarian professionals operating in this vocabulary share a sense that somewhere else, outside or beyond their careful calculations, somebody *else* makes decisions in a different way—exercises political judgment and discretion. This is why the absence of a clear exchange rate for civilian lives is untroubling; if the number is high enough, it will become a political decision.

The Law of War—Do Politicians Think Differently?

This takes us directly to the law of war. Normally, of course, for military professionals, the law of war is far less present. Civilian leadership means leaving questions about the legitimacy of the conflict—the decision to go to war in the first place—to a different, the political, domain.

But, as the law in war has begun to come unstuck, professionals find themselves turning increasingly to the law of war; find themselves unable to assess the legitimacy of wartime violence without assessing the legitimacy of the war itself. We might say that the law of war has become the law in war's destiny. If the use of force is to be proportional—more force for more important objectives—it seems reasonable to think there would be a sliding scale for more and less important wars. Wars for national survival, wars to stop genocide—shouldn't they legitimate more than run of the mill efforts to enforce UN resolutions?

There can be something perverse here—harsher tactics more legitimate in more "humanitarian" campaigns? But once the law of armed conflict becomes relative, a function of the conflict's legitimacy, we must ask whether the vocabulary we use to make the "political" decision to go to war differs in kind from that we use to fight—and restrain—the conflict once underway. Are "political" decisions, in fact, different from decisions of commanding officers and humanitarian advocates?

As it turns out, while the law in war has infiltrated the military profession, the law of war has been engaged in a collateral—and equally successful—campaign to infiltrate the vocabulary of politics. The law about going to war has a history quite parallel to that of humanitarian law. As a result, the distinction between professional and political judgments is far less clear than we might wish.

This story, which can be told in shorter compass, begins with a period of rather fluid justifications expressed in a mixed vocabulary of justice and sovereign right. It is not clear, that 17th-century "unjust" war ideas ever really limited the use of military force. They may well have done more to de-legitimate the enemy and justify the cause.

In any event, by the late 19th century, international law had very little to say about the decision to go to war, a silence rooted in the assumption that war was an unrestrained prerogative of sovereign power. The modern law of war is a century long pragmatic reaction against this 19th-century legal silence.

The right and capacity to make war was so central to the late 19th-century legal definition of sovereignty that even in the 1920s, we still find jurists assessing the international legal personality of the League of Nations by asking whether it has the "right" to make war. But the League's purpose was another.

The diplomats who made the League sought to replace legal doctrines with a political institution that could sanction and deter aggression, while providing a framework for peaceful change and the peaceful settlement of "disputes." The brave new world of institutional management was born.

After the Second World War, again in the name of pragmatism, this scheme matured into a comprehensive constitutional system. As we all know, the UN Charter aimed to establish an international monopoly of force, placing responsibility for maintaining the peace with the Security Council. War was prohibited—except as authorized by the UN Charter. Not as authorized by the United Nations, but as authorized by the Charter.

Like a constitution, the Charter was drafted in broad strokes and would need to be interpreted. Over the years, what began as an effort to monopolize force has become a constitutional regime of legitimate justifications for war.

This modern vocabulary of force has a jurisprudence—an attitude about the relationship between law and power. It is the flexible jurisprudence of principles and policies, of balancing conflicting considerations, familiar from many domestic constitutional systems.

Legal scholar Oscar Schachter gave perhaps the best description in his eulogy for Dag Hammarskjold, who epitomized the new jurisprudential spirit:

> Hammarskjold made no sharp distinction between law and policy; in this he departed clearly from the prevailing positivist approach. He viewed the body of law not merely as a technical set of rules and procedures, but as the authoritative expression of principles that determine the goals and directions of collective action. . . . It is also of significance in evaluating Hammarskjold's flexibility that he characteristically expressed basic principles in terms of opposing tendencies (applying, one might say, the philosophic concept of polarity or dialectical opposition). He never lost sight of the fact that a principle, such as that of observance of human rights, was balanced by the concept of non-intervention, or that the notion of equality of States had to be considered in a context which included the special responsibilities of the great Powers. The fact that such precepts had contradictory implications meant that they could not provide automatic answers to particular problems, but rather that they served as criteria which had to be weighed and balanced in order to achieve a rational solution of

> the particular problem. . . . He did not, therefore, attempt to set law against power. He sought rather to find within the limits of power the elements of common interest on the basis of which joint action and agreed standards could be established.[11]

There is no doubt that this system of principles has legitimated a great deal of warfare. Indeed, it is hard to think of a use of force that could not be legitimated in these terms. It is a rare statesman who launches a war simply to be aggressive. There is almost always something else to be said—the province is actually ours; our rights have been violated; our enemy is not, in fact, a State; we were invited to help; they were about to attack us; we are promoting the purposes and principles of the United Nations. Something.

As the law in war became a matter of standards, balancing, and pragmatic calculation, the difficult, discretionary decisions were exported to the political realm. As the political vocabulary has itself become a matter of constitutional interpretation, our understanding of the political process has also been transformed.

This convergence of humanitarianism and militarism has transformed our understanding of international politics. Idealism no longer provides a standpoint external to the ebbs and flows of the policy conversation. Action legitimates norms, norms legitimate action. Humanitarians and statesmen, idealists and realists are in the same game, and are increasingly difficult to distinguish from one another.

International Politics: a Conversation about Legitimacy

In the international world, we imagine this shared vocabulary of principles and policy judgment to operate through conversation. States, private actors, NGOs, and national courts are participants in an ongoing conversation about the legitimacy of State behavior—legitimacy judged by their compatibility with UN Charter principles.

Conversing before the court of world public opinion, statesmen not only assert their prerogatives, they also test and establish those prerogatives through action. Political assertions come armed with little packets of legal legitimacy, just as legal assertions carry a small backpack of political corroboration. As lawyers must harness enforcement to their norms, States must defend their prerogatives to keep them—must back up their assertions with action to maintain their credibility. A great many military campaigns have been undertaken for just this kind of credibility—missiles become missives.

It was, after all, in this spirit that President Bush went to the United Nations to announce that he would enforce the Charter; and if he succeeded and the Iraq regime were to change and democracy and freedom released, the legitimacy deposit in his account would be a direct transfer from the United Nations. Of course, it was a risk; but the United Nations was also daring, and risking in resisting.

When the United Nations withholds approval or refuses to participate, it may de-legitimate the military campaign. Let us suppose it does not stop it; a determined coalition pushes ahead in the name of Charter principles. In the easy cases, the campaign succeeds; the United Nations has missed out. Or the campaign fails; the United Nations is vindicated.

The difficult case is now ours. The occupation is more difficult than anticipated, the post-conflict/post-war/peace-building/nation-building phase holds hostage the ultimate success or failure of the campaign. Op-ed writers urge all parties to ignore sunk costs, to focus on the future. Surely, they argue, we all have a stake in a successful outcome, and it makes sense for the United States and the international community to cooperate.

Perhaps, but sunk costs cannot be ignored so readily. Seen dynamically, it makes sense for Bush to resist relying on the United Nations to make good his original wager as precedent for the next case; just as it makes sense for the United Nations to resist engagement. It is no accident that we sometimes feel the Europeans want the project to fail, and sometimes they do, for in this game of meaning and precedent, to ignore sunk costs and get with the program is to take a legitimacy hit.

Either way, Iraqi citizens are paying the price, not in the "great game" of 19th-century diplomacy, but in the "great conversation" of 20th-century legitimacy.

If, interpreting the law in war, humanitarians were loath to speak about the civilians who might legitimately be killed—"you just can't target civilians"—they also resist the suggestion in the law of war that they, like military planners, decide when to draw down and when to pay into their legitimacy stockpile, and, therefore, when to accept civilian casualties as necessary for longer term objectives.

Although humanitarians talk about the long-run benefits of building up the UN system or promoting the law of force, they do not make such long-run calculations. Current costs are discounted, future benefits promised as if there were nothing to weigh against expansion of humanitarian institutions and ideas; no civilians who needed to be allowed to die for the legitimacy of the United Nations. But in this, we depart from pragmatic calculation altogether and move into the domain of absolute virtue. We are back speaking truth to power.

When I speak to civilian audiences, there is something scandalous about presenting an aircraft carrier sailing off to war as the realization of international humanitarianism. Aircraft carriers are the instruments of statesmen. Civilians prefer to think of humanitarians as gentle civilizers, lawyers whispering in the admiral's ear, protesters marching in the streets for peace, scholars documenting the norms and standards of humanitarian law, teachers instructing soldiers in the limits to warfare. Humanitarian rulership is often rulership denied.

The transformation of the law of war into a set of constitutional standards at once defined and enforced through an ex-post assessment of legitimacy earned and spent offers an open-ended vocabulary for diplomatic and military conversation. Any and all criteria that turn out to affect the legitimacy of the action in the eyes of those with the power to affect its success will, retrospectively, turn out to have been persuasive requirements of the law of war. Like the "preferences" we think stand behind market behavior, standards of legitimacy are inevitably subjective when we look forward, objective when we look back. Professionalism has, in this sense, taken us as far as it can—fully occupying the field.

Yet this new vocabulary has its own limits, blind spots, biases. Not all voices are equally heard, not all concerns equally calculated by the group of elites we call "the international community."

Those in the loop are likely to focus too much on the United Nations as proxy for world public opinion. Were opponents of the Iraq war serious when they claimed their objection to the war was the lack of UN approval? Would the war really have made more sense to them had France had a different government?

I worry when great debates about war and peace, staged in the vocabulary of the Charter, capture our attention. One unfortunate result: it has become routine to say that international law had little effect on the Iraq war. Arguments made by a few international lawyers that the war was illegal failed to stop the American administration and its allies, who were determined to go ahead, and who had, after all, their own international lawyers.

But this lets international law off the hook too easily. If we expand the aperture from the decision to invade, war looks ever more to be a product of law: the laws in war that legitimated targeting, the laws of war that provided the vocabulary for assessing its legitimacy, the laws of sovereignty that defined and limited Saddam's prerogatives and have structured the occupation, not to mention commercial rules, financial rules, and private law regimes through which Iraq gamed the sanctions system and through which the coalition built its response. The UN law of force makes these background rules seem matters of fact, rather than points of choice.

The Charter scheme encourages us to think of global policy as a combination of short multilateral police actions and humanitarian assistance. It distracts our attention from the economic side of the story—and from the development policy that comes with an invasion. It shortens our sense of how long and how difficult war to build nations or change regimes is likely to be.

In the Iraq case, international law and the UN Charter focused our attention on weapons, which when not forthcoming, de-legitimated the entire enterprise.

International law urges us to respect Iraqi sovereignty, making it all too easy to think our intervention in Iraqi affairs began with the invasion and ended with the handover of the bundle of rights we have decided to call "sovereignty."

The vocabulary of the Charter can make it more difficult to address the motives for war and devise alternative policies. Let us say the administration's hawks were right; suppose that after 9/11 it was necessary to "change regimes" from eastern Turkey to western Pakistan. In the months before the war, the international community found it difficult to discuss regime change straightforwardly. Ideas about sovereignty, the limits of the Charter, core humanitarian commitments to the renunciation of empire; all placed regime change outside legitimate debate.

Yet supposedly sovereign regimes are already entangled with one another. They struggle every day to change one another's regimes in all manner of legitimate ways. Why should this all become taboo when force is added to the mix, unless war is no longer, in fact, in Clausewitz's terms, "a continuation of political intercourse, with a mixture of other means."[12]

When it comes to force, the Charter vocabulary offered an easy and irresponsible way out. We never needed to ask how should the regimes in the Middle East—our regimes—be changed? Is Iraq the place to start? Is military intervention the way to do it? How do we compare various ways of combining military and non-military "means" to the end of regime change?

Had the Europeans not had the United Nations to shield them, not felt the geography of the European Union (EU) marked a legitimate boundary to their global responsibilities, they might well have drawn on their own experiences with "regime change" in Spain, Portugal and Greece in the '80s, with the old East Germany in the '90s, and now with the ten new member States in central and eastern Europe. Why not EU membership for Turkey, Morocco, Jordan, Palestine, Israel, Egypt—regime change through the promise and example of social and economic inclusion rather than military force.

Had our debates not been framed by the laws of war, we might well have found other solutions and escaped the limited choices of UN sanctions, humanitarian aid and war—in short, thought outside the box.

Decisionism: Command Responsibility, Leadership and Politics

I began this morning with a worry about the relationship between the military and humanitarian professions. Should we celebrate their merger in a new pragmatism or should we reinvigorate the pacifist impulse to stand outside and denounce?

The choice turns out to be a false one. The military and humanitarian professions have merged in a shared practice of making and unmaking the distinctions of war and peace that once marked the line between their respective domains. If ours has become a culture of violence, it is a shared culture, a product of military and humanitarian hands. If ours is history's most humane empire, that also is the collaborative achievement of humanitarian and military professionals.

The laws of force increasingly provide the vocabulary not only for restraining the violence and incidence of war, but also for waging war and deciding to go to war. We should be clear; this bold new vocabulary beats ploughshares into swords as often as the reverse. It forecloses our attention to other causes, consequences and alternatives to warfare.

The problem for humanitarians is no longer an unwillingness to be tough; humanitarians have advocated all manner of tough and forceful action in the name of humanitarian pragmatism, and their words have legitimated still more. The problem is an unwillingness to do so responsibly—facing squarely the dark sides, risks and costs of what they propose.

The problem for military professionals is no longer a lack of humanitarian commitment. The military has built humanitarianism into its professional routines. The problem is loss of the human experience of responsible freedom, of discretion to kill, and a loss of the political experience of free decision.

The worry I find most unsettling is the difficulty of locating a moment of responsible political discretion in the broader process. We are all experts, humanitarians, military professionals and statesmen, speaking a common military and humanitarian vocabulary.

The way out will not be to tinker with doctrines of the laws of force. The way forward will require a new posture and professional sensibility among those who work in this common language. When speaking to civilian audiences, I use the vocabulary of decisionism to evoke what I have in mind. Rather than fleeing from the exercise of responsible decision to the comfortable interpretive routines of their professional discourse, humanitarians should, I argue, learn to embrace the exercise of power, acknowledge their participation in governance, and cultivate the experience of professional discretion and the posture of ethically responsible personal freedom. International humanitarians, I argue, inside and outside the military, have sought power, but have not accepted responsibility. They have advocated and denounced, mobilized and killed, while remaining content that others governed and others decided.

The military vocabulary of command responsibility and leadership evokes many of the same ideas. The new law of armed conflict requires a different collaboration between the legal and military professions. The lawyer is brought along to carry the briefcase of rules and restrictions rather than as a participant in discussions of strategy for which he or she would share ethical, if not command, responsibility.

But military and humanitarian professionals alike, however close their partnership, however flexible, fluid and strategic their approach to law, yearn for an external judgment—by political leaders or others—that what they have gotten up to is, in fact, an ethically responsible national politics. In a sense, the commander who offloads responsibility for warfare to the civilian leadership is no different from the foot soldier who cites failures of leadership, or the lawyer who faults limitations in the rules.

The posture of professionalism against decision, or in contrast to responsibility, is only plausible so long as the ethicists and politicians are speaking another language. But they no longer do. Our language has become the language of politics and the language of ethics. The challenge for all of us is to recapture the freedom, and the responsibility, of discretion. Clausewitz was right; war is the continuation of political intercourse. When we make war, humanitarian and military professionals together, let us experience politics as our vocation.

Notes

1. CARL VON CLAUSEWITZ, ON WAR 402 (J. Graham trans., Penguin Books 1968) (1832).
2. Abraham Lincoln, Address before the Young Men's Lyceum of Springfield, Illinois (Jan. 27, 1838), *available at* http://www.presidentialrhetoric.com/historicspeeches/lincoln/lyceumaddress.html.
3. Abraham Lincoln, Gettysburg Address (Nov. 19, 1863), *available at* http://www.presidentialrhetoric.com/historicspeeches/lincoln/gettysburg.html.
4. Paris Declaration Respecting Maritime Law, Apr. 16, 1856, 115 Consol. T.S., *reprinted in* THE LAWS OF ARMED CONFLICTS 1055 (Dietrich Schindler & Jiri Toman eds., 4th ed. 2004).
5. Legality of the Threat or Use of Nuclear Weapons, Advisory Opinion, 1996 I.C.J. 226 (July 8, 1996).
6. Instructions for the Government of Armies of the United States in the Field, General Orders No. 100 (Apr. 24, 1863), *reprinted in* THE LAWS OF ARMED CONFLICTS, *supra* note 4, at 3.
7. Office of the Judge Advocate General, Canadian National Defence Joint Doctrine Manual, Law Of Armed Conflict at the Operational and Tactical Levels [B-GJ-005-104/FP-021] para. 1702, at 17-2 (Aug. 13, 2001), *available* at http://www.dcds.forces.ca/jointDoc/docs/LOAC_3.pdf.
8. Thom Shanker, *The Struggle For Iraq: Strategy*, NEW YORK TIMES, Apr. 11, 2004, at 1.
9. Dexter Filkins, *Either Take a Shot or Take a Chance*, NEW YORK TIMES, Mar. 29, 2003, at A1, B4.
10. CLAUSEWITZ, *supra* note 1, at 402.
11. Oscar Schachter, *Dag Hammarskjold and the Relation of Law to Politics*, 56 AMERICAN JOURNAL OF INTERNATIONAL LAW 1, 2–7 (1962).
12. CLAUSEWITZ, *supra* note 1.

PART II

CUSTOMARY INTERNATIONAL HUMANITARIAN LAW: THE ICRC STUDY

II

Study on Customary International Humanitarian Law: A Contribution to the Understanding and Respect for the Rule of Law in Armed Conflict

Jean-Marie Henckaerts*

Abstract

This article explains the rationale behind a study on customary international humanitarian law recently undertaken by the International Committee of the Red Cross (ICRC) at the request of the International Conference of the Red Cross and Red Crescent. It describes the methodology used and how the study was organized and summarizes some major findings. It does not, however, purport to provide a complete overview or analysis of these findings.

Introduction

In the 50 years or so since the adoption of the Geneva Conventions of 1949, mankind has experienced an alarming number of armed conflicts affecting almost every continent. During this time, the four Geneva Conventions and their Additional

* Legal Adviser, Legal Division, International Committee of the Red Cross (ICRC). The views in this article are those of the author and do not necessarily reflect those of the ICRC. This article was first published in the *International Review of the Red Cross*, Volume 87, Number 857, March 2005, at page 175 and is reprinted with permission.

Protocols of 1977 have provided legal protection to persons not or no longer participating directly in hostilities (the wounded, sick and shipwrecked, persons deprived of their liberty for reasons related to an armed conflict, and civilians). Even so, there have been numerous violations of these treaties, resulting in suffering and death which might have been avoided had international humanitarian law been better respected.

The general opinion is that violations of international humanitarian law are not due to the inadequacy of its rules. Rather, they stem from an unwillingness to respect the rules, from insufficient means to enforce them, from uncertainty as to their application in some circumstances and from a lack of awareness of them on the part of political leaders, commanders, combatants and the general public.

The International Conference for the Protection of War Victims, convened in Geneva in August–September 1993, discussed in particular ways to address violations of international humanitarian law but did not propose the adoption of new treaty provisions. Instead, in its Final Declaration adopted by consensus, the Conference reaffirmed "the necessity to make the implementation of humanitarian law more effective" and called upon the Swiss government "to convene an open-ended intergovernmental group of experts to study practical means of promoting full respect for and compliance with that law, and to prepare a report for submission to the States and to the next session of the International Conference of the Red Cross and Red Crescent."[1]

The Intergovernmental Group of Experts for the Protection of War Victims met in Geneva in January 1995 and adopted a series of recommendations aimed at enhancing respect for international humanitarian law, in particular by means of preventive measures that would ensure better knowledge and more effective implementation of the law. Recommendation II of the Intergovernmental Group of Experts proposed that:

> The ICRC be invited to prepare, with the assistance of experts in IHL [international humanitarian law] representing various geographical regions and different legal systems, and in consultation with experts from governments and international organizations, a report on customary rules of IHL applicable in international and non-international armed conflicts, and to circulate the report to States and competent international bodies.[2]

In December 1995, the 26th International Conference of the Red Cross and Red Crescent endorsed this recommendation and officially mandated the ICRC to prepare a report on customary rules of international humanitarian law applicable in international and non-international armed conflicts.[3] Nearly ten years later, in 2005, after extensive research and widespread consultation of experts, this report, now referred to as the study on customary international humanitarian law, has been published.[4]

Purpose

The purpose of the study on customary international humanitarian law was to overcome some of the problems related to the application of international humanitarian treaty law. Treaty law is well developed and covers many aspects of warfare, affording protection to a range of persons during wartime and limiting permissible means and methods of warfare. The Geneva Conventions and their Additional Protocols provide an extensive regime for the protection of persons not or no longer participating directly in hostilities. The regulation of means and methods of warfare in treaty law goes back to the 1868 St. Petersburg Declaration, the 1899 and 1907 Hague Regulations and the 1925 Geneva Gas Protocol, and has most recently been addressed in the 1972 Biological Weapons Convention, the 1977 Additional Protocols, the 1980 Convention on Certain Conventional Weapons and its five Protocols, the 1993 Chemical Weapons Convention and the 1997 Ottawa Convention on the Prohibition of Anti-personnel Mines. The protection of cultural property in the event of armed conflict is regulated in detail in the 1954 Hague Convention and its two Protocols. The 1998 Statute of the International Criminal Court contains, *inter alia*, a list of war crimes subject to the jurisdiction of the Court.

There are, however, two serious impediments to the application of these treaties in current armed conflicts and which explain why a study on customary international humanitarian law is necessary and useful. First, treaties apply only to the States that have ratified them. This means that different treaties of international humanitarian law apply in different armed conflicts depending on which treaties the States involved have ratified. While the four Geneva Conventions of 1949 have been universally ratified, the same is not true for other treaties of humanitarian law, for example the Additional Protocols. Even though Additional Protocol I has been ratified by more than 160 States, its efficacy today is limited because several States that have been involved in international armed conflicts are not party to it. Similarly, while nearly 160 States have ratified Additional Protocol II, several States in which non-international armed conflicts are taking place have not done so. In these non-international armed conflicts, common Article 3 of the four Geneva Conventions often remains the only applicable humanitarian treaty provision. The first purpose of the study was therefore to determine which rules of international humanitarian law are part of customary international law and therefore applicable to all parties to a conflict, regardless of whether or not they have ratified the treaties containing the same or similar rules.

Second, humanitarian treaty law does not regulate in sufficient detail a large proportion of today's armed conflicts, that is non-international armed conflicts, because these conflicts are subject to far fewer treaty rules than are international conflicts. Only a limited number of treaties apply to non-international armed conflicts, namely the Convention on Certain Conventional Weapons as amended, the Statute of the International Criminal Court, the Ottawa Convention on the Prohibition of Anti-personnel Mines, the Chemical Weapons Convention, the Hague Convention for the Protection of Cultural Property and its Second Protocol and, as already mentioned, Additional Protocol II and Article 3 common to the four Geneva Conventions. While common Article 3 is of fundamental importance, it only provides a rudimentary framework of minimum standards. Additional Protocol II usefully supplements common Article 3, but it is still less detailed than the rules governing international armed conflicts in the Geneva Conventions and Additional Protocol I.

Additional Protocol II contains a mere 15 substantive articles, whereas Additional Protocol I has more than 80. While numbers alone do not tell the full story, they are an indication of a significant disparity in regulation by treaty law between international and non-international armed conflicts, particularly when it comes to detailed rules and definitions. The second purpose of the study was therefore to determine whether customary international law regulates non-international armed conflict in more detail than does treaty law and if so, to what extent.

Methodology

The Statute of the International Court of Justice describes customary international law as "a general practice accepted as law."[5] It is widely agreed that the existence of a rule of customary international law requires the presence of two elements, namely State practice (*usus*) and a belief that such practice is required, prohibited or allowed, depending on the nature of the rule, as a matter of law (*opinio juris sive necessitatis*). As the International Court of Justice stated in the *Continental Shelf* case: "It is of course axiomatic that the material of customary international law is to be looked for primarily in the actual practice and *opinio juris* of States."[6] The exact meaning and content of these two elements have been the subject of much academic writing. The approach taken in the study to determine whether a rule of general customary international law exists was a classic one, set out by the International Court of Justice, in particular in the *North Sea Continental Shelf* cases.[7]

State Practice

State practice must be looked at from two angles: what practice contributes to the creation of customary international law (selection of State practice) and whether this practice establishes a rule of customary international law (assessment of State practice).

Selection of State Practice

Both physical and verbal acts of States constitute practice that contributes to the creation of customary international law. Physical acts include, for example, battlefield behavior, the use of certain weapons and the treatment afforded to different categories of persons. Verbal acts include military manuals, national legislation, national case law, instructions to armed and security forces, military communiqués during war, diplomatic protests, opinions of official legal advisers, comments by governments on draft treaties, executive decisions and regulations, pleadings before international tribunals, statements in international fora, and government positions on resolutions adopted by international organizations. This list shows that the practice of the executive, legislative and judicial organs of a State can contribute to the formation of customary international law.

The negotiation and adoption of resolutions by international organizations or conferences, together with the explanations of vote, are acts of the States involved. It is recognized that, with a few exceptions, resolutions are normally not binding in themselves and therefore the value accorded to any particular resolution in the assessment of the formation of a rule of customary international law depends on its content, its degree of acceptance and the consistency of related State practice.[8] The greater the support for the resolution, the more importance it is to be accorded.

Although decisions of international courts are subsidiary sources of international law,[9] they do not constitute State practice. This is because, unlike national courts, international courts are not State organs. The decisions of international courts were nevertheless included in the study because a finding by an international court that a rule of customary international law exists constitutes persuasive evidence to that effect. In addition, because of the precedential value of their decisions, international courts can also contribute to the emergence of a rule of customary international law by influencing the subsequent practice of States and international organizations.

The practice of armed opposition groups, such as codes of conduct, commitments made to observe certain rules of international humanitarian law and other statements, does not constitute State practice as such. While such practice may contain evidence of the acceptance of certain rules in non-international armed conflicts, its legal significance is unclear and, as a result, was not relied upon to prove the existence of customary international law. Examples of such practice were listed under "other practice" in Volume II of the study.

Assessment of State Practice

State practice has to be weighed to assess whether it is sufficiently "dense" to create a rule of customary international law.[10] To establish a rule of customary international law, State practice has to be virtually uniform, extensive and representative.[11] Let us look more closely at what this means.

First, for State practice to create a rule of customary international law, it must be *virtually uniform*. Different States must not have engaged in substantially different conduct. The jurisprudence of the International Court of Justice shows that contrary practice which, at first sight, appears to undermine the uniformity of the practice concerned, does not prevent the formation of a rule of customary international law as long as this contrary practice is condemned by other States or denied by the government itself. Through such condemnation or denial, the rule in question is actually confirmed.[12]

This is particularly relevant for a number of rules of international humanitarian law for which there is overwhelming evidence of verbal State practice in support of a rule, alongside repeated evidence of violations of that rule. Where violations have been accompanied by excuses or justifications by the party concerned and/or condemnation by other States, they are not of a nature to challenge the existence of the rule in question. States wishing to change an existing rule of customary international law have to do so through their official practice and claim to be acting as of right.

Second, for a rule of general customary international law to come into existence, the State practice concerned must be both *extensive and representative*. It does not, however, need to be universal; a "general" practice suffices.[13] No precise number or percentage of States is required. One reason it is impossible to put an exact figure on the extent of participation required is that the criterion is in a sense *qualitative* rather than quantitative. That is to say, it is not simply a question of how many States participate in the practice, but also *which* States.[14] In the words of the International Court of Justice in the *North Sea Continental Shelf* cases, the practice must "include that of States whose interests are specially affected."[15]

This consideration has two implications: (1) if all "specially affected States" are represented, it is not essential for a majority of States to have actively participated, but they must have at least acquiesced in the practice of "specially affected States"; and (2) if "specially affected States" do not accept the practice, it cannot mature into a rule of customary international law, even though unanimity is not required as explained.[16] Who is "specially affected" under international humanitarian law may vary according to circumstances. Concerning the legality of the use of blinding laser weapons, for example, "specially affected States" include those identified as having been in the process of developing such weapons, even though other States could potentially become the objects of their use. Similarly, States whose population is in need of humanitarian aid are "specially affected" just as are States which frequently provide such aid. With respect to any rule of international humanitarian law, countries that participated in an armed conflict are "specially affected" when their practice examined for a certain rule was relevant to that armed conflict. Although there may be specially affected States in certain areas of international humanitarian law, it is also true that all States have a legal interest in requiring respect for international humanitarian law by other States, even if they are not a party to the conflict.[17] In addition, all States can suffer from means or methods of warfare deployed by other States. As a result, the practice of all States must be considered, whether or not they are "specially affected" in the strict sense of that term.

The study took no view on whether it is legally possible to be a "persistent objector" in relation to customary rules of international humanitarian law. While many commentators believe that it is not possible to be a persistent objector in the case of rules of *jus cogens*, there are others who doubt the continued validity of the persistent objector concept altogether.[18] If one accepts that it is legally possible to be a persistent objector, the State concerned must have objected to the emergence of a new norm during its formation and continue to object persistently afterwards; it is not possible to be a "subsequent objector."[19]

While some time will normally elapse before a rule of customary international law emerges, there is no specified timeframe. Rather, it is the accumulation of a practice of sufficient density, in terms of uniformity, extent and representativeness, which is the determining factor.[20]

Opinio Juris

The requirement of *opinio juris* in establishing the existence of a rule of customary international law refers to the legal conviction that a particular practice is carried out "as of right." The form in which the practice and the legal conviction are expressed may well differ depending on whether the rule concerned contains a prohibition, an obligation or merely a right to behave in a certain manner.

During work on the study, it proved very difficult and largely theoretical to strictly separate elements of practice and legal conviction. Often, the same act reflects both practice and legal conviction. As the International Law Association pointed out, the International Court of Justice "has not in fact said in so many words that just because there are (allegedly) distinct elements in customary law the same conduct cannot manifest both. It is in fact often difficult or even impossible to disentangle the two elements."[21] This is particularly so because verbal acts, such as military manuals, count as State practice and often reflect the legal conviction of the State involved at the same time.

When there is sufficiently dense practice, an *opinio juris* is generally contained within that practice and, as a result, it is not usually necessary to demonstrate separately the existence of an *opinio juris*. In situations where practice is ambiguous, however, *opinio juris* plays an important role in determining whether or not that practice counts towards the formation of custom. This is often the case with omissions, when States do not act or react but it is not clear why. It is in such cases that both the International Court of Justice and its predecessor, the Permanent Court of International Justice, have sought to establish the separate existence of an *opinio juris* in order to determine whether instances of ambiguous practice counted towards the establishment of customary international law.[22]

In the area of international humanitarian law, where many rules require abstention from certain conduct, omissions pose a particular problem in the assessment of *opinio juris* because it has to be proved that the abstention is not a coincidence but based on a legitimate expectation. When such a requirement of abstention is indicated in international instruments and official statements, the existence of a legal requirement to abstain from the conduct in question can usually be proved. In addition, such abstentions may occur after the behavior in question created a certain controversy, which also helps to show that the abstention was not coincidental, although it is not always easy to prove that the abstention occurred out of a sense of legal obligation.

Impact of Treaty Law

Treaties are also relevant in determining the existence of customary international law because they help shed light on how States view certain rules of international law. Hence, the ratification, interpretation and implementation of a treaty, including reservations and statements of interpretation made upon ratification, were included in the study. In the *North Sea Continental Shelf* cases, the International Court of Justice clearly considered the degree of ratification of a treaty to be relevant to the assessment of customary international law. In that case, the Court stated that "the number of ratifications and accessions so far secured [39] is, though respectable, hardly sufficient", especially in a context where practice outside the treaty was contradictory.[23] Conversely, in the *Nicaragua* case, the Court placed a great deal of weight, when assessing the customary status of the non-intervention rule, on the fact that the Charter of the United Nations was almost universally ratified.[24] It can even be the case that a treaty provision reflects customary law, even though the treaty is not yet in force, provided that there is sufficiently similar practice, including by specially affected States, so that there remains little likelihood of significant opposition to the rule in question.[25]

In practice, the drafting of treaty norms helps to focus world legal opinion and has an undeniable influence on the subsequent behavior and legal conviction of States. The International Court of Justice recognized this in its judgment in the *Continental Shelf* case in which it stated that "multilateral conventions may have an important role to play in recording and defining rules deriving from custom, or indeed in developing them."[26] The Court thus confirmed that treaties may codify pre-existing customary international law but may also lay the foundation for the development of new customs based on the norms contained in those treaties. The Court has even gone so far as to state that "it might be that . . . a very widespread and representative participation in [a] convention might suffice of itself, provided it included that of States whose interests were specially affected."[27]

The study took the cautious approach that widespread ratification is only an indication and has to be assessed in relation to other elements of practice, in particular the practice of States not party to the treaty in question. Consistent practice of States not party was considered as important positive evidence. Contrary practice of States not party, however, was considered as important negative evidence. The practice of States party to a treaty vis-à-vis States not party is also particularly relevant.

Thus, the study did not limit itself to the practice of States not party to the relevant treaties of international humanitarian law. To limit the study to a consideration of the practice of only the 30-odd States that have not ratified the Additional Protocols, for example, would not comply with the requirement that customary international law be based on widespread and representative practice. Therefore, the assessment of the existence of customary law took into account that, at the time the study was published, Additional Protocol I had been ratified by 162 States and Additional Protocol II by 157 States.

It should be stressed that the study did not seek to determine the customary nature of each treaty rule of international humanitarian law and, as a result, did not necessarily follow the structure of existing treaties. Rather, it sought to analyse issues in order to establish what rules of customary international law can be found inductively on the basis of State practice in relation to these issues. As the approach chosen does not analyse each treaty provision with a view to establishing whether or not it is customary, it cannot be concluded that any particular treaty rule is *not* customary merely because it does not appear as such in the study.

Organization of the Study

To determine the best way of fulfilling the mandate entrusted to the ICRC, the authors consulted a group of academic experts in international humanitarian law, who formed the Steering Committee of the study.[28] The Steering Committee adopted a plan of action in June 1996, and research started the following October. Research was conducted using both national and international sources reflecting State practice and focused on the six parts of the study identified in the plan of action:

- Principle of distinction
- Specifically protected persons and objects
- Specific methods of warfare
- Weapons
- Treatment of civilians and persons *hors de combat*
- Implementation

Research in National Sources

Since national sources are more easily accessible from within a country, it was decided to seek the cooperation of national researchers. To this end, a researcher or group of researchers was identified in nearly 50 States (9 in Africa, 11 in the Americas, 15 in Asia, 1 in Australasia and 11 in Europe) and asked to produce a report on their respective State's practice.[29] Countries were selected on the basis of geographic representation, as well as recent experience of different kinds of armed conflict in which a variety of methods of warfare had been used.

The military manuals and national legislation of countries not covered by the reports on State practice were also researched and collected. This work was facilitated by the network of ICRC delegations around the world and the extensive collection of national legislation gathered by the ICRC Advisory Service on International Humanitarian Law.

Research in International Sources

State practice gleaned from international sources was collected by six teams, each of which concentrated on one part of the study.[30] These teams researched practice in the framework of the United Nations and other international organizations, including the African Union (formerly the Organization of African Unity), the Council of Europe, the Gulf Cooperation Council, the European Union, the League of Arab States, the Organization of American States, the Organization of the Islamic Conference and the Organization for Security and Co-operation in Europe. International case law was also collected to the extent that it provides evidence of the existence of rules of customary international law.

Research in ICRC Archives

To complement the research carried out in national and international sources, the ICRC looked into its own archives relating to nearly 40 recent armed conflicts (21 in Africa, 2 in the Americas, 8 in Asia and 8 in Europe).[31] In general, these conflicts were selected so that countries and conflicts not dealt with by a report on State practice would also be covered.

The result of this three-pronged approach—research in national, international and ICRC sources—is that practice from all parts of the world is cited. In the nature of things, however, this research cannot purport to be complete. The study focused in particular on practice from the last 30 years to ensure that the result would be a restatement of contemporary customary international law, but, where still relevant, older practice was also cited.

Expert Consultations

In a first round of consultations, the ICRC invited the international research teams to produce an executive summary containing a preliminary assessment of customary international humanitarian law on the basis of the practice collected. These executive summaries were discussed within the Steering Committee at three meetings in Geneva in 1998. The executive summaries were duly revised and, during a second round of consultations, submitted to a group of academic and governmental experts from all regions of the world. These experts were invited in their personal capacity by the ICRC to attend two meetings with the Steering Committee in Geneva in 1999, during which they helped to evaluate the practice collected and indicated particular practice that had been missed.[32]

Writing of the Report

The assessment by the Steering Committee, as reviewed by the group of academic and governmental experts, served as a basis for the writing of the final report. The authors of the study re-examined the practice, reassessed the existence of custom, reviewed the formulation and the order of the rules and drafted the commentaries. These draft texts were submitted to the Steering Committee, the group of academic and governmental experts and the ICRC Legal Division for comment. The text was further updated and finalized, taking into account the comments received.

Summary of Findings

The great majority of the provisions of the Geneva Conventions, including common Article 3, are considered to be part of customary international law.[33] Furthermore, given that there are now 192 parties to the Geneva Conventions, they are binding on nearly all States as a matter of treaty law. Therefore, the customary nature of the provisions of the Conventions was not the subject as such of the study. Rather, the study focused on issues regulated by treaties that have not been universally ratified, in particular the Additional Protocols, the Hague Convention for the Protection of Cultural Property and a number of specific conventions regulating the use of weapons.

The description below of rules of customary international law does not seek to explain why these rules are customary, nor does it present the practice on the basis of which this conclusion was reached. The explanation of why a rule is considered customary can be found in Volume I of the study, while the corresponding practice can be found in Volume II.

International Armed Conflicts

Additional Protocol I codified pre-existing rules of customary international law but also laid the foundation for the formation of new customary rules. The practice collected in the framework of the study bears witness to the profound impact of Additional Protocol I on the practice of States, not only in international but also in non-international armed conflicts (see below). In particular, the study found that the basic principles of Additional Protocol I have been very widely accepted, more widely than the ratification record of Additional Protocol I would suggest.

Even though the study did not seek to determine the customary nature of specific treaty provisions, in the end it became clear that there are many customary rules which are identical or similar to those found in treaty law. Examples of rules found to be customary and which have corresponding provisions in Additional Protocol I include: the principle of distinction between civilians and combatants and between civilian objects and military objectives;[34] the prohibition of indiscriminate attacks;[35] the principle of proportionality in attack;[36] the obligation to take feasible precautions in attack and against the effects of attack;[37] the obligation to respect and protect medical and religious personnel, medical units and transports,[38] humanitarian relief personnel and objects,[39] and civilian journalists;[40] the obligation to protect medical duties;[41] the prohibition of attacks on non-defended localities and demilitarized zones;[42] the obligation to provide quarter and to safeguard an enemy *hors de combat*;[43] the prohibition of starvation;[44] the prohibition of attacks on objects indispensable to the survival of the civilian population;[45] the prohibition of improper use of emblems and perfidy;[46] the obligation to respect the fundamental guarantees of civilians and persons *hors de combat*;[47] the obligation to account for missing persons;[48] and the specific protections afforded to women and children.[49]

Non-international Armed Conflicts

Over the last few decades, there has been a considerable amount of practice insisting on the protection of international humanitarian law in this type of conflicts. This body of practice has had a significant influence on the formation of customary law applicable in non-international armed conflicts. Like Additional Protocol I, Additional Protocol II has had a far-reaching effect on this practice and, as a result, many of its provisions are now considered to be part of customary international law. Examples of rules found to be customary and which have corresponding provisions in Additional Protocol II include: the prohibition of attacks on civilians;[50] the obligation to respect and protect medical and religious personnel, medical units and transports;[51] the obligation to protect medical duties;[52] the prohibition of starvation;[53] the prohibition of attacks on objects indispensable to the survival of the civilian population;[54] the obligation to respect the fundamental guarantees of civilians and persons *hors de combat*;[55] the obligation to search for and respect and protect the wounded, sick and shipwrecked;[56] the obligation to search for and protect the dead;[57] the obligation to protect persons deprived of their liberty;[58] the prohibition of forced movement of civilians;[59] and the specific protections afforded to women and children.[60]

However, the most significant contribution of customary international humanitarian law to the regulation of internal armed conflicts is that it goes beyond the provisions of Additional Protocol II. Indeed, practice has created a substantial number of customary rules that are more detailed than the often rudimentary provisions in Additional Protocol II and has thus filled important gaps in the regulation of internal conflicts.

For example, Additional Protocol II contains only a rudimentary regulation of the conduct of hostilities. Article 13 provides that "the civilian population as such, as well as individual civilians, shall not be the object of attack . . . unless and for such time as they take a direct part in hostilities." Unlike Additional Protocol I, Additional Protocol II does not contain specific rules and definitions with respect to the principles of distinction and proportionality.

The gaps in the regulation of the conduct of hostilities in Additional Protocol II have, however, largely been filled through State practice, which has led to the creation of rules parallel to those in Additional Protocol I, but applicable as customary law to non-international armed conflicts. This covers the basic principles on the conduct of hostilities and includes rules on specifically protected persons and objects and specific methods of warfare.[61]

Similarly, Additional Protocol II contains only a very general provision on humanitarian relief for civilian populations in need. Article 18(2) provides that "if the civilian population is suffering undue hardship owing to a lack of the supplies essential for its survival . . . relief actions for the civilian population which are of an exclusively humanitarian and impartial nature and which are conducted without any adverse distinction shall be undertaken." Unlike Additional Protocol I, Additional Protocol II does not contain specific provisions requiring respect for and protection of humanitarian relief personnel and objects and obliging parties to the conflict to allow and facilitate rapid and unimpeded passage of humanitarian relief for civilians in need and to ensure the freedom of movement of authorized humanitarian relief personnel, although it can be argued that such requirements are implicit in Article 18(2) of the Protocol. These requirements have crystallized, however, into customary international law applicable in both international and non-international armed conflicts as a result of widespread, representative and virtually uniform practice to that effect.

In this respect it should be noted that while both Additional Protocols I and II require the consent of the parties concerned for relief actions to take place,[62] most of the practice collected does not mention this requirement. It is nonetheless self-evident that a humanitarian organization cannot operate without the consent of the party concerned. However, such consent must not be refused on arbitrary grounds. If it is established that a civilian population is threatened with starvation and a humanitarian organization which provides relief on an impartial and non-discriminatory basis is able to remedy the situation, a party is obliged to give consent.[63] While consent may not be withheld for arbitrary reasons, practice recognizes that the party concerned may exercise control over the relief action and that humanitarian relief personnel must respect domestic law on access to territory and security requirements in force.

Issues Requiring Further Clarification

The study also revealed a number of areas where practice is not clear. For example, while the terms "combatants" and "civilians" are clearly defined in international armed conflicts,[64] in non-international armed conflicts practice is ambiguous as to whether, for purposes of the conduct of hostilities, members of armed opposition groups are considered members of armed forces or civilians. In particular, it is not clear whether members of armed opposition groups are civilians who lose their protection from attack when directly participating in hostilities or whether members of such groups are liable to attack as such. This lack of clarity is also reflected in treaty law. Additional Protocol II, for example, does not contain a definition of civilians or of the civilian population even though these terms are used in several provisions.[65] Subsequent treaties, applicable in non-international armed conflicts, similarly use the terms civilians and civilian population without defining them.[66]

A related area of uncertainty affecting the regulation of both international and non-international armed conflicts is the absence of a precise definition of the term "direct participation in hostilities." Loss of protection against attack is clear and uncontested when a civilian uses weapons or other means to commit acts of violence against human or material enemy forces. But there is also considerable practice which gives little or no guidance on the interpretation of the term "direct participation," stating, for example, that an assessment has to be made on a case-by-case basis or simply repeating the general rule that direct participation in hostilities causes civilians to lose protection against attack. Related to this issue is the question of how to qualify a person in case of doubt. Because of these uncertainties, the ICRC is seeking to clarify the notion of direct participation by means of a series of expert meetings that began in 2003.[67]

Another issue still open to question is the exact scope and application of the principle of proportionality in attack. While the study revealed widespread support for this principle, it does not provide more clarification than contained in treaty law as to how to balance military advantage against incidental civilian losses.

Selected Issues on the Conduct of Hostilities

Additional Protocols I and II introduced a new rule prohibiting attacks on works and installations containing dangerous forces, even where these objects are military objectives, if such attack may cause the release of dangerous forces and consequent severe losses among the civilian population.[68] While it is not clear whether these specific rules have become part of customary law, practice shows that States are conscious of the high risk of severe incidental losses which can result from attacks against such works and installations when they constitute military objectives. Consequently, they recognize that in any armed conflict particular care must be taken in case of attack in order to avoid the release of dangerous forces and consequent severe losses among the civilian population, and this requirement was found to be part of customary international law applicable in any armed conflict.

Another new rule introduced in Additional Protocol I is the prohibition of the use of methods or means of warfare that are intended, or may be expected, to cause widespread, long-term and severe damage to the natural environment. Since the adoption of Additional Protocol I, this prohibition has received such extensive support in State practice that it has crystallized into customary law, even though some States have persistently maintained that the rule does not apply to nuclear weapons and that they may, therefore, not be bound by it in respect of nuclear weapons.[69] Beyond this specific rule, the study found that the natural environment is considered to be a civilian object and as such it is protected by the same principles and rules that protect other civilian objects, in particular the principles of distinction and proportionality and the requirement to take precautions in attack. This means that no part of the natural environment may be made the object of attack, unless it is a military objective, and that an attack against a military objective which may be expected to cause incidental damage to the environment which would be excessive in relation to the concrete and direct military advantage anticipated is prohibited. In its advisory opinion in the *Nuclear Weapons* case, for example, the International Court of Justice stated that "States must take environmental considerations into account when assessing what is necessary and proportionate in the pursuit of legitimate military objectives."[70] In addition, parties to a conflict are required to take all feasible precautions in the conduct of hostilities to avoid, and in any event to minimize, incidental damage to the environment. Lack of scientific certainty as to the effects on the environment of certain military operations does not absolve a party to the conflict from taking such precautions.[71]

There are also issues that are not as such addressed in the Additional Protocols. For example, the Additional Protocols do not contain any specific provision concerning the protection of personnel and objects involved in a peacekeeping mission. In practice, however, such personnel and objects were given protection against attack equivalent to that of civilians and civilian objects respectively. As a result, a rule prohibiting attacks against personnel and objects involved in a peacekeeping mission in accordance with the Charter of the United Nations, as long as they are entitled to the protection given to civilians and civilian objects under international humanitarian law, developed in State practice and was included in the Statute of the International Criminal Court. It is now part of customary international law applicable in any type of armed conflict.[72]

A number of issues related to the conduct of hostilities are regulated by the Hague Regulations. These regulations have long been considered customary in international armed conflict.[73] Some of their rules, however, are now also accepted as customary in non-international armed conflict. For example, the long-standing rules of customary international law that prohibit (1) destruction or seizure of the property of an adversary, unless required by imperative military necessity, and (2) pillage apply equally in non-international armed conflicts. Pillage is the forcible taking of private property from the enemy's subjects for private or personal use.[74]

Both prohibitions do not affect the customary practice of seizing as war booty military equipment belonging to an adverse party.

Under customary international law, commanders may enter into non-hostile contact through any means of communication, but such contact must be based on good faith. Practice indicates that communication may be carried out via intermediaries known as *parlementaires* but also by various other means, such as telephone and radio. A *parlementaire* is a person belonging to a party to the conflict who has been authorized to enter into communication with another party to the conflict and who is, as a result, inviolable. The traditional method of making oneself known as a *parlementaire* by advancing bearing a white flag has been found to be still valid. In addition, it is recognized practice that the parties may appeal to a third party to facilitate communication, for example a protecting power or an impartial and neutral humanitarian organization acting as a substitute, in particular the ICRC, but also an international organization or a peacekeeping force. Collected practice shows that various institutions and organizations have acted as intermediaries in negotiations in both international and non-international armed conflicts, and that this is generally accepted. The rules governing *parlementaires* go back to the Hague Regulations and have long been considered customary in international armed conflict. On the basis of practice in the last 50 years or so, they have become customary in non-international armed conflicts as well.[75]

Practice reveals two strains of law that protect cultural property. A first strain dates back to the Hague Regulations and requires that special care be taken in military operations to avoid damage to buildings dedicated to religion, art, science, education or charitable purposes and historic monuments, unless they are military objectives. It also prohibits seizure of or destruction or willful damage to such buildings and monuments. While these rules have long been considered customary in international armed conflicts, they are now also accepted as customary in non-international armed conflicts.

A second strain is based on the specific provisions of the 1954 Hague Convention for the Protection of Cultural Property, which protects "property of great importance to the cultural heritage of every people" and introduces a specific distinctive sign to identify such property. Customary law today requires that such objects not be attacked nor used for purposes which are likely to expose them to destruction or damage, unless imperatively required by military necessity. It also prohibits any form of theft, pillage or misappropriation of, and any acts of vandalism directed against, such property. These prohibitions correspond to provisions set forth in the Hague Convention and are evidence of the influence the Convention has had on State practice concerning the protection of important cultural property.

Weapons

The general principles prohibiting the use of weapons that cause superfluous injury or unnecessary suffering and weapons that are by nature indiscriminate were found to be customary in any armed conflict. In addition, and largely on the basis of these principles, State practice has prohibited the use (or certain types of use) of a number of specific weapons under customary international law: poison or poisoned weapons; biological weapons; chemical weapons; riot-control agents as a method of warfare; herbicides as a method of warfare;[76] bullets which expand or flatten easily in the human body; anti-personnel use of bullets which explode within the human body; weapons the primary effect of which is to injure by fragments which are not detectable by X-rays in the human body; booby-traps which are in any way attached to or associated with objects or persons entitled to special protection under international humanitarian law or objects that are likely to attract civilians; and laser weapons that are specifically designed, as their sole combat function or as one of their combat functions, to cause permanent blindness to unenhanced vision.

Some weapons which are not prohibited as such by customary law are nevertheless subject to restrictions. This is the case, for example, for landmines and incendiary weapons.

Particular care must be taken to minimize the indiscriminate effects of landmines. This includes, for example, the principle that a party to the conflict using landmines must record their placement, as far as possible. Also, at the end of active hostilities, a party to the conflict which has used landmines must remove or otherwise render them harmless to civilians, or facilitate their removal.

With over 140 ratifications of the Ottawa Convention, and others on the way, the majority of States are treaty-bound no longer to use, produce, stockpile and transfer anti-personnel landmines. While this prohibition is not part of customary international law because of significant contrary practice of States not party to the Convention, almost all States, including those that are not party to the Ottawa Convention and are not in favor of their immediate ban, have recognized the need to work towards the eventual elimination of anti-personnel landmines.

The anti-personnel use of incendiary weapons is prohibited, unless it is not feasible to use a less harmful weapon to render a person *hors de combat*. In addition, if they are used, particular care must be taken to avoid, and in any event to minimize, incidental loss of civilian life, injury to civilians and damage to civilian objects.

Most of these rules correspond to treaty provisions that originally applied only to international armed conflicts. That trend has gradually been reversed, for example by the amendment of Protocol II to the Convention on Certain Conventional Weapons in 1996, which also applies to non-international armed conflicts and, most recently, by the amendment of the Convention on Certain Conventional Weapons in 2001 to extend the scope of application of Protocols I–IV to non-international armed conflicts. The customary prohibitions and restrictions referred to above apply in any armed conflict.

When the ICRC received the mandate to undertake the study on customary international humanitarian law, the International Court of Justice was considering the legality of the threat or use of nuclear weapons, following a request for an advisory opinion on the issue from the UN General Assembly. The ICRC decided therefore not to embark on its own analysis of this question. In its advisory opinion, the International Court of Justice held unanimously that "a threat or use of nuclear weapons should also be compatible with the requirements of the international law applicable in armed conflict, particularly those of the principles and rules of international humanitarian law."[77] This finding is significant given that a number of States undertook the negotiation of Additional Protocol I on the understanding that the Protocol would not apply to the use of nuclear weapons. The opinion of the Court, however, means that the rules on the conduct of hostilities and the general principles on the use of weapons apply to the use of nuclear weapons. In application of these principles and rules, the Court concluded, "the threat or use of nuclear weapons would generally be contrary to the rules of international law applicable in armed conflict, and in particular the principles and rules of humanitarian law."[78]

Fundamental Guarantees

Fundamental guarantees apply to all civilians in the power of a party to the conflict and who do not or have ceased to take a direct part in hostilities, as well as to all persons who are *hors de combat.* Because fundamental guarantees are overarching rules that apply to all persons, they were not sub-divided in the study into specific rules relating to different types of persons.

These fundamental guarantees all have a firm basis in international humanitarian law applicable in both international and non-international armed conflicts. In the study, most of the rules relating to fundamental guarantees are couched in traditional humanitarian law language, because this best reflected the substance of the corresponding customary rule.[79] Some rules, however, were drafted so as to capture the essence of a range of detailed provisions relating to a specific subject, in particular the rules prohibiting uncompensated or abusive forced labor, enforced disappearances and arbitrary detention and the rule requiring respect for family life.[80]

Where relevant, practice under international human rights law was included in the study and in particular in the chapter on fundamental guarantees. This was done because international human rights law continues to apply during armed conflicts, as expressly stated in the human rights treaties themselves, although some provisions may, subject to certain conditions, be derogated from in time of public emergency. The continued applicability of human rights law during armed conflict has been confirmed on numerous occasions in State practice and by human rights bodies and the International Court of Justice.[81] Most recently, the Court, in its advisory opinion on the legal consequences of the construction of a wall in the occupied Palestinian territories, confirmed that "the protection offered by human rights conventions does not cease in case of armed conflict" and that while there may be rights that are exclusively matters of international humanitarian law or of human rights law, there are others that "may be matters of both these branches of international law."[82] The study does not set out, however, to provide an assessment of customary human rights law. Instead, practice under human rights law has been included in order to support, strengthen and clarify analogous principles of international humanitarian law.

Implementation

A number of rules on the implementation of international humanitarian law have become part of customary international law. In particular, each party to the conflict must respect and ensure respect for international humanitarian law by its armed forces and other persons or groups acting in fact on its instructions or under its direction or control. As a result, each party to the conflict, including armed opposition groups, must provide instruction in international humanitarian law to its armed forces. Beyond these general obligations, it is less clear to what extent other specific implementation mechanisms that are binding upon States are also binding upon armed opposition groups. For example, the obligation to issue orders and instructions to the armed forces which ensure respect for international humanitarian law is clearly set forth in international law for States but not so for armed opposition groups. Similarly, there is an obligation on States to make legal advisers available, when necessary, to advise military commanders at the appropriate level on the application of international humanitarian law, but not on armed opposition groups.

A State is responsible for violations of international humanitarian law attributable to it and is required to make full reparation for the loss or injury caused by such violations. It is unclear whether armed opposition groups incur an equivalent responsibility for violations committed by their members and what the consequences of such responsibility would be. As stated above, armed opposition groups must respect international humanitarian law and they must operate under a "responsible command."[83] As a result, it can be argued that armed opposition groups incur responsibility for acts committed by persons forming part of such groups. The consequences of such responsibility, however, are not clear. In particular, it is unclear to what extent armed opposition groups are under an obligation to make full reparation, even though in many countries victims can bring a civil suit for damages against the offenders.

When it comes to individual responsibility, customary international humanitarian law places criminal responsibility on all persons who commit, who order the commission of or who are otherwise responsible as commanders or superiors for the commission of war crimes. The implementation of the war crimes regime, that is, the investigation of war crimes and the prosecution of the suspects, is an obligation incumbent upon States. States may discharge this obligation by setting up international or mixed tribunals to that effect.

Conclusion

The study did not attempt to determine the customary nature of each treaty rule of international humanitarian law but sought to analyse issues in order to establish what rules of customary international law can be found inductively on the basis of State practice in relation to these issues. A brief overview of some of the findings of the study nevertheless shows that the principles and rules contained in treaty law have received widespread acceptance in practice and have greatly influenced the formation of customary international law. Many of these principles and rules are now part of customary international law. As such, they are binding on all States regardless of ratification of treaties and also on armed opposition groups in case of rules applicable to all parties to a non-international armed conflict.

The study also indicates that many rules of customary international law apply in both international and non-international armed conflicts and shows the extent to which State practice has gone beyond existing treaty law and expanded the rules applicable to non-international armed conflicts. The regulation of the conduct of hostilities and the treatment of persons in internal armed conflicts is thus more detailed and complete than that which exists under treaty law. It remains to be explored to what extent, from a humanitarian and military perspective, this more detailed and complete regulation is sufficient or whether further developments in the law are required.

As is the case for treaty law, effective implementation of the rules of customary international humanitarian law is required through dissemination, training and enforcement. These rules should be incorporated into military manuals and national legislation, wherever this is not already the case.

The study also reveals areas where the law is not clear and points to issues which require further clarification or agreement, such as the definition of civilians in non-international armed conflicts, the concept of direct participation in hostilities and the scope and application of the principle of proportionality.

In the light of the achievements to date and the work that remains to be done, the study should not be seen as the end but rather as the beginning of a new process aimed at improving understanding of and agreement on the principles and rules of international humanitarian law. In this process, the study can form the basis of a rich discussion and dialogue on the implementation, clarification and possible development of the law.

Notes

1. International Conference for the Protection of War Victims, Geneva, Aug. 30–Sept. 1, 1993, *Final Declaration*, 296 INTERNATIONAL REVIEW OF THE RED CROSS 381 (1993).
2. Meeting of the Intergovernmental Group of Experts for the Protection of War Victims, Geneva, Jan. 23–27, 1995, *Recommendation II*, 310 INTERNATIONAL REVIEW OF THE RED CROSS 84 (1996).
3. 26th International Conference of the Red Cross and Red Crescent, Geneva, Dec. 3–7, 1995, Resolution 1, International humanitarian law: From law to action; Report on the follow-up to the International Conference for the Protection of War Victims, 310 INTERNATIONAL REVIEW OF THE RED CROSS 58 (1996).
4. JEAN-MARIE HENCKAERTS & LOUISE DOSWALD-BECK, CUSTOMARY INTERNATIONAL HUMANITARIAN LAW (2005) (2 volumes: Volume I, Rules; Volume II, Practice (2 Parts)).
5. Statute of the International Court of Justice, art. 38.1(b), June 26, 1945, 33 U.N.T.S. 993.
6. Continental Shelf (Libya v. Malta), Judgment, 1985 I.C.J. 13, 29–30 (June 3).
7. North Sea Continental Shelf (F.R.G. v. Den.; F.R.G. v. Neth.), Judgment, 1969 I.C.J. 3 (Feb. 20).
8. The importance of these conditions was stressed by the International Court of Justice. Legality of the Threat or Use of Nuclear Weapons, Advisory Opinion, 1996 I.C.J. 226, 254–255 (July 8).
9. Statute of the International Court of Justice, *supra* note 5, art. 38.1(b).
10. The expression "dense" in this context comes from Sir Humphrey Waldock, *General Course on Public International Law*, *in* 106 COLLECTED COURSES OF THE HAGUE ACADEMY OF INTERNATIONAL LAW 44 (1962).
11. North Sea Continental Shelf, *supra* note 7, at 43.
12. *See* Military and Paramilitary Activities (Nicar. v. U.S.), Merits, Judgment, 1986 I.C.J. 14, 98 (June 27).
13. International Law Association, Final Report of the Committee on the Formation of Customary (General) International Law, Statement of Principles Applicable to the Formation of General Customary International Law, Report of the Sixty-Ninth Conference 23 (Principal 14) (2000), *available at* http://www.ila-hq.org/pdf/CustomaryLaw.pdf [hereinafter ILA Report].
14. *Id.* at 25–26 (commentary (d) and (e) to Principle 14).
15. North Sea Continental Shelf, *supra* note 7, at 43.
16. ILA Report, *supra* note 13, at 26 (commentary (e) to Principle 14).
17. *See* HENCKAERTS & DOSWALD-BECK, *supra* note 4, Vol. I, commentary to Rule 144.

18. For an in-depth discussion of this issue, see Maurice H. Mendelson, *The Formation of Customary International Law*, *in* 272 COLLECTED COURSES OF THE HAGUE ACADEMY OF INTERNATIONAL LAW 227–244 (1998).
19. ILA Report, *supra* note 13, at 27 (commentary (b) to Principle 15).
20. *Id.* at 20 (commentary (b) to Principle 12).
21. *Id.* at 7 (para. 10(c)). For an in-depth analysis of this question, see Peter Haggenmacher, *La doctrine des deux éléments du droit coutumier dans la pratique de la Cour internationale*, 90 REVUE GÉNÉRALE DE DROIT INTERNATIONAL PUBLIC 5 (1986).
22. *See, e.g.*, S.S. Lotus (Fr. v. Turk.), Judgment, P.C.I.J. Ser. A, No. 10, at 28 (Sept. 7) (the Court found that States had not abstained from prosecuting wrongful acts aboard ships because they felt prohibited from doing so); North Sea Continental Shelf, *supra* note 7, at 43–44 (the Court found that States that had delimited their continental shelf on the basis of the equidistance principle had not done so because they felt obliged to); ILA Report, *supra* note 13, at 36–38 (Principle 17(iv) and commentary).
23. North Sea Continental Shelf, *supra* note 7, at 42.
24. Military and Paramilitary Activities, *supra* note 12, at 99–100. Another important factor in the decision of the Court was that relevant UN General Assembly resolutions had been widely approved, in particular Resolution 2625 (XXV) on friendly relations between States, which was adopted without a vote.
25. Continental Shelf, *supra* note 6, at 33. (The Court considered that the concept of an exclusive economic zone had become part of customary international law, even though the United Nations Convention on the Law of the Sea had not yet entered into force, because the number of claims to an exclusive economic zone had risen to 56, which included several specially affected States.)
26. Continental Shelf, *supra* note 6, at 29–30.
27. North Sea Continental Shelf, *supra* note 7, at 42; see also ILA Report, *supra* note 13, at 43–54 (Principles 20–21, 24, 26 and 27).
28. The Steering Committee consisted of Professors Georges Abi-Saab, Salah El-Din Amer, Ove Bring, Eric David, John Dugard, Florentino Feliciano, Horst Fischer, Françoise Hampson, Theodor Meron, Djamchid Momtaz, Milan Šahović and Raúl Emilio Vinuesa.
29. Africa: Algeria, Angola, Botswana, Egypt, Ethiopia, Nigeria, Rwanda, South Africa and Zimbabwe; Americas: Argentina, Brazil, Canada, Chile, Colombia, Cuba, El Salvador, Nicaragua, Peru, United States of America and Uruguay; Asia: China, India, Indonesia, Iran, Iraq, Israel, Japan, Jordan, Republic of Korea, Kuwait, Lebanon, Malaysia, Pakistan, Philippines and Syria; Australasia: Australia; Europe: Belgium, Bosnia and Herzegovina, Croatia, France, Germany, Italy, Netherlands, Russian Federation, Spain, United Kingdom and Yugoslavia.
30. Principle of distinction: Professor Georges Abi-Saab (rapporteur) and Jean-François Quéguiner (researcher); Specifically protected persons and objects: Professor Horst Fischer (rapporteur) and Gregor Schotten and Heike Spieker (researchers); Specific methods of warfare: Professor Theodor Meron (rapporteur) and Richard Desgagné (researcher); Weapons: Professor Ove Bring (rapporteur) and Gustaf Lind (researcher); Treatment of civilians and persons *hors de combat*: Françoise Hampson (rapporteur) and Camille Giffard (researcher); Implementation: Eric David (rapporteur) and Richard Desgagné (researcher).
31. Africa: Angola, Burundi, Chad, Chad–Libya, Democratic Republic of the Congo, Djibouti, Eritrea–Yemen, Ethiopia (1973–1994), Liberia, Mozambique, Namibia, Nigeria–Cameroon, Rwanda, Senegal, Senegal–Mauritania, Sierra Leone, Somalia, Somalia–Ethiopia, Sudan, Uganda and Western Sahara; Americas: Guatemala and Mexico; Asia: Afghanistan, Cambodia, India (Jammu and Kashmir), Papua New Guinea, Sri Lanka, Tajikistan, Yemen and Yemen–

Eritrea (also under Africa); Europe: Armenia–Azerbaijan (Nagorno-Karabakh), Cyprus, Former Yugoslavia (conflict in Yugoslavia (1991–1992), conflict in Bosnia and Herzegovina (1992–1996), conflict in Croatia (Krajinas) (1992–1995)), Georgia (Abkhazia), Russian Federation (Chechnya) and Turkey.

32. The following academic and governmental experts participated in their personal capacity in this consultation: Abdallah Ad-Douri (Iraq), Paul Berman (United Kingdom), Sadi Çaycý (Turkey), Michael Cowling (South Africa), Edward Cummings (United States of America), Antonio de Icaza (Mexico), Yoram Dinstein (Israel), Jean-Michel Favre (France), William Fenrick (Canada), Dieter Fleck (Germany), Juan Carlos Gómez Ramírez (Colombia), Jamshed A. Hamid (Pakistan), Arturo Hernández-Basave (Mexico), Ibrahim Idriss (Ethiopia), Hassan Kassem Jouni (Lebanon), Kenneth Keith (New Zealand), Githu Muigai (Kenya), Rein Müllerson (Estonia), Bara Niang (Senegal), Mohamed Olwan (Jordan), Raul C. Pangalangan (Philippines), Stelios Perrakis (Greece), Paulo Sergio Pinheiro (Brazil), Arpád Prandler (Hungary), Pemmaraju Sreenivasa Rao (India), Camilo Reyes Rodríguez (Colombia), Itse E. Sagay (Nigeria), Harold Sandoval (Colombia), Somboon Sangianbut (Thailand), Marat A. Sarsembayev (Kazakhstan), Muhammad Aziz Shukri (Syria), Parlaungan Sihombing (Indonesia), Geoffrey James Skillen (Australia), Guoshun Sun (China), Bakhtyar Tuzmukhamedov (Russia) and Karol Wolfke (Poland).

33. Legality of the Threat or Use of Nuclear Weapons, *supra* note 8, at 257–258 (with respect to the Geneva Conventions) and Military and Paramilitary Activities, *supra* note 12, at 114 (with respect to common Article 3).

34. *See* HENCKAERTS & DOSWALD-BECK, *supra* note 4, Vol. I, Rules 1 and 7.

35. *See id.*, Rules 11–13.

36. *See id.*, Rule 14.

37. *See id.*, Rules 15–24.

38. *See id.*, Rules 25 and 27–30.

39. *See id.*, Rules 31–32.

40. *See id.*, Rule 34.

41. *See id.*, Rule 26.

42. *See id.*, Rules 36–37.

43. *See id.*, Rules 46–48.

44. *See id.*, Rule 53.

45. *See id.*, Rule 54.

46. *See id.*, Rules 57–65.

47. *See id.*, Rules 87–105.

48. *See id.*, Rule 117.

49. *See id.*, Rules 134–137.

50. *See id.*, Rule 1.

51. *See id.*, Rules 25 and 27–30.

52. *See id.*, Rule 26.

53. *See id.*, Rule 53.

54. *See id.*, Rule 54.

55. *See id.*, Rules 87–105.

56. *See id.*, Rules 109–111.

57. *See id.*, Rules 112–113.

58. *See id.*, Rules 118–119, 121 and 125.

59. *See id.*, Rule 129.

60. *See id.*, Rules 134–137.

61. *See, e.g., id.*, Rules 7–10 (distinction between civilian objects and military objectives), Rules 11–13 (indiscriminate attacks), Rule 14 (proportionality in attack), Rules 15–21 (precautions in attack); Rules 22–24 (precautions against the effects of attack); Rules 31–32 (humanitarian relief personnel and objects); Rule 34 (civilian journalists); Rules 35–37 (protected zones); Rules 46–48 (denial of quarter); Rules 55–56 (access to humanitarian relief) and Rules 57–65 (deception).
62. *See* Protocol Additional (I) to the Geneva Convention of 12 August 1949, and Relating to the Protection of Victims of International Armed Conflicts, art. 70(1), June 8, 1977, 1125 U.N.T.S. 3 [hereinafter Additional Protocol I] and Protocol Additional (II) to the Geneva Conventions of 12 August 1949, and Relating to the Protection of Victims of Non-International Armed Conflicts, art. 18(2), June 8, 1977, art. 18(2), 1125 U.N.T.S. 609, [hereinafter Additional Protocol II], *reprinted in* DOCUMENTS ON THE LAWS OF WAR (Adam Roberts & Richard Guelff eds., 3d ed. 2000) at 422 and 483, respectively.
63. *See* COMMENTARY ON THE ADDITIONAL PROTOCOLS OF 8 JUNE 1977 TO THE GENEVA CONVENTIONS OF 12 AUGUST 1949, at para. 4885 (Yves Sandoz, Christophe Swinarski, Bruno Zimmermann eds., 1987); *see also* para. 2805.
64. *See* HENCKAERTS & DOSWALD-BECK, *supra* note 4, Vol. I, Rule 3 (combatants), Rule 4 (armed forces) and Rule 5 (civilians and civilian population).
65. Additional Protocol II, *supra* note 62, arts. 13–15, 17–18.
66. *See, e.g.*, Amended Protocol II to the Convention on Certain Conventional Weapons, art. 3(7)–(11), May 3, 1996, 35 INTERNATIONAL LEGAL MATERIALS 1206; Protocol III to the Convention on Certain Conventional Weapons, art. 2, Oct. 10, 1980, 1342 U.N.T.S. 137; Ottawa Convention on the Prohibition of Anti-personnel Mines, preamble, Sept. 18, 1997, 36 INTERNATIONAL LEGAL MATERIALS 1507; Statute of the International Criminal Court, *supra* note 5, art. 8(2)(e)(i), (iii) and (viii).
67. *See, e.g.*, Direct Participation in Hostilities under International Humanitarian Law, Report prepared by the International Committee of the Red Cross (Sept. 2003), *available at* www.icrc.org.
68. Additional Protocol I, *supra* note 62, art. 56(1) (followed, however, by exceptions in paragraph 2) and Additional Protocol II, *supra* note 62, art. 15 (with no exceptions).
69. *See* HENCKAERTS & DOSWALD-BECK, *supra* note 4, Vol. I, Rule 45.
70. Legality of the Threat or Use of Nuclear Weapons, *supra* note 8, para. 30.
71. *See* HENCKAERTS & DOSWALD-BECK, *supra* note 4, Vol. I, Rule 44.
72. *See id.*, Rule 33.
73. International Military Tribunal at Nuremberg, Case of the Major War Criminals, Judgment, Oct. 1, 1946, Official Documents, Vol. I, pp. 253–254.
74. *See* Statute of the International Criminal Court, *supra* note 5, art. 8(2)(b)(xvi) and (e)(v) (Elements of Crimes for the International Criminal Court, Pillage as a war crime).
75. *See* HENCKAERTS & DOSWALD-BECK, *supra* note 4, Vol. I, Rules 67–69.
76. This rule incorporates a reference to a number of other rules of customary international law, namely the prohibition of biological and chemical weapons; the prohibition of attacks against vegetation that is not a military objective; the prohibition of attacks that would cause incidental loss of civilian life, injury to civilians, damage to civilian objects, or a combination thereof, which may be expected to be excessive in relation to the concrete and direct military advantage anticipated; and the prohibition on causing widespread, long-term and severe damage to the natural environment. *See id.*, Rule 76.
77. Legality of the Threat or Use of Nuclear Weapons, *supra* note 8, at 226.
78. *Id.*; *see also* United Nations General Assembly, 51st session, First Committee, Statement by the International Committee of the Red Cross, UN Doc. A/C.1/51/PV.8, 18 October 1996, p. 10,

reprinted in 316 INTERNATIONAL REVIEW OF THE RED CROSS 118–119 (1997) ("the ICRC finds it difficult to envisage how a use of nuclear weapons could be compatible with the rules of international law").

79. These rules include the fundamental guarantees that civilians and persons *hors de combat* be treated humanely and without adverse distinction; the prohibition of murder; the prohibition of torture, cruel or inhuman treatment and outrages upon personal dignity, in particular humiliating and degrading treatment; the prohibition of corporal punishment; the prohibition of mutilation, medical or scientific experiments; the prohibition of rape and other forms of sexual violence; the prohibition of slavery and the slave trade in all their forms; the prohibition of hostage-taking; the prohibition of the use of human shields; fair trial guarantees; the prohibition of collective punishments; and the requirement to respect the convictions and religious practices of civilians and persons *hors de combat*. *See* HENCKAERTS & DOSWALD-BECK, *supra* note 4, Vol. I, Rules 87–94, 96–97 and 100–104.

80. *See id.*, Rules 95, 98–99 and 105.

81. *See id.*, Introduction to Chapter 32, Fundamental Guarantees.

82. Legal Consequences of the Construction of a Wall in the Occupied Palestinian Territory, Advisory Opinion, (July 9, 2004), 43 INTERNATIONAL LEGAL MATERIALS 1009, para. 106 at 1038, *available at* http://www.icj-cij.org/icjwww/idocket/imwp/imwpframe.htm.

83. Additional Protocol II, *supra* note 62, art. 1(1).

Annex

List of Customary Rules of International Humanitarian Law

Note. This list is based on the conclusions set out in Volume I of the study on customary international humanitarian law. As the study did not seek to determine the customary nature of each treaty rule of international humanitarian law, it does not necessarily follow the structure of existing treaties. The scope of application of the rules is indicated in square brackets. The abbreviation IAC refers to customary rules applicable in international armed conflicts and the abbreviation NIAC to customary rules applicable in non-international armed conflicts. In the latter case, some rules are indicated as being "arguably" applicable because practice generally pointed in that direction but was less extensive.

The Principle of Distinction

Distinction between Civilians and Combatants

Rule 1. The parties to the conflict must at all times distinguish between civilians and combatants. Attacks may only be directed against combatants. Attacks must not be directed against civilians. [IAC/NIAC]

Rule 2. Acts or threats of violence the primary purpose of which is to spread terror among the civilian population are prohibited. [IAC/NIAC]

Rule 3. All members of the armed forces of a party to the conflict are combatants, except medical and religious personnel. [IAC]

Rule 4. The armed forces of a party to the conflict consist of all organized armed forces, groups and units which are under a command responsible to that party for the conduct of its subordinates. [IAC]

Rule 5. Civilians are persons who are not members of the armed forces. The civilian population comprises all persons who are civilians. [IAC/NIAC]

Rule 6. Civilians are protected against attack, unless and for such time as they take a direct part in hostilities. [IAC/NIAC]

Distinction between Civilian Objects and Military Objectives

Rule 7. The parties to the conflict must at all times distinguish between civilian objects and military objectives. Attacks may only be directed against military objectives. Attacks must not be directed against civilian objects. [IAC/NIAC]

Rule 8. In so far as objects are concerned, military objectives are limited to those objects which by their nature, location, purpose or use make an effective contribution to military action and whose partial or total destruction, capture or neutralization, in the circumstances ruling at the time, offers a definite military advantage. [IAC/NIAC]

Rule 9. Civilian objects are all objects that are not military objectives. [IAC/NIAC]

Rule 10. Civilian objects are protected against attack, unless and for such time as they are military objectives. [IAC/NIAC]

Indiscriminate Attacks

Rule 11. Indiscriminate attacks are prohibited. [IAC/NIAC]

Rule 12. Indiscriminate attacks are those:

(a) which are not directed at a specific military objective;

(b) which employ a method or means of combat which cannot be directed at a specific military objective; or

(c) which employ a method or means of combat the effects of which cannot be limited as required by international humanitarian law;

and consequently, in each such case, are of a nature to strike military objectives and civilians or civilian objects without distinction. [IAC/NIAC]

Rule 13. Attacks by bombardment by any method or means which treats as a single military objective a number of clearly separated and distinct military objectives located in a city, town, village or other area containing a similar concentration of civilians or civilian objects are prohibited. [IAC/NIAC]

Proportionality in Attack

Rule 14. Launching an attack which may be expected to cause incidental loss of civilian life, injury to civilians, damage to civilian objects, or a combination thereof, which would be excessive in relation to the concrete and direct military advantage anticipated, is prohibited. [IAC/NIAC]

Precautions in Attack

Rule 15. In the conduct of military operations, constant care must be taken to spare the civilian population, civilians and civilian objects. All feasible precautions must be taken to avoid, and in any event to minimize, incidental loss of civilian life, injury to civilians and damage to civilian objects. [IAC/NIAC]

Rule 16. Each party to the conflict must do everything feasible to verify that targets are military objectives. [IAC/NIAC]

Rule 17. Each party to the conflict must take all feasible precautions in the choice of means and methods of warfare with a view to avoiding, and in any event to minimizing, incidental loss of civilian life, injury to civilians and damage to civilian objects. [IAC/NIAC]

Rule 18. Each party to the conflict must do everything feasible to assess whether the attack may be expected to cause incidental loss of civilian life, injury to civilians, damage to civilian objects, or a combination thereof, which would be excessive in relation to the concrete and direct military advantage anticipated. [IAC/NIAC]

Rule 19. Each party to the conflict must do everything feasible to cancel or suspend an attack if it becomes apparent that the target is not a military objective or that the attack may be expected to cause incidental loss of civilian life, injury to civilians, damage to civilian objects, or a combination thereof, which would be excessive in relation to the concrete and direct military advantage anticipated. [IAC/NIAC]

Rule 20. Each party to the conflict must give effective advance warning of attacks which may affect the civilian population, unless circumstances do not permit. [IAC/NIAC]

Rule 21. When a choice is possible between several military objectives for obtaining a similar military advantage, the objective to be selected must be that the attack on which may be expected to cause the least danger to civilian lives and to civilian objects. [IAC/arguably NIAC]

Precautions against the Effects of Attacks

Rule 22. The parties to the conflict must take all feasible precautions to protect the civilian population and civilian objects under their control against the effects of attacks. [IAC/NIAC]

Rule 23. Each party to the conflict must, to the extent feasible, avoid locating military objectives within or near densely populated areas. [IAC/arguably NIAC]

Rule 24. Each party to the conflict must, to the extent feasible, remove civilian persons and objects under its control from the vicinity of military objectives. [IAC/arguably NIAC]

Specifically Protected Persons And Objects

Medical and Religious Personnel and Objects

Rule 25. Medical personnel exclusively assigned to medical duties must be respected and protected in all circumstances. They lose their protection if they commit, outside their humanitarian function, acts harmful to the enemy. [IAC/NIAC]

Rule 26. Punishing a person for performing medical duties compatible with medical ethics or compelling a person engaged in medical activities to perform acts contrary to medical ethics is prohibited. [IAC/NIAC]

Rule 27. Religious personnel exclusively assigned to religious duties must be respected and protected in all circumstances. They lose their protection if they commit, outside their humanitarian function, acts harmful to the enemy. [IAC/NIAC]

Rule 28. Medical units exclusively assigned to medical purposes must be respected and protected in all circumstances. They lose their protection if they are being used, outside their humanitarian function, to commit acts harmful to the enemy. [IAC/NIAC]

Rule 29. Medical transports assigned exclusively to medical transportation must be respected and protected in all circumstances. They lose their protection if they are being used, outside their humanitarian function, to commit acts harmful to the enemy. [IAC/NIAC]

Rule 30. Attacks directed against medical and religious personnel and objects displaying the distinctive emblems of the Geneva Conventions in conformity with international law are prohibited. [IAC/NIAC]

Humanitarian Relief Personnel and Objects

Rule 31. Humanitarian relief personnel must be respected and protected. [IAC/NIAC]

Rule 32. Objects used for humanitarian relief operations must be respected and protected. [IAC/NIAC]

Personnel and Objects Involved in a Peacekeeping Mission

Rule 33. Directing an attack against personnel and objects involved in a peacekeeping mission in accordance with the Charter of the United Nations, as long as they are entitled to the protection given to civilians and civilian objects under international humanitarian law, is prohibited. [IAC/NIAC]

Journalists

Rule 34. Civilian journalists engaged in professional missions in areas of armed conflict must be respected and protected as long as they are not taking a direct part in hostilities. [IAC/NIAC]

Protected Zones

Rule 35. Directing an attack against a zone established to shelter the wounded, the sick and civilians from the effects of hostilities is prohibited. [IAC/NIAC]

Rule 36. Directing an attack against a demilitarized zone agreed upon between the parties to the conflict is prohibited. [IAC/NIAC]

Rule 37. Directing an attack against a non-defended locality is prohibited. [IAC/NIAC]

Cultural Property

Rule 38. Each party to the conflict must respect cultural property:

A. Special care must be taken in military operations to avoid damage to buildings dedicated to religion, art, science, education or charitable purposes and historic monuments unless they are military objectives.

B. Property of great importance to the cultural heritage of every people must not be the object of attack unless imperatively required by military necessity.

[IAC/NIAC]

Rule 39. The use of property of great importance to the cultural heritage of every people for purposes which are likely to expose it to destruction or damage is prohibited, unless imperatively required by military necessity. [IAC/NIAC]

Rule 40. Each party to the conflict must protect cultural property:

A. All seizure of or destruction or willful damage done to institutions dedicated to religion, charity, education, the arts and sciences, historic monuments and works of art and science is prohibited.

B. Any form of theft, pillage or misappropriation of, and any acts of vandalism directed against, property of great importance to the cultural heritage of every people is prohibited.

[IAC/NIAC]

Rule 41. The occupying power must prevent the illicit export of cultural property from occupied territory and must return illicitly exported property to the competent authorities of the occupied territory. [IAC]

Works and Installations Containing Dangerous Forces

Rule 42. Particular care must be taken if works and installations containing dangerous forces, namely dams, dykes and nuclear electrical generating stations, and other installations located at or in their vicinity are attacked, in order to avoid the release of dangerous forces and consequent severe losses among the civilian population. [IAC/NIAC]

The Natural Environment

Rule 43. The general principles on the conduct of hostilities apply to the natural environment:

A. No part of the natural environment may be attacked, unless it is a military objective.

B. Destruction of any part of the natural environment is prohibited, unless required by imperative military necessity.

C. Launching an attack against a military objective which may be expected to cause incidental damage to the environment which would be excessive in relation to the concrete and direct military advantage anticipated is prohibited.

[IAC/NIAC]

Rule 44. Methods and means of warfare must be employed with due regard to the protection and preservation of the natural environment. In the conduct of military operations, all feasible precautions must be taken to avoid, and in any event to minimize, incidental damage to the environment. Lack of scientific certainty as to the effects on the environment of certain military operations does not absolve a party to the conflict from taking such precautions. [IAC/arguably NIAC]

Rule 45. The use of methods or means of warfare that are intended, or may be expected, to cause widespread, long-term and severe damage to the natural environment is prohibited. Destruction of the natural environment may not be used as a weapon. [IAC/arguably NIAC]

Specific Methods Of Warfare

Denial of Quarter

Rule 46. Ordering that no quarter will be given, threatening an adversary therewith or conducting hostilities on this basis is prohibited. [IAC/NIAC]

Rule 47. Attacking persons who are recognized as *hors de combat* is prohibited. A person *hors de combat* is:

(a) anyone who is in the power of an adverse party;

(b) anyone who is defenseless because of unconsciousness, shipwreck, wounds or sickness; or

(c) anyone who clearly expresses an intention to surrender;

provided he or she abstains from any hostile act and does not attempt to escape. [IAC/NIAC]

Rule 48. Making persons parachuting from an aircraft in distress the object of attack during their descent is prohibited. [IAC/NIAC]

Destruction and Seizure of Property

Rule 49. The parties to the conflict may seize military equipment belonging to an adverse party as war booty. [IAC]

Rule 50. The destruction or seizure of the property of an adversary is prohibited, unless required by imperative military necessity. [IAC/NIAC]

Rule 51. In occupied territory:

(a) movable public property that can be used for military operations may be confiscated;

(b) immovable public property must be administered according to the rule of usufruct; and

(c) private property must be respected and may not be confiscated;

except where destruction or seizure of such property is required by imperative military necessity. [IAC]

Rule 52. Pillage is prohibited. [IAC/NIAC]

Starvation and Access to Humanitarian Relief

Rule 53. The use of starvation of the civilian population as a method of warfare is prohibited. [IAC/NIAC]

Rule 54. Attacking, destroying, removing or rendering useless objects indispensable to the survival of the civilian population is prohibited. [IAC/NIAC]

Rule 55. The parties to the conflict must allow and facilitate rapid and unimpeded passage of humanitarian relief for civilians in need, which is impartial in character and conducted without any adverse distinction, subject to their right of control. [IAC/NIAC]

Rule 56. The parties to the conflict must ensure the freedom of movement of authorized humanitarian relief personnel essential to the exercise of their functions. Only in case of imperative military necessity may their movements be temporarily restricted. [IAC/NIAC]

Deception

Rule 57. Ruses of war are not prohibited as long as they do not infringe a rule of international humanitarian law. [IAC/NIAC]

Rule 58. The improper use of the white flag of truce is prohibited. [IAC/NIAC]

Rule 59. The improper use of the distinctive emblems of the Geneva Conventions is prohibited. [IAC/NIAC]

Rule 60. The use of the United Nations emblem and uniform is prohibited, except as authorized by the organization. [IAC/NIAC]

Rule 61. The improper use of other internationally recognized emblems is prohibited. [IAC/NIAC]

Rule 62. Improper use of the flags or military emblems, insignia or uniforms of the adversary is prohibited. [IAC/arguably NIAC]

Rule 63. Use of the flags or military emblems, insignia or uniforms of neutral or other States not party to the conflict is prohibited. [IAC/arguably NIAC]

Rule 64. Concluding an agreement to suspend combat with the intention of attacking by surprise the enemy relying on that agreement is prohibited. [IAC/NIAC]

Rule 65. Killing, injuring or capturing an adversary by resort to perfidy is prohibited. [IAC/NIAC]

Communication with the Enemy

Rule 66. Commanders may enter into non-hostile contact through any means of communication. Such contact must be based on good faith. [IAC/NIAC]

Rule 67. *Parlementaires* are inviolable. [IAC/NIAC]

Rule 68. Commanders may take the necessary precautions to prevent the presence of a *parlementaire* from being prejudicial. [IAC/NIAC]

Rule 69. *Parlementaires* taking advantage of their privileged position to commit an act contrary to international law and detrimental to the adversary lose their inviolability. [IAC/NIAC]

Weapons

General Principles on the Use of Weapons

Rule 70. The use of means and methods of warfare which are of a nature to cause superfluous injury or unnecessary suffering is prohibited. [IAC/NIAC]

Rule 71. The use of weapons which are by nature indiscriminate is prohibited. [IAC/NIAC]

Poison

Rule 72. The use of poison or poisoned weapons is prohibited. [IAC/NIAC]

Biological Weapons

Rule 73. The use of biological weapons is prohibited. [IAC/NIAC]

Chemical Weapons

Rule 74. The use of chemical weapons is prohibited. [IAC/NIAC]

Rule 75. The use of riot-control agents as a method of warfare is prohibited. [IAC/NIAC]

Rule 76. The use of herbicides as a method of warfare is prohibited if they:

a) are of a nature to be prohibited chemical weapons;

b) are of a nature to be prohibited biological weapons;

c) are aimed at vegetation that is not a military objective;

d) would cause incidental loss of civilian life, injury to civilians, damage to civilian objects, or a combination thereof, which may be expected to be excessive in relation to the concrete and direct military advantage anticipated; or

e) would cause widespread, long-term and severe damage to the natural environment.

[IAC/NIAC]

Expanding Bullets

Rule 77. The use of bullets which expand or flatten easily in the human body is prohibited. [IAC/NIAC]

Exploding Bullets

Rule 78. The anti-personnel use of bullets which explode within the human body is prohibited. [IAC/NIAC]

Weapons Primarily Injuring by Non-detectable Fragments

Rule 79. The use of weapons the primary effect of which is to injure by fragments which are not detectable by X-rays in the human body is prohibited. [IAC/NIAC]

Booby-traps

Rule 80. The use of booby-traps which are in any way attached to or associated with objects or persons entitled to special protection under international humanitarian law or with objects that are likely to attract civilians is prohibited. [IAC/NIAC]

Landmines

Rule 81. When landmines are used, particular care must be taken to minimize their indiscriminate effects. [IAC/NIAC]

Rule 82. A party to the conflict using landmines must record their placement, as far as possible. [IAC/arguably NIAC]

Rule 83. At the end of active hostilities, a party to the conflict which has used landmines must remove or otherwise render them harmless to civilians, or facilitate their removal. [IAC/NIAC]

Incendiary Weapons

Rule 84. If incendiary weapons are used, particular care must be taken to avoid, and in any event to minimize, incidental loss of civilian life, injury to civilians and damage to civilian objects. [IAC/NIAC]

Rule 85. The anti-personnel use of incendiary weapons is prohibited, unless it is not feasible to use a less harmful weapon to render a person *hors de combat.* [IAC/NIAC]

Blinding Laser Weapons

Rule 86. The use of laser weapons that are specifically designed, as their sole combat function or as one of their combat functions, to cause permanent blindness to unenhanced vision is prohibited. [IAC/NIAC]

Treatment of Civilians and Persons Hors de Combat

Fundamental Guarantees

Rule 87. Civilians and persons *hors de combat* must be treated humanely. [IAC/NIAC]

Rule 88. Adverse distinction in the application of international humanitarian law based on race, color, sex, language, religion or belief, political or other opinion, national or social origin, wealth, birth or other status, or on any other similar criteria is prohibited. [IAC/NIAC]

Rule 89. Murder is prohibited. [IAC/NIAC]

Rule 90. Torture, cruel or inhuman treatment and outrages upon personal dignity, in particular humiliating and degrading treatment, are prohibited. [IAC/NIAC]

Rule 91. Corporal punishment is prohibited. [IAC/NIAC]

Rule 92. Mutilation, medical or scientific experiments or any other medical procedure not indicated by the state of health of the person concerned and not consistent with generally accepted medical standards are prohibited. [IAC/NIAC]

Rule 93. Rape and other forms of sexual violence are prohibited. [IAC/NIAC]

Rule 94. Slavery and the slave trade in all their forms are prohibited. [IAC/NIAC]

Rule 95. Uncompensated or abusive forced labor is prohibited. [IAC/NIAC]

Rule 96. The taking of hostages is prohibited. [IAC/NIAC]

Rule 97. The use of human shields is prohibited. [IAC/NIAC]

Rule 98. Enforced disappearance is prohibited. [IAC/NIAC]

Rule 99. Arbitrary deprivation of liberty is prohibited. [IAC/NIAC]

Rule 100. No one may be convicted or sentenced, except pursuant to a fair trial affording all essential judicial guarantees. [IAC/NIAC]

Rule 101. No one may be accused or convicted of a criminal offence on account of any act or omission which did not constitute a criminal offence under national or international law at the time it was committed; nor may a heavier penalty be imposed than that which was applicable at the time the criminal offence was committed. [IAC/NIAC]

Rule 102. No one may be convicted of an offence except on the basis of individual criminal responsibility. [IAC/NIAC]

Rule 103. Collective punishments are prohibited. [IAC/NIAC]

Rule 104. The convictions and religious practices of civilians and persons *hors de combat* must be respected. [IAC/NIAC]

Rule 105. Family life must be respected as far as possible. [IAC/NIAC]

Combatants and Prisoner-of-War Status

Rule 106. Combatants must distinguish themselves from the civilian population while they are engaged in an attack or in a military operation preparatory to an attack. If they fail to do so, they do not have the right to prisoner-of-war status. [IAC]

Rule 107. Combatants who are captured while engaged in espionage do not have the right to prisoner-of-war status. They may not be convicted or sentenced without previous trial. [IAC]

Rule 108. Mercenaries, as defined in Additional Protocol I, do not have the right to combatant or prisoner-of-war status. They may not be convicted or sentenced without previous trial. [IAC]

The Wounded, Sick and Shipwrecked

Rule 109. Whenever circumstances permit, and particularly after an engagement, each party to the conflict must, without delay, take all possible measures to search for, collect and evacuate the wounded, sick and shipwrecked without adverse distinction. [IAC/NIAC]

Rule 110. The wounded, sick and shipwrecked must receive, to the fullest extent practicable and with the least possible delay, the medical care and attention required by their condition. No distinction may be made among them founded on any grounds other than medical ones. [IAC/NIAC]

Rule 111. Each party to the conflict must take all possible measures to protect the wounded, sick and shipwrecked against ill-treatment and against pillage of their personal property. [IAC/NIAC]

The Dead

Rule 112. Whenever circumstances permit, and particularly after an engagement, each party to the conflict must, without delay, take all possible measures to search for, collect and evacuate the dead without adverse distinction. [IAC/NIAC]

Rule 113. Each party to the conflict must take all possible measures to prevent the dead from being despoiled. Mutilation of dead bodies is prohibited. [IAC/NIAC]

Rule 114. Parties to the conflict must endeavour to facilitate the return of the remains of the deceased upon request of the party to which they belong or upon the request of their next of kin. They must return their personal effects to them. [IAC]

Rule 115. The dead must be disposed of in a respectful manner and their graves respected and properly maintained. [IAC/NIAC]

Rule 116. With a view to the identification of the dead, each party to the conflict must record all available information prior to disposal and mark the location of the graves. [IAC/NIAC]

Missing Persons

Rule 117. Each party to the conflict must take all feasible measures to account for persons reported missing as a result of armed conflict and must provide their family members with any information it has on their fate. [IAC/NIAC]

Persons Deprived of their Liberty

Rule 118. Persons deprived of their liberty must be provided with adequate food, water, clothing, shelter and medical attention. [IAC/NIAC]

Rule 119. Women who are deprived of their liberty must be held in quarters separate from those of men, except where families are accommodated as family units, and must be under the immediate supervision of women. [IAC/NIAC]

Rule 120. Children who are deprived of their liberty must be held in quarters separate from those of adults, except where families are accommodated as family units. [IAC/NIAC]

Rule 121. Persons deprived of their liberty must be held in premises which are removed from the combat zone and which safeguard their health and hygiene. [IAC/NIAC]

Rule 122. Pillage of the personal belongings of persons deprived of their liberty is prohibited. [IAC/NIAC]

Rule 123. The personal details of persons deprived of their liberty must be recorded. [IAC/NIAC]

Rule 124.

A. In international armed conflicts, the ICRC must be granted regular access to all persons deprived of their liberty in order to verify the conditions of their detention and to restore contacts between those persons and their families.

B. In non-international armed conflicts, the ICRC may offer its services to the parties to the conflict with a view to visiting all persons deprived of their liberty for reasons related to the conflict in order to verify the conditions of their detention and to restore contacts between those persons and their families.

[IAC (A)/NIAC (B)]

Rule 125. Persons deprived of their liberty must be allowed to correspond with their families, subject to reasonable conditions relating to frequency and the need for censorship by the authorities. [IAC/NIAC]

Rule 126. Civilian internees and persons deprived of their liberty in connection with a non-international armed conflict must be allowed to receive visitors, especially near relatives, to the degree practicable. [IAC/NIAC]

Rule 127. The personal convictions and religious practices of persons deprived of their liberty must be respected. [IAC/NIAC]

Rule 128.

A. Prisoners of war must be released and repatriated without delay after the cessation of active hostilities.

B. Civilian internees must be released as soon as the reasons which necessitated internment no longer exist, but at the latest as soon as possible after the close of active hostilities.

C. Persons deprived of their liberty in relation to a non-international armed conflict must be released as soon as the reasons for the deprivation of their liberty cease to exist.

The persons referred to may continue to be deprived of their liberty if penal proceedings are pending against them or if they are serving a sentence lawfully imposed. [IAC (A&B)/NIAC (C)]

Displacement and Displaced Persons

Rule 129.

A. Parties to an international armed conflict may not deport or forcibly transfer the civilian population of an occupied territory, in whole or in part, unless the security of the civilians involved or imperative military reasons so demand.

B. Parties to a non-international armed conflict may not order the displacement of the civilian population, in whole or in part, for reasons related to the conflict, unless the security of the civilians involved or imperative military reasons so demand.

[IAC (A)/NIAC (B)]

Rule 130. States may not deport or transfer parts of their own civilian population into a territory they occupy. [IAC]

Rule 131. In case of displacement, all possible measures must be taken in order that the civilians concerned are received under satisfactory conditions of shelter, hygiene, health, safety and nutrition and that members of the same family are not separated. [IAC/NIAC]

Rule 132. Displaced persons have a right to voluntary return in safety to their homes or places of habitual residence as soon as the reasons for their displacement cease to exist. [IAC/NIAC]

Rule 133. The property rights of displaced persons must be respected. [IAC/NIAC]

Other Persons Afforded Specific Protection

Rule 134. The specific protection, health and assistance needs of women affected by armed conflict must be respected. [IAC/NIAC]

Rule 135. Children affected by armed conflict are entitled to special respect and protection. [IAC/NIAC]

Rule 136. Children must not be recruited into armed forces or armed groups. [IAC/NIAC]

Rule 137. Children must not be allowed to take part in hostilities. [IAC/NIAC]

Rule 138. The elderly, disabled and infirm affected by armed conflict are entitled to special respect and protection. [IAC/NIAC]

Implementation

Compliance with International Humanitarian Law

Rule 139. Each party to the conflict must respect and ensure respect for international humanitarian law by its armed forces and other persons or groups acting in fact on its instructions, or under its direction or control. [IAC/NIAC]

Rule 140. The obligation to respect and ensure respect for international humanitarian law does not depend on reciprocity. [IAC/NIAC]

Rule 141. Each State must make legal advisers available, when necessary, to advise military commanders at the appropriate level on the application of international humanitarian law. [IAC/NIAC]

Rule 142. States and parties to the conflict must provide instruction in international humanitarian law to their armed forces. [IAC/NIAC]

Rule 143. States must encourage the teaching of international humanitarian law to the civilian population. [IAC/NIAC]

Enforcement of International Humanitarian Law

Rule 144. States may not encourage violations of international humanitarian law by parties to an armed conflict. They must exert their influence, to the degree possible, to stop violations of international humanitarian law. [IAC/NIAC]

Rule 145. Where not prohibited by international law, belligerent reprisals are subject to stringent conditions. [IAC]

Rule 146. Belligerent reprisals against persons protected by the Geneva Conventions are prohibited. [IAC]

Rule 147. Reprisals against objects protected under the Geneva Conventions and Hague Convention for the Protection of Cultural Property are prohibited. [IAC]

Rule 148. Parties to non-international armed conflicts do not have the right to resort to belligerent reprisals. Other countermeasures against persons who do not or who have ceased to take a direct part in hostilities are prohibited. [NIAC]

Responsibility and Reparation

Rule 149. A State is responsible for violations of international humanitarian law attributable to it, including:

(a) violations committed by its organs, including its armed forces;

(b) violations committed by persons or entities it empowered to exercise elements of governmental authority;

(c) violations committed by persons or groups acting in fact on its instructions, or under its direction or control; and

(d) violations committed by private persons or groups which it acknowledges and adopts as its own conduct.

[IAC/NIAC]

Rule 150. A State responsible for violations of international humanitarian law is required to make full reparation for the loss or injury caused. [IAC/NIAC]

Individual Responsibility

Rule 151. Individuals are criminally responsible for war crimes they commit. [IAC/NIAC]

Rule 152. Commanders and other superiors are criminally responsible for war crimes committed pursuant to their orders. [IAC/NIAC]

Rule 153. Commanders and other superiors are criminally responsible for war crimes committed by their subordinates if they knew, or had reason to know, that the subordinates were about to commit or were committing such crimes and did not take all necessary and reasonable measures in their power to prevent their commission, or if such crimes had been committed, to punish the persons responsible. [IAC/NIAC]

Rule 154. Every combatant has a duty to disobey a manifestly unlawful order. [IAC/NIAC]

Rule 155. Obeying a superior order does not relieve a subordinate of criminal responsibility if the subordinate knew that the act ordered was unlawful or should have known because of the manifestly unlawful nature of the act ordered. [IAC/NIAC]

War Crimes

Rule 156. Serious violations of international humanitarian law constitute war crimes. [IAC/NIAC]

Rule 157. States have the right to vest universal jurisdiction in their national courts over war crimes. [IAC/NIAC]

Rule 158. States must investigate war crimes allegedly committed by their nationals or armed forces, or on their territory, and, if appropriate, prosecute the suspects. They must also investigate other war crimes over which they have jurisdiction and, if appropriate, prosecute the suspects. [IAC/NIAC]

Rule 159. At the end of hostilities, the authorities in power must endeavour to grant the broadest possible amnesty to persons who have participated in a non-international armed conflict, or those deprived of their liberty for reasons related to the armed conflict, with the exception of persons suspected of, accused of or sentenced for war crimes. [NIAC]

Rule 160. Statutes of limitation may not apply to war crimes. [IAC/NIAC]

Rule 161. States must make every effort to cooperate, to the extent possible, with each other in order to facilitate the investigation of war crimes and the prosecution of the suspects. [IAC/NIAC]

III

An Australian Perspective on the ICRC Customary International Humanitarian Law Study

Timothy L. H. McCormack*

Introduction

It is a pleasure for me to be here to participate in this panel discussion on the International Committee of the Red Cross's (ICRC's) *Customary International Humanitarian Law* study (hereinafter the Study) for several reasons. I have great respect for the Naval War College and its important contributions to the development of the law of armed conflict (LOAC) over many years. This is the first opportunity I have had to travel to Newport to participate in the annual International Law Conference and I am indebted to the Stockton Professor Charles Garraway and to Professor Dennis Mandsager for their invitation to me to make the trip from Down Under. I have also had a long association with the ICRC customary law study and have been looking forward to the opportunity to engage with others in response to the Study in a public forum such as this.

I also confess that Newport, Rhode Island has a reverential aura about it in the hearts of Aussies like me. It was in this place in 1983 that *Australia II* with its infamous winged keel came from three races down to wrest the "Auld Mug" from the

* Professor McCormack is the Foundation Australian Red Cross Professor of International Humanitarian Law and also the Foundation Director of the Asia-Pacific Centre for Military Law, University of Melbourne, Melbourne, Australia.

New York Yacht Club—the fiercely competitive custodians of the America's Cup. The Cup had never left American hands since it was won by *America* (hence the Cup's name in honor of its inaugural winner) in the inaugural race against the Royal Yacht Squadron around the Isle of Wight in 1851, until, after 132 years and multiple unsuccessful challenges, the Aussies finally broke the US stranglehold. It is fair, although nationally unpalatable, to concede that we were unable to match anything like the US ability to successfully defend the Cup against successive challenges (24 in total). In 1987 Dennis Connor regained the Cup and returned it to the United States—this time to the San Diego Yacht Club—before it was won by the Kiwis and now the Swiss. The Aussies have never come close to retrieving it since. All this to say that it is special to be here in Newport and I do not take the opportunity for granted.

My intention is to briefly explain the nature of my involvement with the customary law study before I move to more substantive observations. I want to offer some thoughts on positive benefits of the Study—some potential and others already manifest—as a way of congratulating the ICRC on the publication of the Study. Then I will add some of my own thoughts on reasons why the ICRC ought not be surprised by the level of criticism of the Study which has already emerged and which, in my view, will continue largely unabated.

Personal Involvement with the Study

As the incumbent of the Australian Red Cross Chair of International Humanitarian Law, it is sometimes wrongly assumed that I am an official apologist for not only the Australian Red Cross but also for the entire Red Cross Movement including the ICRC. The assumption is wrong because my appointment is to the University of Melbourne and not to the Australian Red Cross. It was agreed at the time the Chair was established that the incumbent would exercise academic freedom as an employee of the University and would not necessarily act as a spokesperson for the Australian Red Cross. On many occasions I have participated in the Australian public debate on international humanitarian law related issues on behalf of the Australian Red Cross but it is also true that on other occasions I have had to distance myself somewhat—either because I disagree with the position of the national society or, more commonly, because the decision to speak out publicly about certain issues conflicts with one or more of the Fundamental Principles of the Red Cross Movement. I accept that the "wearing of different hats" invites confusion and can be a recipe for misunderstanding but I am learning to live with those negatives. I am a firm believer in the Red Cross Movement and not because of the Chair I occupy. That belief does not translate automatically into support for every position the ICRC takes. When it comes to the customary law study I would characterize myself as cautiously supportive and I intend to explain what I mean by that general characterization in due course.

I was responsible for the preparation of the Australian national report constituting one of the forty-seven such national reports forming the primary source of evidence of State practice and expressions of *opinio juris* upon which the ICRC has reached its conclusions. The process of searching for and identifying evidence of Australian practice and national expressions of *opinio juris* in the areas of international humanitarian law covered by the Study was a novel one for Australia. I will say more of my observations of the benefits of undertaking this national study later. It is sufficient here to say that having worked hard to finalize the Australian report and then having handed it over to the ICRC early in 1998, I anticipated the publication of the Study much sooner than 2005. It is obvious from the sheer magnitude of the published Study just how massive an undertaking this project really was. Now I can see that I was entirely unrealistic to have expected to see the published version of the Study years earlier. Then though, as the years slipped by post-1998, I remember growing increasingly disappointed by the passage of time, particularly because of my acute awareness that so much more national Australian practice had occurred in the course of military operations in East Timor, in Afghanistan, in Iraq, in Bougainville and in the Solomon Islands, in inter-governmental fora around the world and in Canberra itself in the intervening period since the Australian report had been submitted to the ICRC.

The ICRC worked hard to cover developments in State practice up to the cut-off date of 2002 but I am convinced that their own staff could not have accessed the same documentation as had been possible during the preparation of the national reports. The authors of the Study make a concession to this effect in their "Introduction" when they acknowledge that "the purpose of the additional research was also to make sure that the study would be *as up-to-date as possible* and would, *to the extent possible*, take into account developments up to December 31, 2002" having earlier acknowledged that "national sources are more easily accessible from within a country."[1]

Consequently, when Yves Sandoz speaks of a "still photograph of reality,"[2] it seems to me that the photo is from the late 1990s with some touching up in 2000–2002 and that there has already been a prodigious amount of State practice and many expressions of *opinio juris* since then which are not reflected in the Study. If I am correct in that assessment it will very soon be a decade since the still photograph was taken and questions will inevitably be raised about the currency of the Study.

Some Positive Observations

I do want to take this opportunity to congratulate the ICRC on the completion of this enormous project. The more than 5,000 pages of the Study in three separate volumes is so detailed and vast that there must have been many opportunities for the individuals involved in the Project, as well as for the ICRC as an institution, to seriously doubt whether the Study would ever be concluded and appear in print. The fact that it has been published at all is testament to the commitment of the ICRC, not only to grasp the initiative and to resource the project, but also to see it through to its completion. I offer the following observations about some of the positive contributions the Study has already made or is likely to make in the near future.

Providing a Significant Australian National Catalyst

Yves Sandoz proposes his own test for the success of the Study by suggesting that "this study will have achieved its goal only if it is considered not as an end of a process but as a beginning."[3] It is my observation that the beginning of the process of reflection, discussion and debate on both the content of customary international humanitarian law, as well as on its more effective implementation, commenced much earlier than at the moment of publication of the Study. In Australia's case, the announcement by the ICRC of its decision to undertake the Study and the invitation to Australia to prepare a national report on evidence of State practice and expressions of *opinio juris* presented an unprecedented opportunity. There had never been a comprehensive audit of Australia's approach to customary international humanitarian law and this particular exercise resulted in a unique collaboration between the key Australian Government Departments of Defence, Foreign Affairs and Trade and the Attorney-General.

The preparation of the Australian study exposed examples of inconsistency and inaccuracy on national approaches to aspects of international humanitarian law. Two examples will help illustrate my meaning. Rule 70 of the ICRC Study is the prohibition on the use of weapons which are of a nature to cause unnecessary suffering or superfluous injury.[4] In Volume II of the Study the ICRC provides the substantiating State practice and *opinio juris* to support the articulation of the Rule in Volume I. In the assessment of national support for the existence of customary Rule 70 the editors of the Study cite, *inter alia*, the "Australian Military Manual,"[5] which states in relevant part that "weapon use will be unlawful under LOAC when it breaches the principle of proportionality by causing unnecessary suffering or injury."[6] On one reading of this sentence there is clear confusion between the rule of proportionality and the rule on superfluous injury or unnecessary suffering. The rule of proportionality is intended to protect the civilian population from the deleterious effects of armed conflict. The use of weapons violates the rule of proportionality when the expected loss of civilian life and/or damage to civilian property is excessive relative to the expected military advantage from an attack.[7] In contrast, the rule on superfluous injury or unnecessary suffering is intended to benefit combatants by prohibiting the use of weapons of a nature to cause superfluous injury or unnecessary suffering to those combatants who might otherwise be subjected to attack from such weapons. It is also possible to read the offending sentence to mean superfluous injury or unnecessary suffering to the civilian population, e.g., that the expected loss of civilian life or damage to civilian property is excessive (superfluous or unnecessary) relative to the expected military advantage to be gained. On the first reading, the assertion is wrong in law and on the second reading, the choice of terminology is confusing and unhelpful. On either interpretation, the preparation of the Australian national report helped to flush out examples such as this which can now be rectified and improved.

My second example also relates to the Rule of Proportionality—incorporated in Rule 14 of the ICRC Study. Again in the assessment of State practice to substantiate the existence of the customary law rule[8] the authors cite, *inter alia*, the "Australian Military Manual" that states in relevant part that:

> Collateral damage may be the result of military attacks. This fact is recognised by LOAC and, accordingly, it is not unlawful to cause such injury and damage. The principle of proportionality dictates that the results of such action must not be excessive in light of the military advantage anticipated from the attack.[9]

There is no ambiguity here. This particular articulation of the rule of proportionality wrongly asserts that the test for proportionality is whether the *actual* loss of civilian life and/or damage to civilian property is excessive in relation to the *anticipated* military advantage. Articles 51(5)(b) and 57(2)(b) of Additional Protocol I[10] both explicitly speak of the *expected* loss of civilian life and/or damage to civilian property weighed against the *anticipated* concrete military advantage. The Australian military has not suddenly altered its legal position on the test for proportionality in attack. The official position of the Government is that the test at treaty law (pursuant to the above-mentioned provisions of Additional Protocol I) and at customary international law (as encapsulated in the ICRC's Rule 14) is indeed the *expected* loss of civilian life weighed against the *anticipated* military advantage and certainly not the *actual* loss of civilian life weighted against the *anticipated* military advantage. The preparation of the Australian national report helped to expose this inaccuracy in the Australian military publication on the law of armed conflict.

The preparation of the Australian national report involved the identification of literally hundreds of government documents—many of them classified and requiring official approval for release. As representatives from different government departments poured over the documents identified by research teams, it became increasingly obvious that many of the documents had never been retrieved from files once those files had been stored. This process proved to be cathartic for those involved as we read through statements of Australian Government positions taken in various multilateral fora in the past. Now that the ICRC Study has been published, Australia has the opportunity to revisit the preparation of its national report and to measure the ICRC's articulation of customary rules against more recent Australian State practice not covered by the Australian national report. This opportunity would not exist but for the ICRC initiative and, in my view, acknowledgement ought to be made and gratitude expressed to the ICRC for it. I would be surprised if at least some of the other 46 States which also prepared national reports for the ICRC Study have not had similar experiences to the Australian one I have described.

Creating a Rich Source of Comparative Primary Material

The prodigious effort of the ICRC and the Study's editors to complete the project has resulted in over 4,400 pages (in the two volumes of the so-called "Practice" section of the Study) of references to national (and, in some cases international) legislation, case law, military manuals and statements of national government representatives in relevant inter-governmental conferences. There is simply no resource like this in the field of international humanitarian law. The *Yearbook of International Humanitarian Law* provides a helpful and detailed annual survey of State practice which effectively supplements the ICRC Study. The *Yearbook* material takes the form of "Country Reports" on State practice and developments around the world in national approaches to international humanitarian law.[11] However, this annual report obviously only covers national developments within the calendar year of each volume of the *Yearbook* and is sorted by country name in English alphabetical order—certainly not by ICRC rule in the customary law study. I am not suggesting that the *Yearbook* obviates the need for the ICRC to update its own Study. Rather, I am suggesting that apart from the "Country Reports" section of the *Yearbook* I know of no other attempt to gather primary source material from States and that reality places the ICRC Study in a unique position.

It is not difficult to conceive circumstances in which the comparative material on State practice in the Study will be extremely useful. In my capacity as *amicus curiae* on international law issues in the trial of Slobodan Milošević, for example, I can imagine that the Study's two Practice volumes could provide an invaluable source of references to a range of case law, legislation and military manuals on national approaches to the criminalization and prosecution of the war crimes of murder, willful killing, torture, willfully causing grave suffering, cruel treatment, wanton destruction of villages and plunder of public and private property. I am not suggesting that the two Practice volumes would be the sole source of investigation, but the fact that they exist and are structured on the basis of topic—corresponding with the articulation of the customary law rules in Volume I of the Study—ensures that these volumes will be consulted regularly.

I am surely not alone in this view. Others practicing in the area of international criminal law—judges, prosecutors, defense lawyers and registry staff—are all regularly referring to national case law and/or legislation to flesh out the substance of this ever-emerging body of international law. It is undoubtedly the case that as the international jurisprudence proliferates there is increasing reliance on international sources. But, it is also the reality that practitioners in this field of international law are often required to resort to national legislation and jurisprudence to supplement international sources. The natural tendency has been to rely upon the practitioner's own national sources because they are more familiar and accessible and for want of entrée into other national sources. I suspect that the ICRC Study will provide a welcome starting point for comparative criminal law research.

Of course it is far too simplistic to suggest that only international criminal lawyers will rely on the comparative material in the Study. Copies of this Study will be routinely pulled off the shelves of government legal advisers in foreign ministries, in defense establishments and in justice ministries. The sheer size of the Study will ensure that the advice of those government lawyers who do take the time to familiarize themselves with the contents of the Study will be eagerly sought.

Sparking a Global Discussion

The publication of the long-awaited Study has already spawned a succession of conferences and seminars focused on the results of the Study and reactions to it. Our own panel discussion here follows on from sessions at Chatham House, at the Annual Meeting of the American Society of International Law, in The Hague and precedes planned events in Bangkok, Brussels, Montreal, New Delhi, San Remo and Warsaw. The rush to discuss, to analyze, to question and to criticize on every continent in the world is all indicative of the intensity of anticipation of the final tabling of the Study and, perhaps more importantly for most observers, a keen desire for clarification as to how the Study might be utilized, how it will be received and the regard it will come to have in the future. It is in this sense that I entirely agree with Yves Sandoz's view that the publication of the Study is not the end but the beginning of a process and the ICRC is right to ask for as much feedback, debate and testing of its findings as it can receive.

The arrival of the Study also seems to have spawned a new debate on customary international law itself—what it is, how it is formed, what sources should be relied upon to determine its content, the identification of the precise relationship between treaty law and the development of custom. This debate is redolent, even if smaller in scale, of the debate following the decision of the International Court of Justice (ICJ) in the *Nicaragua* case. Now, of course, almost 20 years after that decision, there is a new generation of international lawyers involved in the debate. That is surely a healthy development and one for which the ICRC should be congratulated.

The Inevitability of Criticism for Articulating Customary International Law Rules

Despite the many ways in which the Study will be utilized and relied upon, the ICRC ought not be surprised either by the intensity of, or by the specific details of, the criticism directed against the Study. The "notorious imprecision" of customary international law acknowledged by Judge Koroma of the International Court of Justice in his "Foreword" to the Study[12] is a double-edged sword for the ICRC. The Study represents a laudable attempt to clarify some of the inherent imprecision but the reality of that imprecision emboldens others to challenge the ICRC's attempts at clarification. The applicability of the adage "we know it when we see it but cannot quite pin it down" to customary international humanitarian law may leave many academic international lawyers dissatisfied while simultaneously providing a sense of confidence to national government legal advisers. I am not suggesting that such advisers can tell their governments that the content of customary international law on a specific issue is whatever the government wants it be. Rather, one attraction of the "notorious imprecision" is the slight ambiguity, the elasticity at the edges of the specific detail of a rule. Any attempt to introduce precision and certainty in the articulation of the specifics of the law will inevitably draw criticism as interested parties, particularly States, will simply not agree with some of what has been included and also with some of what has been omitted.

Irrespective of the Authority of the Articulating Organization

All those involved in the study and practice of international law in the latter half of the 1980s are unlikely to forget the deluge of academic articles following the delivery of the Court's judgment in the *Nicaragua* case. It was as if the Judgment breached a dam wall unleashing a torrent of criticism and condemnation—some of it focused on the Court's decision on jurisdiction and some of it on the merits, but much of it directed at the Court's reasoning in relation to the formation of customary international law and on the process of identifying the content of customary rules on the use of force by States.[13] Just the titles of some of the articles are descriptive enough: "Icy Day at the ICJ";[14] "Between a Rock and a Hard Place: The United States, The International Court and the *Nicaragua* case";[15] "*Nicaragua* and International Law: The 'Academic' and the 'Real'";[16] and "The International Court of Justice at the Crossroads."[17]

Hilary Charlesworth's criticisms are particularly pertinent to our present discussion and I reproduce some of them in detail. Charlesworth claimed that:

> Generally, in *Nicaragua,* the Court appears to expand the category of activities that can constitute state practice. Its analysis is not easy to follow for the discussion of state practice and *opinio juris* is often elided and it is sometimes uncertain whether the Court regards a particular action as state practice, *opinio juris,* or as doing service to both. The Court relies upon the acceptance of treaty obligations as state practice. While this is a generally accepted source of state practice, the Court places special emphasis on the fact that both Nicaragua and the United States have accepted particular treaty obligations as evidence that they at least are firmly bound by such norms. Unlike jurists such as D'Amato, who regard only actions which have physical consequences as state practice, the Court accepts General Assembly resolutions and resolutions of other international organisations, particularly those in which Nicaragua and the United States participated, as forms of state practice. This approach accords with that of many jurists. The Court, however, does not appear to discriminate between international fora, nor does it discriminate between resolutions based on *lex lata* and *lex ferenda.* The Court places considerable reliance on the Declaration on Friendly Relations which is couched in legislative language. But it also relies on other resolutions and agreements whose language is not mandatory.[18]

Even if the Court in *Nicaragua* had been more precise about its delimitation between evidence of State practice and expressions of *opinio juris*, it is likely that the judgment would have been criticized by those who disagreed with the judges' assessment of the material falling into either category. The criticism has been exacerbated in substantial part by the Court's lack of clarity as to categorization, as well as by its apparent failure to accord appropriate weight on the basis of a more nuanced and discerning approach to the material it considered.

The key point here is that in its attempt to bring precision to the "notoriously imprecise" customary international law, the ICJ was subjected to a barrage of criticism. If the ICJ was subjected to such a formidable assault, the ICRC ought not expect to be immune from a similar intensity of opposition in relation to its methodology, the material it seeks to rely upon and the conclusions it has reached.

Another example of criticism of a body articulating customary international law on a particular topic involved the drafting and subsequent adoption of the Statute for the International Criminal Tribunal for the Former Yugoslavia (ICTY). The UN Security Council had called for a report from the UN Secretary-General with a Statute for the proposed Tribunal to be attached.[19] The Office of the Legal Adviser to the UN prepared the Draft Statute on the basis of customary international law explaining that:

> The international tribunal should apply rules of International Humanitarian Law which are beyond any doubt part of customary law so that the problem of adherence of some but not all States to specific conventions does not arise. This would appear to be particularly important in the context of an international tribunal prosecuting persons responsible for serious violations of International Humanitarian Law.[20]

That stated rationale for the adopted approach could hardly be disputed. If the jurisdiction *ratione personae* of the ICTY was to extend to all persons allegedly responsible for violations of the Statute on the physical territory of the Former Yugoslavia, it was essential that members of paramilitary organizations and other non-State entities be covered. In any case, even for those members of State militaries and police forces, State succession issues at the time of the dissolution of the Former Federal Republic of Yugoslavia ensured some uncertainties as to the precise treaty obligations of the newly independent former Federal republics.

Understandably, the UN Office of the Legal Adviser took a cautious approach to the definition of the crimes within the ICTY Statute. The principal criticism leveled against the Draft Statute (which was, perhaps surprisingly, adopted without amendment by the UN Security Council[21]) has been that it was too conservative in its approach. The Appeals Chamber of the ICTY is the source of the best-known criticism of the drafting of the Statute. In the course of the trial of Dusko Tadić the Appeals Chamber had to decide whether or not to accept the challenge of the accused to the Tribunal's exercise of jurisdiction over him. In relation to Article 5 of the ICTY Statute defining Crimes Against Humanity, the Appeals Chamber stated that:

> It is by now a settled rule of customary international law that crimes against humanity do not require a connection to international armed conflict. Indeed, as the Prosecutor points out, customary international law may not require a connection between crimes against humanity and any conflict at all. Thus, by requiring that crimes against humanity be committed in either internal or international armed conflict, the Security

Council may have defined the crime in Article 5 more narrowly than necessary under customary international law.[22]

Prima facie this criticism is tempered and relatively benign. Coming as it does, though, from an international judicial body, the criticism was taken very seriously indeed. At the negotiations for the Statute of the International Criminal Court in Rome, for example, reference was made to both the text of the Statute of the International Criminal Tribunal for Rwanda, which omits a requisite nexus with armed conflict in the definition of crimes against humanity, as well as the ICTY Appeals Chamber decision in *Tadić* as bases for departing from the approach in Article 5 of the ICTY Statute.[23]

The drafting of the Statute for the ICTY and the criticism leveled against it was clearly on a significantly smaller scale than the response to the ICJ decision in the *Nicaragua* case. That is at least partly explicable on the basis that the ICJ made general declarations on the nature of customary international law and how it is formed—with significant implications for future cases before the Court as well as more generally. In the case of the Statute of the ICTY, that instrument established an important precedent for future international criminal tribunals but the customary international law implications were limited to the subject matter of international criminal law.

The fact remains, however, that both the ICJ and the Office of the Legal Adviser found themselves the subject of criticism in response to respective efforts to articulate the content of customary international law in a particular area and, in the ICJ's case, in response to the Court's articulation of the process for the development of customary international law rules. Given that highly regarded institutions such as these have been subjected to intense scrutiny and criticism, the ICRC should not expect to be immune.

It is possible that my analysis is flawed. I have suggested that criticism is inevitable regardless of the authority of the articulating organization. Perhaps that is incorrect. An organization no one takes seriously might purport to articulate the content of customary law on a particular issue and receive no critical feedback precisely because of the lack of respect for the articulating institution. That is surely not the case in relation to the ICRC. The publication of the customary law study under the imprimatur of the ICRC ensures that the Study will be taken very seriously indeed—precisely because of the international standing of the institution. Had the Study been prepared by an academic institution, for example, or by a non-governmental organization (quite apart from the obvious question of how any such institution would have gathered the material from States as effectively as the ICRC), it is much less likely that the Study would have attracted anything like the scrutiny it is receiving. But, since it is the ICRC that has published the Study, States cannot act as the proverbial ostrich with their heads in the sand, simply ignoring the Study in the pretence that it will have no effect or in the hope that it will conveniently disappear.

Irrespective of the Rigor of the Process Leading to the Articulation

Criticism of the Study is also inevitable despite the attempt by the ICRC to be as rigorous as possible in its approach to the identification and compilation of relevant State material and to its assessment and articulation of the content of customary international humanitarian law. The editors of the Study explain in some detail the steps in the process of preparing the Study—the establishment and oversight of the Study at all stages by the Steering Committee, the undertaking of 47 national studies, the additional collection of material from relevant international organizations (including from the ICRC's own archives), the supplementary collection of material from the countries the subject of national reports as well as from other States not the subject of national reports and the establishment and work of the Academic and Governmental Expert Advisory Group.[24] I am sure that many will appreciate the efforts of the ICRC to undertake the Study on the basis of a clear, transparent and defensible approach. Those efforts will undoubtedly translate into greater weight and authority extended to the Study. But, those efforts, while admirable, will not eliminate criticism of the Study.

Many examples of State practice are, in fact, the acts of individual advisers within national delegations in the context of multilateral *fora*—with the blessing of their national governments of course. Individual members of delegations regularly act on the basis of agreed broad national parameters. National statements are usually carefully checked through an interagency process in national capitals but the reality is that individual members of national delegations—particularly senior members of delegations—have broad discretion in the pursuit of national priorities. In particular, individuals within national delegations become involved in the minutiae of multilateral negotiations and develop specialist knowledge about the nuances of a negotiated text. In circumstances where such individuals become the national experts in relation to particular issues in sustained multilateral negotiations, those individuals often also assume the mantle of national institutional memory. Those individuals know exactly what was meant by a particular intervention, how an intervention was received by other States, the differences between some States' articulated positions and their true intentions (or the failure to reveal true intentions). The authors of the ICRC Study have had to make decisions about the wording of some customary rules derived in part from treaty provisions. Some individuals involved in the specific treaty negotiations have criticized the ICRC for misunderstanding the context of negotiations and for misrepresenting specific national acts to support the ICRC version of the customary rule.

One of the best examples, to my knowledge, of this phenomenon is the intervention by Hays Parks at the Annual Meeting of the American Society of International Law in April 2005. Parks was on a panel to discuss the ICRC Study and, having only received his personal copy a few days before, undertook what he characterized as a "biopsy" on some of the conventional weapons issues he had been extensively involved with for almost two and half decades as a member of the US delegation to the Certain Conventional Weapons Convention[25] (CCW) negotiations in Geneva. Parks looked first at incendiary weapons and expressed surprise to see that the Study quotes a USSR Statement to the effect that Moscow was "in favour of the prohibition of means of warfare which were particularly cruel, because their use was incompatible with the norms of international law. One such means was napalm."[26] Parks asserts that the Study, at least on this issue, lacks a sense of context in relying as it does upon the Soviet Statement as if that represented a statement of State policy. The United States had changed its position late in the conference process and announced that it would support a protocol regulating the use of incendiary weapons. Parks explains that that change of US policy threw the Soviet delegation into disarray. The Soviet Ambassador, Victor Israelyen, conceded subsequently to Parks that the very statement which the ICRC Study relies upon in part to support the emergence of a customary rule on incendiary weapons was in fact a smokescreen. The Soviets assumed that the United States would not compromise and accept a protocol on incendiary weapons and so were hiding behind the original US position. The change of US policy exposed the real Soviet position and Parks claims that "the Soviet Union had no intention of accepting a prohibition on incendiary weapons, as the Warsaw Pact had huge stocks it fully intended to employ."

Whether or not the Soviet Statement tips the balance one way or the other in terms of the ICRC claiming the existence of the customary rule is hardly the critical point here. What is at stake is the nature of the material the ICRC has relied upon in order to assert the formulation of customary rules. The explicit reliance upon a statement that, in fact, did not reflect either State practice or *opinio juris* to support a customary rule will inevitably increase skepticism about what other materials may have been relied upon in the Study. Parks claims that statements seem to take priority over the actual practice of States in armed conflict. He questions why the Study fails to refer to and discuss the North Vietnamese use of flamethrowers in its 1968 Tet offensive, for example, or the Soviet use of incendiaries in Afghanistan and the Russian use of incendiaries in Chechnya.[27] Parks makes similar claims about exploding bullets. The ICRC is uncomfortable about the widespread use of the Raufoss 12.7 mm multipurpose round, which the institution claims can explode on impact with the human body. Parks, and other government lawyers, dispute this finding. Parks asserts that the Study fails to mention that more than two dozen States include the Raufoss 12.7 mm multipurpose round in their inventories and that at least some of those States have communicated to the ICRC that they have undertaken legal reviews of the round and believe that the continued use of the round is compatible with existing legal obligations.[28]

These are serious criticisms and, in my view, more of them are likely to flow. As those individuals, like Parks, who have been intimately involved in the development of the law take the time to read the detail of the Study—not only the articulation of the rules themselves but also the supporting material—the ICRC will increasingly be subjected to criticism that it has overlooked, misinterpreted or misrepresented the material it claims supports the assertion that "State practice establishes this rule as a norm of customary international law."

Particularly When Rules Are Articulated in Absolute Terms

I have referred a number of times to Yves Sandoz's claim that:

> [T]he study will have achieved its goal only if it is considered not as the end of a process but as a beginning. It reveals what has been accomplished but also what remains unclear and what remains to be done. . . . [T]he study makes no claim to be the final word.[29]

There is a welcome self-effacing here and no doubt Sandoz is absolutely genuine in his request that the Study be read, be discussed and be commented upon. However, it seems to me that there is a measure of incongruity in the claim that the Study reveals what is unclear and what remains to be done—that it does not represent the last word on customary international humanitarian law—and the manner in which the 161 Rules themselves are worded. All of them are written in absolute terms followed by a summary statement which invariably includes an absolute finding that State practice establishes this rule as a norm of customary international law (either in international or non-international armed conflicts or in both). Occasionally there is a reference to an issue which is not covered by the Study. Rule 155 on obedience to superior orders is an example. The Study specifically mentions that other defenses, including the defense of duress, may apply but are not covered by the Study,[30] demonstrating that the Study does not purport to be exhaustive. However, in relation to the issues which are covered by the Study, the language used is absolute.

Others have commented upon this aspect of the Study. Daniel Bethlehem, for example, notes the *pro forma* approach of following the formulation of the customary rule with a "summary":

> which, almost without exception, asserts 'State practice establishes this rule as a norm of customary international law. . . .' There are occasions in which this affirmation is followed by a statement noting ambiguity or controversy in respect of some element of the rule, but the affirmation of customary status stands fast.[31]

I imagine that it would have been unpalatable for the ICRC to formulate rules of customary international humanitarian law other than in absolute terms. An equivocal approach to formulation may have undermined the purpose of the Study by creating a sense of uncertainty and ambiguity—something the ICRC as an institution is rightly committed to avoiding. But in the existing approach to formulation of the rules there seems little room for acknowledging dissent or opposition to the emergence of a particular rule. I am unable to shake the sense that the formulation of rules in the absolute terms that appear in the Study invites disagreement and criticism rather than discussion and constructive comment. I hope I am proved wrong.

Notes

1. JEAN-MARIE HENCKAERTS & LOUISE DOSWALD-BECK, CUSTOMARY INTERNATIONAL HUMANITARIAN LAW xlv–xlvi (2005) (2 volumes: Volume I, Rules; Volume II, Practice (2 Parts)) (emphasis added).
2. Yves Sandoz, *Foreword*, *in id.*, Vol. I, at xvii.
3. *Id.*
4. *See id.*, Vol. I, Chap. 20, at 237.
5. This language is contentious as the Australian Government does not consider the cited document to constitute a military manual as such. The document cited is Australian Defence Force, *Law of Armed Conflict*, OPERATIONS PUBLICATIONS SERIES (1994) (hereinafter ADFP 37).
6. *See* HENCKAERTS & DOSWALD-BECK, *supra* note 1, Vol. II, Part 1, at 1510 citing paragraph 207 of ADFP37, *supra* note 5.
7. *See id.*, Rule 14, Vol. I, at 46.
8. *See id.*, Vol. II, Part 1, at 299.
9. ADFP 37, *supra* note 5 at para. 535.
10. Protocol Additional to the Geneva Conventions of 12 August 1949, and Relating to the Protection of Victims of International Armed Conflict, June 8, 1977, 1125 U.N.T.S. 3, *reprinted in* DOCUMENTS ON THE LAWS OF WAR 422 (Adam Roberts & Richard Guelff eds., 3rd ed. 2000).
11. The *Yearbook*, produced by the Asser Instituut in The Hague and published by Cambridge University Press, includes an extremely useful "Country Reports" section every year. That section is prepared by correspondents in-country around the world and is the only ongoing collection of evidence of State practice in International Humanitarian Law of which I am aware. The "Country Reports" section is not and does not purport to be exhaustive of all relevant State

practice. The preparation of the material is dependent on the work of volunteer correspondents and for many States no suitable correspondent has been found. The Asser Instituut does not purport to be supplementing the ICRC Study's Practice volume. I am offering my own characterization of the effect of the Section.

12. Dr. Abdul G. Koroma, *Foreword* in HENCKAERTS & DOSWALD-BECK, *supra* note 1, at xii.

13. *See, for example,* the Symposium, *Appraisals of the ICJ's Decision: Nicaragua v. United States,* 81 AMERICAN JOURNAL OF INTERNATIONAL LAW (1987). The following authors contributed to that issue: Keith Highet, at 1; Herbert W. Briggs, at 77; Anthony D'Amato, at 101; Michael J. Glennon, at 121; Edward Gordon, at 129; John Lawrence Hargrove, at 135; Frederic L. Kirgis Jr., at 146; John Norton Moore, at 151; Fred L. Morrison, at 160; W. Michael Reisman, at 166; Fernando R. Teson, at 173. Other articles, include those in the following footnotes, and for example, Abram Chayes, *Nicaragua, the United States and the World Court,* 79 COLUMBIA LAW REVIEW 1445 (1985); James P. Rowles, *Nicaragua Versus the United States: Issues of Law and Policy,* 20 THE INTERNATIONAL LAWYER 1245 (1986); Keith Highet, *You Can Run But You Can't Hide: Reflections on the United States Position in the Nicaragua Case,* 27 VIRGINIA JOURNAL OF INTERNATIONAL LAW 551 (1987); Hilary Charlesworth, *Customary International Law and the Nicaragua Case,* 11 AUSTRALIAN YEARBOOK OF INTERNATIONAL LAW 1 (1984–87); Anthea Elizabeth Roberts, *Traditional and Modern Approaches to Customary International Law: A Reconciliation,* 95 AMERICAN JOURNAL OF INTERNATIONAL LAW 757 (2001).

14. Thomas M. Franck, *Comment: Icy Day at the ICJ,* 79 AMERICAN JOURNAL OF INTERNATIONAL LAW 379 (1985).

15. Keith Highet, *Between a Rock and a Hard Place – the U.S., the International Court and the Nicaragua Case,* 21 THE INTERNATIONAL LAWYER 1083 (1987).

16. Anthony D'Amato, *Comment: Nicaragua and International Law: The "Academic" and the "Real,"* 79 AMERICAN JOURNAL OF INTERNATIONAL LAW 657 (1985).

17. This was the title of Lori Fisler Damrosch's book on the implications of the *Nicaragua* case published by Transnational Publishers in 1987.

18. Hilary Charlesworth, *supra* note 13, at 18.

19. *See* UN Security Council Resolution 808, 48 UN SCOR, UN Doc. S/RES/808 (Feb. 22, 1993).

20. *See* Report of the UN Secretary-General, UN Doc. S/25704 (May 3, 1993), para 34. The text of the Report is annexed to the text of UNSC Resolution 827.

21. *See* UN Security Council Resolution 827, 48 UN SCOR, UN Doc. S/RES/827 (May 25, 1993).

22. *See* Prosecutor v. Dusko Tadić a/k/a "Dule", Decision on the Defence Motion for Interlocutory Appeal on Jurisdiction, Case No. IT-94-1-T, Oct. 2, 1995.

23. *See, for example,* Herman von Hebel & Daryl Robinson, *Crimes within the Jurisdiction of the Court, in* THE INTERNATIONAL CRIMINAL COURT: THE MAKING OF THE ROME STATUTE – ISSUES, NEGOTIATIONS, RESULTS 92–93 (Roy S. Lee ed., 1999).

24. See "Organisation of the Study" in the authors' *Introduction, in* HENCKAERTS & DOSWALD-BECK, *supra* note 1, Vol. 1, at xlv–li.

25. Convention on Prohibitions or Restrictions on the Use of Certain Conventional Weapons Which May be Deemed to be Excessively Injurious or to Have Indiscriminate Effects, Oct. 10, 1980, 1342 U.N.T.S. 137, *reprinted in* DOCUMENTS ON THE LAWS OF WAR, *supra* note 10, at 520.

26. W. Hays Parks, *The ICRC Customary Law Study: A Preliminary Assessment,* 99 PROCEEDINGS OF THE ANNUAL MEETING OF THE AMERICAN SOCIETY OF INTERNATIONAL LAW 209 (2005).

27. *Id.* at 210.

28. *Id.* at 211.

29. Sandoz, *supra* note 2, Vol. I, at xvii.
30. HENCKAERTS & DOSWALD-BECK, *supra* note 1, Vol. I, at 565.
31. Daniel Bethlehem, *The ICRC Customary Law Study: An Assessment*, paper presented to the Seminar on The Law of Armed Conflict: Problems and Prospects, Chatham House, London, Apr. 18–19, 2005, *available at* www.chathamhouse.org.uk/index.php?id=261.

IV

The ICRC Customary International Humanitarian Law Study

Yoram Dinstein*

The Study

The publication in 2005 of an impressive Study of Customary International Humanitarian Law (IHL) by the International Committee of the Red Cross (ICRC) (hereinafter the Study)[1] is undoubtedly an important landmark. The Study—done in two parts (Rules and Practice)—is bound to be scrutinized, cited and debated for a long time to come. It will leave its imprints in the future both in the case law and in the legal literature, and, whatever one's view is of the overall success of the enterprise, no scholar or practitioner can afford to ignore it.

The mandate for the preparation of the Study came exactly ten years prior to its publication (1995), from the 26th International Conference of the Red Cross and Red Crescent. For an entire decade, the ICRC spared no effort to put the Study together. The project was based, *inter alia*, on extensive consultations with academic and government experts; nearly fifty reports of individual States' practice, submitted by national research teams; research on the practice of international organizations produced by several additional teams; and further archival research pursued by the ICRC itself. The resulting two volumes (for reasons of sheer size, Volume II (Practice) is published in two separately bound parts) comprise more than 5,000 printed

---

* Yanowicz Professor of Human Rights and Pro-President, Tel Aviv University (Israel). This article was first published in volume 36 of the *Israel Yearbook on Human Rights* (2006) and is reprinted with permission.

pages (621 covering Rules and commentary thereon; and 4,411 encompassing Practice and appendices). The final product represents the largest scholarly undertaking (on any theme) ever undertaken in the long history of the ICRC.

Since this article is an unadorned critique of the Study, I would like to emphasize two important personal points. First, I was marginally involved in the enterprise: I am responsible for the Israeli country report; I have participated in subsequent consultations convened by the ICRC; and I have been given ample opportunity—which I liberally used—to express reservations about earlier drafts of Volume I (although I had not seen Volume II prior to publication). Secondly, and even more significantly, I feel that the initiative was absolutely right, even if I do not approve of some of the results. Indeed, I take credit for being probably the first to have put on record the idea of launching a project with a view to examining the text of Additional Protocol I[2] of 1977 against the background of customary international law. I first raised the proposal publicly in 1987, in a conference convened in Geneva on the 10th anniversary of the conclusion of the two Additional Protocols of 1977, where I said:

> I happen to believe that it is very important to try to pinpoint those provisions of Protocol I, which are either reflective of existing customary international law or at least are non-controversial to such an extent that there is every reason to believe that they will crystallize as customary international law in the near future.

A year later, in another International Colloquium held at Bad Homburg in 1988 (the proceedings of which have been published), I reiterated the argument:

> The insertion of clauses like Article 44 in the Protocol is lamentable. All the same, these clauses should not overshadow other provisions reflecting customary *lex lata* or widely supported *lex ferenda*. To my mind, an attempt ought to be made to identify in an authoritative way those sections of the Protocol which are declaratory or non-controversial (I should hasten to add that, in my assessment, the great majority of the norms of the Protocol – perhaps as many as 85% – qualify as declaratory or non-controversial). Such an evaluation of the Protocol's text could be undertaken by informal meetings of experts like the present one, and it will prove invaluable not only to Israel but also to other countries – primarily, the United States – which are not expected to become contracting parties in the foreseeable future.
>
> I have broached this idea before, but have failed to persuade the ICRC representatives that it has much merit.[3]

In other words, my main concern was to bridge over what I like to call the "Great Schism,"[4] dividing Contracting from Non-Contracting Parties of Additional

Protocol I because of the 15% or so of the text (such as Article 44, which will be adverted to below) thoroughly rejected by the latter States. The ICRC in the late 1980s was unenthusiastic; its apprehension being that such an exercise might undermine the authority of Additional Protocol I as a treaty.

Admittedly, the Study goes in several different directions, compared to my own idea. A critical segment of the Study relates to non-international armed conflicts and Additional Protocol II[5] (something that did not occur to me in the 1980s but I find most useful today). There are also sections dealing with law of armed conflict norms contained in treaties other than Additional Protocols I and II, particularly those dealing with prohibited weapons (an addition which has merit, although it has certainly complicated the process). Conversely, not every clause of Additional Protocol I is dealt with (an omission that I find puzzling) and not much attention is given to *lex ferenda* stipulations that seem to be non-controversial (for instance, those provisions dealing with civil defense).[6] From the subjective angle of my original idea, the entire project is upside down. Instead of systematically examining Protocol I article by article, what is presented in the Study is a set of independent Rules with only the commentary indicating the relationship (if any) to provisions of Protocol I. Still, much as I may have wished the Study to be differently structured, the three volumes have to be taken as they are.

The Methodology

Let me start with some comments about Volume II (Practice). This is the methodological underpinning of the Rules plus commentary, and its size is not just daunting; it is overwhelming. However, when one tries to get into the thicket of literally tens of thousands of cites, one begins to get underwhelmed for reasons that will become apparent in the ensuing text of the present article. Indeed, to my mind, Volume II is proof positive of the adage that sometimes more is less.

The preliminary question that must be addressed is: what is customary international law? The classical definition of international custom is encapsulated in the well-known formula of Article 38(1)(b) of the Statute of the International Court of Justice: "international custom, as evidence of a general practice accepted as law."[7] The *font et origo* of customary international law is, in essence, the general practice of States. States are the main actors in the international arena, and it is their general practice that constitutes the core of custom. Without State practice there is no general customary international law.

What does State practice consist of? There is much scholarly debate over the question of whether conduct constitutes the sole expression of custom-making practice, and whether statements—at times referred to as mere "claims"[8] or as "verbal (as distinct from "physical") acts"[9]—count. I share the view of the authors of the Study that "[b]oth physical and verbal acts of States constitute practice that contributes to the creation of customary international law."[10] Nevertheless, not every statement counts: it all depends on who is making the statement, when, where and in what circumstances. The Study has attached an import to statements in a most comprehensive generic fashion. I strongly believe that this is going way too far: the gamut of admissible statements—as grist to the mill of State practice—must be much more focused and filtered.

The Study includes much State practice but a lot besides. One cannot cavil that the Study incorporates the practice of inter-governmental international organizations (IGOs). To some extent, this is due to the fact that IGOs may have an international legal personality of their own,[11] but additionally it must not be forgotten that IGOs are comprised of States. Member States of an IGO may therefore contribute to State practice through their conduct and statements within the fold of the organization. As pronounced by the International Court of Justice in its Advisory Opinion on *Nuclear Weapons*, UN General Assembly resolutions (not binding as such) "can, in certain circumstances, provide evidence important for establishing the existence of a rule or the emergence of an *opinio juris*."[12]

In contradistinction to IGOs, the role of non-governmental organizations (NGOs) in international law-making is confined to a consultative status,[13] not to mention lobbying and other behind-the-scenes activities vis-à-vis States. NGOs, whatever their standing, can never contribute directly through their own practice to the creation of customary norms. This is true even of the most important—and unique—NGO, the ICRC. Admittedly, the ICRC is assigned by IHL important functions to carry out.[14] But that fact does not turn the ICRC into a State-like entity. It is therefore surprising (and inappropriate) that the authors of the Study give a lot of attention to the practice of the ICRC itself[15] (and occasionally even to that of other NGOs, such as Amnesty International[16]). ICRC reports, communications, press releases, statements and the like—recapitulated at some length in Volume II of the Study—are simply not germane to customary international law, unless and until they actually impact on State practice. It is true that "the official reactions which ICRC statements elicit are State practice."[17] However, this is not ICRC practice: this is State practice and it should be subsumed under the right heading. The ICRC plays in such circumstances the role of a catalyst for the evolution of State practice, but no more. One problem with the erroneous designation of such practice is that when ICRC appeals exhorting States to action are registered as ICRC practice, the gaze shifts from the actor to the catalyst. If the ICRC is successful in eliciting a positive response from States,[18] no real harm is done. But what happens when the ICRC's appeal evokes no response?[19] At best, the ICRC action proved itself to be irrelevant. At worst, it is an indication *a contrario* that States are not willing to accept the position of the ICRC.

The ICRC practice at least deserves that designation, albeit it does not qualify in the context of the term of art "practice" employed in the definition of customary international law. But, in a manner bordering on the bizarre, the Study goes far beyond anything remotely resembling practice. How can one refer to resolutions of the *Institut de Droit International*—weighty as they indisputably are—as "other practice"?[20] Whose practice? The same question arises, in an even starker way, when the Restatement prepared under the aegis of the American Law Institute is cited as "other practice,"[21] and most egregiously when scholarly books (however prestigious) get a similar classification.[22] When everything is categorized as practice, the reader cannot be blamed for a modicum of skepticism.

There is much reliance in the Study on a host of military manuals, especially where it really counts, *viz.* in Volume I (Rules). Indeed, it appears that the authors themselves—sharing perhaps some of the skepticism re the plethora of items collated in Volume II (Practice)—opted, to be on the safe side, to predicate the Rules more on legislative codes and military manuals than on any other single source of practice. This editorial decision should be commended. Irrefutably, legislative codes and military manuals (i.e., binding instructions to the armed forces) are invaluable sources of genuine State practice. However, are all the documents called manuals in the Study authentic manuals?

From personal knowledge, I can attest that the so-called Israeli Manual on the Laws of War of 1998[23]—cited quite often throughout the Study—is not a genuine manual. As I tried on several occasions to point out to the authors of the Study prior to its publication—to no avail—this is merely a tool used to facilitate instruction and training, and it has no binding or even authoritative standing. The insistence on regarding the text as a manual has led the authors of the Study to a number of errors. Thus, in the context of Rule 65 (whereby "[k]illing, injuring or capturing an adversary by resort to perfidy is prohibited"),[24] I alerted them to the fact that Israel does not accept the words "or capturing" as a reflection of customary international law. They refused to accept this, and, in the commentary on Rule 65, even singled out the so-called Israeli Manual as the "exception" among non-Contracting Parties to Additional Protocol I: other manuals of these countries do not mention "capturing"; the Israeli Manual does.[25] As it turns out, the cite given in a footnote does not refer to the so-called manual at all, but to another booklet.[26] When one checks out the matching material in the Practice volume, it turns out that (a) the paragraph cited does quote the "Manual" (rather than the booklet) but there is no mention of "capturing" at all; (b) a previous paragraph (not the one cited) refers to capture, but the quote is from that other booklet (rather than the

"Manual"), and, for that matter, it is based on a secondary source![27] Thus, in deciding that the "Manual" trumps any and all disclaimers, they went completely astray. Since nobody can afford the time to go through every cite in a Study comprising thousands of pages, I can only express the hope that this wild goose chase is the exception rather than the rule.

But is the Israeli "Manual" the only non-manual? I wonder. It should be mentioned that there are many references to a UK manual of 1981 on the Law of Armed Conflict (listed separately and independently of the 1958 British Military Manual).[28] In reality, there have been only three UK manuals on the subject of the law of armed conflict. The first one (written jointly by L. Oppenheim and Colonel JE Edmonds) was a chapter of the Army Manual of Military Law published in 1914 and revised in 1936. The second (written by Hersch Lauterpacht with the assistance of Colonel Gerald Draper), again a part of the Army Manual of Military Law, came out in 1958. The third (written jointly by several authors), a completely new and separate Manual of the Law of Armed Conflict, was issued by the Ministry of Defence in 2004, not in time for inclusion in the Study. It is not clear what the 1981 text represents.

When the ICRC decided to look into its own (otherwise closed) archives to research some 40 recent armed conflicts, the news was greeted with enthusiasm. Everybody hoped that the research would yield a trove of inaccessible State practice. In the event, the results have been quite disappointing. First off, although the conflicts are specified in a general list,[29] no identification of the State (or rebel group) concerned is made in context. This already diminishes considerably from the weight that one can attach to the practice concerned. Secondly, and even more significantly, the "practice" cited is often of no practical use. What value added to the law of armed conflict in non-international armed conflicts can be derived, for instance, from the following vignette: "The Head of Foreign Affairs of an armed opposition group told the ICRC in 1995 that his group was conscious of the necessity to respect and to spare the civilian population during an armed conflict"?[30] This, lamentably, is quite typical of the kind of statements that the Study distilled from the archives. Even when more specificity is added, the result can be the following: "In 1991, an official of a State rejected an ICRC request to protect the civilian population from pillage by government troops. He replied that as long as they provided a hiding place for rebels, the army would burn the fields if necessary. However, this behaviour was not representative of the general opinion of the military personnel met by the ICRC in this context."[31] If civilian fields are burnt, to deny a hiding place to rebels, why is this legally deemed "pillage"?[32] And, whatever the juridical taxonomy, why does one statement by one unidentified organ of an unknown State—inconsistent with other statements by other organs of the same

State—shed any light on that State's practice? We are not told what actually happened or what the circumstances were; nor are we informed about the relative ranks of the officials adverted to. And so it goes.

The Rules

Having focused so far on methodology, it is necessary to consider some of the Rules—constituting the backbone of the Study—and the commentary thereon. I do not take issue with many of the black-letter Rules and much of the commentary, as presented in Volume I of the Study. But I believe that there are grave errors in the formulation of some of the Rules, and part of the commentary, in ways that adversely affect the ability of the Study to project an image of objective scholarship.

Rule 1 starts off with an unassailable statement that "[t]he parties to the conflict must at all times distinguish between civilians and combatants."[33] But then, in Rule 5, the dichotomy changes from civilians/combatants to civilians/members of the armed forces: "[c]ivilians are persons who are not members of the armed forces."[34] Is that so? Rule 3 rightly states that, in fact, not all members of the armed forces are combatants, since medical and religious personnel are excluded from that category.[35] By the same token, not every person who is not a member of the armed forces is a civilian. In particular, by directly (or actively) participating in hostilities, a person who claims to be a civilian loses that protective mantle and becomes a (perhaps unlawful) combatant.[36] Even Additional Protocol I, in its "Basic rule"—Article 48[37]—distinguishes between the civilian population and combatants; and in its definition of civilians—Article 50(1)[38] —prescribes that civilians are persons who do not belong to certain categories of persons, including the category referred to in Article 4A(2) of Geneva Convention (III) (covering irregular troops).[39] By switching the dichotomy from civilians/combatants to civilians/members of the armed forces, the Study lays the ground to loading the legal dice. If the antonym of civilians under customary international law is members of the armed forces, it follows (as the ICRC believes) that civilians who directly (or actively) participate in hostilities do not lose their classification as civilians. Conversely, if—as I think the right approach is—the antonym of civilians is combatants, civilians who directly (or actively) participate in hostilities may turn themselves into unlawful combatants.

One of the cardinal causes for the "Great Schism"—sharply dividing Contracting and non-Contracting Parties to Additional Protocol I—is the utter and unqualified rejection by the latter countries of those provisions of the Protocol that, to all intents and purposes, eliminate the status of unlawful combatants in all cases except spies and mercenaries.[40] The epicenter of the controversy lies in the combination of Articles 43 and 44.[41] Rule 4 of the Study simply reiterates some of the language of Article 43 of Additional Protocol I: "The armed forces of a party to the conflict consist of all organized armed forces, groups and units which are under a command responsible to that party for the conduct of its subordinates."[42] The commentary treats this definition as customary international law, trying to create the impression that organization and discipline (rather than distinction from civilians) are the gist of the matter; and—whereas the commentary briefly refers to the other, cumulative, Hague and Geneva conditions of lawful combatancy (which non-Contracting Parties to Additional Protocol I continue to regard as of essence)—it makes short shrift of them and somehow manages to convey the message that even Article 44 of the Protocol (one of the key sources of the "Great Schism") hardly presents a real problem.[43] This is plainly misleading.

In a written comment to the ICRC on an earlier (but not much different) version of Rule 4, I stated:

> Rule 4. The text and commentary are highly objectionable. Israel utterly and unreservedly rejects Articles 43–44 of Additional Protocol I as a source of customary international law. Israel adheres to the original texts of the Hague Regulations and the Geneva Conventions and does not accept any and all changes that Articles 43–44 of the Protocol purport to introduce. Allow me to add that the objections to Articles 43–44 lie at the root of the refusal to ratify the Protocol. Should the ICRC attempt to gloss over the fundamental differences of opinion re this crucial issue, the whole study will be irremediably flawed.

The authors of the Study did not heed these cautioning words, nor did they choose to allude to them in the commentary's footnotes. Instead, the commentary—in trying to establish the case for the customary nature of Rule 4 and in attempting to create the false impression that the customary definition is mainly concerned with the discipline and organization of the armed forces—purports to rely even on the practice of non-Contracting Parties to Additional Protocol I: a footnote relies specifically on the practice of the United States.[44] The US text cited (appearing in The Commander's Handbook on the Law of Naval Operations) is quoted in the Practice volume, but lo and behold: it does not confine itself to discipline and organization; it explicitly speaks about members of forces "who are under responsible command and subject to internal military discipline, carry their arms openly, and otherwise distinguish themselves clearly from the civilian population."[45] These last Hague/Geneva conditions are of course the crux of the issue. And, in the Annotated Supplement to The Commander's Handbook, the text is followed by a footnote which mentions expressly the construct of unlawful combatants.[46]

It must be added that when the emergence of customary international law subsequent to a treaty (in this instance, Additional Protocol I) is examined, it is the practice of non-Contracting Parties that carries the day. In the 1969 *North Sea Continental Shelf* cases, the International Court of justice made it amply clear that—in analyzing the post-treaty practice of States, with a view to establishing whether a new custom has been created in the wake of the treaty—it is required to leave aside (and not to consider as a reliable guide) not only the practice of Contracting Parties among themselves but even the practice among States that shortly would become Contracting Parties, since they were all "acting actually or potentially in the application of the Convention."[47] The Court held that "[f]rom their action no inference could legitimately be drawn as to the existence of a rule of customary international law" generated by the treaty.[48] The Court therefore concentrated on the practice of "those States . . . which were not, and have not become parties to the Convention," the goal being to find whether an "inference could justifiably be drawn that they believed themselves to be applying a mandatory rule of customary international law."[49] The authors of the Study are fully aware of this ruling of the Court, although they made a deliberate decision not to confine the Study to the practice of non-Contracting Parties to Additional Protocol I.[50] On the central issue of unlawful combatancy, that decision led them to an overt misreading of customary international law.

There are manifold other issues. For instance, Rule 6 states, as a matter of customary international law, that "[c]ivilians are protected against attack unless and for such time as they take a direct part in hostilities."[51] Nobody would challenge most of the sentence. However, the words "and for such time"—which are based on Article 51(3) of Additional Protocol I[52]—are contested. The Study relies on practice, including that of the United States, but when one takes a look at The Commander's Handbook, which is explicitly cited more than once,[53] it is striking that the text omits the words "and for such time"![54] Moreover, although in my written comments to the ICRC, I had observed: "Rule 6. Israel does not accept the qualifying phrase 'for such time', which—incidentally—has been removed from Article 8 of the Rome Statute . . . ," no account was taken in the Study's commentary either of the remark itself or of the deletion of the words "and for such time" from Article 8(2)(b)(i) of the 1998 Rome Statute of the International Criminal Court.[55]

It is not proposed here to parse every Rule in the Study. However, it is noteworthy that Rule 35 sets forth that "[d]irecting an attack against a zone established to shelter the wounded, the sick and civilians from the effects of hostilities is prohibited."[56] As the commentary mentions, the idea is based on the provisions of Article 23 of Geneva Convention (I)[57] and Articles 14–15 of Geneva Convention (IV)[58] (dealing with hospital zones, safety zones and neutralized zones). But, as the ICRC

Commentary on Geneva Convention (I) states categorically, "[t]he zones will not, strictly speaking, have any legal existence, or enjoy protection under the Convention, until such time as they have been recognized by the adverse Party."[59] The same observation appears in the Commentary on Geneva Convention (IV).[60] Where does the text of Rule 35 even imply that the establishment of a protected zone cannot be effected without the prior consent of the other side?

It seems that the concept of consent is not an easy construct for the framers of the Study. Thus, Rule 55 states *tout court* that "[t]he parties to the conflict must allow and facilitate rapid and unimpeded passage of humanitarian relief for civilians in need, which is impartial in character and conducted without any adverse distinction, subject to their right of control."[61] This obligation is based on Article 70 of Additional Protocol I, except that Article 70 adds the pivotal caveat (missing from Rule 55): "subject to the agreement of the Parties concerned in such relief actions."[62] Even the ICRC Commentary on Additional Protocol I does not claim more than that Article 70 may be construed as precluding refusal of agreement to allow relief for arbitrary or capricious reasons.[63] Surely, as I have argued elsewhere, "[i]t is impossible to assert, at the present point, that a general right to humanitarian assistance has actually crystallized in positive international law."[64] This is a prime example that the Study—instead of looking for a compromise between Contracting and non-Contracting Parties to Additional Protocol I—actually transcends the Protocol (which is *lex lata* for the former States) and moves into the realm of the *lex ferenda* (for both the former and the latter States). Curiously enough, in the commentary on Rule 55, the requirement of consent in Additional Protocol I and Additional Protocol II is explicitly mentioned, but there follows a vague statement that "[m]ost of the practice collected does not mention this requirement."[65] Uncharacteristically, no footnote accompanies the proposition, and it is not spelled out whose practice this is in reference to.

Rule 45 of the Study[66] confirms the customary standing of the provisions of Articles 35(3) and 55(1) of Additional Protocol I, which prohibit the use of methods or means of warfare expected to cause widespread, long-term and severe damage to the natural environment.[67] The commentary on Rule 45 mentions objections by France, the United Kingdom and the United States, adding:

> [T]hese three States are especially affected as far as possession of nuclear weapons is concerned, and their objection to the application of this specific rule to such weapons has been consistent since the adoption of this rule in treaty form in 1997. Therefore, if the doctrine of "persistent objector" is possible in the context of humanitarian rules, these three States are not bound by this specific rule as far as any use of nuclear weapons is concerned.[68]

The extract reveals total confusion between two completely disparate concepts in the modern analysis of customary international law, namely, "persistent objector," on the one hand, and "States whose interests are specially affected," on the other.

The "persistent objector" doctrine (supported by most commentators) maintains that a State, which persistently and unequivocally objects from the outset to the emergence of a new customary rule, cannot be held bound by that rule.[69] A timely "persistent objector" cannot be caught in the net of the new custom, but otherwise that custom will bind the entire international community. In other words, the custom will consolidate—notwithstanding the opposition—although it will not affect the "persistent objector."

The construct of "States whose interests are specially affected" was developed by the International Court of Justice, in the *North Sea Continental Shelf* cases.[70] These are States with priority in contributing to the creation of customary international law (the paradigmatic example being that of the chief maritime States where the law of the sea is concerned). If several "States whose interests are specially affected" object to the formation of a custom, no custom can emerge.

When three nuclear Powers—the United States, the United Kingdom and France—have taken the position that Rule 45 does not reflect customary international law, there is no doubt that they act as "States whose interests are specially affected" (as conceded by the commentary quoted above). By arriving at the conclusion that (at the most) the three Powers can only be viewed as "persistent objectors"—and that, therefore, they will not be bound by the custom which has emerged—the Study gets the law completely wrong. There is no question that, when adopted in 1977, Articles 35(3) and 55(1) were innovative in character.[71] The question, consequently, is whether custom has developed thereafter, and it cannot be denied that three leading members of the small and select "nuclear club" have opposed it vocally since 1977. Surely, as "States whose interests are specially affected," the three countries cannot be relegated to the status of persistent objection. By repudiating the putative custom protecting the environment from all means of warfare, the three nuclear States have not merely removed themselves from the reach of such a custom: they in fact managed to successfully bar its formation (as a minimum, with respect to the employment of nuclear weapons).

Finally, Rule 77 states that "[t]he use of bullets which expand or flatten easily in the human body is prohibited."[72] I explicitly transmitted to the ICRC the official position of Israel re the use of expanding bullets, namely, that it is permissible for domestic law-enforcement purposes, as well as in the fight against terrorists and "suicide bombers" (when every split-second counts and there is a vital need to prevent the completion of their heinous attack). Once more, unfortunately, this is not reflected in the commentary.

Conclusion

In order not to further complicate the discussion, I did not get into specific issues of non-international armed conflicts in this paper. This is not to suggest that the Study is unassailable where such conflicts are concerned. But an examination of the Study's provisions thereon raises different issues and deserves a separate paper.

On the whole, as regards international armed conflicts, I am afraid that the Study clearly suffers from an unrealistic desire to show that controversial provisions of API are declaratory of customary international law (not to mention the occasional attempt to go even beyond API). By overreaching, I think that the Study has failed in its primary mission. After all, there is no practical need to persuade Contracting Parties to API that it is declaratory of customary international law. Whether or not such is the case, Contracting Parties are bound by API by virtue of their consent to ratify or accede to it. But there is a need to persuade non-Contracting Parties that they must comply with a large portion of API: not because it is a treaty but because it is general custom. I do not think that non-Contracting Parties will be persuaded by the conclusions of the Study. Thus, the authors missed a golden opportunity to bring Contracting and non-Contracting Parties to API closer together. Indeed, at least on some central points, far from bridging over the present abyss, the Study will only drive the two sides of the "Great Schism" farther away from each other.

Notes

1. JEAN-MARIE HENCKAERTS & LOUISE DOSWALD-BECK, CUSTOMARY INTERNATIONAL HUMANITARIAN LAW (2005) (2 volumes: Volume I, Rules; Volume II, Practice (2 Parts)).
2. Protocol Additional (I) to the Geneva Conventions of 12 August 1949, and Relating to the Protection of Victims of International Armed Conflicts, June 8, 1977 [hereinafter Additional Protocol I], *reprinted in* DOCUMENTS ON THE LAWS OF WAR 422 (Adam Roberts & Richard Guelff eds., 3d ed. 2000).
3. Yoram Dinstein, *The Application of Customary International Law Concerning Armed Conflicts in the National Legal Order*, *in* NATIONAL IMPLEMENTATION OF INTERNATIONAL HUMANITARIAN LAW: PROCEEDINGS OF AN INTERNATIONAL COLLOQUIUM HELD AT BAD HOMBURG, JUNE 17–19, 1988, at 29, 34 (Michael Bothe ed., 1990).
4. *See* Yoram Dinstein, *International Humanitarian Law and Modern Warfare*, *in* INTERNATIONAL EXPERT CONFERENCE ON COMPUTER NETWORK ATTACKS AND THE APPLICABILITY OF INTERNATIONAL HUMANITARIAN LAW 17, 18–19 (Karin Byström ed., 2004).
5. Protocol Additional (II) to the Geneva Conventions of 12 August 1949, and Relating to the Protection of Victims of Non-International Armed Conflicts, June 8, 1977, 1125 U.N.T.S. 609, [hereinafter Additional Protocol II], *reprinted in* DOCUMENTS ON THE LAWS OF WAR, *supra* note 2, at 483.
6. Additional Protocol I, *supra* note 2, arts. 61–67, at 456–461.

7. Statute of the International Court of Justice, June 26, 1945, 33 U.N.T.S. 993.
8. ANTHONY D'AMATO, THE CONCEPT OF CUSTOM IN INTERNATIONAL LAW 88 (1971).
9. Karol Wolfke, *Some Persistent Controversies Regarding Customary International Law*, 24 NETHERLANDS YEARBOOK OF INTERNATIONAL LAW 1, 3 (1993).
10. HENCKAERTS & DOSWALD-BECK, *supra* note 1, Vol. I, at xxxii.
11. *Id.* at xxxv.
12. Legality of the Threat or Use of Nuclear Weapons, Advisory Opinion, 1996 I.C.J. 226, 254–55 (July 8).
13. *See* 1 OPPENHEIM'S INTERNATIONAL LAW 21 (Robert Jennings & Arthur Watts eds., 9th ed. 1992).
14. *See especially* Additional Protocol I, *supra* note 2, art. 81(1), at 752.
15. This policy is rather briefly and unpersuasively defended in HENCKAERTS & DOSWALD-BECK, *supra* note 1, Vol. I, at xxxv.
16. *See id.*, Vol. II, Part 2, at 400.
17. *Id.*, Vol. I, at xxxv.
18. For an example, *see id.*, Vol. I, at 38 and Vol. II, Part 1, at 266 (regarding the prohibition of indiscriminate attacks).
19. For several instances of such apparently fruitless exhortations, see *id.*, Vol. II, Part 1, at 267–69.
20. *Id.* at 450.
21. *Id.*, Vol. II, Part 2, at 2105.
22. *Id.*, Vol. II, Part 1, at 232, 324–25.
23. *Id.*, Vol. II, Part 2, at 4201.
24. *Id.*, Vol. I, at 221.
25. *Id.* at 225.
26. *Id.* at n.152.
27. *Id.*, Vol. II, Part 1, at 1381.
28. *Id.*, Vol. II, Part 2, at 4206.
29. *Id.*, Vol. I, at xlix–l.
30. *Id.*, Vol. II, Part 1, at 161.
31. *Id.* at 1105.
32. For a definition of pillage emphasizing the private or personal use of the pillaged property, see *id.*, Vol. I, at 185.
33. *Id.* at 3.
34. *Id.* at 17.
35. *Id.* at 11.
36. On unlawful combatancy, see YORAM DINSTEIN, THE CONDUCT OF HOSTILITIES UNDER THE LAW OF INTERNATIONAL ARMED CONFLICT 27–54 (2004).
37. Additional Protocol I, *supra* note 2, at 447.
38. *Id.* at 448.
39. Geneva Convention (III) Relative to the Treatment of Prisoners of War, Aug. 12, 1949, 75 U.N.T.S. 135, *reprinted in* DOCUMENTS ON THE LAWS OF WAR, *supra* note 2, at 244, 246.
40. *See* DINSTEIN, *supra* note 36, at 44–47.
41. Additional Protocol I, *supra* note 2, at 444–45.
42. HENCKAERTS & DOSWALD-BECK, *supra* note 1, Vol. I, at 14 *et seq.*
43. *Id.* at 14, 16.
44. *Id.* at 14, n.91.
45. *Id.*, Vol. II, Part 1, at 93.

46. ANNOTATED SUPPLEMENT TO THE COMMANDER'S HANDBOOK ON THE LAW OF NAVAL OPERATIONS 296 (A. R. Thomas & James C. Duncan eds., 1999) (Vol. 73, US Naval War College International Law Studies).
47. North Sea Continental Shelf, (F.R.G. v. Den.; F.R.G. v. Neth.), 1969 I.C.J 3, 43 (Feb. 20).
48. *Id.*
49. *Id.* at 43–44.
50. HENCKAERTS & DOSWALD-BECK, *supra* note 1, Vol. I, at xliv.
51. *Id*, at 19.
52. Additional Protocol I, *supra* note 2, at 448.
53. HENCKAERTS & DOSWALD-BECK, *supra* note 1, Vol. I, at 20, and Vol. II, Part 1, at 110, 117.
54. ANNOTATED SUPPLEMENT, *supra* note 46, at 484.
55. Rome Statute of the International Criminal Court, July 17, 1998, 2187 U.N.T.S. 90, *reprinted in* 37 INTERNATIONAL LEGAL MATERIALS 999, 1006.
56. HENCKAERTS & DOSWALD-BECK, *supra* note 1, Vol. I, at 119.
57. Geneva Convention (I) for the Amelioration of the Condition of the Wounded and Sick in Armed Forces in the Field, Aug. 12, 1949, 75 U.N.T.S. 31, *reprinted in* DOCUMENTS ON THE LAWS OF WAR, *supra* note 2, at 197, 206.
58. Geneva Convention (IV) Relative to the Protection of Civilian Persons in Time of War, Aug. 12, 1949, 75 U.N.T.S. 287, *reprinted in id.* at 301, 306–07.
59. 1 COMMENTARY ON THE GENEVA CONVENTIONS OF 12 AUGUST 1949, at 215 (Jean S. Pictet ed., 1952).
60. 4 COMMENTARY ON THE GENEVA CONVENTIONS OF 12 AUGUST 1949, at 127 (Oscar M. Uhler & Henri Coursier eds., 1958).
61. HENCKAERTS & DOSWALD-BECK, *supra* note 1, Vol. I, at 193.
62. Additional Protocol I, *supra* note 2, at 462.
63. COMMENTARY ON THE ADDITIONAL PROTOCOLS OF 8 JUNE 1977 TO THE GENEVA CONVENTIONS OF 12 AUGUST 1949, at 819 (Yves Sandoz, Christophe Swinarski, Bruno Zimmermann eds., 1987).
64. Yoram Dinstein, *The Right to Humanitarian Assistance*, 53 NAVAL WAR COLLEGE REVIEW 77 (2000).
65. HENCKAERTS & DOSWALD-BECK, *supra* note 1, Vol. I, at 196.
66. *Id.* at 151–52.
67. Additional Protocol I, *supra* note 2, at 442, 451.
68. HENCKAERTS & DOSWALD-BECK, *supra* note 1, Vol. I, at 154–55.
69. *See* Committee on Formation of Customary (General) International Law, Final Report, International Law Association, 69th Conference 712, 738–39 (2000).
70. North Sea Continental Shelf, *supra* note 47, at 43.
71. *See* HENCKAERTS & DOSWALD-BECK, *supra* note 1, Vol. I, at 152.
72. *Id.* at 268.

PART III

LAW OF ARMED CONFLICT DISSEMINATION

V

The American Red Cross and International Humanitarian Law Dissemination

Lucy Brown*

We heard about Nuremburg—and stuff about World War II in other classes in school, but it didn't really mean anything . . . now I understand why it's important.

Introduction

For well over a decade, the American Red Cross (ARC) has been telling the United States civilian population that international humanitarian law (IHL) is an important subject about which everyone needs to be knowledgeable. The ARC outreach occurs primarily at a grassroots level, through our chapter network around the country, and focuses on dissemination to the general public. It is our hope, and a goal of our dissemination, that the majority of students—as well as adults—in the United States will be able to say, as the high school student quoted above did, that they know what IHL is and they understand why it's important.

IHL Dissemination in the US Context

Since the attacks of 9/11 and the US engagement in Afghanistan and Iraq there has been a marked increase in organizations speaking to the American public about IHL. I think this is very much a "good news/bad news" phenomenon. It is wonderful that Americans are much more interested in a subject that not many found

* Senior Advisor, International Humanitarian Law, American Red Cross.

relevant only a few years ago. What is unfortunate is the reason they find it relevant—that armed conflict now affects many more people in this country.

The Role of the American Red Cross

We are often asked, especially by those in the military, why we say "international humanitarian law" instead of "law of armed conflict" or "law of war." The answer is that while we sometimes use the terms interchangeably, our perspective is the humanitarian one and it is focused primarily on teaching the Geneva Conventions. In our courses we situate IHL within the wider context of international law, including Hague law. Our objective, however, is to increase protection for vulnerable groups in armed conflict and facilitate humanitarian work by raising awareness within the general public about the 1949 Geneva Conventions and their 1977 Protocols. While the content of our training overlaps with the military's law of war training, the military understandably has an additional emphasis on Hague law, focusing on the means and methods of warfare.

In our dissemination we also explain the role of the Red Cross Movement—what it is and what it is not. We have learned that many people think the Red Cross is a human rights organization, and that IHL is synonymous with human rights law. We explain to them, for example, that while the Red Cross is not a human rights organization as such, much of the work it does benefits people's human rights.

Sometimes members of the public are surprised to discover the Red Cross is not an organization whose primary purpose is to promote peace. However, we discuss how a byproduct of Red Cross efforts in conflict regions can help facilitate a return to peace, and a byproduct of Red Cross principles being understood and acted on can help promote peaceful coexistence among antagonistic groups.

Sometimes we have to correct the mistaken notion that the Red Cross is responsible for enforcing the rules of IHL against those who commit violations. I think people imagine some kind of international Red Cross police force and expect to see Red Cross staff providing testimony against war criminals. They do not realize how impossible that would be for a Movement based on the principles of humanity, impartiality and neutrality—whose most powerful weapon may be its ability to be present on both sides of a front line.

One of our challenges over the years is what to call our program. Just the term "international humanitarian law" is a real mouthful and can be very off-putting. That is why we settled on "Humanity in the Midst of War." That phrase comes much closer to expressing the message we want to convey—that respect for IHL helps ensure that the principle of humanity, and humanitarian actions themselves, will continue to exist, even in the midst of war.

We let people in our classes know that they, as individuals, have an important role to play in making this happen. Many people feel a profound sense of helplessness when faced with the brutality and suffering of war. They would like nothing more than to turn away. We tell them IHL makes a difference and that they themselves can make a difference—for humanity.

Why Is the ARC Involved in Dissemination?

Our responsibility for dissemination derives from the Geneva Conventions and our role as an auxiliary to the US Government under our 1905 Congressional Charter. The Statutes of the International Red Cross and Red Crescent Movement explicitly state that national Red Cross and Red Crescent societies are to "disseminate and assist their governments in disseminating international humanitarian law; they take initiatives in this respect."

The American Red Cross began its dissemination program with a 1988 grant from the US Institute of Peace that enabled us to develop our educational materials for the general public. Then in 1991 the International Services Department of the American Red Cross received an internal grant to develop an instructor training curriculum. Starting in 1993 we began a series of instructor training courses.

What Is the Message?

We focus on very basic messages that address protection and human dignity. Examples include:

- That those no longer taking an active part in hostilities—wounded, sick and captured combatants, and civilians—must be protected from harm and treated with respect regardless of what side they are on.

- That people in these protected groups are entitled to humane treatment. We ask a class what rules they think should apply in armed conflict. Then we ask: "How should a prisoner be treated if he has just killed your buddy?" and then "What if the prisoner is your brother?"

- Another message is that governments have the primary responsibility for enforcing IHL and that the Red Cross, the International Committee of the Red Cross in particular, has a role in implementing it.

- We point out that the Geneva Conventions are treaties, agreements negotiated by governments, and they therefore reflect a balance between humanitarian protections and military objectives. This comes as a surprise to some people, who wonder why IHL doesn't just outlaw war.

• We stress the importance of the principle of distinction (combatant vs. noncombatant), but also discuss how civilians can lose protections by participating in the fighting.

• We talk about the US military's own training for soldiers and give examples of how the provisions of the Geneva Conventions have been incorporated into military operational training. We now show a portion of a US Marine Corps law of war training video in our classes and distribute a handout on the "Basic Principles of the Law of War" as provided to Marines. We believe it is essential that the American public understand how seriously the majority in our military takes this body of law.

These are a few of the basic messages we think an informed public needs to know.

Who Do We Want to Reach—What Target Groups?

Our dissemination program is designed primarily for the general public. It is the audience we reach best, as anyone who is familiar with our first aid, CPR or water safety classes, to name a few, understands. It is seen as part of our organization's mission to help communities prevent, prepare for and respond to emergencies.

However, within the general public we have some priority audiences, including: 1) American Red Cross internal audiences and prospective instructor/disseminators; 2) youth and educators; and 3) opinion leaders within the general public, including in the media, academia, and in community leadership positions.

We do offer some programs for more specialized or expert audiences, but these are fewer in number and are mostly dependent upon the level of expertise, motivation and opportunity of individual instructors.

How Do We Do It?

Our dissemination program is based on a national instructor training model through which over 300 American Red Cross instructors have been trained in over 25 training sessions. Since 1993 these instructors have reached over 324,000 people through introductory courses and presentations in communities around the country. These courses and presentations have been organized and coordinated by our network of over 800 local chapters, although, of course, not all our chapters have the capacity to offer IHL instruction. It is important to realize that for the most part instructors are not legal experts, but act instead as *facilitators* to guide and stimulate discussion and learning.

While the IHL courses tend to generate excitement and interest in those who attend, we have had limited human and financial resources from the very beginning of the dissemination effort and our reach has been much smaller than we would like. We hope to change that. We recently streamlined our instructor training model and the IHL course itself to bring them more into alignment with other American Red Cross training models, thereby hopefully expanding the number of people we can reach.

Exploring Humanitarian Law and IHL Dissemination to Youth

A major part of our current strategy is to make IHL dissemination to youth—through a program called "Exploring Humanitarian Law"—a priority.

Why Focus on IHL Dissemination to Youth?

The advantage of exposing young people to the Geneva Conventions at an early age is obvious. As one military lawyer put it rather succinctly, "The last thing we want is for young people to come into the military thinking it's okay to harm prisoners."

Exploring Humanitarian Law (EHL) is the best material I have ever seen for teaching IHL to youth. To date, the feedback from teachers and students has been overwhelmingly positive. As one student said:

> It gives you a whole new perspective . . . a bigger perspective. People don't think about these things because we live in America and war seems so far away . . . but war isn't really far away and all of this is a lot closer than people think. It changed the way I think. . . .

EHL was developed by the ICRC working with the Educational Development Corporation, based in Boston, and the American Red Cross was one of the original pilot sites. It is a resource pack of materials designed to use with adolescents and can be used alone or to enrich existing classroom materials.

EHL teaches students respect for human life and dignity, ethical judgment, life skills, global citizenship, the protections of the Geneva Conventions and the role of the Red Cross. Students learn by actively participating in a series of ethical explorations that look at both historical and contemporary examples and that examine concepts such as:

- Human dignity
- Obstacles to humanitarian behavior
- Dilemmas

- The chain of consequences
- Multiple perspectives

Exploring Humanitarian Law is currently being implemented in 95 countries through national Red Cross and Red Crescent societies and ministries of education. In the United States, it has been aligned with the national standards for high school social studies; but it is also used in other classes, including: psychology, history, anthropology, economics, global studies, geography and political science. Extracurricular groups have begun using the materials, including some Junior Reserve Officer Training Course classes. These materials resonate at the deepest level with both students and teachers.

The American Red Cross is currently seeking funding to expand the program to reach thousands of teachers and millions of students. We are working on the development of an EHL distance-learning course for teachers and exploring ways to include the study of IHL in the curriculum offered by American high schools. It is not an easy task in a country with, in effect, 50 separate departments of education. However, if we can expand EHL into many more classrooms, it will be a major leap forward for IHL dissemination in the United States. We have shared these materials with individuals at the Department of Defense, who have responded very positively.

Conclusion

A few years ago when I was interviewed by MTV for an article they wrote for their online news titled *What Are the Geneva Conventions?* I explained that whoever said "All's fair in love and war" only got it half right. My remark was obviously designed to draw the attention of a young audience to the fact that there are widely agreed upon standards for humane treatment in war. Making these standards much more widely known and accepted is a goal worthy of all our best efforts.

VI

Teaching the Law of Armed Conflict to Armed Forces: Personal Reflections

David Lloyd Roberts*

Introduction

The International Committee of the Red Cross' (ICRC) approach to training the armed forces in the law of armed conflict, as well as some of my personal approaches, will be addressed under the following subheadings:

- Problems that might be faced by armed forces in teaching and applying the law.
- The need to accept that training must be based on the realities and pressures of combat.
- The approach to training soldiers, young officers and senior officers.
- Suggested gaps in the teaching of the law.
- Views on whether that training is accepted and implemented in battle.

The ICRC Approach

In terms of dissemination, the ICRC has a supporting role. Its aim is to assist the military wherever possible in carrying out their responsibilities in relation to training and teaching the law of armed conflict. Its mandate stems directly from the

* Independent consultant and lecturer in the law of armed conflict and human rights law, as well as humanitarian security issues. The views expressed in this article are the author's alone unless reference is made to specific ICRC policy.

Geneva Conventions of 1949[1] and the Additional Protocols of 1977,[2] as well as resolutions stemming from the Fourth Session of the 1974–1977 Diplomatic Conference on the Reaffirmation and Development of International Humanitarian Law Applicable in Armed Conflicts.[3]

How does the ICRC carry out this mandate? In its headquarters in Geneva, the ICRC has a small department dealing with relations with armed and security forces. Then throughout the world there are officers based on regional delegations. These officers are known as "Delegates to the Armed Forces." All are retired and all have seen some form of operational service with their own forces or with the United Nations. Their task is to make contact with the armed forces of the region in which they are working and to explain how and to what extent the ICRC can offer assistance based on their particular requirements. The key is assistance and cooperation. It is certainly not the ICRC's mandate or intention to assume the full responsibility of an armed force to train its own personnel in the law. Many countries have their own system of dissemination in place while others have nothing.

The strategy is essentially one of encouraging armed forces to integrate the law of armed conflict into their training and operations. This is based on initial confidence building, e.g., meetings, briefings and introductory courses. This would be followed by training courses for selected officers resulting in the actual training of trainers. Thereafter, the ICRC might offer assistance in the drawing up of law syllabi so that the law is integrated into all levels of training and operational planning.

The ICRC Delegates to the Armed Forces can offer the following:

- A wide-ranging experience in combat and other military operations. These new and different experiences can be shared with an armed force to broaden knowledge.

- Access to good teaching material, produced by the ICRC in Geneva and specifically tailored to the needs of the particular country. The ICRC's new *Teaching File for Armed Forces* is a good example of this. Its purpose is to provide instructors with the basic tools they require to conduct lessons in the law of armed conflict. It consists of twelve lessons covering the whole subject, including human rights law and standards applicable to the use of force in internal security operations.[4] It has been translated into a number of languages including French, Russian, Chinese, Spanish, Mongolian and Amharic. In order to keep abreast of new developments or simply for more detailed advice on particular issues, the delegates also have access to the large legal department at the ICRC headquarters in Geneva.

- The delegates bring to their instruction their operational experience, but because they are also from the ICRC they are impartial and neutral in what they have to say. It is for the students and staff of colleges and academies to relate the law to their own particular circumstances. It is definitely not the role of the ICRC instructor.

- Because they have been soldiers and because they have sat through lectures at their own military academies or staff colleges, they know how easy it is for lecturers to send students to sleep, particularly when the topic is law. They try therefore to inject realism and interest into their presentations and to motivate their audience by a mix of programming and training aids. Case studies using up-to-date examples are a particularly valuable way of bringing the subject alive and encouraging a cross flow of ideas and discussion. In addition to lectures and courses, the instructors can offer assistance with seminars, training programs and the provision of training booklets. Courses can be tailored to the specific needs of army, navy, air force, paramilitary and police personnel. The human rights law and standards applicable to lower levels of internal violence are more and more in demand, particularly from the military.
- Finally, the ICRC can sponsor senior officers at courses either in Geneva, or more regularly, at the International Institute of Humanitarian Law in San Remo, Italy where they have the opportunity to interact with officers from a range of countries.

Personal Approach

To teach the law you must believe in it. There is no way you could possibly bluff a military audience if you did not. Based on my experiences of conflict, I believe that the law is sound. It is useful when teaching the law to point out that it was born on the battlefield. It is very much soldiers law molded by our ancestors' experiences of battle. The law is rich in military tradition and custom; for example, ruses of war, perfidy, and the truly customary white flag of truce. One of the principles of war is simplicity of action. The law is also simple and straightforward. It is full of good practical guidance. In no way does it hinder your actions on the battlefield or, as some may think, tie one hand behind your back. In no area does it conflict with the principles of war, such as maintenance of momentum, concentration of effort, surprise and so on.

The law to which we're referring is today usually called either international humanitarian law or the law of armed conflict. I still find, however, that soldiers respond more readily to the subject if we refer to it as the "law of war," and that is the term I will use in this article. Knowing the attitude of soldiers to the subject of the law, I like to begin lectures by putting them on the spot and making them think at the very outset about the subject so I begin the very first lecture by saying to them:

> I would like to take a guess at what you're thinking right now. Some probably think that this is an ideal opportunity to catch up on some well-earned rest. You may be saying to yourself "thank goodness I'm not on the assault course or on maneuvers. This is absolutely marvelous. I can switch off and let this instructor ramble on for 45 minutes. I know all about the Geneva Conventions anyway—the law is part of my culture and our military traditions. I really don't need to listen to all this legal mumbo-jumbo."

The more skeptical and cynical might well be thinking along the lines of Cicero, the very famous orator of ancient Rome, who stated, "Laws are silent amidst the clash of arms."[5] In other words, war by its very nature is beyond the law. Wars break out when the rule of law breaks down, so that there are no longer any rules. It's like finding yourself in the middle of a football match without referees or umpires, so just go for it. The mentality becomes, "We have to win at any cost, so let's forget the legal do-gooders."

Some may hold the view that consideration of the law, while of great interest to lawyers, leaves most operational officers, and certainly every soldier, absolutely cold. I am sure that the word "law" on military programs immediately brings to mind dust-covered old books and instills feelings of boredom or remoteness and, to put it quite bluntly, irrelevance.

Some might actually think the law is important for any professional soldier, but they are frightened by it. Becoming conversant with the law represents a massive investment of time and effort. How, on top of all the other commitments, can one be expected to come to grips with the subject?

At this stage, and if time allows, one can pose the question "where do you stand on the issue?" Having heard what the students think and having involved them in the subject from the outset, the time has come to gently point out that they might not be quite as knowledgeable as they originally thought. This is done by running over once again the differing attitudes described above and asking, "This question is for those of you who know all about the Geneva Conventions. If you really do, that is fine, but can you tell me exactly what these mean?" A picture of a soldier holding a white flag appears on a PowerPoint slide, hands flash up and inevitably, the class answer will be "It means I want to surrender." It is not the time to teach just yet, so we put the class on hold with the reply, "Let's see later in our lessons if you were right or wrong." We move on to the next slide and here few, if any, students know what the symbol of large orange circles is designed to protect.[6] The lesson continues in this vein. For example, we can then ask the class if they are sure about their exact duties in relation to the following categories of persons and objects: captured combatants, civilians, the Red Cross protective emblem, and the wounded, both military and civilian.

To those who may be among the skeptics and believe that war must be fought without rules, we ask:

> Perhaps you would like to consider whether it would be useful to you in battle for some provisions of the law to protect you, if you have been captured, from torture while under interrogation, or from poisonous gas attacks from your opponent; or to protect you if you are a civilian.

And to those who think the subject is dull and irrelevant, we can ask:

> Are you absolutely sure what your legal responsibilities are when planning an attack? Are you sure how and when you can use weapons such as booby traps and flamethrowers? How does the law of war differ from the law applicable to internal security operations? Are there any differences?

I end this introduction by saying, "I hope that this has allowed you to focus on the relevance of the law of war—to you and to those under your command." By now, most are fully awake and most are now fully aware of their shortcomings in the subject and motivated to learn more.

It is important in this approach to training that the instructor has credibility with his military audience. An instructor who has experienced conflict will have a head start in getting the subject across to the audience. The rapport and understanding in both directions will be immediate and will make any teaching more relevant and acceptable. Even the language and jargon used will be more digestible and acceptable to the audience. This, as I mentioned earlier, is exactly the approach used by the ICRC.

Problems Faced by Armed Forces in Teaching and Applying the Law

In training armed forces, one must accept that there are certain problems that have to be taken into account. Even in the very best of armed forces there will always be constraints on training time. At a military academy or a staff college, the commandant will always be pulled in numerous directions to include more of this or that in the syllabus. It is a brave commandant who insists on maintaining a module on the law of war. Yet it is in these very institutions that a nation's future high command must be instructed in the provisions of the law that are one day likely to influence them and their decisions as commanders. Ignorance of the law in light of a nation's obligation under the Geneva Conventions to teach the law is inexcusable. It is in peacetime that we have time to consider the law; once the balloon goes up it is then too late.

Commanders must believe in the law and demonstrate by their interest and emphasis on training in peacetime, and, of course, by their behavior in battle that they respect the law. Commanders must be trained to know the law and their responsibilities within it. Setting a bad example or giving unclear, ambiguous orders has certainly caused problems in the past and has been a principal root cause of grave breaches of the law.

Once when teaching a bunch of young cadets we came to the coffee break. We were sitting with the commandant and his senior officers, separated, thankfully, from the cadets. "What you are saying David is all very well but at the end of the day I have found that the only way to get information out of a terrorist is to break his legs!" I could see and tell from the reaction of my students that they were interested and receptive. However, with this sort of barracks room attitude or culture, my message would soon be adjusted—"OK, forget what you have just been told. This is the way we do it here!"

Another real problem is that there is indeed a great deal of skepticism and cynicism out there at the coalface of the law of war. Most audiences will say, "We accept what you are telling us. It's all very well us abiding by the law, which of course we do. But what about our opponents? They continually break the law and get away with it." That is the old "eye for an eye, tooth for a tooth" argument. They ask, "Have you been to teach in country XYZ (a potential opposing belligerent) as well? Why don't you, the ICRC, or the UN do something about those who abuse the law?" Sometimes it is very difficult to accept that in the long run it is better to adopt the high moral ground when you know that today your opponent has a policy of using suicide bombers and a "no quarter" policy!

Following on from this is the general feeling that the law is toothless. When, as is so often the case, it is abused, the chances of any international body such as the United Nations putting an end to it are slim. The powerful can get away with violations. There is not a great deal of faith in the United Nations. Often audiences will refer to UN resolutions, which are ignored or circumvented. There is also much cynicism surrounding the International Criminal Court. No doubt, this will diminish as the court finds its feet and produces results; for the present, however, this cynicism remains.

At a course in Africa, I came face to face with this general feeling of cynicism. It was at the end of a two-week session for a very bright group of officers. A senior commander arrived from the Ministry of Defense for the farewell speech. We spoke a little beforehand and I had told him what I had been doing with the ICRC.

In front of the assembled officers, he thanked me very much for my lectures and noted that I had spent many years teaching armed forces in Third World countries. He said, "Of course we know all about the law of war and have always applied the rules in our fighting with our neighbors. May I suggest that the ICRC's time would be better spent educating the more civilized nations in this subject who it would seem need it more than us!" My course coincided with the disclosures in the written press and television of the alleged abuses of prisoners in Abu Ghraib.

Training Must Be Based on the Realities and Pressures of Combat

It is important in training to accept that there are sometimes severe difficulties and pressures placed upon a soldier in battle that might incline them to disregard the rules they are supposed to obey. There may be fear, tiredness, frustration, anger, hunger and stress. There may be the need to overcome the inclination for revenge or retribution. This must be controlled by good training, and good clear orders which are enforced by good commanders at all levels.

Let us take a look at some of the pressures. We know that every member of the armed forces, whatever his or her rank, has a personal responsibility to comply with the law and to ensure that it is complied with by others and to take action in the event of violations.[7] If you break the rules, you can be tried, and not just by your own courts.[8]

It is no defense to a war crime to say that the act was committed in compliance with a superior order. A soldier who carries out an order that is illegal under the law of war is guilty of a war crime, provided that he or she was aware of the circumstances which made that order unlawful or could reasonably have been expected to be aware of them.[9]

This point is of great significance to any soldier. It is a simple point to make but much more difficult for soldiers to carry out in the field. It means they must refuse a command if they believe it to be plainly unlawful. Surely unflinching loyalty and obedience to superior commanders are fundamental to any armed force. This is true, but there is clearly a higher loyalty, to your State and its laws. The duty of all soldiers not to comply with unlawful orders is quite clearly established in international law. During the Nuremberg and Tokyo trials that followed the Second World War, the defense of superior orders, while considered a mitigating factor in relation to sentencing, in no way excused law breakers. The principle has been reaffirmed in modern tribunals such as those set up to deal with war crimes committed in the former Yugoslavia and Rwanda. If an order is plainly unlawful, a soldier has a duty not to carry it out. Superior orders might be used in mitigation of an offense, and might result in reduced punishment, but not as an excuse for an offense.

Let's take a look at some other pressures. How about dealing with prisoners of war (POW) or other categories of captured persons? Whether they have surrendered or not, they become protected persons under the law the instant they fall into the power of the adverse party. The law clearly states that it is forbidden to kill or mistreat a combatant who has been taken prisoner or who is *hors de combat*. That's fine on paper but how does it translate onto the battlefield? During and immediately after combat, soldiers are still hyped up; the adrenaline is running very high. One minute they may be required to kill the enemy and the next they have to treat him with kid gloves even though he might well have killed or wounded some of their comrades.

This is obviously a difficult situation, but professional soldiers must cope. The best way is to put yourself in the prisoners' position. "Do unto others as you would have others do unto you." How would you like to be treated if you had been captured? As professional soldiers who now have the upper hand, the time has come to show humanity and respect for your opponents.

The POWs are no doubt tired, disorientated and very frightened. No good soldier or commander should take advantage of their plight or vulnerability. Bullying or mistreatment of POWs is a real problem immediately after capture. Anger and frustration might result in this being vented against the prisoner.

Misguided attempts by unprofessional soldiers to gain information can lead to problems. The law is quite clear on this. No coercion whatsoever may be used to force a prisoner to give information. Torture, both physical and mental, inhumane or degrading treatment or punishment is absolutely prohibited.[10]

The argument of military necessity can never be used to justify torture. For example, we can never say that we needed to torture someone because we knew they had vital information that might save the lives of others (sometimes referred to as the "ticking bomb scenario"). In combat, torture is not only illegal; it serves little military purpose except perhaps to vent anger. It is far more sensible to send a suspect to the rear where trained interrogators can use their skills within the law to gain information. Battlefield interrogation, or as it is sometimes called "tactical questioning" can waste valuable time and in most cases will be futile. A well-trained and motivated soldier will tell you nothing or, even worse, try to mislead you. A frightened prisoner might tell you anything just to ease his plight; so again the information is unreliable. Anyway, who will do the questioning? Are they qualified interrogators? Do they know what they are doing? Is the information you gain reliable?

Prisoners must therefore be moved as soon as possible to the rear and must not be unnecessarily exposed to danger in the meantime. They must not be compelled to engage in activities of a military character, for example clearing the way through a minefield. They must be protected against acts of violence, intimidation, insults or public curiosity. For example, television crews may take pictures of the group as a whole, but only on condition that no prisoner of war is individually identifiable. This has not been the case in recent history, with those on both sides flouting the law.

Training Methodology

Soldiers

For soldiers to understand and implement the law it must be presented in a credible and digestible way. It is in peacetime that we have time to consider the law, to teach and to train. Once the fighting has started, it is too late. For soldiers, the law needs to be a part of normal behavior in action. Just as they are taught to fire weapons, to employ camouflage and concealment, etc., as a matter of routine, they should also be taught the basics of the law so that it becomes second nature, a reflex action. In battle, a soldier cannot be overburdened with complicated legal jargon or rules. He needs simple and understandable guidelines, especially if he is to respect the law in a combat environment. The KISS approach (Keep It Simple Stupid) is certainly the best. Long lectures will not be appreciated. The best approach is one based on short practical exercises or demonstrations to bring out points and then making sure they are repeated in training. Ambush drills, section attacks, and fighting in built-up areas exercises can all have a small element of law of war training incorporated into them. The scope is simply dependent on the interest and enthusiasm of the instructor. For example, exercises could easily include capture drills; correct treatment of prisoners of war; treatment and evacuation of the wounded (yours and the enemy's); and respect for the civilian population and protected property. Drills for dealing with the white flag of truce and dealing with humanitarian aid convoys are further examples. All of these scenarios can be built into field exercises without too much difficulty; indeed, they tend to make field training much more interesting.

In this way, tactics and law of war issues are seen to be part and parcel of the same subject. They become accepted routine procedures, i.e., a matter of normal behavior in action. Classroom instruction for soldiers should be kept to the minimum. Some lectures will be necessary to set the scene. Perhaps one or two periods as a maximum, any more and they are likely to prove counterproductive. Here the use of playlets to demonstrate a point is particularly useful, for example, the right and wrong way to deal with a captured combatant. In addition, up-to-date examples of law of war issues, pictures of real events, video clips—sometimes from war movies—and so on are important in maintaining interest. Many nations have produced their own law of war training videos; they find them particularly useful in getting key messages on the law across to soldiers.

Junior Officers

Training of junior officers is, in my view, probably the most important aspect of all. These future commanders must be given the opportunity to learn and reflect on the subject from the outset. The time spent on this training need not be long. If done properly a young officer can be taught all the law of war lessons he really needs to know for the whole of his career. Eight to ten periods covering will give them the background knowledge they need. There is a need to set the scene and explain the background to the law—how it originated, its status today, its aims and when the law applies. The principles of the law, in particular those relating to distinction, military necessity, proportionality and limitation are very important and if taught to junior officers will act as a foundation for all future training, planning and operations. There must be a period on command responsibility. Commanders must be trained in the law and their responsibilities within it. The law in relation to the conduct of operations is of course of paramount importance. Periods on weapons and the law and logistics and rear areas, including prisoner of war camps, should be included. Today, the law of belligerent occupation might be quite important. Perhaps the law applicable to lower levels of violence should be included so that the differences in approach and in the rules are known from the outset. Internal security operations, post-conflict situations of restoring law and order or UN peacekeeping (as opposed to peace enforcement) operations come to mind. Field exercises and model room exercises can incorporate law of war aspects to reinforce this teaching. Case studies and military history can also be used to draw out lessons on the law as the course progresses. I think it is also very important that junior officers are left in no doubt as to their responsibilities to teach the law to their subordinates and perhaps to give them some ideas and tools to do that.

Senior Officers and Staff Officers

Staff colleges and war colleges are ideal places to reinforce the lessons learned as a cadet and junior officer and to consider broader issues of the law. The officers at these places of learning will be filling important posts in the future and some will be destined for high command. Case studies of recent conflicts can be used to highlight not only tactical or strategic issues but also law of war concerns. Topics could include command responsibility. Indeed, there are a number of useful case studies in this area resulting from recent experiences in Iraq and in the former Yugoslavia. Targeting and the law would be another important topic, in particular recent lessons relating to the principle of proportionality and distinction, the avoidance of collateral damage, the problems caused to planners and commanders by dual-use targets, and the need for good intelligence on which to base targeting decisions. There are a number of good case studies resulting from the conflicts in Kosovo, Afghanistan and Iraq. Logistic implications of the law are areas worthy of study at this higher level. For example, the treatment, handling and back loading of prisoners of war or casualties. Then there are UN operations/coalition operations and the law. There is plenty to cover.

Gaps in Teaching the Law

Do armed forces actually pay the required attention to the law? How much training actually takes place? Will they apply it in battle? All these are hard to assess. How many armed forces insist on a formal qualification in the law from their soldiers? Almost all countries require everyone to pass a written and practical test in the law before he or she can drive a car. How many soldiers that we send into combat have to pass a test on the laws of war? We know that States have undertaken to respect and to ensure respect for the Geneva Conventions in all circumstances, but how many actually do?

To a very large extent the international community relies on the ICRC to disseminate the law to armed forces. They do a good job but with some 20 delegates devoted to the task, and a few "on call" consultants, their impact on armies that in some cases exceed one million persons might be considered a pinprick. Some in the United Nations and large non-governmental organizations may believe that as "guardians" of the Geneva Conventions, the law of war is very much the ICRC's responsibility and that they should not interfere. If we are to rely exclusively on the ICRC then their efforts and staff devoted to this particular task must be greatly increased. Of course, we should not rely on them entirely. It is a nation's responsibility to ensure their armed forces are fully aware of their legal responsibilities in combat. It is a national responsibility to enforce and ensure respect for the law.

I have found a thirst for knowledge of the law that applies to the levels of conflict below the threshold for the application of the international law of war. It is in these lower levels of conflict that domestic law and international human rights law and standards come into play. There is, in my view, a definite gap here that must be filled. Many nations are facing situations of internal violence and disturbances, or as the military terms them, internal security situations. Many are interested in the law applicable to peacekeeping and post-conflict situations, i.e., where restraint and minimum force are required, the opposite of what is required of a soldier in conventional warfare. Although such situations will, in the main, be the responsibility of the police, there are occasions when the armed forces might be called upon to assist, or in some cases take over completely until law and order can be restored. This is occurring more and more frequently. If the armed forces are deployed into these situations with no knowledge of the law, with inadequate training and without the equipment necessary to produce a graduated response, then mistakes are likely which might well make the situation worse.

Acceptance and Implementation of the Law

Finally, I think it is important to consider whether and how well the law is actually being accepted and implemented by soldiers in battle even if training is perfect and the gaps are all filled. The cynical and skeptical might, as mentioned at the outset, agree with Cicero that in the reality of the recent conflicts in Afghanistan, Iraq and the ongoing "war on terror" the rules are indeed very often "Silent midst the clash of arms."

Is the situation that bad? Based on my experience, when it comes to practical law of war issues such as prisoner of war treatment, prohibition of torture, guidelines for attack, use of weapons, etc., I never had anyone arguing the toss[11] with the content of the law, which says a great deal about its practicality and common sense. Superior orders sometimes cause problems and I have covered that.

We mostly only hear the bad things. As someone once said, "If a dog bites a man, it's hardly news. On the other hand, if a man bites a dog, then it's going to be extensively reported." There have indeed been numerous reports of violations of the law, but very rarely are reports made on how well it is being applied, on how much effort is being put into target planning to avoid collateral damage, or on efforts to spare and protect the civilian population.

Perhaps from a cynical standpoint one could point out that the armed forces and civilian political leaders are now much more aware of their responsibilities and the dangers of breaking the law because of the CNN, BBC or "Al Jazeera" factor. It can make a commander's eyes water as he sees his promotion prospects disappearing when having to explain a mistake to CNN's Christiana Amanpour or BBC's John Simpson.

We cannot rest on our laurels, the gaps must be closed and we must make continued and indeed greater efforts to teach and ensure all combatants understand the law and apply it on operations. Offenders must be brought to justice, punished and be seen to be punished. At the end of the day, if soldiers in tight situations know as a reflex action how they should react then we have achieved our aim.

Notes

1. *See* Convention for the Amelioration of the Condition of the Wounded and Sick in Armed Forces in the Field, Aug. 12, 1949, 75 U.N.T.S. 31 [Geneva Convention I]; Convention for the Amelioration of the Condition of the Wounded, Sick and Shipwrecked Members of the Armed Forces at Sea, Aug. 12, 1949, 75 U.N.T.S. 85 [Geneva Convention II]; Convention Relative to the Treatment of Prisoners of War, Aug. 12, 1949, 75 U.N.T.S. 135 [Geneva Convention III]; Convention Relative to the Protection of Civilian Persons in Time of War, Aug. 12, 1949, 75 U.N.T.S. 287 [Geneva Convention IV]; all *reprinted in* DOCUMENTS ON THE LAWS OF WAR (Adam Roberts & Richard Guelff eds., 3d ed. 2000), at 197, 122, 244 and 301, respectively. The following appears in Geneva Convention I at Article 47, Geneva Convention II at Article 48, Geneva Convention III at Article 127, and Geneva Convention IV at Article 144:

> The High Contracting Parties undertake, in time of peace as in time of war, to disseminate the text of the Convention as widely as possible in their respective countries, and, in particular, to include the study thereof in their programmes of military and, if possible, civil instruction, so that the principles thereof may be known to the entire population, in particular to the armed fighting forces, medical personnel and chaplains.

2. Protocol Additional to the Geneva Conventions of 12 August 1949, and Relating to the Protection of Victims of International Armed Conflicts, Jun. 8, 1977, 1125 U.N.T.S. 3, *reprinted in* Roberts & Guelff, *supra* note 1, at 422 [Additional Protocol I]. Article 83 provides:

> 1. The High Contracting Parties undertake, in time of peace as in time of armed conflict, to disseminate the Conventions and this Protocol as widely as possible in their respective countries, and, in particular, to include the study thereof in their programmes of military instruction and to encourage the study thereof by the civilian population, so that those instruments may become known to the armed fighting forces and to the civilian population.
>
> 2. Any military or civilian authorities who, in time of armed conflict, assume responsibilities in respect of the application of the Conventions and this Protocol shall be fully acquainted with the text thereof.

Article 6 adds:

> 1. The high Contracting Parties shall, also in peacetime, endeavour, with the assistance of the national Red Cross (Red Crescent, Red Lion and Sun) Societies, to train qualified personnel to facilitate the application of the Conventions and of this Protocol, and in particular the activities of the Protecting Powers.

Article 82 states:

> The High Contracting Parties at all times, and the Parties to the conflict in time of armed conflict, shall ensure that legal advisers are available, when necessary, to advise military commanders at the appropriate level on the application of the Conventions and this Protocol and on the appropriate instruction to be given to the armed forces on this subject.

3. See Resolution 21 of the Fourth session of the 1974–1977 Diplomatic Conference on the Reaffirmation and Development of International Humanitarian Law Applicable in Armed Conflicts: "The Diplomatic Conference encourages the authorities concerned to plan and give effect, if necessary with the assistance and advice of the ICRC to arrangements to teach international humanitarian law, particularly to the armed forces." *Reprinted in* COMMENTARY

ON THE ADDITIONAL PROTOCOLS OF 8 JUNE 1977 to the Geneva Conventions of 12 August 1949, at 1525 (Yves Sandoz, Christophe Swinarski & Bruno Zimmerman eds., 1987).

4. David Lloyd Roberts, International Committee of the Red Cross, Unit for Relations with Armed and Security Forces, The Law of Armed Conflict – Teaching File for Instructors (Knut Dormann ed., 2002).

5. Marcus Tullius Cicero, Quotes, *available at* http://www.brainyquote.com/quotes/authors/m/marcus_tullius_cicero.html.

6. Three bright orange circles placed on the same axis identify works and installations containing dangerous forces. *See* Additional Protocol I, *supra* note 2, art. 56 and Annex I, art. 16.

7. JEAN-MARIE HENCKAERTS & LOUISE DOSWALD-BECK, CUSTOMARY INTERNATIONAL HUMANITARIAN LAW, Vol. I, Rule 151: Individual Responsibility, at 551 (2005).

8. *See* Geneva Convention I, *supra* note 1, art. 49; Geneva Convention II, *supra* art. 50; Geneva Convention III, *supra* art. 120; and Geneva Convention IV, *supra* art. 146. *See also* Additional Protocol I, *supra* note 2, arts. 85, 86.

9. HENCKAERTS & DOSWALD-BECK, *supra* note 7, Rules 154 & 155, at 563–567.

10. Geneva Convention I, *supra* note 1, arts. 12, 50; Geneva Convention II, *supra* arts. 12, 51; Geneva Convention III, *supra* arts 17, 87, 130. Geneva Convention IV, *supra* arts. 32, 100, 118, 147; Protocol Additional I, *supra* note 2, art. 75; Protocol Additional to the Geneva Conventions of 12 August 1949, and Relating to the Protection of Victims of Non-International Armed Conflicts art. 4, June 8, 1977, 1125 U.N.T.S. 609, *reprinted in* Roberts & Guelff, *supra* note 1, at 483.

11. "Disagree" when translated from the King's English.

PART IV

MODERN WEAPONRY AND WARFARE

VII

War, Technology and the Law of Armed Conflict

Michael N. Schmitt*

War, technology, and the norms governing warfare have influenced each other dramatically since the beginning of organized conflict.[1] Technology determines how wars can be fought. When the resulting hostilities run counter to prevailing values or interests, law and other prescriptive strictures often emerge to restrain them.[2] This occurs either through treaties or as the result of policy decisions by belligerents (generally States) to conduct themselves in a particular manner. In the latter case, the practice matures into customary international law when it becomes "general" (widespread) and "accepted as law" by States.[3] Finally, as the norms governing war become outdated, law is reinterpreted, ignored, or discarded.

In the 21st century, the pace of technological change in warfare has quickened. This article asks how war and law are likely to react to, and upon, one another in the near future. It begins with a brief survey of the normative architecture governing

---

* Professor of International Law, George C. Marshall European Center for Security Studies, Garmisch-Partenkirchen, Germany. The views expressed herein are those of the author in his personal capacity and should not be construed as the official position of either the Federal Republic of Germany or the United States. This article was previously published as an Occasional Paper by the Program on Humanitarian Policy and Conflict Research (HPCR) (Summer 2005) and is reprinted with permission.

methods (tactics) and means (weapon systems) of warfare. Technology is then reviewed, with particular emphasis on current weapons development programs and overall trends. The article concludes with an analysis of how this technology may influence the application and interpretation of the law of armed conflict.

The Law Relevant to Technology

In 1996, the International Court of Justice (ICJ) recognized the law of armed conflict's two "cardinal" principles in *Legality of the Threat or Use of Nuclear Weapons.*[4] Distinction, the first, provides that "States must never make civilians the object of attack and must consequently never use weapons that are incapable of distinguishing between civilian and military targets." In other words, weapons must be both capable of discrimination and used discriminately. The second disallows weapons that cause combatants unnecessary suffering. Nearly all law of armed conflict prohibitions related to the conduct of hostilities, whether treaty-based or customary, find their genesis in these principles.

The 1868 St. Petersburg Declaration, which dealt with explosive projectiles, ushered in the modern era of limitations on methods and means of warfare with its pronouncement:

> That the only legitimate object which States should endeavour to accomplish during war is to weaken the military forces of the enemy;
>
> That for this purpose it is sufficient to disable the greatest possible number of men;
> That this object would be exceeded by the employment of arms which uselessly aggravate the sufferings of disabled men, or render their death inevitable;
>
> That the employment of such arms would, therefore, be contrary to the laws of humanity. . . .[5]

Other efforts to restrict military technology followed[6]—projectiles and explosives dropped from balloons (1899 and 1907); gas and chemicals (1899, 1925, 1993); expanding bullets (1899); submarine mines (1907); biological weapons (1972); environmental modification techniques (1976); non-detectable fragments (1980); mines & booby traps (1980, 1996, and 1997); incendiary weapons (1980); and blinding lasers (1995).[7]

Undoubtedly, further attempts to regulate weaponry will be launched. Possible topics include depleted uranium shells, cluster munitions, computer network attacks, non-lethal weapons, and space-based offensive operations.[8] The prospect of States agreeing to accept limits on their weaponry depends on variables ranging from whether they possess or are likely to be attacked with them, to the degree of international and domestic concern about their impact on the civilian population.

The international community also regulates methods and means of warfare through non-weapon specific law of armed conflict principles. Two early compilations were the Regulations annexed to the 1899 and 1907 Hague Conventions on the Laws and Customs of War on Land.[9] These regulations set forth the most basic limitation on the conduct of hostilities, that "[t]he right of belligerents to adopt means of injuring the enemy is not unlimited."[10] Other relevant provisions include a ban on poison[11] and "arms, projectiles, or material calculated to cause unnecessary suffering";[12] acceptance of ruse;[13] and a requirement to take "all necessary steps" to "spare, as far as possible, buildings dedicated to religion, art, science, or charitable purposes, historic monuments, hospitals, and places where the sick and wounded are collected, provided they are not being used at the time for military purposes."[14]

The most comprehensive codification governing methods and means of warfare is the 1977 Protocol Additional to the 1949 Geneva Conventions (Additional Protocol I) which governs international armed conflict.[15] Although key States such as Israel, India, and the United States are not party to the instrument, they recognize many of the Protocol's provisions as reflective of the customary law of armed conflict.[16]

Article 35 restates the basic Hague principles that there are limits on methods and means of warfare and that weapons causing superfluous injury or unnecessary suffering are banned.[17] More significant, is Article 48, which sets forth the core law of armed conflict principle, distinction: "In order to ensure respect for and protection of the civilian population and civilian objects, the Parties to the conflict shall at all times distinguish between the civilian population and combatants and between civilian objects and military objectives and accordingly shall direct their operations only against military objectives." Articles 51 and 52 build on this requirement.

> *Article 51:* (2) The civilian population as such, as well as individual civilians, shall not be the object of attack. Acts or threats of violence the primary purpose of which is to spread terror among the civilian population are prohibited.
>
> (3) Civilians shall enjoy the protection afforded by this Section, unless and for such time as they take a direct part in hostilities.
>
> *Article 52:* (1) Civilian objects shall not be the object of attack or of reprisals. Civilian objects are all objects which are not military objectives as defined in paragraph 2.
>
> (2) Attacks shall be limited strictly to military objectives. In so far as objects are concerned, military objectives are limited to those objects which by their nature,

location, purpose or use make an effective contribution to military action and whose total or partial destruction, capture or neutralization, in the circumstances ruling at the time, offers a definite military advantage.

In a related prohibition, Article 51.4 bans "indiscriminate" attacks on civilians, defining them as:

(a) those which are not directed at a specific military objective;

(b) those which employ a method or means of combat which cannot be directed at a specific military objective; or

(c) those which employ a method or means of combat the effects of which cannot be limited as required by this Protocol; and consequently, in each such case, are of a nature to strike military objectives and civilians or civilian objects without distinction.

Subpart (a) of the article contemplates the indiscriminate use of a weapon system capable of being aimed or otherwise controlled, i.e., one that is by nature discriminate. Iraq's launch of SCUD missiles against Israeli population centers during the 1990–91 Gulf War constitutes the textbook example.[18] The remaining subparts address indiscriminate weapons, the use of which is prohibited altogether. Subpart (b) deals with weapon systems incapable of being aimed directly at a military objective. A long-range missile with a guidance system so rudimentary or unreliable that its chances of striking a military objective are almost happenstance illustrates this category.[19] By contrast, subpart (c) outlaws use of aimable weapons that produce uncontrollable effects. A biological contagion that spreads uncontrollably through a civilian population, albeit initially targeted against combatants, epitomizes such weapons.[20]

Even if an attack is directed at a combatant or other military objective, and the weapon system employed is both discriminate by nature and used discriminately, it must be proportionate. Codified in Article 51.5(b), the principle of proportionality prohibits attacks which "may be expected to cause incidental loss of civilian life, injury to civilians, damage to civilian objects, or a combination thereof, which would be excessive in relation to the concrete and direct military advantage anticipated."[21] The law of armed conflict styles injury or death of civilians as "incidental injury," whereas damage or destruction of civilian property is labeled "collateral damage."

Finally, attackers must take "precautions in attack" to minimize harmful effects on civilians and civilian objects caused during an otherwise lawful strike. Article 57 sets out the requirements, the bulk of which represent customary law of armed conflict.[22] The principle requires "those who plan or decide upon an attack" to do "everything feasible" to ensure they are not attacking civilians, civilian objects, or items or individuals who enjoy special protection; to "take all feasible precautions" when choosing weapons and tactics in order to minimize incidental injury and collateral damage; and to select that military objective from among those yielding a "similar military advantage" that "may be expected to cause the least danger to civilian lives and to civilian objects."

Beyond the general principles, Additional Protocol I extends special protection to specified objects, most notably medical establishments, cultural objects, places of worship, objects indispensable to the civilian population, the natural environment, and works and installations containing dangerous forces.[23] Also proving increasingly significant is the prohibition on perfidy. Perfidy occurs when one party feigns protected status to kill, injure, or capture the enemy.[24] Examples include feigning: an intent to negotiate under a flag of truce or surrender; civilian status; being sick or wounded; and protected status (indicated by uniform or emblem) of the United Nations or a State not party to the conflict.[25]

In addition to treaty law, the customary law of armed conflict imposes certain restrictions on methods and means of warfare. Given the fact that the applicability provisions found in law of armed conflict treaties preclude their operation in many conflicts, customary law provides the key constraints on warfare.[26] In this regard, recall the Martens Clause, the contemporary formulation of which is found in Article 1.2 of Additional Protocol I: "In cases not covered by this Protocol or by other international agreements, civilians and combatants remain under the protection and authority of the principles of international law derived from established custom, from the principles of humanity and from dictates of public conscience."[27]

The dilemma with customary law lies in determining its content. The International Committee of the Red Cross recently released its *Customary International Humanitarian Law* study. Based on extensive surveys of State practice and pronouncements, the study attempts to capture the current customary law of armed conflict in writing.[28] Although somewhat controversial, it represents the only comprehensive attempt to do so in any systematic, internationally vetted fashion.

The study reiterates most norms described above, drawing heavily on the text of Additional Protocol I. Chapter 21 restates the ban on the use of methods or means "of a nature to cause superfluous injury or unnecessary suffering" and on indiscriminate weapons.[29] The subsequent chapters prohibit poison, biological weapons, chemical weapons, riot-control agents as a method of warfare, certain uses of herbicides, expanding bullets, exploding anti-personnel bullets, weapons with non-detectable fragments, specified uses of booby-traps, and laser weapons designed to cause blindness.[30]

Part I of the study sets out the broad law of armed conflict prohibitions: attacking or terrorizing civilians (unless directly participating in hostilities);[31] attacking other than military objectives;[32] perfidy;[33] and indiscriminate attacks, including the use of indiscriminate weapons, using discriminate weapons indiscriminately, and treating distinct military objectives in a concentration of civilians or civilian objects as a single target.[34] It further contains the principles of proportionality[35] and precautions in attack.[36] Rules governing medical, religious, humanitarian relief, and peacekeeping personnel and objects; journalists; protected zones; cultural property; works and installations containing dangerous forces; and the natural environment are found in Part II.[37]

The aforementioned instruments and principles represent the core normative boundaries applicable to methods and means of warfare . . . and which they will influence. Before turning to these dynamics, it is useful to consider 21st-century military technology.

The Technology Relevant to Law

Too often, thinking about war focuses on weaponry. Yet, weapons are simply one component of a "weapon system," i.e., "a combination of one or more weapons with all related equipment, materials, services, personnel, and means of delivery and deployment (if applicable) required for self-sufficiency."[38] It is the weapon system, often incorporating technology more complex than the weapon itself, which determines success or failure. For instance, in an air-to-ground engagement against a fleeting target, the intelligence assets that allow the target to be identified and the communications, command, and control networks that make rapid attack possible are as essential to mission success as the aircraft and the bomb it drops. Simply put, fully understanding combat operations requires consideration of *all* the technologies having a direct causal relationship to weapons employment. Therefore, this article adopts an inclusive approach to the technology of future war, looking first at specific development programs and then at general trends.

Specific Programs: Since the United States armed forces enjoys a technological edge over every other military in the world (a gap that will certainly widen), the best indicator of technology's vector lies in US military research and development programs.[39] Within the Department of Defense, the Defense Advanced Research Projects Agency (DARPA) oversees future technologies.[40] DARPA's current research centers around eight "strategic thrusts."[41] Because they provide a feel for the technology likely to be fielded on the 21st-century battlefield, it is useful to briefly review each category.

1) Detection, Precision Identification, Tracking, and Destruction of Elusive Surface Targets. Today, weapons fielded by advanced militaries are highly accurate. However, target detection, identification, and tracking continue to present

major hurdles to even the best-equipped forces. The unsuccessful decapitation campaign against Iraqi leadership during Operation Iraqi Freedom (OIF) offers a classic illustration. US air forces conducted 50 highly accurate strikes, yet failed to kill even a single targeted individual.[42] The problem lay both in the unreliability of some intelligence and the inability to leverage reliable information quickly enough.

In response to such challenges, DARPA hopes to find ways to collapse the current sequential targeting process (find, fix, track, target, engage, and assess results) into an uninterrupted and continuous one that adapts to battlefield events.[43] For instance, new technologies will blur the traditional distinction between intelligence (gather and process information), plans (determine what to do in response to that information), and operations (execute the plan). Platforms that carry both sensors and weapons, like the Predator, are merely the tip of the iceberg.[44] In the near future, systems will operate without human input; in other words, a single platform will search for, identify, and destroy targets autonomously.[45]

Networking represents the other thread in this strategic thrust. DARPA envisages developing systems that will first "connect more and more sensors, platforms, and weapons with a variety of communications links," and later permit "computers and commanders" to "take advantage of the massive amounts of data available to increase the speed, accuracy, agility, and capability" of combat forces.[46] In a simple illustration, a Predator might use video to track a target. When it enters an area of heavy foliage, the networked system would automatically switch to foliage penetrating radar. In response to the radar returns, 3D LADAR (laser detection and ranging) sensors would produce a detailed three-dimensional image which can be compared to computerized geometric models to accurately identify the target. Technology will have seamlessly linked sensors to sensors to shooters.

2) Robust, secure self-forming tactical networks. Although this strategic thrust supports the previous one, it is not limited to target destruction. "Network centric" operations "turn information superiority into combat power so that the United States and its allies have better information and can plan and conduct operations far more quickly and effectively than any adversary."[47] Doing so depends on highly advanced command, control, communications, computers, intelligence, surveillance, and reconnaissance (C4ISR) systems integrated into a single network.[48] The goal is an ability to rapidly gather, process, and react to information about an opponent, while hindering its efforts to do the same. In military terms, this is known as "getting inside the enemy's observe-orient-decide-act (OODA) loop."[49] Once inside, you control the flow, pace, and direction of battle. Eventually, disorientation paralyzes your adversary.[50]

DARPA is pursuing a number of systems along these lines. For instance, it has developed prototype self-forming, self-healing networks, such as the Small Unit

Operations Situational Awareness System (SUO SAS). SUO SAS will be used at the squad level to allow soldiers in complex physical environments such as cities and jungles to securely communicate with each other and monitor the location of fellow squad members.

3) Networked manned and unmanned systems. This thrust teams manned and unmanned systems to leverage the unique qualities each offers. An example is the backpack portable Micro Air Vehicle, which will perform intelligence, surveillance, and reconnaissance functions for small units. Another is the Unmanned Ground Combat Vehicle, a system providing fire support missions for ground forces.[51] Unmanned systems are especially useful in high threat environments or where the alternative (e.g., manned aerial reconnaissance) is labor intensive, costly, or in short supply.[52]

4) Urban Area Operations. Because of the advantages US forces enjoy on the open battlefield, adversaries increasingly confront them in urban areas where they can take advantage of clutter and proximity to civilians and civilian objects to mask their location or shield their activities. Events in Iraq have shaped the direction of research in this area. Present studies include systems to detect enemy forces, explosives (including suicide bombers and improvised explosive devices), and weapons of mass destruction (WMD); distinguish combatants from civilians and threats from civilian objects in crowded areas; "tag" a potential target (individual or object) to allow it to be monitored; employ weapons of variable effectiveness (non-lethal to lethal) to minimize collateral damage; and make individual soldiers and unmanned systems vertically mobile. An illustrative example is the Boomerang shooter detection system, which calculates the direction from which shots have been fired at a moving vehicle to enable effective return fire. Another is the Command Post of the Future (CPOF). Presently, command and control (C2) is exercised from a distinct physical location—a command post. CPOF creates a virtual, mobile, distributed, collaborative C2 system in which key participants operate from different locations, but still collaborate effectively in real time.

5) Detection, Characterization, and Assessment of Underground Structures. In light of US capabilities to accurately target aboveground structures, adversaries are using underground facilities for such purposes as hiding weapons (including WMD), protecting leadership, C2, and mustering forces. They range from the caves used by the Taliban and al Qaeda to the huge underground bunkers found in Iraq.[53]

DARPA has responded with the Counter-Underground Facility program. The program will develop ground and airborne seismic, acoustic, electromagnetic, optical, and chemical sensors that locate underground facilities; analyze their construction, layout, and vulnerabilities; and conduct post-attack battle damage assessment to determine the need for reattack.

6) Assured Use of Space. Operations like those taking place in Afghanistan and Iraq would be unimaginable without space-based communications, navigation, surveillance, reconnaissance, and weather systems. From satellite imagery to hand-held global positioning system locators, space is integral to every facet of high-tech warfare. To leverage space, and deny enemies the same opportunity, DARPA has focused efforts in five areas: rapid and affordable space access; situational awareness in space (what is there and what is it doing); protecting US spaced-based assets; preventing adversaries from using space-based assets; and using space in support of earth-based operations.

Numerous programs are underway. Orbital Express involves automated spacecraft to refuel, upgrade, and maintain other spacecraft. The Space Surveillance Telescope is a ground-based telescope with the capability to search space for small objects. Perhaps most significant is the Falcon program's Hypersonic Cruise Vehicle, which will traverse space to speed travel.

7) Cognitive Computing. Cognitive computing reverses the process whereby computer users adapt to computers by creating computers that adapt to users. Such computers "learn" from their experiences and adjust their activities accordingly. For instance, they can be used in operations centers to deal with fast-paced, complex situations by using past experiences to filter and prioritize information and craft responses thereto. When this occurs, the possibility of surprise diminishes significantly. An example is the Personalized Assistant that Learns (PAL). PAL will anticipate an individual's (e.g., decision-makers or intelligence analysts) needs based on previous experiences and prepare materials for them before being tasked to do so.

8) The Bio-revolution. This DARPA strategic thrust envisions technologies that either work with the human body or imitate nature. Examples of the former include programs that maintain physical and mental performance despite stress, environmental conditions like heat or altitude, lack of sleep, or insufficient nutrients. "Legged" robots able to traverse rough terrain better than wheeled vehicles (in one case modeled on a cockroach), optics based on the eye, and sensors inspired by insects that calculate room temperature exemplify the latter.

9) Miscellaneous Programs. DARPA works in areas other than its strategic thrusts. Three merit particular mention. The first is materials.[54] One current effort is the Structural Amorphous Metals program, which studies materials with amorphous microstructures that yield hardness and strength previously unattainable. Such materials might be of use, for example, in replacing the depleted uranium shells that have generated so much controversy. Other possibilities include an

unobtrusive external skeleton for soldiers carrying heavy backpacks and "morphing" aircraft structures that change shape while airborne to vary the flight envelope (much as the body of a bird does).

Microsystems comprise a second area of interest, one that gives the United States much of its current technological edge. In particular, microtechnology dramatically increases the functions performable by computer chips, thereby enhancing the processing capabilities of military systems. Similarly, smaller weapon systems on aircraft or vehicles yield greater range, mobility, and carrying capacity. This allows striking more targets with fewer platforms.

The third area is information technology. Present projects include peta-scale computing,[55] autonomous vehicle navigation, and collaboration between humans and robots or robots and robots. The High Productivity Computing Systems program is improving computer efficacy in activities such as cryptanalysis and weather forecasting by a factor of 10 to 40. Also noteworthy is the Improving Warfighter Information Intake under Stress program, which non-invasively monitors human cognitive load so information provided to the warfighter does not overload thought processes.

General trends: The aforementioned programs offer a real-world glimpse into the technology of future war. Some are understandable reactions to current challenges, such as the urban warfare and underground facility programs, while others reflect weaponry trends already underway. Since the characteristics of weapon systems, not individual systems, determine conflict's character, it is useful to summarize those trends most likely to persist.

1) Precision. Precision must be distinguished from accuracy. Accuracy is the ability of a weapon to strike a specified location, known as the aimpoint.[56] Precision, by contrast, involves identifying targets in a timely fashion and striking them accurately.

Many weapons are highly accurate, with circular error probable (CEP) calculations now measured in feet.[57] Accuracy lessens the risk of causing collateral damage and incidental injury, not only because weapons hit closer to their intended aimpoints, but also because the more accurate they are, the less explosive charge needed to achieve the desired probability of damage (PD).[58] While we can expect CEPs to progressively improve, the unfortunate reality is that few States can afford the "precision guided munitions" and associated launch platforms necessary to conduct truly accurate operations.[59] This being so, the task for research and development is *affordable* accuracy.[60]

A more prevalent trend in precision warfare is improved ability to locate, identify, and track targets—transparency of the battlefield. Today's warfighters benefit from an array of information sources: imagery intelligence (IMINT); human intelligence (HUMINT); signals intelligence (SIGINT); measurement and signature intelligence (MASINT); open-source intelligence (OSINT); technical intelligence (TECHINT); and counterintelligence (CI).[61] Moreover, aircraft such as the AWACs, JSTARS, and UAVs offer transparency in real-time,[62] while equipment like night vision goggles allow soldiers and airmen to locate and target the enemy in adverse conditions like darkness and poor weather. All indicators point to continued improvements in this area.

2) Coordination, command, and control. Another discernable trend is improved coordination horizontally and better command and control vertically. DARPA's work in network centric warfare is illustrative, for it demonstrates that future high-tech militaries will fight as networked entities, rather than hierarchical organizations.

Networking permits quicker collection, fusion, analysis, and dissemination of critical information (such as the location of a fleeting target); better decisions about the platforms able to respond most effectively to it; greater control over an ongoing operation; increased ability to coordinate operations in real-time with other friendly forces; enhanced responsiveness to unanticipated events that arise as the operation unfolds; less risk of friendly operations interfering with each other; and greater ability to deal with enemy threats. Taken together, networking is one of two keys to operating within the enemy's OODA loop.

An example is Blue-Force Tracker, a satellite-based tracking and communication system that allows computerized data integration and dissemination to troops in the field. With Blue-Force Tracker, all echelons of command and staff can follow a battle and provide combat support. Using a combination of computer maps, real-time automated data updates (on friendly and enemy locations, as well as other battlefield information), and chat room coordination, troops engaging the enemy no longer have to rely on preplanned support or that which happens to be "on-station" (in the vicinity). Instead, they can draw on the full range of theater assets, near simultaneously.[63] Blue-Force tracker, currently fielded in Afghanistan and Iraq, is merely the tip of the iceberg in terms of the networking likely to characterize tomorrow's battlefield.[64]

3) Transparency. As mentioned, transparency is the current focus of efforts to improve precision attack. But transparency also allows warfighters to anticipate enemy actions and proactively counter them. It is the second key to getting inside an adversary's OODA loop. Equipped with improved command and control, transparency, precision, and the ability to operate at night and in all-weather conditions, the high-tech military can sculpt the course of most ongoing battles against lesser-equipped foes.

Space enjoys particular importance in this regard, not only as the ultimate "high ground" from which to observe the enemy, but also as a medium through which information may be transmitted (e.g., by communications and navigation satellites); hence the centrality of space in US development programs. Transparency also undergirds efforts to link sensors for persistent battlefield coverage, as well as the fielding of unmanned systems to maintain coverage in high threat environments.

4) Soldier effectiveness. Several of the programs described earlier will dramatically improve the effectiveness of individual soldiers relative to their opponents. The bio-revolution and cognitive computing thrusts are illustrative, with potential further gains from research in tactical networking, manned-unmanned collaboration, materials, and microsystems. These programs cap a long-record of providing individual soldiers competitive advantages over their foes, represented by such currently fielded systems as night-vision goggles, light weight body armor, global positioning systems, individual weapons equipped with advanced sighting, and hand-free communications capability. The relative effectiveness and survivability of the individual soldier in militaries capable of acquiring such technology will only increase over time.

5) Unmanned and man-out-of-the-loop systems. Unmanned systems have become common on the modern battlefield (and off in the global war on terror). Although early systems provided rudimentary battlefield surveillance and reconnaissance,[65] UAVs are evolving into weapons platforms. A variant of the Predator, the MQ-1, is now armed with two Hellfire missiles, allowing it to directly engage targets it locates, as in the CIA-controlled strike on a car carrying Qaed Senyan al-Harthi, al Qaeda's senior operative in Yemen, in 2002.[66] It is only a matter of time before UAVs and other unmanned systems conduct attacks without the involvement of a human decision-maker.

6) Variable lethality and destructiveness. As noted, DARPA is assessing weapons of variable lethality for use in urban areas. This effort builds on the extensive non-lethal systems (more accurately labeled less-than-lethal) research done to date.[67] The difference is that in the past such systems were viewed primarily as useful in crowd control and other low-intensity situations. However, urban combat in Iraq has demonstrated the utility of weapons with differing destructiveness and lethality even in relatively intensive combat. This is particularly true when civilians and civilian objects are used as shields. Thus, field commanders are actively seeking ways to effectively attack the enemy in an urban setting while limiting collateral damage and incidental injury.

7) Other significant trends. As warfare becomes more complex, technology may outpace the ability of uniformed personnel to develop and maintain proficiency in

its operation. Some technologies, such as computer network or space operations, require education that the average member of the armed forces lacks. Or, given the limited numbers of a particular system in the inventory, it may be cost prohibitive to develop training programs for military personnel. Whatever the case, technological complexity suggests a greater civilianization of the battlefield and a closer nexus between civilians and the conduct of hostilities.

Future battlefields will also be less cluttered with military personnel and equipment. Simple cost calculations put massive inventories of equipment beyond the reach of most countries, as does the per item cost of advanced weapon systems. A B-2 bomber, for instance, has a life cycle cost of 2.5 billion dollars.[68] At this price, only the United States can field the aircraft in sufficient numbers to make risking it in combat reasonable. And high-tech weapons are much more effective than their low-tech counterparts, thereby requiring the use of fewer weapons platforms to achieve a given objective.

At the same time, militaries throughout the world are downsizing, usually for political and economic reasons. Compensatory technology has also made reductions possible. Unmanned systems are but one example. Additionally, the more technology allows penetration of an enemy's OODA loop, the less important raw troop strength is to effective combat operations.

Finally, although not a specific DARPA focus, future weapons will be employable from ever-greater distances and altitudes. Current systems are frequently launched beyond visual range (BVR).[69] For instance, during Operation Iraqi Freedom, naval vessels launched 802 Tomahawk Land Attack Missiles (BGM-109), which have a range of 690 miles. US forces also launched, *inter alia*, over 900 AGM-65 Maverick air-to-ground missiles, with a range of over 17 miles, and 408 AGM-88 HARM (high speed anti-radiation missile), with a 30-mile range.[70] The frequency of BVR engagements will only increase as those with long-range precision systems leverage them to stay outside the enemy's threat envelope.

Range, the ability to locate and fix distant enemies, and penetrable enemy defenses,[71] have made battlefields four dimensional (land, sea, air/space, and cyberspace) and spatially unlimited. War is no longer necessarily linear, i.e., fought along fixed lines of troops; instead, it may encompass the opponent's entire territory—from day one. Battlefields have been replaced by "battlespaces."

The Impact of Technology on Law

The technologies described above are dramatically influencing the application and interpretation of the law of armed conflict. They will continue to do so in the future. First and foremost, such technologies exacerbate the asymmetry that already challenges certain key law of armed conflict principles. Second, they complicate efforts to distinguish combatants and other military objectives from civilians and civilian objects. Third, and somewhat paradoxically, modern technology empowers militaries to avoid collateral damage, incidental injuries, and mistaken attacks. As it does so, however, troubling expectations regarding casualties are surfacing, expectations that endanger current understandings of the law of armed conflict.

Asymmetry: The technologies of war already on the battlefield, and development programs like those described above, will create a degree of asymmetry between the high and low-tech forces that has seldom been observed in military history.[72] High-tech forces locate their enemies more easily; observe their actions with better understanding; anticipatorily react to those actions with greater speed, coordination, and effectiveness; field weapons systems and soldiers that are infinitely more survivable and better able to neutralize enemy defenses; employ weapons that strike their aimpoint with a degree of force precisely metered to achieve the desired level of destruction; and assess the results of their actions, and readjust if necessary, very quickly and with a high degree of reliability. And, as first demonstrated during Operation Enduring Freedom in Afghanistan, technology has reached the point where these tasks can be performed around-the-clock.[73]

Even numerically superior low-tech militaries with positional advantage cannot prevail against such forces in conventional combat. At the start of the recent conflict, Iraq fielded a ground force of nearly 400,000.[74] It was defeated in six weeks by one less than half its size.[75] Further demonstrating the impact of asymmetry, the Iraqi air force never even left the ground. Meanwhile Coalition aircraft flew 20,733 fighter/bomber sorties over territory with an air defense system that was robust by contemporary standards. Only one fixed wing aircraft, an A-10 Warthog, was lost to hostile fire.[76] And in its most inhospitable environment, the urban battlefield, technology prevailed. For instance, during the battle for Fallujah, US Marines killed nearly 1,200 insurgents while suffering only 50 casualties.[77]

Cynics will point out that weapons advances historically either find their way to the enemy or soon fall victim to effective countermeasures.[78] As an example, Iraqi insurgents are using mobile phones to rapidly coordinate attacks on Coalition forces and detonate roadside bombs. Similarly, complex US Department of Defense systems are regularly the target of cyberattacks. But the prospects of disadvantaged forces turning the tables on their high-tech opponents in the near term remain slight.

Low-tech forces face two basic challenges in modern warfare: 1) how to perform the most basic function in combat, survival; and 2) how to engage the enemy, either to defeat it or to so alter its cost-benefit calculations that it withdraws from the fray voluntarily.

Consider survival. Facing an adversary armed with advanced C4ISR and immediately available precision weaponry, the best survival option is to avoid being spotted in the first place. Lawful methods to avoid discovery include, *inter alia*, camouflage, ruses, jamming, and spoofing.[79] As demonstrated during the unsuccessful Coalition decapitation strikes, simply staying on the move can frustrate advanced detection systems.[80] And militaries have always used physical features such as jungle canopy, mountainous areas, caves, underground bunkers and tunnels, and urban areas, as well as night and weather, to mask their presence.

But, as noted, research is underway on systems to counter each of these tactics, from jam resistant networked information networks to chemicals capable of mapping caves. So how does the out-teched side survive? Increasingly, it does so by blurring or even discarding law of armed conflict principles. Iraq is the paradigmatic example. During the first Gulf War, Coalition forces slaughtered Iraqi military units wherever they met in open battle.[81] By 2003, the technology available to US forces had radically improved, while the Iraqi military had not recovered from its earlier defeat and the ensuing sanctions regime. Wisely, then, the Iraqi army avoided open confrontations.

To keep the Coalition troops from identifying them, many Iraqi soldiers promptly discarded their uniforms.[82] The tactic has no *de jure* relationship to the prohibition on attacking civilians, but it endangered them in the sense that Coalition soldiers were less certain about who posed a threat, thereby heightening the risk of mistaken uses of force against innocents. Because such mistakes of fact are more reasonable than would be the case where civilians and combatants are clearly distinguishable, the law of armed conflict's deterrent effect was effectively weakened.

In fairness, members of the military who merely wear civilian clothes do not violate the law of armed conflict. Rather, they lose combatant status because they lack the prerequisites thereof set forth in Article 4 of the Third Geneva Convention.[83] Article 4A(1) provides that members of the armed forces enjoy combatant status. Article 4A(2) sets forth four cumulative conditions which members of a militia not forming part of the armed forces (and members of other volunteers corps, including resistance fighter) must meet to be lawful combatants. Because these conditions are inherent in the meaning of "armed forces," they apply equally to those encompassed in Article 4A(1).[84] The relevant criterion in this context is "having a fixed distinctive sign recognizable at a distance," one typically met through uniform wear.

Two consequences attach to the loss of this status. First, those captured do not qualify as prisoners of war.[85] Second, because only combatants have the right to "directly participate" in hostilities,[86] others enjoy no combatant immunity for their actions during the hostilities. While it is not a war crime to attack the enemy, doing so may amount to a criminal offense (e.g., murder) under the national law of capturing forces. Lacking immunity, they may be prosecuted in the courts of any State with subject matter over the offense and personal jurisdiction over the offender.[87]

Another technique for avoiding identification is feigning specially protected status. Iraqi regular and irregular forces did so, for instance, by misusing protective emblems. One recurring tactic was to seize ambulances and use them as scout vehicles. Iraqi militia forces also marked the Ba'ath Party building in Basra with the emblem of the International Committee of the Red Cross (ICRC). Party buildings were regularly used as military supply depots and mustering points.[88] The law of armed conflict expressly prohibits the display of the distinctive emblems of medical and religious personnel, transports, and units, or the personnel, property, and activities of the International Movement of the Red Cross and Red Crescent, for other than their intended purposes.[89]

Sometimes one cannot avoid being identified by the enemy. When that is the case, an increasingly common survival tactic is "counter-targeting," i.e., the use of civilians and civilian objects as shields.[90] Shields may serve voluntarily or involuntarily, an important distinction vis-à-vis the law of armed conflict.

The war in Iraq is illustrative. Iraqi forces, especially the paramilitary Fedayeen, frequently forced humans, including women and children, to shield their activities. For instance, in one common tactic, they drove their vehicles next to those of civilians whenever they observed Coalition helicopters in the area.[91]

Article 51(7) of Additional Protocol I forbids the use of "[t]he presence or movements of the civilian population or individual civilians . . . to render certain points or areas immune from military operations, in particular in attempts to shield military objectives from attacks or to shield, favor or impede military operations,"[92] a prohibition that is unquestionably customary.[93] Violation of this norm by one side does not impose an absolute obligation on the other to refrain from attacking the shielded object or persons, but neither does it release the attacker from its own obligations.[94] Therefore, the principle of proportionality applies to attacks on shielded targets; if the likely injuries to (or death of) the shields, together with any other incidental injury or collateral damage caused, is excessive in relation to the resulting concrete and direct military advantage, attack is prohibited.[95] Voluntary shields are an exception, for they lose their law of armed conflict immunity from attack by "directly participating" in hostilities.[96] Obviously, since direct participants may be attacked, it would be incongruent to suggest they should nevertheless count in proportionality calculations.[97]

Civilian objects are also useful in counter-targeting. Iraqi forces often located military equipment and troops in or near civilian buildings, including specially protected locations. For instance, as Coalition forces moved north the Fedayeen used such protected locations as al-Nasiriyya Surgical Hospital, the Baghdad Red Crescent Maternity Hospital, the Imam Ali mosque in al-Najaf, and the Abu Hanifa mosque as bases for operations.[98] Later, during the battle for Fallujah, 60 of the city's 100 mosques and three medical facilities were so used.[99]

Although no express provision on using civilian objects as shields exists in the law of armed conflict, such actions violate Additional Protocol I's Article 58 obligations to "endeavour to remove the civilian population, individual civilians and civilian objects under their control from the vicinity of military objects; avoid locating military objectives within or near densely populated areas; [and] take the other necessary precautions to protect the civilian population, individual civilians and civilian objects under their control against the dangers resulting from military operations," albeit only "to the maximum extent feasible."[100] It is always "feasible" to refrain from intentionally placing military equipment and personnel in or near civilian objects in order to keep the former from being attacked.

Even more clearly a law of armed conflict violation is misuse of specially protected objects to compensate for technological disadvantage. The First Geneva Convention provides in Article 19 that "responsible authorities shall ensure that . . . medical establishments and units are, as far as possible, situated in such a manner that attacks against military objectives cannot imperil their safety." Additional Protocol I is plainer still: "Under no circumstances shall medical units be used in an attempt to shield military objectives from attack."[101] Further, "historic monuments, works of art or places of worship which constitute the cultural or spiritual heritage of peoples" receive analogous protections under the Protocol.[102] The Iman Ali and Abu Hanifa Mosques, mentioned above, qualify, for they are important Shia and Sunni shrines respectively.[103]

Absent special protection, civilian objects can become military objectives due to their militarily significant *location*, through *use* for military actions, or when their future *purpose* is military.[104] Moreover, each treaty granting specially protected status withdraws it upon misuse.[105] Thus, as a matter of *law*, shielding with civilian objects has little effect aside from influencing proportionality calculations.

Assuming the technologically weaker forces survive, they still need to attack the enemy. One logical, albeit unlawful, tactic for doing so is perfidy. Iraqi forces adopted a number of other perfidious tactics to offset the Coalition's technological superiority. Recall that Iraqi forces regularly fought in civilian clothes, a perfidious act if done as an element of an attack tactic. Of course, this is precisely why soldiers usually don civilian clothes. Additionally, they feigned surrender and used stolen ambulances to approach Coalition forces, hoping their opponents would make themselves more vulnerable by lowering their guard.[106]

Another tactic adopted in Iraq is suicide bombing. The increasing frequency of bombings attests either to the success of the tactic against superior forces or the relative lack of alternatives in the face of such superiority.[107] Although lawful if directed against combatants and military objectives,[108] when the bomber feigns protected status to approach targets, as is the norm, the attack is perfidious. Typically, though, civilians (unlawful combatants) carry out suicide attacks. Their *mens rea* determines whether doing so constitutes perfidy. If merely attacking, their actions comprise direct participation in hostilities. On the other hand, if the wearing of civilian clothing forms an integral part of their attack tactics, they have committed perfidy.[109]

Eventually, the technologically disadvantaged side may conclude that it is unlikely to prevail and reframe the conflict by shifting attention towards a center of gravity other than the military.[110] As Clausewitz recognized, war is the continuation of politics by other means. This being so, when facing overwhelming odds, it is quite rational to abandon the principle of distinction altogether and attack civilians as a center of gravity.

Both practicalities and objectives compel adoption of such a strategy. From a practical perspective, it is impossible to protect the civilian population effectively, no matter how robust one's technological wherewithal. Crippled by technology in a classic fight, the disadvantaged side responds asymmetrically by attacking its opponent's vulnerabilities.

Attacking civilians is also appealing when the objective is to take the fight out of an enemy without defeating it militarily. For instance, the goal may be to rupture a coalition, as in Iraqi targeting of Israeli cities in 1991.[111] Attacking civilians may also be intended to affect non-governmental and intergovernmental organizations. In Iraq, for instance, insurgents attacked the UN and ICRC headquarters in an effort to force their withdrawal. Similarly, civilian targeting can make the conflict appear too costly to belligerent States and citizens. The kidnapping and murder of foreign hostages in Iraq is designed to convince US partners to leave Iraq; such crimes are proving effective. Or, the "target" population might be the attacker's own. One goal of the attacks against Iraqi civilians is to convince the population it will be safer without Coalition forces. More directly, attacks against civilian politicians, judicial officials, and law enforcement personnel are designed to deter cooperation with the Coalition. Whatever the motivation, attacking civilians is a sadly frequent asymmetrical method of countering battlefield technological advantage.

Beyond unlawful *methods*, the technologically weaker side may resort to compensatory *means* of warfare. Two at the center of discussion are computer network attack (CNA)[112] and weapons of mass destruction.

CNA represents "war on the cheap" for an otherwise technology starved belligerent, for cost is limited to acquisition of off-the-shelf computers and exploitation software, access to the target network, and computer expertise. Moreover, the higher-tech an opponent, the more vulnerable it is to such attacks. Terrorist groups are already effectively using websites to conduct information campaigns, the broadcast of beheadings representing the extreme example. Concerted, organized offensive use of information technology will soon follow.

There is nothing unlawful per se about cyberattacks. On the contrary, when computer network attack assets are readily available, the law of armed conflict's precautions in attack requirements may sometimes mandate their use because CNA usually risks less collateral damage and incidental injury than kinetic weapons.[113] That said, the proportionality principle applies to CNA, as it does in all attacks. This is a particularly meaningful limitation on CNA because civilian systems are often linked to military networks (thereby risking the spread of viruses and other computer contagions),[114] and because many potential CNA targets are dual-use entities (e.g., power grids).[115]

As suggested by DARPA's programs, high-tech militaries have recognized this threat and are developing robust defenses. This may have the ironic effect of turning attention towards more penetrable civilian networks. In a networked world, the consequences of such attacks could be disastrous. Imagine cyberattacks against global financial networks, air traffic control systems, water treatment and distribution facilities, nuclear power plants, oil refineries and pipelines, or medical data systems.

The issue of whether attacks on civilian networks violate the law of armed conflict has generated an interesting debate. Some experts argue that all CNA operations against civilian networks violate the principle of distinction.[116] The better view is that the law of armed conflict only prohibits those rising to the level of an "attack." Although Article 48 of Additional Protocol I requires Parties to "direct their *operations* only against military objectives," every other relevant Protocol prohibition cites "attack" as its operative criterion.[117] "Attack" is a term of art defined in Article 49 as "acts of violence against the adversary, whether in offence or in defence."

Given advances in military technology, it would be unreasonable to further interpret the term "attacks" as being limited to those conducted through kinetic means. Indeed, universal consensus exists that non-kinetic biological, chemical, and radiological operations qualify as attacks. But at the same time, the express reference to violence can only be interpreted as implying violent *consequences.*[118] Thus, a military operation causing injury to humans (or severe mental suffering) or physical damage to property is an attack.[119] Mere inconvenience would not suffice. Universal acceptance of the proportionality principle as considering "incidental loss of civilian *life*, *injury* to civilians [and] *damage* to civilian objects" supports this interpretation.

In addition to exploiting the cyber-vulnerabilities of technology dependent societies, disadvantaged foes may fight asymmetrically with WMD. A number of States are acquiring WMD ostensibly to deter attack by technologically advantaged militaries, most notably North Korea.[120] Doing so is a predictable response on the part of those facing militarily dominant rivals.

The law of armed conflict outlaws chemical and biological weapons use for States party to the various instruments cited above. Arguably, customary law does the same for the rest.[121] That States do not have great confidence in these normative prohibitions is attested to by the extensive efforts they take to be able to operate in contaminated environments. This is understandable, for biological and chemical weapons are relatively low-tech, cheap, accessible, and easily deployable.[122]

Yet, it is not battlefield use that generates the greatest concern. The dynamic of asymmetry operates in the biological and chemical context in much the same way it does vis-à-vis CNA. Facing militaries equipped to withstand biological and chemical attacks, opponents may decide civilians pose the more attractive target. Thus, beyond the general prohibition on use, violation of the distinction principle logically (albeit not lawfully) results from severe disadvantage in conventional weapons systems.

The case of nuclear weapons is more complicated. In its 1996 advisory opinion on *The Threat or Use of Nuclear Weapons*, the International Court of Justice opined that their use "would generally be contrary to the rules of international law applicable in armed conflict, and in particular the principles and rules of humanitarian law." However, it added the caveat that it could not "conclude definitively whether the threat or use of nuclear weapons would be lawful or unlawful in an extreme circumstance of self-defence, in which the very survival of a State would be at stake."[123]

These conclusions demonstrate a relative misunderstanding of nuclear warfare.[124] Clearly, there are circumstances in which the use of such weapons would comply with the principle of distinction, including proportionality.[125] That there are probably nine nuclear powers, including all five of the permanent members of the Security Council, further draws the Court's conclusions into question.[126] For these and related reasons, the *Customary International Humanitarian Law* study wisely refrained from asserting that the use of nuclear (in contrast to chemical and biological) weapons violates the customary law of armed conflict.[127]

But the days of imaging nuclear warfighting generally faded away with the Cold War. Today, a limited number of nuclear weapons would not be decisive in a battle against determined high-tech forces like those of the United States. Therefore, beyond deterrent saber-rattling, the most likely nuclear scenario in the early 21st century is use of a small, low-yield, unsophisticated weapon against a population center, for holding the population at risk (or attacking it) offers the greatest leverage over an opponent. The perverse logic of technological asymmetry yet again leads, at least in theory, the disadvantaged belligerent towards extreme measures violating the law of armed conflict.

Each of the dynamics of asymmetry sketched out thus far centers on technology possessed by one side impelling its lesser-equipped opponent beyond the boundaries of the law of armed conflict. But the effect of technological asymmetry may be subtler, resulting in shifting interpretations of the law, rather than outright violation. Most significantly, the scope of military objectives and the principle of proportionality are likely to be so affected.

Recall that the principle of distinction limits attacks to combatants and military objectives.[128] Military objectives are objects that "make an effective contribution to military action," the attack on which will yield a "definite military advantage." Typically, the concept is interpreted narrowly, requiring a relatively direct nexus between the object attacked and the conduct of hostilities.[129] But to the extent military assets are difficult to attack due to an adversary's technological edge, an incentive exists to characterize entities with a weaker nexus to combat, but which are more vulnerable, as military objectives. Thus, for instance, while all would agree that a munitions factory qualifies, a disadvantaged side might argue that other industries providing income to finance the war effort do as well.

In fact, the United States may have inadvertently strengthened the position of those who would so argue by adopting a broad interpretation of military objectives in the Navy, Marine Corps and Coast Guard's *The Commander's Handbook on the Law of Naval Warfare*. In that manual, military objectives are described as objects contributing to the enemy's warfighting or war-sustaining capability. The Handbook goes on to note that "[e]conomic targets of the enemy that indirectly but effectively support and sustain the enemy's war-fighting capability may also be attacked." In light of this interpretation, which is labeled customary, it is difficult to contest adoption of a similar approach by a technologically weaker opponent determined to impose costs on its superior enemy.[130]

Paradoxically, militaries that outclass their adversaries may also see merit in a broad interpretation of the concept of military objectives. Technology, particularly when not possessed by an opponent, makes possible strategies that otherwise might not be viable. Most notable in this regard are coercive strategies, which seek not to defeat the enemy militarily, but rather to coerce it into engaging in a particular course of conduct (or desisting from one) through imposition of unacceptable costs. The archetypal example is Operation Allied Force, NATO's 1999 air campaign to force the Federal Republic of Yugoslavia to quit killing Kosovar Albanians and negotiate a political settlement on the basis of the Rambouillet Accords.[131] NATO never harbored a desire to defeat Yugoslavia militarily. On the contrary, President Clinton famously announced that NATO had no intention of sending in ground forces.[132] Instead, the aim was to employ force to alter the cost-benefit calculations of the Yugoslavian leadership, particularly Slobodan Milosevic.

From a law of armed conflict perspective, the predicament with coercive campaigns is that destruction of military targets may not affect the enemy leadership as much as holding its political power base, the civilian population, or personal financial assets (*inter alia*) at risk. This being so, there is an incentive to define military objectives as encompassing attractive coercion targets. Indeed, one distinguished commentator has gone so far as to suggest that elements of the principle of distinction should be abandoned altogether to permit targeting along these lines.[133]

The adoption of effects-based operations (EBO)—a targeting approach that replaces attrition strategies that progressively destroy enemy forces with surgical strikes designed to achieve particular well-defined effects—coincided with the rise of thinking about coercive strategies.[134] Advanced technology, especially precision, stealth, and C4ISR, has rendered effects-based operations feasible by making it possible to reliably deconstruct enemy systems, identify those aspects thereof that can yield a defined effect, and penetrate enemy territory to conduct precision strikes.[135]

Inevitably, concentrating on effects will lead to strategies aimed at achieving them without necessarily destroying the enemy's military as the means of doing so. As discussed, there are already suggestions along these lines with overtly coercive campaigns. A closely related doctrine with the potential for operationalizing this tendency is axiological targeting. Made possible by advanced technologies, axiological operations distinguish between utility and value targets.[136] Utility is the future usefulness of a prospective target to the enemy, whereas value constitutes its relative worth. In utility targeting, the attacker seeks to deny enemy forces what they need to operate by striking military objects such as airfields, vehicles, troops, headquarters, and command and control.[137] By contrast, axiological operations (although including utility targets) focus on objects the enemy leadership values, prioritizing targets based on the extent to which their destruction (or neutralization) is likely to affect decision-making.[138]

Although affecting cost-benefits calculations is often one mission planning goal, axiological operations elevate it to the central purpose. As with coercive strategies, viewing military operations in this manner drives one towards interpreting the concept of military objectives very liberally or, perhaps, even ignoring the principle of distinction.

Application of the proportionality principle may also be affected in subtle ways by technological disadvantage. Understandably, the technologically weaker side tends to view all victories over its superior opponent as momentous. To some extent they may be, for even minor successes by the weaker side embolden one's own troops and can demoralize an adversary. As a result, the weaker side might overvalue military advantage when determining whether incidental injury and collateral damage are excessive. Conversely, facing defeat, the weaker side may undervalue collateral damage and incidental injury, for risk to enemy civilians is unlikely to resonate as forcefully given its own dire straits.

The technologically superior side is liable to reverse these tendencies. Nearly certain of ultimate victory, the importance of any one military success will weigh less heavily in the proportionality calculation. Casualty aversion on the part of dominant forces reflects this dynamic in a slightly different context; the greater the likelihood of victory, the less willing the prevailing side is to place its forces at risk. Similarly, the advantaged belligerent may attribute considerable value to enemy collateral damage and incidental injury because it has more leeway to avoid them without jeopardizing its pending victory. This is particularly true given the media's ability to globally report civilian losses in near real time.

Of course, it is impossible to objectively relate the value of military advantage to collateral damage and incidental injury; they are dissimilar values that cannot be compared meaningfully except in the extreme cases. Be that as it may, the proportionality principle does cause warfighters pause when planning and executing attacks. The degree to which it does so depends in part on the extent of one's combat wherewithal relative to the enemy.

Finally, as we have seen in Iraq and as recognized by DARPA, technological disadvantage drives one from the open battlefield into either terrain that masks location or urban areas. In the case of the former, such as jungle or mountainous terrain, there is seldom risk to civilians, for it is the very remoteness of the areas that appeals to the vulnerable side. But as noted, DARPA is working hard to develop systems that deny the enemy the protection of jungle canopies, caves, etc. As this occurs, disadvantaged forces will be pushed into urban areas where, despite emerging urban warfare technology, the proximity to civilians and the difficulty in distinguishing combatants (who will often wear civilian attire) from civilians will offer greater hope of survival.

It is apparent that technological asymmetry creates faultlines in international humanitarian law. Yet, advanced technology will affect the interpretation and application of the law of armed conflict in ways wholly distinct from asymmetrical warfare.

Hindering Distinction: Technology complicates application of the principle of distinction, but not always as advertised. Much is often made of the fact that many weapons are launched BVR. Further, as described above, systems are now being developed in which an attack occurs without direct involvement of humans. There is a persistent tendency to characterize both BVR and "man-out-of-the-loop" technologies as weakening the ability to distinguish. Their use, so the argument goes, violates the precautions in attack requirements to "do everything feasible to verify that the objectives to be attacked are neither civilians nor civilian objects and are not subject to special protection" and to "take all feasible precautions in the choice of means and methods of attack with a view to avoiding, and in any event minimizing, incidental loss of civilian life, injury to civilians and damage to civilian objects."[139] For instance, some have claimed that an accidental attack on an Albanian refugee column during Operation Allied Force and the bombing of marked ICRC warehouses during Operation Enduring Freedom could have been averted had the pilots flown low enough to see the targets.[140]

While it may be true in individual cases that human involvement enhances target identification and verification and lowers the probability of collateral damage and incidental injury, this is not always the case. Most significantly, getting close enough to actually see the enemy brings with it vulnerability to enemy fire. This fact alone affects one's ability to perceive accurately. So too does taking the evasive maneuvers necessary to avoid being hit, for some precision weapons require a stable launch platform and sufficient time to acquire and lock onto a target. Further, certain precision weapons become more accurate with distance and altitude because there is greater opportunity for the weapon to guide to the target. Finally, there is no scientific basis for concluding that human perception and judgment is necessarily more acute or reliable than that of machines. Even if there was, it is appropriate to consider the safety of one's own forces when assessing the propriety of a strike. Force protection cannot alone outweigh any degree of collateral damage and incidental injury, but it is certainly a proper consideration for the attacker.[141]

A greater obstacle to application of the distinction principle is the growing proximity of military objectives to civilians and civilian objects, a phenomenon caused in part by technology. Perhaps most significantly, the range and precision of weapons, the transparency of the battlefield made possible by advanced ISR, and the ability to generate attacks very quickly using networked C4 have transformed traditional battlefields, on which forces typically engaged along a relatively identifiable line know as the FEBA (forward edge of the battle area). Linearity allowed civilians to distance themselves from the hostilities to some extent, although the advent of airpower dramatically limited their ability to do so.

As noted, current technologies have transformed the linear battlefield into a battlespace, with combat operations often occurring simultaneously on the ground and high seas, in air and space, and through cyberspace.[142] And distance is no longer an obstacle; hi-tech militaries such as those of the United States can mount attacks very quickly almost anywhere they wish. During Operation Iraqi Freedom, for instance, there was no part of the country that the Coalition could not monitor and attack.

The distinction implications are momentous. Because hostilities can take place everywhere, a location to which civilians flee may itself become the site of attacks. In particular, precision has made strikes against targets within populated areas viable. Imprecision ironically protected civilians, for many attacks, especially in urban areas, could not be mounted due to the potential for unacceptable impact on the civilian population. With modern weaponry, this de facto protection disappears since strikes against military objectives near civilians and civilian objects are often possible without causing "excessive" collateral damage and incidental injury. Yet, even with high-tech weaponry, it remains impossible to avoid all collateral damage and incidental injury. Therefore, by opening populated areas to military operations, precision denies civilians risk-free sanctuary therein.

Other aspects of modern weaponry increase the presence of civilians or civilian objects near combat operations. For instance, there are more civilian employees and contractors on the modern battlefield. Downsizing, cost-cutting measures, and unanticipated demands for troops are partially responsible. But advanced technology also drives civilianization. In some cases, there may not be sufficient numbers of advanced systems in the inventory for the military to develop training programs for its own personnel. Thus, weapon systems contracts often include maintenance and operations personnel. Or the systems may simply be so complex that few in the military have the background necessary to be trained to handle them.

Additionally, because of the prohibitive cost of developing high-tech systems, armed forces are turning to "off-the-shelf" (civilian) equipment. Thus, a factory producing items used by the military is a valid target despite its civilian production, unless a strike thereon would violate the principle of proportionality. The same applies to locations where the items are stored. Militaries also increasingly use civilian facilities and functions (such as airfields, electrical generation, civilian transport, communications assets) for their military needs. All such objects and dual-use locations are military objectives by the "use" criterion. To the extent they are planned for use, they become military objectives by virtue of "purpose." In all these cases, attacks will by definition result in collateral damage, and, in many cases, incidental injury to civilians.[143]

Enhancing Distinction: At the same time, technology often fosters distinction. In the first place, collateral damage and incidental injury are typically caused by: incomplete knowledge about what is being attacked; a lack of understanding of how civilians will be affected; inaccuracy; an inability to precisely meter the force applied to ensure no more than necessary is used; and restriking a target because one is unsure whether the desired level of destruction or neutralization has been achieved. The advanced technologies described above, as well as the general trends noted, will counteract these causal factors to varying degrees. Transparency will provide a greater quantity of information about the target and its environs, and it will be increasingly reliable. Similarly, post-strike battle damage assessment will give commanders a more complete picture of when they need to restrike a target, thereby avoiding unnecessary additional attacks that place the civilian population at risk. Improvements in accuracy will steadily reduce the circular error probable and allow the use of smaller charges to achieve the desired level of damage.

Moreover, technological advances are making possible non-kinetic (or non-lethal) alternatives to destructive kinetic attacks. For instance, rather than destroying components of an electrical grid, which may be located near civilians or upon which they depend for power, it is now possible to drop carbon-fiber filaments on power lines to interrupt electricity to a particular military objective, such as a command and control facility. Offering even greater possibilities is computer network attack. Using CNA, power to the target could simply be shut off. It might even be possible to exert some control over enemy command and control (rather than merely disrupting it) by altering, adding, or deleting select information within the system. Doing so might be more advantageous than simply turning off power, for it could create a false picture of the battlespace such that the enemy actually places itself at risk. Obviously, CNA and other technological alternatives to attack with kinetically destructive weapons present the possibility of dramatically limiting collateral damage and incidental injury, while attaining the same or greater military advantage.

Finally, as noted, technology can compensate for numbers in warfare. During World War II, the circular error probable (CEP) of a B-17 dropping gravity bombs was roughly 3,300 feet. This required 1,500 sorties dropping 9,000 bombs before achieving a high probability of damage against a point target.[144] An F-117 armed with laser-guided munitions, by contrast, can now strike its target with an unclassified CEP of approximately 10 feet, good enough for one-bomb, one-target tactics. Obviously, the impact on civilians produced by hundreds of sorties dwarfs that caused by one. Moreover, because technology decreases the number of troops necessary to conduct combat operations, there is less intermingling with the civilian population, and less opportunity for collateral damage and incidental injury.

Technology's ability to enable one to operate within the enemy's OODA loop is also generating positive effects. By controlling the course of battle, the advantaged side can avoid engagements that slow the pace of operations. This is exactly what happened in Iraq. The Coalition, operating within the Iraqi OODA loop, was able to quickly speed north, bypassing urban areas where fighting would have both bogged it down and endangered the civilian population.[145] Since the best way to minimize the impact of combat on civilians is to limit its duration, the technology that makes speedy defeat possible enhances the protections of civilians and other protected persons and objects.[146]

The greatest impact of technology on the law of armed conflict lies in the area of precautions in attack. Recall that those who plan or decide on an attack have to do everything feasible to verify targets are military objectives, choose methods and means of warfare with an eye towards minimizing collateral damage and incidental injury, provide a warning if the circumstances permit, and select that target from among those yielding a similar military advantage that causes the least collateral damage and incidental injury. As discussed, technology is expanding the opportunities for militaries equipped with state of the art equipment to avoid collateral damage and incidental injury by complying with these requirements. They possess more robust systems for reliably locating and tracking military objectives and distinguishing them from civilians and civilian objects, have a greater variety of weapons systems with which to strike the target, can choose from a larger set of possible targets (in part because they have a greater ability to penetrate enemy defenses), and will often have more opportunity to warn because, given their superiority, surprise is not as valuable a commodity to them as it is to their lower-tech adversaries.

But as the technological gap widens, the precautions in attack requirements operate on the belligerents in an increasingly disparate manner. After all, the standards are subjective, not objective; a belligerent is only required to do what is feasible, and feasibility depends on the available technology. The result is normative relativism—the high tech belligerent is held to higher standards vis-à-vis precautions in attack than its opponent. It is, of course, normative relativism by choice because States are under no legal obligation to acquire assets that will permit them to better distinguish between military objectives and the civilian population.

The problem with normative relativism is that States comply with the law of armed conflict in part due to reciprocity, i.e., they agree to be bound because their opponents shoulder identical obligations. The obligations may not impose equivalent burdens in practice, but at least as a matter of law the parties are on equal footing. With precautions in attack, however, the law itself, interpreted in a completely neutral manner, imposes dissimilar duties. This reality creates resentment; the greater the disparity, the greater the dissatisfaction of the belligerent bearing the greater burden of the legal obligation.

Complicating matters are exaggerated expectations on the part of many as to the ability of high-tech forces to avoid either mistakes or collateral damage and incidental injury. Advanced militaries bear part of the responsibility for creating such expectations. Since at least Operation Desert Storm, they have mounted aggressive public affairs campaigns designed to convince the domestic and international public that they are doing everything possible to avoid harming civilians and their property. In the process, they have created the impression that high-tech militaries have an endless supply of precision munitions, when in fact the inventories remain limited. [147]

Moreover, they also inadvertently caused an impression that weapons are flawless. Yet, even when working perfectly, they are not perfectly accurate. The most commonly employed precision munitions used in Iraq (and most accurate) were laser guided. Among these, the most frequently dropped was the GBU-12 Paveway II, which has a circular error probable of nine meters.[148] Although such accuracy is extraordinary, it is far from perfect.

At the same time, tales of satellite photos of individuals taken from space and eavesdropping on cell phone conversations from aircraft circling overhead cause many to believe the battlespace transparency enjoyed by high-tech militaries is comprehensive and fully accurate. Although it is true that transparency is at a level unimaginable even a decade ago (and improving rapidly), it is equally true that it is not absolute, a fact demonstrated by incidents ranging from the attack on the Chinese Embassy in Belgrade, to two strikes against an ICRC warehouse in Afghanistan, to the attack on a wedding party in Iraq.

Critics of recent campaigns, who tend to overrate the ability of high-tech forces, often overlook the fog of war. Increasingly, they view collateral damage and incidental injury (or mistaken attacks) as prima facie evidence of a failure to take precautions in attack. After all, given the high-tech systems at the disposal of advanced militaries, civilian loss "must" have been caused by either a failure to take the necessary precautions or outright recklessness. A rebuttable presumption of negligence in serious collateral damage/incidental injury incidents seems to be emerging vis-à-vis attacks conducted by high-tech attackers, who increasingly bear the burden of persuasion as to having taken appropriate precautions.[149]

Consider the reports written on the air campaigns during Operations Allied Force and Iraqi Freedom.[150] While occasionally questioning attacks on the basis of whether the target was a military objective (most notably media facilities), the bulk of the criticism alleged failure to take adequate precautions in attack. For instance, with regard to Allied Force, Human Rights Watch (HRW) expressed uneasiness over "whether every feasible precaution was taken to accurately distinguish civilians from combatants" and felt there were "questions regarding the decisions to attack on the basis of incomplete and/or seriously flawed information."[151] Commenting on the Dubrava Prison incident, in which 20 prisoners died during NATO attacks on nearby military facilities, HRW argued that "NATO did not apply adequate precautions in executing its airstrikes on nearby military objectives, and therefore must be held accountable for the civilian deaths that occurred as a direct result of those attacks." But the organization failed to cite those precautions the attackers should have taken, beyond a general comment earlier in the report about bombing from altitude.

The same tact was taken vis-à-vis Iraqi Freedom. HRW opined that continuing the decapitation campaign despite the lack of success "can be seen as a failure to take 'all feasible precautions' in choice of means and methods of warfare in order to minimize civilian losses as required by international humanitarian law."[152] Yet, the organization offered no alternatives to those precautions taken, other than not striking at all. This suggestion misstates the law, for the precautions in attack principle only applies to an attack that is otherwise lawful. The central issue is whether the attacker could have done something differently that would have lessened harm to the civilian population without forfeiting military advantage.

Many have been so captured by the wizardry of modern weaponry and so exposed to the horror of civilian suffering through the media that entire campaigns now become tainted by individual incidents. Indeed, scholarly, NGO, and journalistic comment often focuses on specific incidents, such as the Grdelica Gorge Bridge attack in Yugoslavia or the wedding party incident in Iraq, forgetting in the process that overall high-tech warfare is yielding campaigns that are ever-more discriminate.[153] Recall, that the number of weapons dropped during Operation Iraqi Freedom exceeded 10,000 and Allied Force involved the employment of more than 20,000. Yet, Human Rights Watch labeled its report on the former *Off Target* and the latter *Civilian Deaths in the NATO Air Campaign.*

Thus, technology not only actually heightens the legal standards to which high-tech forces must conform, but it creates expectations which, albeit initially without legal valence, create de facto standards which States operating under the media microscope can ill-afford to ignore. Very subtly, these de facto standards will influence application and interpretation of de jure standards as to what is and is not lawful collateral damage and incidental injury, the nature of the duty of care required of those planning and executing attacks, and the reasonableness of mistakes of war.

Conclusions

What is striking about the relationship between the technology, warfare, and the law of armed conflict is that all the news is not good. One would expect technology to increasingly limit the impact of warfare on the civilian population. It certainly does so to an extent, and a number of the technologies described will further distance war from civilians.

Yet, the technology has a negative face as well. Although almost never a purpose of technology, the weapons of war are increasingly placing the principles underpinning the law of armed conflict at risk. In great part, this is the result of an ever-widening divide between the technological "haves" and "have-nots." Faced with near certain defeat, "have-nots" are understandably (albeit inexcusably) rejecting the law of armed conflict as they compensate for their asymmetrical weakness. When one side operates in repeated violation of the law, adherence by the other usually deteriorates in lock-step.

Even the technology itself weakens the ability to safeguard the civilian population and other protected individuals and entities during armed conflict. Whether because it has broken the traditional spatial limitations of conflict or simply placed more civilians on the battlefield, technology has proven it is no panacea.

And sadly, technology has confused many observers of warfare, causing them to adopt unrealistic expectations that seem to be morphing into normative boundaries. Inevitably, militaries will react negatively to this trend, for it places limitations on their activities that were not the product of the careful balancing between military necessity and humanitarian concerns that typically characterize the formation of the law of armed conflict. This division does not bode well for either the military or those who seek to limit its use.

Notes

1. For an interesting article exploring the relationship between war and technology, see Charles J. Dunlap, Jr., *Technology: Recomplicating Moral Life for the Nation's Defenders*, PARAMETERS, Autumn 1999, at 24.
2. For instance, in ancient India the Law Code of Manu proclaimed that when "engaged in battle, (one) must never slay his enemies with weapons that are treacherous, barbed, or laced with poison, or whose tips are ablaze with fire." THE LAW CODE OF MANU (INDIA), ch. VII, v. 90 (Patrick Olivelle trans., Oxford University Press, 2004) (c. 100 BCE). In the fifth century BC, the *koina nomina* (common customs of the Hellenes) forbade the use of "unhoplite" arms. Josiah Ober, *Classical Greek Times, in* THE LAWS OF WAR: CONSTRAINTS ON WARFARE IN THE WESTERN WORLD 12, 13 (Michael Howard et al. eds., 1994). The Second Lateran Council condemned the use of the arc and crossbow in 1139 because it was seen as less than honorable to attack from a distance [Gerald I.A.P. Draper, *The Interaction of Christianity and Chivalry in the*

Historical Development of the Law of War, 5 INTERNATIONAL REVIEW OF THE RED CROSS 3, 19 (1965)], and in 1500 the *Corpus Juris Canonici* outlawed arrows, darts, and catapults on the same rationale. Leslie C. Green, *The Law of War in Historical Perspective*, *in* THE LAW OF MILITARY OPERATIONS 39, 46 (Michael N. Schmitt ed., 1998) (Vol. 72, US Naval War College International Law Studies).

3. Statute of the International Court of Justice, art. 38.1(b), June 26, 1945, 33 U.N.T.S. 993. The Court has noted that customary international law is "looked for primarily in the actual practice and *opinio juris* of States." Continental Shelf (Libya v. Malta), Judgment, 1985 I.C.J. 13, 29 (June 3). *See also* North Sea Continental Shelf (F.R.G. v. Den.; F.R.G. v. Neth.), Judgment, 1969 I.C.J. 3, 44 (Feb. 20). For an excellent summary of the nature and sources of the customary law of armed conflict, see Jean-Marie Henckaerts, *Study on Customary International Humanitarian Law: A Contribution to the Understanding and Respect for the Rule of Law in Armed Conflict*, 87 INTERNATIONAL REVIEW OF THE RED CROSS 175 (2005).

4. Legality of the Threat or Use of Nuclear Weapons, Advisory Opinion, 1996 I.C.J. 226, 257 (July 8).

5. St. Petersburg Declaration Renouncing the Use, in Time of War, of Explosive Projectiles Under 400 Grammes Weight, Dec. 11, 1868, *reprinted in* THE LAWS OF ARMED CONFLICT 91 (Dietrich Schindler & Jiri Toman eds., 4th ed. 2004).

6. Generally, restrictions on military technology were reactive in nature. For instance, the current prohibition on chemical weapons found its first expression in the 1925 Gas Protocol, a reaction to the 1.3 million gas casualties, including 91,000 deaths, during the First World War. Similarly, the Conventional Weapons Convention's anti-personnel mine Protocols of 1980 and 1996, and the 1997 Ottawa Convention, are belated responses to a weapon that had killed some 250,000 individuals since its invention. Occasionally, the international community attempts to constrain technologies before they find their way onto the battlefield. Famously unsuccessful were attempts to limit airpower in the late 19th and early 20th centuries. More successful has been the ban on biological weapons in the 1925 Gas Protocol and the 1972 Biological Weapons Convention, and the 1995 Protocol on blinding lasers to the Conventional Weapons Convention. *See* cites, *infra* note 7.

7. Hague Declaration (IV, 1) to Prohibit, for the Term of Five Years, the Launching of Projectiles and Explosives from Balloons, and Other Methods of Similar Nature, July 29, 1899; Hague Declaration (IV, 2) Concerning Asphyxiating Gases, July 29, 1899; Hague Declaration (IV, 3) Concerning Expanding Bullets, July 29, 1899; Convention (VIII) Relative to the Laying of Automatic Submarine Contact Mines, Oct. 18, 1907; Declaration (XIV) Prohibiting the Discharge of Projectiles and Explosives from Balloons, Oct. 18, 1907; Protocol for the Prohibition of the Use in War of Asphyxiating, Poisonous or other Gases, and of Bacteriological Methods of Warfare, June 17, 1925; Convention on the Prohibition of Development, Production and Stockpiling of Bacteriological (Biological) and Toxin Weapons and on Their Destruction, Apr. 10, 1972; Convention on the Prohibition of Military or any Other Hostile Use of Environmental Modification Techniques (arguably a method, not means, of warfare), Dec. 10, 1976; Convention on Prohibitions or Restrictions on the Use of Certain Conventional Weapons Which may be Deemed to be Excessively Injurious or to have Indiscriminate Effects (hereinafter Conventional Weapons Convention), with its Protocols on Non-Detectable Fragments (I), Mines, Booby Traps and Other Devices (II, amended May 3, 1996), and Incendiary Weapons (III), Oct. 10, 1980; Protocol (IV) to the CCW on Blinding Lasers, Oct. 13, 1995; Convention on the Prohibition of the Development, Production, Stockpiling and Use of Chemical Weapons and on Their Destruction, Jan. 13, 1993; and the Convention on the Prohibition of the Use, Stockpiling, Production and Transfer of Anti-Personnel Mines and on

Their Destruction, Sept. 18, 1997. All *reprinted in* THE LAWS OF ARMED CONFLICT, *supra* note 5, at 309, 95, 99, 1071, 309, 105, 135, 163, 181, 239, and 285, respectively.

Means of warfare have been addressed through other avenues. As noted, in 1996 the ICJ issued an advisory opinion on nuclear weapons. Three decades earlier, the United Nations General Assembly had addressed nuclear weapons in its aspirational 1961 Declaration on the Prohibition of the Use of Nuclear and Thermo-Nuclear Weapons. UNGA Res. 1653 (XVI), Nov. 24, 1961, *reprinted in* THE LAWS OF ARMED CONFLICT, *supra* note 5, at 127. Also noteworthy is the 1979 Conventional Weapons Convention Conference's Resolution on Small-Calibre Weapons. Resolution on Small-Calibre Weapon Systems, adopted by the UN Conference on Prohibitions or Restrictions on the Use of Certain Conventional Weapons, Sept. 28, 1979, *reprinted in* THE LAWS OF ARMED CONFLICT, *supra* note 5, at 237.

8. Various non-governmental organizations (NGOs) are seeking a moratorium (or ban) on the use of cluster munitions. *See, e.g.*, Human Rights Watch, Cluster Munitions and International Humanitarian Law: The Need for Better Compliance and Stronger Rules, Prepared for the Convention on Conventional Weapons (CCW) Group of Governmental Experts on Explosive Remnants of War (ERW), July 5–16, 2004, (no date).

9. Hague Convention (II) with Respect to the Laws and Customs of War on Land, and its Annex: Regulations Respecting the Laws and Customs of War on Land, July 29, 1899, *reprinted in* THE LAWS OF ARMED CONFLICT, *supra* note 5, at 55 [hereinafter Hague II Regulations]; Hague Convention (No. IV) Respecting the Laws and Customs of War on Land and its Annex: Regulations Respecting the Laws and Customs of War on Land, Oct. 18, 1907, *reprinted in* THE LAWS OF ARMED CONFLICT, *supra* note 5, at 55 [hereinafter Hague IV Regulations].

10. *Id.*, art. 22 (both instruments).

11. *Id.*, art. 23(a) (both instruments).

12. *Id.*, art. 23(d) (both instruments). The text is drawn from the 1907 formula. The 1899 provision prohibited employment of "arms, projectiles, or material of a nature to cause superfluous injury." On this issue and variations in modern texts, see YORAM DINSTEIN, THE CONDUCT OF HOSTILITIES IN THE LAW OF INTERNATIONAL ARMED CONFLICT 57–61 (2004).

13. Hague II Regulations, Hague IV Regulations, *supra* note 9, art. 24. Ruses are defined in Additional Protocol I, Article 37:

> Ruses of war are not prohibited. Such ruses are acts which are intended to mislead an adversary or to induce him to act recklessly but which infringe no rule of international law applicable in armed conflict and which are not perfidious because they do not invite the confidence of an adversary with respect to protection under that law. The following are examples of such ruses: the use of camouflage, decoys, mock operations and misinformation.

Ruses must be distinguished from unlawful perfidy (see discussion *infra*). Protocol Additional to the Geneva Convention of 12 August 1949, and Relating to the Protection of Victims of International Armed Conflicts (Protocol I), Dec. 12, 1977, *reprinted in* THE LAWS OF ARMED CONFLICT, *supra* note 5, at 711 [hereinafter Additional Protocol I].

14. Hague II Regulations, Hague IV Regulations, *supra* note 9, art. 27 (both instruments). Note that historical monuments were added in the 1907 version.

15. Additional Protocol I, *supra* note 13.

16. 160 States were party as of May 2005. The US position on Additional Protocol I is authoritatively set out in Memorandum for Assistant General Counsel (International), Office of the Secretary of Defense, 1977 Protocols Additional to the Geneva Conventions: Customary International Law Implications, May 8, 1986 (on-file with author). *See also* Michael J. Matheson, *The United States Position on the Relation of Customary International Law to the 1977 Protocols*

Additional to the 1949 Geneva Conventions, 2 AMERICAN UNIVERSITY JOURNAL OF INTERNATIONAL LAW & POLICY 419 (1987).

17. In unusual placement, this article includes a prohibition on employment of "methods or means of warfare which are intended, or may be expected, to cause widespread, long-term and severe damage to the natural environment."

18. Article 51.5(a)'s ban on "an attack by bombardment by any methods or means which treats as a single military objective a number of clearly separated and distinct military objectives located in a city, town, village or other area containing a similar concentration of civilians or civilian objects" is a variation of this prohibition.

19. Such as the German Vergeltungswaffe (reprisal) 2 rockets of World War II.

20. Of course, biological warfare is separately unlawful through specific prohibition. All weapons must be reviewed to assess their legality prior to being fielded. Additional Protocol I, *supra* note 13, art. 36. Although not a party to Additional Protocol I, US policy mandates such reviews. Deputy Secretary of Defense, Interim Guidance, Defense Acquisition, Memo, Oct. 30, 2002. US military service regulations also require weapons reviews. Army Regulation 27-53, Review of Weapons Under International Law, Jan. 1, 1979; Air Force Instruction 51-402, Weapons Review, May 13, 1994; Secretary of the Navy Instruction 5711.8A, Review of Weapons Under International Law, Jan. 29, 1988. *See also* Isabelle Daoust, Robin Coupeland & Rikke Ishoey, *New Wars, New Weapons? The Obligation of States to Assess the Legality of Means and Methods of Warfare*, 84 INTERNATIONAL REVIEW OF THE RED CROSS 345 (2002).

21. The principle is repeated in Article 57.2(a)(iii) & (b).

22. *See, e.g.*, Jean-Marie Henckaerts & Louise Doswald-Beck, I CUSTOMARY INTERNATIONAL HUMANITARIAN LAW (2005), ch. 5 [hereinafter Customary Law Study]. For an operational expression of this principle in an Additional Protocol I non-party State's military manual, see US Navy, US Marine Corps, US Coast Guard, The Commander's Handbook on the Law of Naval Operations, NWP 1-14M, MCWP 5-2.1, COMDTPUB P5800.7,¶ 8.1.2.1, 1995, reprinted in its annotated version as Volume 73, US Naval War College International Law Studies (1999).

23. Additional Protocol I, *supra* note 13, arts. 12, 53, 54, 55, and 56 respectively. The Customary Law Study suggests that the following are specially protected under the customary law of war: medical and religious personnel and objects, humanitarian relief personnel and objects, journalists, protected zones, cultural property, works and installations containing dangerous forces, the natural environment, and those who are *hors de combat* (wounded, sick, shipwrecked, those who have surrendered, and prisoners of war). Customary Law Study, *supra* note 22, Parts II and V.

24. Additional Protocol I, *supra* note 13, article 37 provides that:

> 1. It is prohibited to kill, injure or capture an adversary by resort to perfidy. Acts inviting the confidence of an adversary to lead him to believe that he is entitled to, or is obliged to accord, protection under the rules of international law applicable in armed conflict, with intent to betray that confidence, shall constitute perfidy. The following acts are examples of perfidy:
>
> (a) the feigning of an intent to negotiate under a flag of truce or of a surrender;
>
> (b) the feigning of an incapacitation by wounds or sickness;
>
> (c) the feigning of civilian, non-combatant status; and
>
> (d) the feigning of protected status by the use of signs, emblems or uniforms of the United Nations or of neutral or other States not Parties to the conflict.

25. These examples are contained in Article 37 itself. The 1907 Hague IV Regulations reference "improper use of a flag of truce, of the national flag or of the military insignia and uniform of the

enemy, as well as distinctive badges of the Geneva Convention," a prohibition that is now unquestionably customary. Hague IV Regulations, *supra* note 9, art. 23(f). Customary Law Study, *supra* note 22, ch. 18; International Military Tribunal (Nuremberg), Judgment and Sentences (1946), 41 AMERICAN JOURNAL OF INTERNATIONAL LAW 172, 218 (1947). The reference is to the Geneva Convention of 1864. Convention for the Amelioration of the Condition of the Wounded in Armies in the Field, Aug. 22, 1864, *reprinted in* THE LAWS OF ARMED CONFLICT, *supra* note 5, at 365.

26. Consider the 2003 war in Iraq. Neither the United States nor Iraq was party to Additional Protocol I. The UK's party status imposed no legal obligations on British forces because Additional Protocol I applies between a party and non-party State only when the latter "accepts and applies the provisions thereof" (art. 96). Iraq had not done so. Since Iraq was not a party to the 1907 Hague Convention (IV), that agreement was inoperative by virtue of its general participation clause (art. 2). Only the 1925 Gas Protocol, 1949 Geneva Conventions, and the 1972 Biological Weapons Convention bound all three major belligerents. The 1993 Chemical Weapons Convention also constrained the United States and the United Kingdom, even though Iraq was not a party, because it prohibits using chemical weapons "under any circumstances" (art. 1.1).

27. A provision along these lines appears in numerous law of armed conflict conventions. Hague II Regulations, *supra* note 9; Hague IV Regulations, *supra* note 9, Preamble; Gas Protocol, *supra* note 7, Preamble; Convention for the Amelioration of the Condition of the Wounded and Sick in Armed Forces in the Field, art. 63, Aug. 12, 1949, 75 U.N.T.S. 31, *reprinted in* THE LAWS OF ARMED CONFLICT, *supra* note 5, at 459 [hereinafter Geneva Convention I]; Convention for the Amelioration of the Condition of the Wounded, Sick, and Shipwrecked Members of Armed Forces at Sea, art. 62, Aug. 12, 1949, 75 U.N.T.S. 85, *reprinted in* THE LAWS OF ARMED CONFLICT, *supra* note 5, at 485 [hereinafter Geneva Convention II]; Convention Relative to the Treatment of Prisoners of War, art. 142, Aug. 12, 1949, 75 U.N.T.S. 135, *reprinted in* THE LAWS OF ARMED CONFLICT, *supra* note 5, at 507 [hereinafter Geneva Convention III]; Convention Relative to the Protection of Civilian Persons in Time of War, art. 158, Aug. 12, 1949, 75 U.N.T.S. 287, *reprinted in* THE LAWS OF ARMED CONFLICT, *supra* note 5, at 575 [hereinafter Geneva Convention IV]; Conventional Weapons Convention, *supra* note 7, para. 5. In its *Nuclear Weapons* advisory opinion, the International Court of Justice stated that the "continuing existence and applicability" of the Martens Clause "is not to be doubted." Nuclear Weapons, *supra* note 4, at 260.

28. Customary Law Study, *supra* note 22.

29. *Id.*, Rules 70 and 71.

30. *Id.*, Rules 72, 73–80, 86. It further cites landmines and incendiaries as requiring particular care. *Id.*, Rules 81–85.

31. *Id.*, Rules 1–2, 6.

32. *Id.*, Rules 7–8 (adopting the Additional Protocol I, art. 52.2, definition thereof).

33. *Id.*, Rule 65.

34. *Id.*, Rules 11–13.

35. *Id.*, Rule 14.

36. *Id.*, Rules 15–21.

37. *Id.*, Rules 25–30.

38. Chairman Joint Chiefs of Staff, Department of Defense Dictionary of Military and Associated Terms, Joint Publication 1-02, as amended through May 9, 2005, *available at* www.dtic.mil/doctrine/jel/doddict/.

39. The US defense budget for 2003 (most recent comparative figures available) was 404.9 billion dollars. Compare this figure with: Germany, 35.1b$; the United Kingdom, 42b$; France 45.7b$; China, 55.9b$; and Russia, 65.2b$. International Institute of Strategic Studies, STRATEGIC BALANCE 2004–2005. The United States spent 26.2% of this amount on investment (research, development, acquisition). Available comparable figures for Germany and the United Kingdom are 18.5% and 24.4%, respectively. NATO Press Release 146 (2003).
40. Initially set up in response to the 1957 Soviet launch of Sputnik, DARPA's current mission is twofold: "to prevent technological surprise to the US" and "to create technological surprise" for US adversaries. Defense Advanced Research Agency, Bridging the Gap, Feb. 2005, para 1 [hereinafter DARPA Mission]. The agency was instrumental in conception and development of such systems as the F-117 stealth fighter and the Global Hawk and Predator unmanned aerial vehicles. Most notably, DARPA created the ARPANet and its network protocol architecture, the precursor to today's Internet. The following discussion of strategic thrusts is drawn primarily from this document. On the organization, see http://www.darpa.mil/.
41. DARPA Mission, *supra* note 40, at ch. 3. On the agency's programs, see also Statement by Tony Tether, Director DARPA, to the Subcommittee on Terrorism, Unconventional Threats and Capabilities, House Armed Services Committee, House of Representatives, Mar. 10, 2005, *available at* www.darpa.mil/body/news/2005/darpa_hasc_3_10_05_final.pdf; Institute for Defense Analyses, Transformation and Transition: DARPA's Role in Fostering an Emerging Revolution in Military Affairs (Paper P-3698), April 2003.
42. For a discussion of these strikes and their law of armed conflict implications, see Michael N. Schmitt, *The Conduct of Hostilities during Operation Iraqi Freedom: An International Humanitarian Law Assessment*, 6 YEARBOOK OF INTERNATIONAL HUMANITARIAN LAW 73 (2003).
43. DARPA Mission, *supra* note 40, fig. 6.
44. The RQ-1 Predator is an unmanned aerial vehicle (UAV) that provides surveillance, reconnaissance, and target acquisition services over long periods of time. Its detection capabilities include a TV camera, an infrared camera, and synthetic aperture radar for looking through smoke, clouds or haze.
45. See Raydon Gates, *Towards 2015: Challenges for a Medium Navy—An Australian Perspective*, which is Chapter XIII in this volume, at 262–263.
46. DARPA Mission, *supra* note 40, para. 3.1.
47. *Id.*, para. 3.2.
48. Intelligence is "the *product* resulting from the collection, processing, integration, analysis, evaluation, and interpretation of available information concerning foreign countries or areas." Surveillance is the "*systematic observation* of aerospace, surface, or subsurface areas, places, persons, or things, by visual, aural, electronic, photographic, or other means." Reconnaissance is "a *mission* undertaken to obtain, by visual observation or other detection methods, information about the activities and resources of an enemy or potential enemy, or to secure data concerning the meteorological, hydrographic, or geographic characteristics of a particular area." DoD Dictionary, *supra* note 38.
49. Colonel J. Boyd, USAF, coined the term. Operating within an opponent's OODA loop is a decision-making concept in which one party, maintaining constant situational awareness, assesses a situation and acts on it more rapidly than its opponent. When this happens, the opponent is forced into a reactive mode, thereby allowing the first party to maintain the initiative. As the process proceeds, the opponent eventually begins to react to actions that no longer bear on the immediate situation. The resulting confusion causes paralysis. Boyd's ideas

were set out in a briefing titled "Patterns of Conflict," which he delivered hundreds of times at numerous venues.

50. The 2004 US National Military Strategy specifically adopts this approach by emphasizing the criticality of decision superiority:

> Decision superiority – the process of making decisions better and faster than an adversary – is essential to executing a strategy based on speed and flexibility. Decision superiority requires new ways of thinking about acquiring, integrating, using and sharing information. It necessitates new ideas for developing architectures for command, control, communications and computers (C4) as well as the intelligence, surveillance and reconnaissance assets that provide knowledge of adversaries. Decision superiority requires precise information of enemy and friendly dispositions, capabilities, and activities, as well as other data relevant to successful campaigns. Battlespace awareness, combined with responsive command and control systems, supports dynamic decision-making and turns information superiority into a competitive advantage adversaries cannot match.

Chairman of the Joint Chiefs of Staff, National Military Strategy of the United States 17 (2004).

51. Fire support consists of firing artillery or other weapons in support of forces engaging the enemy.

52. Robots are also being developed, some of which are already fielded in Iraq to deal with roadside bombs. For a description of the robotics development program, see Tim Weiner, *Arsenal of the Future: Robots in Combat*, NEW YORK TIMES, Feb. 16, 2005, at A1.

53. CNN.com, Huge Underground Hideout Uncovered in Iraq, June 5, 2005, *available at* www.cnn.com/2005/WORLD/meast/06/05/iraq.main/. The air-conditioned 503,000 square foot bunker contained a large supply of weapons and ammunition, and contained living spaces for Iraqi forces.

54. DARPA was instrumental in developing stealth materials for aircraft.

55. Peta as a prefix refers to 10 to the 15th power. In computing, it is one quadrillion (one thousand million million) bytes.

56. An aimpoint is "[a] precise point associated with a target and assigned for a specific weapon impact to achieve the intended objective and level of destruction. [It] may be defined descriptively (e.g., vent in center of roof) by grid reference or geolocation." Chairman of the Joint Chiefs of Staff, Joint Doctrine for Targeting, Joint Publication 3-60, Jan. 17, 2002, at G-6.

57. CEP is the radius of a circle within which 50% of the weapons will strike.

58. Probability of damage (PD) expresses the statistical probability (percentage or decimal) that specified damage criteria can be met assuming the probability of arrival. United States Air Force, Intelligence Targeting Guide, AF Pamphlet 14-210, at 59–60, Feb. 1, 1998. For non-nuclear weapons, damage criteria include F-Kill (Fire-power Kill), M-Kill (Mobility Kill), K-Kill (Catastrophic Kill), FC-Kill (Fire Control Kill), PTO-Kill (Prevent Takeoff Kill), I-Kill (Interdiction Kill), SW-Kill (Seaworthiness Kill), and Cut and Block. *Id.* at 58.

59. For instance, a single cruise missile costs over $1,000,000. Federation of American Scientists, BGM-109 Tomahawk, *available at* www.fas.org/man/dod-101/sys/smart/bgm-109.htm. Per unit cost for forces already equipped to employ these systems is approximately $500,000.

60. The joint direct attack munition (JDAM) is a major first step. JDAMs consist of an existing unguided bomb to which a guidance tail kit is attached. Using global positioning system (satellite) and inertial navigation guidance, the resulting weapon has an unclassified CEP of approximately 20 feet from as far away as 15 miles. Most aircraft can be easily modified to employ the system. At a cost of roughly $20,000, JDAM brings accuracy within the reach of many nations.

During Operation Iraqi Freedom, 5,086 JDAM GBU-31s (2,000 pound) were dropped between March 19 and April 18, 2003. In addition, US forces dropped 768 JDAM GBU 32s (1,000 pound) and 675 GBU 35s (1,000 pound penetrator). US Central Command Air Forces, Assessment and Analysis Division, Operation Iraqi Freedom—By the Numbers, Apr. 30, 2003, at 11, *available at* www.globalsecurity.org/military/library/report/2003/uscentaf_oif_report_30apr2003.pdf.

61. Chairman of the Joint Chiefs of Staff, Doctrine for Intelligence Support to Joint Operations, Joint Publication 2-0, Mar. 9, 2000, fig. II-2

62. The E-3 Sentry is an airborne warning and control system (AWACS) providing surveillance, command, weapons control, battle management, and communications services in the aerial environment. Defensively, AWACS detects enemy aircraft or missiles and directs fighters to intercept them. Offensively, it can monitor the battlespace, providing real-time location and identification of enemy and friendly aircraft and naval vessels to users at the tactical, operational, and strategic levels of warfare. The E-8C Joint Surveillance Target Attack Radar System (JSTARS) is an airborne battle management, command and control, intelligence, surveillance and reconnaissance aircraft that provides ground and air commanders with information that supports attacks on enemy ground forces. Unmanned Aerial Vehicles (UAV) are aircraft without a crew that can (depending on the system) perform surveillance, reconnaissance, and target acquisition and attack functions.

63. Interview with senior US Army officer with recent combat experience. DARPA has also demonstrated the capability for establishing Internet connectivity with tactical aircraft which will allow ground station operators to access, as needed, data from sensors (e.g., electro-optical and infrared video) on the aircraft. DARPA, DARPA Demonstrates Internet Connection for Tactical Aircraft, News Release, Jun. 28, 2004.

64. Networking significantly affects command and control. On the one hand, it pushes authority and responsibility down the chain of command because the underlying premise of a networked system is rapid response to information through enhanced horizontal cooperation (e.g., by passing data directly from the sensor to the "shooter"). Yet, the technology that makes transparency possible and improves communications speed and reliability also allows those up the chain to become involved in even minor tactical engagements. Senior commanders can literally watch soldiers enter buildings from thousands of miles away and talk to those soldiers as they do so.

65. Over time, UAVs have become more robust. For instance, the Global Hawk can fly to an area over 1,000 miles away and remain on station for 24 hours. Equipped with synthetic aperture radar, a ground moving target indicator, and high-resolution electro-optical and infrared sensors, it collects information that is transmitted to users in near real-time. Because it operates at high altitude, the Global Hawk is highly survivable and can monitor huge areas on earth.

66. Anthony Dworkin, The Yemen Strike, Nov. 14, 2002, *available at* www.crimesofwar/onnews/news-yemen.html.

67. Non-lethal weapons are "[w]eapons that are explicitly designed and primarily employed so as to incapacitate personnel or material, while minimizing fatalities, permanent injury to personnel, and undesired damage to property and the environment." DOD Dictionary, *supra* note 38. The United States has established the Joint Non-Lethal Weapons Program to "provide warfighters a family of Non-Lethal Weapon (NLW) systems with a range of optional non-lethal capabilities across the full spectrum of threats and crisis." *See generally*, NLWP website, *available at* www.jnlwd.usmc.mil/mission.asp.

68. In then-year dollars. B-2 Bomber: Status of Cost, Development, and Production, General Accounting Office, GAO/NSIAD-95-164, Aug. 1995.

69. I.e., without the shooter actually seeing the target. Also labeled an "over the horizon" attack.
70. Through April 18, 2003. By the Numbers, *supra* note 60. Or consider computerized counter-battery radar systems that identify an incoming shell at the apex of its flight and immediately calculate its source. Fire is returned quickly, presumably before the enemy has an opportunity to relocate.
71. Using advanced defensive and offensive technologies such as stealth aircraft (e.g., B-2 Spirit and F-117 Nighthawk), anti-radar missiles (e.g., AGM-88 HARM high speed anti-radiation missile), and jamming (e.g., with an EA6-B Prowler aircraft).
72. Steven Metz and Douglas Johnston have usefully described asymmetry as follows:

> In the realm of military affairs and national security, asymmetry is acting, organizing, and thinking differently than opponents in order to maximize one's own advantages, exploit an opponent's weaknesses, attain the initiative, or gain greater freedom of action. It can be political-strategic, military strategic, or a combination of these. It can entail different methods, technologies, values, organizations, time perspectives, or some combination of these. It can be short-term or long-term. It can be deliberate or by default. It can be discrete or pursued in combination with symmetric approaches. It can have both psychological and physical dimensions.

Steven Metz & Douglas V. Johnson II, ASYMMETRY AND U.S. MILITARY STRATEGY: DEFINITION, BACKGROUND, AND STRATEGIC CONCEPTS (US Army War College, Strategic Studies Institute, Jan. 2001). The instant article limits discussion to technological asymmetry. Other useful material on asymmetry includes Stephen J. Blank, RETHINKING ASYMMETRIC THREATS, (US Army War College, Strategic Studies Institute, Sept. 2003); Ivan Arrequin-Toft, *How the Weak Win Wars: A Theory of Asymmetric Conflict*, INTERNATIONAL SECURITY, Summer 2001, at 19; Steven J. Lambakis, *Reconsidering Asymmetric Warfare*, JOINT FORCE QUARTERLY, Dec. 2004, at 102; Montgomery C. Meigs, *Unorthodox Thoughts about Asymmetric Warfare*, PARAMETERS, Summer 2003, at 4; R.V. Gusentine, *Asymmetric Warfare—On Our Terms*, PROCEEDINGS OF THE UNITED STATES NAVAL INSTITUTE, Aug. 2002, at 58.
73. NORMAN FRIEDMAN, TERRORISM, AFGHANISTAN, AND AMERICA'S NEW WAY OF WAR 166 (2004).
74. International Institute for Strategic Studies, THE MILITARY BALANCE 2002–2003, at 97 (2003).
75. 183,000. BOB WOODWARD, PLAN OF ATTACK 401 (2004).
76. By the Numbers, *supra* note 60, at 3, 7–8. Losses also included four Apache and two Cobra helicopters. *Id.* Iraqi air defenses had been degraded by Operations Northern Watch and Southern Watch air strikes prior to commencement of Operation Iraqi Freedom. These operations monitored the no-fly zones in northern and southern Iraq.
77. November 2004. Estimates of casualties vary somewhat. *See, e.g.*, Anthony Shadid, *Baghdad Suffers a Day of Attacks*, WASHINGTON POST, Nov. 21, 2004, at A30; *US Casualties Surge in Iraq, but Public Impact is Muffled*, AGENCE FRANCE PRESSE, Nov. 30, 2004; Iraq Coalition Casualty Count, icasualties.org/oif/Stats.aspx (filter by place and month).
78. The United States specifically noted this possibility in its 2004 National Military Strategy.

> Dual-use civilian technologies, especially information technologies, high-resolution imagery and global positioning systems are widely available. These relatively low cost, commercially available technologies will improve the disruptive and destructive capabilities of a wide range of state and non-state actors. Advances in automation and information processing will allow some adversaries to locate and attack targets both overseas and in the United States. Software tools for network-attack, intrusion and

> disruption are globally available over the Internet, providing almost any interested adversary a basic computer network exploitation or attack capability.

National Military Strategy, *supra* note 50, at 6.

79. Jamming impedes the enemy's use of the electromagnetic spectrum. Spoofing involves creating signals that imitate those of the enemy or others.

80. In this case, intercepting mobile phone signals.

81. *See generally* US Department of Defense, Final Report to Congress: Conduct of the Persian Gulf War (1992).

82. Human Rights Watch, Off Target: The Conduct of the War and Civilian Casualties in Iraq 78–79 (Dec. 2003), *available at* www.hrw.org/reports/2003/usa1203/. Since the denial of combatant status to Taliban fighters and publication of photos of US Special Forces soldiers attired in indigenous clothing during Operation Enduring Freedom, the "requirement" to wear uniforms has evoked much discussion. *See, e.g.*, Michelle Kelly & Morten Rostrup, *Identify Yourselves: Coalition Soldiers in Afghanistan are Endangering Air Workers*, GUARDIAN (London), Feb. 1, 2002, at 19. For a comprehensive legal analysis of the subject, see W. Hays Parks, *Special Forces' Wear of Non-Standard Uniforms*, 4 CHICAGO JOURNAL OF INTERNATIONAL LAW 493 (2003).

83. The relevant provisions of Article 4 exclude the following from civilian status:

> (1) Members of the armed forces of a Party to the conflict, as well as members of militias or volunteer corps forming part of such armed forces.
>
> (2) Members of other militias and members of other volunteer corps, including those of organized resistance movements, belonging to a Party to the conflict and operating in or outside their own territory, even if this territory is occupied, provided that such militias or volunteer corps, including such organized resistance movements, fulfill the following conditions:
>
> (a) that of being commanded by a person responsible for his subordinates;
>
> (b) that of having a fixed distinctive sign recognizable at a distance;
>
> (c) that of carrying arms openly;
>
> (d) that of conducting their operations in accordance with the laws and customs of war.

Geneva Convention III, *supra* note 27. On the wear of "distinctive" attire, see also Hague IV Regulations, *supra* note 9, art. 1.2; Geneva Convention I, *supra* note 27, art. 13(2)(b); Geneva Convention II, *supra* note 27, art. 13(2)(b). Article 44.3 of Additional Protocol I relaxes the uniform requirement in "situations in armed conflicts where, owing to the nature of hostilities an armed combatant cannot so distinguish himself." In such circumstances, he or she must carry arms openly during military engagements and while visible to the adversary during "a military deployment preceding the launch of an attack." This provision is not customary law of armed conflict, and therefore does not supercede the Geneva criteria for non-party States.

84. Michael Bothe (et al.) have noted that, "[i]t is generally assumed that these conditions were deemed, by the 1874 Brussels Conference and the 1899 and 1907 Hague Peace Conferences, to be inherent in the regular armed forces of States. Accordingly, it was considered unnecessary and redundant to spell them out in the Conventions." MICHAEL BOTHE ET AL., NEW RULES FOR VICTIMS OF ARMED CONFLICT 234 (1982). See also discussion in Customary Law Study, *supra* note 22, at 15. Case law is supportive. *See, e.g.*, Mohammed Ali et al. v. Public Prosecutor (1968), [1969] AC 430, 449; Ex parte Quirin et al., 317 U.S. 1 (1942). For a superb analysis of the subject, see Kenneth Watkin, WARRIORS WITHOUT RIGHTS? COMBATANTS, UNPRIVILEGED

BELLIGERENTS, AND THE STRUGGLE OVER LEGITIMACY, Program on Humanitarian Policy and Conflict Occasional Paper No. 2, Winter 2005.
85. This point is reflected in Customary Law Study, *supra* note 22, Rule 106.
86. "Members of the armed forces of a party to a conflict (other than medical personnel and chaplains covered by Article 33 of the Third Convention) are combatants, that is to say, they have the right to participate directly in hostilities." Additional Protocol I, *supra* note 13, art. 43.2.
87. The classic article on the subject is Richard R. Baxter, *So-called "Unprivileged Belligerency": Spies, Guerrillas and Saboteurs*, 1952 BRITISH YEARBOOK OF INTERNATIONAL LAW 323, *reprinted in* MILITARY LAW REVIEW (Bicentennial Issue) 487 (1975). For a contemporary treatment of the issue of direct participation, see Michael N. Schmitt, *Humanitarian Law and Direct Participation in Hostilities by Private Contractors or Civilian Employees*, 5 CHICAGO JOURNAL OF INTERNATIONAL LAW 511 (2005); Michael N. Schmitt, *"Direct Participation in Hostilities" and 21st Century Armed Conflict*, *in* CRISIS MANAGEMENT AND HUMANITARIAN PROTECTION: FESTSCHRIFT FUR DIETER FLECK 505 (Horst Fischer et al. eds., 2004).
88. Off Target, *supra* note 82, at 70.
89. The prohibition dates from the 1863 Lieber Code, and appears in the 1899 and 1907 Hague Regulations; 1906, 1929, and 1949 Geneva Conventions; and Additional Protocol I. General Order No. 100, US Department of Army, Instructions for the Government of Armies of the United States in the Field (Lieber Code), art. 117, *reprinted in* THE LAWS OF ARMED CONFLICT, *supra* note 5, at 3; Hague II Regulations, *supra* note 9, art. 23(f); Hague IV Regulations, *supra* note 9, art. 23(f); Convention for the Amelioration of the Condition of the Wounded in Armies in the Field, arts. 27–28, July 6, 1906, *reprinted in* THE LAWS OF ARMED CONFLICT, *supra* note 5, at 385; Convention for the Amelioration of the Condition of the Wounded in Armies in the Field, arts. 24 & 28, July 27, 1929, *reprinted in* THE LAWS OF ARMED CONFLICT, *supra* note 5, at 409; Geneva Convention I, *supra* note 27, arts. 39, 44, 53, 54; Geneva Convention II, *supra* note 27, arts. 41, 44, 45; Additional Protocol I, *supra* note 13, art. 38.1. See also the military manuals of many nations. E.g., Commander's Handbook, *supra* note 22, para. 11.9.6; UK Ministry of Defence, The Manual of the Law of Armed Conflict, para. 5.10(a) (2004). Permitted purposes are set forth in Geneva Convention I, *supra* note 27, arts. 24–27, 38–44; Geneva Convention II, *supra* note 27, arts. 22, 24–25, 27, 36–39, 41–44; Geneva Convention IV, *supra* note 27, arts. 18–22; Additional Protocol I, *supra* note 13, arts. 8, 18, 22–23. The prohibition is self-evidently customary in nature today. *See, e.g.*, Customary Law Study, *supra* note 22, Rule 59. When the purpose of the misuse goes beyond merely "hiding" from the enemy to the use of the emblem to treacherously attack, the separate violation of perfidy occurs. *See, e.g.*, Commander's Handbook, *supra* note 22, para. 12.2.; Federal Ministry of Defence (Germany), Humanitarian Law in Armed Conflicts Manual, sec. 640 (1992).
90. Counter-targeting is "preventing or degrading detection, characterization, destruction, and post-strike assessment." Defense Intelligence Agency, Saddam's Use of Human Shields and Deceptive Sanctuaries: Special Briefing for the Pentagon Press Corps, Feb. 26, 2003, *available at* www.defenselink.mil/news/Feb2003/g030226-D-9085M.html.
91. Todd S. Purdum, *Night Time Ambush in Iraqi City*, NEW YORK TIMES, Apr. 5, 2003, at 1; Dexter Filkins, *In the Field Choosing Targets: Iraqi Fighters Or Civilians? Hard Decision for Copters*, NEW YORK TIMES, Mar. 31, 2003, at 5.
92. This prescription tracks that found in the 1949 Fourth Geneva Convention, Article 28: "The presence of a protected person may not be used to render certain points or areas immune from military operations." The prohibition only applies vis-à-vis those who "find themselves . . . in the hands of a Party to the conflict or Occupying Party of which they are not nationals." It would not apply to Iraqi forces using Iraqis as shields. Geneva Convention IV, *supra* note 27, art. 4.

93. Customary Law Study, *supra* note 22, Rule 97. *See also* Commander's Handbook, *supra* note 22, para. 11.2; Rome Statute of the International Criminal Court (Rome Statute), art. 8.2(b)(xxiii), July 17, 1998, *reprinted in* THE LAWS OF ARMED CONFLICT, *supra* note 5, at 1309. The customary nature is further evidenced by the widespread condemnation that results whenever shields are used. The UN General Assembly labeled Iraq's use of human shields during the first Gulf War as a "most grave and blatant violation of Iraq's obligations under international law" GA Res. 46/134 (Dec. 17, 1991). In May 1995, Bosnian Serbs seized United Nations Protection Force (UNPROFOR) peacekeepers and used them as human shields against NATO air strikes. In response, the UN condemned the action, demanded release, and authorized the creation of a rapid reaction force to handle such situations. SC Res. 998 (June 16, 1995).

94. A principle enshrined in Article 51.8 of Additional Protocol I: "Any violation of these prohibitions [includes the prohibition on shielding] shall not release the Parties to the conflict from their legal obligations with respect to the civilian population and civilians. . . ."

95. Those taking the opposite stance on involuntary shields reasonably and accurately point out that it creates an incentive for the use of shields because an opponent can effectively render a military objective immune from attack simply by placing enough civilians at risk (by virtue of operation of the proportionality principle). A.P.V. Rogers has argued that:

> [A] tribunal considering whether a grave breach has been committed [a disproportionate attack] would be able to take into account when considering the rule of proportionality the extent to which the defenders had flouted their obligation to separate military objectives from civilian objects and to take precautions to protect the civilian population . . . the proportionality approach taken by the tribunals should help to redress the balance which would otherwise be tilted in favour of the unscrupulous.

A.P.V. ROGERS, LAW ON THE BATTLEFIELD 129 (2d ed. 2004). *See also* W. Hays Parks, *Air War and the Law of War*, 32 AIR FORCE LAW REVIEW 1, 163 (1992).

96. As noted in Article 51.3 of Additional Protocol I, "[c]ivilians shall enjoy the protection afforded by this Section, *unless and for such time as they take a direct part in hostilities.*" The Rome Statute adopts this standard by making it a war crime to intentionally attack civilians unless they are "taking direct part in hostilities." *Supra* note 93, art. 8.2(b)(i). The United States correctly takes the position that as direct participants, they become targetable (although there will seldom be any reason to directly attack them) and, more important, are excluded in the estimation of incidental injury when assessing proportionality.

> And then, the other target category that is a challenge for us is where the human shields that we've talked of before might be used. And you really have two types of human shields. You have people who volunteer to go and stand on a bridge or a power plant or a water works facility, and you have people that are placed in those areas not of their own free will. In the case of some of the previous use of human shields in Iraq, Saddam placed hostages, if you will, on sensitive sites in order to show that these were human shields, but, in fact, they were not there of their own free will. Two separate problems to deal with that, and it requires that we work very carefully with the intelligence community to determine what that situation might be at a particular location.

US Department of Defense, Background Briefing on Targeting, Mar. 5, 2003, *available at* www.defenselink.mil/news/Mar2003/t03052003_t305targ.html. Human Rights Watch takes the opposite position. Human Rights Watch, International Humanitarian Law Issues in a Potential War in Iraq, Feb. 20, 2002, *available at* www.hrw.org/backgrounder/arms/iraq0202003.htm#1. Children legally lack the mental capacity to form the intent to voluntarily shield military objectives. Israeli forces do not use live ammunition against children. Justus R. Weiner,

Co-existence Without Conflict: The Implementation of Legal Structures for Israeli-Palestinian Cooperation Pursuant to the Interim Peace Agreements, 26 BROOKLYN JOURNAL OF INTERNATIONAL LAW 591 n.407 (2000).

97. International volunteer shields traveled to Iraq prior to Operation Iraqi Freedom. All departed once they realized the seriousness of their actions and the Iraqi Government's desire to use them as shields for military objectives. Those who suggest that shielding is not direct participation forget that, in the CNN age, shielding may be a more effective defense against attack than weaponry.

98. Off Target, *supra* note 82, at 72–73.

99. Marine Expeditionary Force & Multi-National Corps-Iraq, Telling the Fallujah Story to the World, Briefing Slides, Nov. 20, 2004 (on file with author).

100. *See also* Customary Law Study, *supra* note 22, ch. 6.

101. Additional Protocol I, *supra* note 13, art. 12.4.

102. *Id.*, art. 53(b). *See also* Hague IV Regulations, *supra* note 9, art. 27.

103. Off Target, *supra* note 82, at 72–73. On misuse of religious locations, *see also Regime Shows Disregard for Historical, Religious Sites in Holy City*, US Central Command News Release No. 03-04-28, Apr. 2, 2003; *Regime Use of Baghdad Mosques And Hospitals*, US Central Command News Release No. 03-04-65, Apr. 6, 2003.

104. Additional Protocol I, *supra* note 13, art. 52.2. According to the ICRC Commentary on the definition of military objective, "[t]he criterion of purpose is concerned with the intended future use of an object, while that of use is concerned with its present function." COMMENTARY ON THE ADDITIONAL PROTOCOLS OF 8 JUNE 1977 TO THE GENEVA CONVENTIONS OF 12 AUGUST 1949, at para. 2022 (Yves Sandoz, Christophe Swinarski & Bruno Zimmerman eds., 1987). For instance, an apartment building's use as a unit headquarters transforms it into an attackable military facility. Any collateral damage or incidental injury that might be caused during an attack thereon would be governed by the principle of proportionality.

105. *See also* Rome Statute, *supra* note 93, art. 8.2(b)(ix).

106. *See, e.g.*, Glenn Collins, *Allied Advances, Tougher Iraqi Resistance, and a Hunt in the Tigris*, NEW YORK TIMES, Mar. 24, 2003, at 1; Brian Knowlton, *Bush Tells of 'Good Progress' But Says War has Just Begun*, INTERNATIONAL HERALD TRIBUNE, Mar. 24, 2003, at 6. The prohibition is set forth in Article 37.1(a), Additional Protocol I. *See also* Lieber Code, *supra* note 89, art. 71; Project of an International Declaration Concerning the Laws and Customs of War (1874 Brussels Declaration), art. 13, *reprinted in* THE LAWS OF ARMED CONFLICT, *supra* note 5, at 21; The Laws of War on Land (1880 Oxford Manual), at 9(b), reprinted in THE LAWS OF ARMED CONFLICT, *supra* note 5, at 29; Hague II Regulations, *supra* note 9, art. 23(c); Hague IV Regulations, *supra* note 9, art. 23(c); Additional Protocol I, *supra* note 13, art. 41.2(b). Violation is a grave breach pursuant to Additional Protocol I, Article 85.3(e). A flag is not the sole means of communicating intent to surrender; any technique that so informs the enemy suffices. Surrendering forces are *hors de combat* and entitled to immunity from attack.

107. On the increasing use of suicide bombings in Iraq, see Robert A. Pape, *Blowing Up an Assumption*, INTERNATIONAL HERALD TRIBUNE, May 19, 2005, at 8. *See also* ROBERT A. PAPE, DYING TO WIN: THE STRATEGIC LOGIC OF SUICIDE TERRORISM (2005). Pape looked at 315 suicide bombings, concluding that suicide bombers are seldom religious fanatics. On the contrary, the majority of bombings are conducted as part of a political or military campaign, often intended to motivate democracies to leave territory that the bombers consider their homeland. *See also* Dan Eggen & Scott Wilson, *Suicide Bombs Potent Tools of Terrorist*, WASHINGTON POST, July 17, 2005, at A1.

108. As illustrated by the kamikaze in the Second World War. *See* Yoram Dinstein, *Jus in Bello Issues Arising in the Hostilities in Iraq in 2003*, 34 ISRAEL YEARBOOK ON HUMAN RIGHTS 1, 4–5 (2004), for a discussion of the legal issues in the context of the war in Iraq.

109. See Schmitt, Humanitarian Law and Direct Participation, *supra* note 87, at 520–21.
110. Centers of gravity consist of "[t]hose characteristics, capabilities, or sources of power from which a military force derives its freedom of action, physical strength, or will to fight." DoD Dictionary, *supra* note 38.
111. To draw Israel into the conflict, thereby disrupting the Coalition, which included Arab States such as Syria.
112. CNA consists of "[o]perations to disrupt, deny, degrade, or destroy information resident in computers and computer networks, or the computers and networks themselves. . . . CNA relies on the data stream to execute the attack. . . ." An example is "sending a code or instruction to a central processing unit that causes the computer to short out the power supply." DoD Dictionary, *supra* note 38. On computer network attack, see COMPUTER NETWORK ATTACK AND INTERNATIONAL LAW (Michael N. Schmitt & Brian O'Donnell eds., 2002) (Vol. 76, US Naval War College International Law Studies); Michael N. Schmitt, *Wired Warfare: Computer Network Attack and International Law*, 84 INTERNATIONAL REVIEW OF THE RED CROSS 365 (2002); Michael N. Schmitt, Heather A. Harrison-Dinniss & Thomas C. Winfield, *Computers and War: The Legal Battlespace*, Harvard Program on Humanitarian Policy and Conflict Research, International Humanitarian Law Research Initiative Briefing Paper (June 2004), *available at* www.ihlresearch.org/ihl/pdfs/schmittetal.pdf; Michael N. Schmitt, *CNA and the Jus in Bello: An Introduction, in* INTERNATIONAL EXPERTS CONFERENCE ON COMPUTER NETWORK ATTACK AND THE APPLICABILITY OF INTERNATIONAL HUMANITARIAN LAW: PROCEEDINGS 101 (Karin Brystrom ed., 2005).
113. Recall that Article 57.2(a)(ii) of Additional Protocol I requires those who plan or decide upon an attack to "take all feasible precautions in the choice of means and methods of attack with a view to avoiding, and in any event to minimizing, incidental loss of civilian life, injury to civilians and damage to civilian objects."
114. If the computer contagions are designed to spread randomly in a way that may cause injury to civilians or damage to civilian objects, they constitute prohibited indiscriminate weapon.
115. Dual-use objects are those used for both military and civilian purposes.
116. *See, e.g.*, Knut Dormann, *Applicability of the Additional Protocols to Computer Network Attack*, in INTERNATIONAL EXPERTS CONFERENCE, *supra* note 112, at 139, 145.
117. For instance, "the civilian population as such, as well as individual civilians, shall not be the object of attack" (51.2); "civilian objects shall not be the object of attack" (52.1); "indiscriminate attacks are forbidden" (51.4); "attacks shall be limited strictly to military objectives" (52.2); etc.
118. This position is consistent with other aspects of Additional Protocol I. For instance, Article 51, which provides that the "civilian population and individual civilians shall enjoy general protection against *dangers* arising from military operations," and which prohibits "acts or threats of *violence* the primary purpose of which is to spread terror among the civilian population," as well as the commentary to Article 48, which notes that "the word 'operation' should be understood in the context of the whole of the Section; it refers to military operations during which violence is used." Additional Protocol I, *supra* note 13, art. 51.1-2; COMMENTARY, *supra* note 104, para. 1875.
119. A point supported by the prohibition on attacks intended to terrorize the civilian population in Additional Protocol I, art. 51.2.
120. *See, e.g.*, James Brooke, *North Koreans Claim to Extract Weapons Grade Fuel for Bombs*, NEW YORK TIMES, May 12, 2005, at 1.
121. This is the position taken by the Customary Law Study, *supra* note 22.
122. For a threat analysis of biological weapons, see Milton Leitenberg, *Biological Weapons and "Bioterrorism" in the First Years of the 21st Century*, 21:2 POLITICS AND THE LIFE SCIENCES 3 (2002).
123. Nuclear Weapons, *supra* note 4, para. 105E.

124. *See generally*, Michael N. Schmitt, *The International Court of Justice and the Use of Nuclear Weapons*, NAVAL WAR COLLEGE REVIEW, Spring 1998, at 91, *reprinted in* 7 JOURNAL OF LEGAL STUDIES 57 (1997).
125. For instance, use of nuclear mines in remote areas of the high seas against enemy ballistic missile submarines or low-yield battlefield nuclear weapons employed against armor forces in remote parts of the desert when there is no wind. The situations are rare, but not unimaginable.
126. Additional States include Israel, Pakistan, India, and North Korea.
127. *See* Customary Law Study, *supra* note 22, ch. 22.
128. The term extends to members of the armed forces. It is not limited to objects. COMMENTARY, *supra* note 104, at para. 2017.
129. The official ICRC COMMENTARY, discussing the term "definite military advantage," states "it is not legitimate to launch an attack which offers only potential or indeterminate advantages." COMMENTARY, *supra* note 104, para. 2024.
130. Commander's Handbook, *supra* note 22, para. 8.1.1. This assertion is labeled a "statement of customary international law." The Handbook cites General Counsel, Department of Defense, Letter of September 22, 1972, *reprinted in* 67 AMERICAN JOURNAL OF INTERNATIONAL LAW 123 (1973), as the basis for this characterization. US joint doctrine reinforces this approach by providing that "[c]ivilian objects consist of all civilian property and activities other than those used to support or sustain the adversary's warfighting capability." Joint Publication 3-60, *supra* note 56, at A-2. The term "war sustaining" also appears in the Instructions for the US Military Commission at Guantanamo. Department of Defense, Military Commission Instruction No. 2, Crimes and Elements for Trials by Military Commission, Apr. 30, 2003, para. 5D.
131. NATO's demands were set forth in a Statement of the Extraordinary Meeting of the North Atlantic Council on April 12, 1999, and reaffirmed by the Heads of State and Government at Washington on April 23. They included a cessation of military action, as well as ending violence and repression of the Kosovar Albanians; withdrawal from Kosovo of military, police, and paramilitary forces; an international military presence in Kosovo; safe return of refugees and displaced persons and unhindered access to them by humanitarian aid organizations; and the establishment of a political framework agreement on the basis of the Rambouillet Accords. Press Release M-NAC-1(99)51, Apr. 12, 1999, *available at* www.nato.int/docu/pr/1999/p99-051e.htm; Press Release S-1(99)62, Apr. 23, 1999, *available at* www.nato.int/docu/pr/1999/p99-062e.htm.
132. Christopher Marquis, *In Wartime, Some Argue, Commanders in Chief Do Best When They Really Command*, NEW YORK TIMES, Feb. 10, 2004, at 18.
133. *See, e.g.*, Charles J. Dunlap, Jr., *The End of Innocence: Rethinking Noncombatancy in the Post-Kosovo Era*, STRATEGIC REVIEW 14 (Summer 2000).
134. Effects based operations are "[a]ctions taken against enemy systems designed to achieve specific effects that contribute directly to desired military and political outcomes." US Air Force, Air Force Glossary (AF Doctrine Document 1-2) 26 (Aug. 24, 2004). Consider electrical power. Command and control usually relies to some degree on the civilian electrical grid. Therefore, in the past, neutralizing C2 often led to strikes against power substations and generating plants. However, the effect sought was not destruction of the electrical grid, but merely interference with command and control. An effects-based analysis would deconstruct the electrical grid to identify that discrete component thereof depriving C2, and little more, of electricity. Only that component would be attacked. A focus on effects has now been included in the National Military Strategy: "Force application focuses more on generating the right effects to achieve objectives than on generating overwhelming numbers of forces." National Military Strategy, *supra* note 50, at 15.
135. On effects-based operations, see DAVID A. DEPTULA, EFFECTS-BASED OPERATIONS: CHANGE IN THE NATURE OF WAR (2001); Department of Defense, Effects-based Operations

Briefing, Mar. 19, 2003, *available at* www.defenselink.mil/news/Mar2003/g030318-D-9085.html. On EBO and law, see Michael N. Schmitt, *Aerial Effects-Based Operations and the Law of Armed Conflict*, paper presented at a conference to mark the launch of the UK Manual of the Law of Armed Conflict, Oxford University, July 2004. The articles presented at the conference will appear in a compilation to be edited by Steven Haines.

136. *See generally* Peter W.W. Wijninga & Richard Szafranski, *Beyond Utility Targeting: Towards Axiological Operations*, AEROSPACE POWER JOURNAL, Winter 2000, at 45.

137. Proponents of axiological operations cite Colonel John Warden's model, in which the enemy is attacked as a system consisting of five concentric circles (leadership, organic or system essentials, infrastructure, population, and fielded forces), as an example of sophisticated utility targeting. In Warden's approach, the intent is to cause the system to malfunction such that paralysis sets in. On Warden's theory, see JOHN A. WARDEN III, THE AIR CAMPAIGN: PLANNING FOR COMBAT (Brassey's rev. ed., 1998).

138. Recall the comments by NATO air commander, Lieutenant General Michael Short, regarding Operation Allied Force air attacks against Belgrade: "I felt that on the first night the power should have gone off, and major bridges around Belgrade should have gone into the Danube, and the water should be cut off so the next morning the leading citizens of Belgrade would have got up and asked 'Why are we doing this?' and asked Milosevic the same question." Short realized that Milosevic most feared losing the support of the population, and thereby political power; in axiological operations terms, popular support for the regime was the value to be attacked to most effectively create the effects sought—incentivizing compliance with NATO demands. C.R. Whitney, *The Commander; Air Wars Won't Stay Risk-Free, General Says*, NEW YORK TIMES, June 18, 1999, at A1.

139. Additional Protocol I, *supra* note 13, art. 57.2.

140. For example, Human Rights Watch specifically discussed the Djakovica Road incident in its report on Operation Allied Freedom, concluding that because "higher altitude seems to have impeded a pilot from adequately identifying a target" . . . "inadequate precautions were taken to avoid civilian casualties." Human Rights Watch, Civilian Deaths in the NATO Air Campaign, Feb. 2000, *available at* www.hrw.org/reports/2000/nato/index.htm#TopOfPag.

141. As noted by Michael Bothe et al., "[t]he term military advantage involves a variety of considerations, including the security of the attacking force." BOTHE ET AL., *supra* note 84, para. 2.4.4. *See also*, A.P.V. Rogers, *Zero-Casualty Warfare*, 82 INTERNATIONAL REVIEW OF THE RED CROSS 165 (2000).

142. The term "battlespace" has been formally adopted in the National Military Strategy, *supra* note 50, at 16.

143. Some argue (albeit contentiously) that even future potential use meets the purpose criterion, although the better position is that there must be a reasonable belief that such use is highly likely before an object or location may be characterized as a military objective and attacked.

144. Effects-based Operations Briefing, *supra* note 135. To take another example, during Operation Cobra, the breakout from Normandy, US air forces dropped 14,600 500-pound bombs on one German division, destroying 66 tanks and 11 heavy guns. During Desert Storm, the US dropped 9,800 precision guided munitions, destroying 2,500 tanks, heavy artillery pieces, and armored personnel carriers—a ratio of bombs to equipment destroyed 50 times that of Operation Cobra. Robert A. Pape, *Hit or Miss: What Precision Air Weapons do Precisely*, FOREIGN AFFAIRS, Sept./Oct. 2004, at 160, 163.

145. For general discussions of the conduct of the war in Iraq, see JOHN KEEGAN, THE IRAQ WAR (2004); ANTHONY H. CORDESMAN, THE WAR IN IRAQ: STRATEGY, TACTICS, AND MILITARY LESSONS (2003); WILLIAMSON MURRAY & ROBERT H. SCALES, JR., THE IRAQ WAR: A MILITARY HISTORY (2003).

146. This temporal aspect was recognized in the Lieber Code, which noted "[t]he more vigorously wars are pursued the better it is for humanity. Sharp wars are brief." Lieber Code, *supra* note 89, art. 29.
147. For instance, during Desert Storm, a mere 8.8% of the munitions dropped were precision. WILLIAM M. ARKIN ET AL., ON IMPACT: MODERN WARFARE AND THE ENVIRONMENT, A CASE STUDY OF THE GULF WAR 78 (1991). By Operation Iraqi Freedom this figure had only grown to 68%. By the Numbers, *supra* note 60. For an excellent summary of the precision aspects of the campaign in Kosovo, see US Department of Defense, Report to Congress, Kosovo/Operation Allied Force After-Action Report, Jan. 31, 2000.
148. 7,114 of the 19,948 guided munitions dropped. By the Numbers, *supra* note 60, at 11.
149. For a discussion of Operation Iraqi Freedom, see Schmitt, *supra* note 42.
150. Office of the Prosecutor, International Criminal Tribunal for the Former Yugoslavia, Final Report to the Prosecutor by the Committee Established to Review the NATO Bombing Campaign Against the Federal Republic of Yugoslavia, June 13, 2000, *reprinted in* 39 INTERNATIONAL LEGAL MATERIALS 1257, 1258 (2000); Amnesty International, "Collateral Damage" or Unlawful Killings? Violations of the Laws of War by NATO during Operation Allied Force, AI Index: EUR 70/18/00, June 2000, *available at* www.amnesty.org/ailib/intcam/kosovo/docs/natorep_all.doc.; Civilian Deaths, *supra* note 140; Off Target, *supra* note 82.
151. Civilian Deaths, *supra* note 140.
152. Off Target, *supra* note 82, at 40.
153. On the Grdelica attack, *see* Final Report, *supra* note 150; Civilian Deaths, *supra* note 140; Collateral Damage, *supra* note 150. On the wedding party incident, *see* Dexter Filkins & Edward Wong, *Disputed Strike by U.S. Leaves 40 Iraqis Dead,* NEW YORK TIMES, May 20, 2004, at 1.

VIII

Modern Weaponry and Warfare: The Application of Article 36 of Additional Protocol I by Governments

Marie Jacobsson*

Introduction

The basic rules directly addressing the use of weapons as reflected in Additional Protocol I to the 1949 Geneva Conventions are found in Articles 35 and 36.[1] Needless to say, there are other articles in the Protocol (primarily those relating to targeting) and, of course, other conventions that also address matters relating to the use of weapons. Regulating and restricting the use of weapons is not only a matter that is dealt with in the context of international humanitarian law, disarmament law and human rights law are also relevant.

Neither the 1949 Geneva Conventions nor the 1977 Additional Protocols prohibit a specific, easily identifiable weapon. This conclusion is by no means controversial. On the contrary, the International Committee of the Red Cross's (ICRC's) *Commentary* to the Additional Protocol I clearly concluded that "[t]he Protocol does not impose a specific prohibition on any specific weapon. The prohibitions are those of customary law, or are contained in other international agreements."[2] The ICRC's *Customary International Humanitarian Law*[3] study draws the same conclusion.

* Principal Legal Adviser on International Law to the Swedish Ministry for Foreign Affairs. The ideas presented in this paper do not necessarily reflect the views of the Swedish Government.

In many States, soldiers are taught that it is prohibited to use certain types of weapons.[4] A section on prohibited weapons also has a natural part in any decent presentation to the public of the contents of international humanitarian law.[5] As a result of such education, as well as media coverage, many people are aware that certain weapons are prohibited, such as gas, dum-dum bullets and anti-personnel land mines. In short, the general public has the perception (however vague it might be) that the laws of warfare prohibit and restrict the use of weapons. Or perhaps it would be better to say that the prohibitions and restrictions are nothing but a reflection of "the laws of humanity and the dictates of the public conscience."[6]

However, when a lawyer, or for that matter, any interested person, attempts to list prohibited weapons, the result may be described in two diametrical ways. It is either possible to conclude that the list is depressingly short, or to conclude that it is impressively long; it all depends on the perspective. When viewed from that of humanitarian law, the list can be characterized as depressingly short; from that of international disarmament law, the list can be characterized as impressively long.

Although the ICRC *Commentary* is clear (and the *Customary International Humanitarian Law* study somewhat less clear)[7] when it concludes that Additional Protocol I does not impose a specific prohibition on any specific weapon, the second paragraph of Article 35 of the Protocol declares that "It is prohibited to employ weapons, projectiles and material and methods of warfare of a nature to cause superfluous injury or unnecessary suffering." This is nothing short of a clear-cut prohibition on certain types of *means of warfare* (weapons, projectiles and material), as well as a clear-cut prohibition of certain *methods of warfare.*

It is well known that the language of this article catches the essence of the long-standing prohibition under international law that certain weapons are unacceptable (to phrase it in *ethical* and *moral* terms) and hence such weapons are prohibited (to phrase it in *normative* and *legal* terms).

However, the Geneva Conventions and the Additional Protocols do not offer much practical guidance as to which particular weapons are prohibited. These conventions leave it to the States themselves to identify the weapons that fall under the prohibition. Attempts by individual States and individual nongovernmental organizations to propose an independent "international scrutinizing mechanism" have never met with support. What was left from the Diplomatic Conference in the 1970s was the obligation imposed on States to determine whether the employment of a particular weapon "would, in some or all circumstances, be prohibited by this Protocol or by any other rule of international law."[8]

In fact, even that provision must be regarded as a diplomatic success, given the resistance on the part of some States to include such a provision in the Protocol. Unfortunately, very few States undertake such an examination before employing new means and methods of warfare, despite the fact that the obligation relates to the initial stages, i.e., the "study" and "development" of a new weapon.

The ICRC has attempted to assist States—and put pressure on States—to establish evaluation procedures to meet the obligation in Article 36. The first attempt was made through the so-called SIrUS project.[9] That was not very successful.

More successful was the initiative taken at the 28th International Conference of the Red Cross and Red Crescent in 2003. The Conference invited States that have review procedures in place to cooperate with the ICRC with a view to facilitating the voluntary exchange of experience on review procedures.[10] The purpose of the "exchange of experience" is to disseminate knowledge of, and information about, how Article 36 is implemented, with the goal that more and more States would establish Article 36 procedures. Such processes of informal exchanges of experience have already commenced, including several meetings and workshops.[11]

The Swedish Delegation for International Law Monitoring of Arms Projects

The Swedish Delegation for International Law Monitoring of Arms Projects was set up by the Government in 1974 to meet the requirements of international humanitarian law concerning the potential effects of conventional (mainly anti-personnel) weapons for unnecessary suffering and indiscriminate use. Sweden and the United States were the first States to set up such a mechanism.

The reason the Delegation was set up should be seen against the efforts made by Sweden, particularly during the early 1970s, as regards restrictions and use of certain excessively inhumane weapons. It was noted that the Swedish efforts were met by growing international response. It was therefore considered that future Swedish requisition of arms for the military defense needed to be judged and scrutinized from the perspective of international law (hence, not only humanitarian law). It was deemed that such examination was best undertaken in conjunction with the then existing technical-economical examination. It was therefore decided that the Delegation should consist of experts on international and national law, military and technical experts, experts on arms technology and scientists. The Delegation is today an independent "authority." It is not subordinated to the Swedish Defence Forces or any other authority or ministry.

The Delegation monitors planned purchases or modifications of military weapons or applications of means and methods of warfare to assess whether they would be dubious from the point of view of international law (primarily humanitarian law), human rights law and disarmament law.

After monitoring, the Delegation makes either approval or non-approval decision. The Delegation may combine a negative decision with a request that modifications of the construction of the weapon or ammunition be made, or that the applicant consider an alternative weapon system or restrict the operational use of the weapon in order to meet the requirements of international law. The decisions can be appealed to the Government.

The mandate of the Delegation developed over time. It has become more and more precise—but also wider. It was clear from the outset that the Delegation should not only look at what was already forbidden under international law, but also on international discussions that could lead to further prohibitions. Hence, the mandate(s) has/have clearly reflected not only *de lege lata* requirements, but also *de lege ferenda* tendencies.

For example, the year after the establishment of the Delegation, in 1975, following the Lucerne and Lugano conferences that preceded the negotiations on the Additional Protocols, the Ministry of Defence amended the instructions for the Delegation with regard to projected means of warfare to direct that it should particularly examine whether they could result in unnecessary suffering or have indiscriminate effects.

Some features of the mandate have been particularly noteworthy. Among those is the requirement that the Delegation, in examining weapons projects, should not only take into account existing law, but also international treaties that had not yet entered into force, but which Sweden had signed or ratified.

Consideration should also be given to proposals that Sweden had put forward at international conferences.

In addition, attention should also be given to the limited resources of Sweden as regards weapons acquisition. The Delegation should make sure that the possibility of Sweden to be part of the development in weapons technology was not impeded. The Delegation had, particularly in the 1980s, contacts with the Swedish weapon industry.

The present mandate of the Delegation is formulated under a separate ordinance that stems from 1994. In that year, the Delegation became an independent authority under the Ministry of Defence. According to the ordinance, all Swedish authorities (e.g., the Swedish Armed Forces, the Coast Guard and the Swedish Police Authority) that intend to purchase weapons must report their intended purchases to the Delegation, which then monitors the project. As a result, the Delegation has examined the acquisition of so-called pepper spray and certain ammunition to be used by the Swedish police, the Swedish Coast Guard, and the Swedish Prison and Probation Service.

Finally, it should be mentioned that the Delegation has a right to initiate monitoring even if the Swedish authorities have not reported planned purchases or use.

What Kind of Comments Has the Delegation Made?

The Delegation often requests more information or requires more tests to be made if it believes that the test results either do not meet scientific criteria or are difficult to interpret. Moreover, it often sets out conditions for the use of a certain weapon, for example, that a certain projectile must be used only for anti-materiel purposes; that development of a weapon may continue only if certain conditions are met; or that only a described combination of a weapon and ammunition is allowed, and if changes are made, a new application must be submitted.

The analysis comprises both primary and secondary effects, possible indiscriminate effects, whether Sweden (or any other State) has put forward a proposal that could lead to a prohibition, and implications of allowing civil authorities such as the Swedish police or the Coast Guard, but not military personnel, to use a specific weapon.

Since the Delegation primarily focuses on anti-personnel weapons or weapons that can have anti-personnel effects, the two notions of superfluous injury and unnecessary suffering are of particular interest. The Delegation has not established specific criteria of its own, but evaluates the weapons much along the lines that are described in the *Customary International Humanitarian Law* study.[12]

The extended mandate of the Delegation has been both a challenging and meaningful exercise. It is challenging because the traditional ethical norms transformed into international humanitarian law rules do not correspond with the norms expressed in human rights law. Tear gas and pepper spray are clearly prohibited under disarmament law and international humanitarian law as means and methods of warfare, but perfectly acceptable in a police enforcement situation.

Although the mandate has been extended, it does not cover export control. It is the Swedish Inspectorate of Strategic Products that is entrusted with the task of ensuring that the export of weapons is in conformity with Swedish laws and regulations. However, it does not fall under the competence of the Inspectorate to examine whether or not a weapon would contravene humanitarian law rules.

This has raised some concern. The Swedish Government, together with the Swedish Red Cross, and the other Nordic States, therefore issued a Pledge at the 28th International Conference of the Red Cross and Red Crescent in 2003 to

> undertake a review of national legislation and policies on arms transfer, in order to explore the possibilities to take international humanitarian law into consideration as one of the criteria on which arms transfer decisions are made and to examine appropriate ways of assessing an arms recipient's likely respect for international humanitarian law.[13]

The Nordic States also pledged "to use the result of the review as a basis in order to explore the possibilities to develop a model for the incorporation of international humanitarian law criteria in national arms transfer decision-making."[14] Sweden has commenced working to achieve the goals set out in the Pledge.

There are various references to "Swedish needs" in relation to the mandate of the Delegation. This might be surprising to those who believe the illusion that Sweden has taken advocated strong positions in all weapons contexts (disarmament, as well as international humanitarian law) on the ground that Sweden did not have a national security interest to protect. Such an assumption is incorrect.

On the contrary, Sweden, in the 1970s aiming at proclaimed neutrality in war time, had all the more reason to ensure that it could secure its own weapon production and, as a consequence, that the industry was strong enough to export its products and survive. At the same time, Sweden had at long-standing ideological record in the context of disarmament, humanitarian law and human rights values. Instead of disconnecting what on the surface appear to be contradictory policies, all Swedish Governments attempted to combine them—and still do. Faced with a relatively new political context (judged from the perspective of a history of nearly 200 years of almost uninterrupted neutrality in wartime), namely, the fall of the Berlin Wall and new political requirements, including its membership in the European Union, Sweden has started to take a new and fresh look at the weapons issues.

To limit the rights of combatants to use certain new weapons is often interpreted as "telling the industry" not to develop certain types of weapons. That is to cast an obligation in the negative. Instead, it gives the producers an opportunity to interpret the prohibition in a positive manner, i.e., develop weapons that fall into the framework of Article 36! This can be part of the producers' policy on corporate responsibility.

But it is not enough that the Governments and the producers are collaborating. Weapons technology is still developing at an impressive speed. The manufacturers quickly respond to the demands of the market, irrespective of whether the market consists of States, organizations or individuals. Indeed, this is yet another area where the market economy has proven to be "successful." At the same time, States focus their discussions on existing weapons and remnants of weapons that cause problems today. Of tomorrow's weapons we hear nothing—at least not in the context of discussing their legality or legitimacy. The real challenge is to get States to focus on "new weapons" and "methods of warfare."

All weapons need to be reviewed from a humanitarian perspective. The difficult challenge is whether or not the same norms should apply when considering a weapon used by one combatant against another combatant, as when we consider a weapon or ammunition to be used by a police enforcement official against a civilian.

Previously, it seemed easy to argue that there is a built-in distinction between a combatant-to-combatant situation (a traditional armed conflict) and a police enforcement situation. In the first situation, the combatant is simply not allowed to attack a civilian. In the second, the entire rationale for the police operation is to restore civil order and security for individuals by, albeit as a last resort, the use of force. The objective of the military operation is to weaken the enemy by disabling his combatants. Today such a distinction is more difficult to uphold, for example, the UN operation may be exclusively one of peacekeeping or one that contains elements of both peacekeeping and police enforcement or even an Operation Other Than War (OOTW).

In this context, it is interesting to note that, despite the almost daily reports on the development and employment of so-called non-lethal (or less lethal) weapons, virtually no discussion on the political and legal implications of these weapons has been held on a State-to-State basis, either at a civil or military level. It is worrying that the legally shallow argument, "it is always better to be wounded than dead," is resurfacing in the discussion on less lethal weapons.

There are a number of critical issues that need to be addressed at an international level. These include high-power microwaves, millimeter waves, thermobaric devices and improvised explosive devices. Addressing them does not imply that the weapons should be prohibited. But given the obligation imposed on all States to evaluate the legality of the weapons used, it is reasonable to discuss the matter in a multilateral context.

Conclusion

I would like to encourage States to:

- Set up Article 36 mechanisms;
- Get medical, military, technical, industry experts, lawyers and scientists involved;
- Establish a transparent view;
- Be prepared to review the mandate;
- Cooperate with other States—not only with allies.

Finally, be a step ahead. Look not just at existing weapons and methods of warfare but at the new weapons and new warfighting methods that rapidly evolving technological capabilities are now and will continue to produce. International humanitarian law and the "dictates of public conscience" require that these weapons and methods of warfare be examined to ensure they are consistent with the law and do not unnecessarily add to the suffering inherent in war.

Notes

1. Protocol Additional to the Geneva Conventions of 12 August 1949, and Relating to the Protection of Victims of International Armed Conflicts (Protocol I), June 8, 1977, 1125 U.N.T.S. 3, *reprinted in* DOCUMENTS ON THE LAWS OF WAR 422 (Adam Roberts & Richard Guelff eds., 3d ed. 2000). Article 35 (Basic rules) reads provides:

> 1. In any armed conflict, the right of the Parties to the conflict to choose methods or means of warfare is not unlimited.
>
> 2. It is prohibited to employ weapons, projectiles and material and methods of warfare of a nature to cause superfluous injury or unnecessary suffering.
>
> 3. It is prohibited to employ methods or means of warfare which are intended, or may be expected, to cause widespread, long-term and severe damage to the natural environment.

Id. at 422.

Article 36 (New weapons) provides:

> In the study, development, acquisition or adoption of a new weapon, means or method of warfare, a High Contracting Party is under an obligation to determine whether its employment would, in some or all circumstances, be prohibited by this Protocol or by any other rule of international law applicable to the High Contracting Party.

Id.

2. COMMENTARY TO THE ADDITIONAL PROTOCOLS OF 8 JUNE 1977 TO THE GENEVA CONVENTIONS OF 12 AUGUST 1949, at 399 (Yves Sandoz, Christopher Swinarski & Bruno Zimmermann eds., 1987) (hereinafter ICRC COMMENTARY). The *Commentary* hastens to add: "The rules of the Protocol must be interpreted in good faith at every level." *Id.*

3. JEAN-MARIE HENCKAERTS & LOUISE DOSWALD-BECK, CUSTOMARY INTERNATIONAL HUMANITARIAN LAW (2005) (2 volumes: Volume I, Rules; Volume II, Practice (2 Parts)) (hereinafter CUSTOMARY LAW STUDY). "Although there is general agreement on the existence of the rule, views differ on how it can actually be determined that a weapon causes superfluous injury or unnecessary suffering." *Id.*, Vol. I, at 240.

4. See, for example, *Krigets lagar & soldatregler* (The laws of war and the soldiers' rules), published by the Swedish Armed Forces in 2001. This pocket friendly booklet contains eight basic soldiers' rules and two additional references to the law of naval warfare and the law of air warfare. The second rule refers to the prohibition to use certain means and methods of warfare.

5. ROY GUTMAN & DAVID RIEFF, CRIMES OF WAR. WHAT THE PUBLIC SHOULD KNOW (1999).

6. The formulation of the famous Martens clause as it appears in the preamble to Hague Convention (IV) Respecting the Laws and Customs of War on Land, Oct. 18, 1907, *reprinted in* DOCUMENTS ON THE LAWS OF WAR, *supra* note 1, at 70.

7. CUSTOMARY LAW STUDY, *supra* note 3, at Vol. I, at 242.

8. Additional Protocol I, Article 36 (New weapons) provides:

> In the study, development, acquisition or adoption of a new weapon, means or method of warfare, a High Contracting Party is under an obligation to determine whether its

> employment would, in some or all circumstances, be prohibited by this Protocol or by any other rule of international law applicable to the High Contracting Party.

DOCUMENTS ON THE LAWS OF WAR, *supra* note 1, at 442.

9. International Committee of the Red Cross, The SIRUS Project: Towards a Determination of which Weapons Cause "Superfluous Injury or Unnecessary Suffering" (Robin M. Coupland ed., 1997).

10. The invitation was proposed action 2.5.3 of Final Goal 2.5 of the Agenda for Humanitarian Action. The text is available at http://www.icrc.org/Web/Eng/siteeng0.nsf/htmlall/p1103/$File/ICRC_002_1103.PDF!Open.

11. These include a seminar hosted by the Canadian Ministry of Foreign Affairs, Ministry of Defence and the Canadian Red Cross. The seminar took place in Ottawa on February 9–10, 2005, and indeed provided valuable input.

12. CUSTOMARY LAW STUDY, *supra* note 3, Vol. I, Part IV, at 240–296.

13. Joint Pledge P105, *available at* http://www.icrc.org/Applic/p128e.nsf/pbk/UCOE-5TVNNP?openDocument&section=PBP

14. *Id.*

IX

Chemical Agents and "Expanding" Bullets: Limited Law Enforcement Exceptions or Unwarranted Handcuffs?

Kenneth Watkin*

Introduction

Modern armed conflict has entered a particularly dangerous, and in many ways, chaotic phase. The post–September 11, 2001 period has witnessed significant debate concerning the ability of existing humanitarian norms to regulate 21st-century warfare, and in particular the "war on terror."[1] In an international system of "order" based on the nation-State much of today's conflict is taking place on the fringes of what Clausewitz might have viewed as war between "civilized peoples."[2]

Certainly as the 2003 Iraq campaign demonstrated, traditional conflict between States is still a reality. Here, the "black and white" treaty law provides a well established, if not perfect, normative structure known as the law of armed conflict or international humanitarian law.[3] Customary international law also sets out the obligations of States in international armed conflict. Determination of the exact scope of this second body of law is more challenging as is evidenced in the continuing dialogue over which of the provisions of Additional Protocol I are to be viewed

* Brigadier General, Canadian Forces. The opinions expressed in this article are those of the author and do not necessarily reflect the views of the Government of Canada, the Canadian Forces, or the Office of the Judge Advocate General.

as customary international law.[4] However, notwithstanding this dialogue, there is a significant commonality in the understanding of the obligations on States during the conduct of hostilities.[5]

However, much of contemporary conflict is occurring in what can be termed a "gray" zone. There are four situations where the military forces of the State are required to conduct operations at the interface between warfare and policing: occupation, non-international armed conflict, peace support operations and the international campaign against terrorism. Consistent with the term "gray zone," the determination of the normative framework to be applied is not always clear. While there is often a common theme of violence being applied between State and non-State actors, the lack of clarity as to what rules should be followed occurs in two ways. First, there is the question of the degree to which the law of armed conflict, designed for inter-State conflict, can or should regulate violence between State and non-State actors. Secondly, there is the inevitable interface between the law of armed conflict and human rights norms. In simpler terms: the rules governing armed conflict versus those applying to law enforcement.

Resolving the question of which normative framework applies is extremely important. For the personnel involved, identification of the correct normative framework governing the decision to use force can be literally a matter of life and death. Complying with that framework means military personnel are not only acting "legally," but also in accordance with the value system demanded by modern States of its "warriors."[6] The importance for soldiers, sailors and airmen to act according to the standards of society, both broader society as well as military society, cannot be overstated.

In dealing with this challenge of applying the law, military and civilian government legal advisors can take some solace from the fact that they are not alone in their struggle to do the right thing in the complex security situations confronting States. Non-governmental organizations and other humanitarian groups are also wrestling with what law or norms should be applied to 21st-century conflict.[7] Just as military forces are changing their understanding and approaches towards armed conflict, human rights and humanitarian groups are being confronted with having to apply long-cherished norms in an uncertain operational environment. One scholar from the humanitarian law community has written "[i]t is debatable whether the challenges of asymmetrical war can be met with the current law of war. If war between States is on the way out, perhaps the norms of international law that were devised for them are becoming obsolete as well."[8] This observation provides an indication that the ability of existing codified law to meet the challenges of 21st-century warfare is being opened up to considerable debate.

The purpose of this article is to look at two discrete areas of weapons usage—chemical agents and "expanding" bullets—in order to identify some of the challenges presented in determining the law governing their use during complex security operations. Such operations often straddle the armed conflict and law enforcement paradigms. In this analysis, particular reference will be made to the 2005 International Committee of the Red Cross *Customary International Humanitarian Law* study (hereinafter the Study).[9] This ambitious Study seeks to outline customary international law rules for both international and non-international armed conflict, as well as provide an important compendium of State practice. In seeking to clarify the customary law of armed conflict rules that apply to non-international armed conflict, the Study represents the most fulsome attempt to date to do something that the courts, academics and the militaries themselves have increasingly attempted to do over the past few decades.[10] That being said, the Study offers a starting point for discussion rather than the definitive word on what constitutes customary international humanitarian law. The ultimate test for such statements of customary international law, and particularly those dealing with the law of armed conflict, may be whether they can be practically applied by governments and the military forces who act on their behalf.

This exploration of the law surrounding the use of chemical agents and "expanding" bullets in contemporary conflict is divided into four parts. The first part outlines the law of armed conflict governing the use of these weapons. Particular emphasis is placed on identifying the restrictions on their use set out in treaty law. However, as will be noted, those prohibitions are not absolute as both chemical agents and "expanding" bullets are permitted in law enforcement situations. The second part identifies two approaches to analyzing contemporary armed conflict. The first more formal approach sets out distinct categories of conflicts such as international armed conflict, non-international armed conflict and domestic disturbances that are often analyzed independently of one another. However, the second approach notes armed conflict is increasingly being viewed in a less structured manner, thereby recognizing greater potential for overlap between the law of armed conflict and human rights normative regimes.

This then leads to the third area of analysis: the challenge of applying the law of armed conflict rules governing chemical agents and "expanding" bullets in contemporary conflict. The final part outlines State practice in applying the "spirit and principle" of the law of armed conflict rather than the formal rules governing large-scale inter-State conflict. In effect, there is a more flexible application of the law than a rule-based system of international armed conflict otherwise provides. In the final analysis, it is suggested the complex 21st-century security environment may require a re-analysis of rules governing the use of less lethal weapons such as riot control agents and "expanding" bullets.

Broad Prohibitions?

In dealing with chemical weapons and "expanding" bullets across the broad spectrum of conflict, it will be helpful to first review the provisions of the law as they apply to international armed conflict.

Chemical Weapons

As is noted in the Study, there is a broad treaty prohibition against the use of chemical weapons in international armed conflict, including: the 1899 Hague Declaration Concerning Asphyxiating Gases,[11] the 1925 Geneva Gas Protocol,[12] the 1993 Chemical Weapons Convention[13] and the 1998 Statute of the International Criminal Court.[14] For example, there are only 13 States that are not a "party to either the Geneva Gas Protocol or the Chemical Weapons Convention."[15] Strong support for suggesting that such a ban is customary is found in domestic legislation, military manuals and the statements of governments and national case law.[16]

Similarly, in respect of non-international armed conflict, the Chemical Weapons Convention, Article I broad prohibition framed as "under any circumstances" reflects a more general trend "towards reducing the distinction between international and non-international armed conflicts for the purposes of the rules governing the conduct of hostilities."[17] Many of the contemporary abuses, perhaps most infamously the use of chemical weapons by Saddam Hussein against the Kurds in 1988,[18] have occurred in non-international armed conflict. In terms of a normative prohibition there appears to be a broad consensus, including a strong statement by the International Criminal Tribunal for the former Yugoslavia Appeal Chamber in the *Tadic* decision against the use of such weapons in non-international armed conflict.[19]

However, not all military use of "chemicals" is prohibited. It is, after all, a "weapons" convention involving "toxic chemicals and their precursors."[20] As a result, military purposes "not connected with the use of chemical weapons and not dependent upon the use of the toxic properties of chemicals as method of warfare" are not prohibited.[21] This is not the end of the discussion. The use of "chemical agents" is not absolutely forbidden for all purposes by States seeking to control violence. There is a significant exception regarding the use of such agents. Among the purposes not prohibited under the Convention is "[l]aw enforcement including domestic riot control purposes."[22] However, "riot control agents" will not be used as a method of warfare.[23] A rationale provided for the prohibition of what is otherwise an effective, less-lethal means of warfare, and one particularly suited to certain activities such as forcing an enemy out of caves, bunkers and confined spaces, is "the fact that use of tear gas . . . 'runs the danger of provoking the use of other more dangerous chemicals' . . . since a party 'may think it is being attacked by deadly chemicals and resort to the use of chemical weapons.'"[24]

Riot control agents have traditionally been associated with CS and CN gases as well as vomiting agents.[25] The clarification over the use of chemical agents for law enforcement found in the Chemical Weapons Convention ended long-standing controversy over the scope of the 1925 Gas Protocol. The Study indicates the vast majority of States were of the view the Protocol did apply to riot control agents; however, there were notable exceptions.[26] The United States took the view that the Gas Protocol did not apply to agents with temporary effects and used such agents during the Vietnam conflict.[27] The United Kingdom clarified its position in 1970 to indicate "CS and other such gases accordingly as being outside the scope of the Geneva Protocol."[28]

The exception regarding the use of chemical agents for law enforcement purposes is reflected, perhaps too narrowly, in the Study in Rule 75 which states "[t]he use of riot-control agents as a method of warfare is prohibited." It should be noted that under the Chemical Weapons Convention "law enforcement" is a broader concept than "riot control."[29] These provisions reflect State practice where certain chemical agents are used against citizens for law enforcement purposes, primarily as a less lethal alternative to using deadly force.[30] Not all such agents are used as "riot control agents" as chemical substances such as "pepper spray" may be used for self-defense and for subduing of violent suspects.[31]

In addition to riot control agents, chemical incapacitants can include malodorants[32] and calmatives.[33] The use of the latter led to tragic consequences during the 2002 Moscow Theatre hostage rescue operation when Russian security forces attempted to incapacitate Chechen terrorists with gas.[34]

"Expanding" Bullets

The second area where the law of armed conflict and law enforcement can interface is in respect of the prohibition against using "bullets which expand or flatten easily in the human body."[35] This prohibition is linked to the 1899 Hague Declaration[36] and Additional Protocol I, Article 35(2) in that it is prohibited "to employ weapons, projectiles and material and methods of warfare of a nature to cause superfluous injury or unnecessary suffering."[37] The use of bullets "which expand or flatten easily in the human body, such as bullets with a hard envelope which does not entirely cover the core or is pierced with incisions" is listed as a "war crime" in the

1998 Rome Statute of the International Criminal Court (ICC Statute) in respect of international armed conflicts.[38]

The question of whether "expanding" bullets may be used in non-international armed conflict is a more interesting one. In respect of the Study it is noted that the prohibition against the use of "expanding" bullets "in any armed conflict is set out in several military manuals"[39] and that "[n]o official contrary practice was found with respect to either international armed conflict or non-international armed conflict."[40]

Since Canada was one of the countries whose manual was identified as supporting this principle, it is important to note that the Canadian manual approaches the application of the law of armed conflict to internal armed conflict situations in a much more nuanced fashion than the Study suggests. The Canadian manual does not make a broad statement suggesting that "expanding" bullets are prohibited as a matter of law in non-international armed conflict situations. *The Law of Armed Conflict at the Operational and Tactical Level* does state that expanding bullets are prohibited weapons under the law of armed conflict.[41] However, the application of the law of armed conflict to non-international armed conflict is specifically discussed in terms of common Article 3[42] and Additional Protocol II.[43] As the Canadian manual indicates, "[t]oday a significant number of armed conflicts in which the CF may be involved are non-international in nature. As stated, the law applicable to such conflicts is limited. It is CF policy, however, that the CF will, as a minimum, apply the spirit and principles of the LOAC during all operations other than domestic operations."[44]

This is not to suggest that "expanding" bullets are permitted as a means of warfare in non-international armed conflict. However, the rules of the law of armed conflict may have a far more nuanced application in complex security situations where a significant part of the duties of military forces may also involve law enforcement and other public security duties. In this regard, it must be noted that the Appeals Chamber in the *Tadic* decision warned that two limitations would apply to the application of humanitarian law rules to non-international armed conflict. Those limitations were "(i) only a number of rules and principles governing international armed conflicts have gradually been extended to apply to internal conflicts; and (ii) this extension has not taken place in the form of a full and mechanical transplant of those rules to internal conflicts; rather, the general essence of those rules, and not the detailed regulation they may contain, has become applicable to internal conflicts."[45]

There is also a further indication that the broad extension of the law of armed conflict to non-international conflict found in the Study may not fully reflect the contemporary consensus of States. In this respect, unlike the provision making the use of "expanding" bullets a war crime during international armed conflict, there is no similar provision in the ICC statute in respect of "conflicts not of an international character."[46] As with the use of chemical agents, it is also notable that there is a "law enforcement" exception regarding the use of "expanding" bullets. While this exception is not written in any treaty, it is specifically referred to in the Study.[47] Unfortunately, in the Study it is phrased in terms of "several" States having decided to use such ammunition for domestic law enforcement purposes. There seems to be a significantly broader practice than this wording suggests, extending even to the development of "fragible" ammunition. "Expanding" ammunition appears to be used by security forces in Canada, the United States and the United Kingdom primarily for reasons related to the ammunition being "less susceptible to ricochet and the concomitant creation of unintended collateral casualties."[48]

Law Enforcement Operations

It is these exceptions to the prohibitions of chemical agents and "expanding" bullets that raise some of the most significant challenges to the contemporary law of armed conflict. Both chemical agents and "expanding" bullets options are employed in law enforcement operations with humanitarian goals in mind. For chemical agents, it is the opportunity to apply less lethal means. Regarding the use of "expanding" ammunition, sometimes, but far too inclusively, referred to as "hollow point" bullets, it is concerns over collateral damage and injury that favor their use. When these means are not allowed, particularly where armed conflicts and law enforcement responsibilities interface, a situation can be created where a less "humane" option is imposed on combatants. As a result, uninvolved civilians may be exposed to greater risk of death or injury because of the application of rules that are approximately a century old in their genesis and which were designed specifically for State versus State conflict. The circumstances under which these moral and legal challenges arise are particularly evident is the complex operational environment of contemporary conflict. In that respect, the analysis will now turn to looking at how modern conflict is impacting on the application of normative regimes governing the use of these less lethal weapons.

"Paper Worlds" and the Categorization of Conflict

The application of the law of war is dependent upon the categorization of conflict. While Michael Walzer has noted "lawyers have created a paper world which fails at crucial points to correspond to the world the rest of us live in,"[49] the establishment of law and order is ultimately dependent upon the drawing of jurisdictional lines.

However, the determination of when and how the law of war applies is impacted by two often divergent perspectives.

One more traditional approach sees conflict divided into three formal categories of: international armed conflict, non-international armed conflict and "situations of internal disturbances and tensions."[50] International armed conflict is governed by the extensive treaty and customary law regime of the law of war, while the last category is controlled by a law enforcement/human rights regime. The boundaries of each of these two categories are fairly well prescribed. International armed conflict is largely defined by inter-State conflict, while non-international armed conflict is usually separated from normal law enforcement by the requirement for the conflict to be between "organized armed groups" controlling territory and exercising a semblance of governance. It should also be noted Additional Protocol I provides recognition that international armed conflict can occur between States and non-State actors.[51] However, there is a generally recognized view that most non-State groups will not be able to avail themselves of its provisions.[52]

Under a traditional interpretation of the law, the law of armed conflict operates during international armed conflict as a *lex specialis* to the exclusion of human rights norms.[53] Even though there is a growing body of case law and opinion that places the law of war in a more tightly woven relationship with human rights norms, even during international armed conflict,[54] in many instances this idea of overlap continues to be rejected particularly where it is suggested that human rights treaties have extra-territorial application.[55]

Finally, in respect of non-international armed conflict, it is the provisions of common Article 3 to the 1949 Geneva Conventions[56] and Additional Protocol II[57] which are applied. The scope of internal armed conflict can be quite broad ranging from civil war to conflict just outside the scope of purely criminal activity.[58] A particular challenge has been identifying the limits to the application of common Article 3 which does not have the territorial control; organized armed forces with a responsible command; or "sustained and concerted military operations" criteria of Additional Protocol II.[59] While neither of these law of armed conflict codifications provides as extensive a list of legal provisions as the law applicable to inter-State conflict, they inject basic standards of humanity into conflicts where States still view their non-State opponents as "criminals."[60]

The second perspective on the application of the law of war appears to be neither as definitive nor exclusionary as the first, more formal, model. Here, as is reflected in the more general wording of common Article 3 to the 1949 Geneva Conventions, the dividing lines between the categories of armed conflict are less well defined. Particularly, among humanitarian and human rights groups there is a reluctance to clearly identify when common Article 3 applies either by associating it with Additional Protocol II, or definitively outlining how it interfaces with the lower standard of "internal disturbances and tensions."[61] It is these groups which have also pressed to have international human rights standards apply concurrently with the law of armed conflict. In addition, the existence of an armed conflict can be viewed as having a quite limited temporal existence. For example, in *Juan Carlos Abella v. Argentina*, the Inter-American Commission on Human Rights appeared to view the "armed conflict," the retaking of a military barracks from rebels, as being limited in time to the actual operation.[62]

This second, less well defined, delineation of armed conflict has been significantly influenced in the post Cold War construct of armed conflict. The breakup of Yugoslavia forced the International Criminal Tribunal for the Former Yugoslavia (ICTY) to address the interface between international and non-international armed conflict resulting in a ruling in the *Tadic* case that the law of armed conflict applied to non-international conflicts.[63] The impetus for this change was a shift from a sovereignty based approach to one placing emphasis on "human beings."[64]

The reality is that some aspects of contemporary armed conflict have changed. The events of 9/11 have highlighted the often complex interface between armed conflict and normal policing. The categorization of the post-9/11 events included assessments that the conflict was international, non-international or internationalized non-international armed conflict.[65] Another category known as "transnational armed conflict" has been suggested primarily, it would appear, to avoid admitting international armed conflict can occur between States and non-State actors.[66] Some scholars have seen the attacks as only being amenable to a law enforcement response.[67] However, it is possible to conclude that "[i]n many respects, global terrorism seems to straddle the law enforcement and armed conflict paradigms. Engagement in criminal activity by terrorist groups, warlords, and other non-State actors to finance their operations adds significantly to the perception of an overlap between law enforcement and the conduct of hostilities."[68]

The current emphasis on extending the laws of armed conflict to non-international armed conflict, while seeking to expand the application of human rights norms, sets the scene for a conflict of normative regimes. This could have significant and quite unintended results in the effort to expand humanitarian and human rights protection. The extension of the law of armed conflict not only brings with it a legal regime designed to protect uninvolved civilians, it also expands on the level of violence that can be used by the State to counter an insurgency threat. At the same time, the interface with the human rights-based regime extends the potential for the application of chemical agents and "expanding" bullets in the context of law enforcement.

Perhaps the most graphic example of this potential blurring of law of armed conflict and human rights norms can be found in the United Nations Secretary-General's Bulletin *Observance by United Nations Forces of International Humanitarian Law.*[69] The Bulletin states that the "fundamental principles and rules of international humanitarian law" are applicable in situations of armed conflict, which are stated to include "enforcement actions, or in peacekeeping operations when the use of force is permitted in self-defence."[70] It appears that the use of force during a United Nations operation, even in self-defense, is equated to "combat." However, it is not clear that would always be the case, nor is it evident that the level of violence confronted during a peace support operation would necessarily rise to that of an armed conflict.

While the use of "weapons or methods of combat of a nature to cause unnecessary suffering" is prohibited under the Secretary-General's Bulletin, it is equally evident that the use of riot-control agents for law enforcement purposes is contemplated during United Nations operations. A 2002 Chemical and Biological Weapons (CBW) Conventions Bulletin, "*Law Enforcement" and the CWC*,[71] recognizes law enforcement under the Chemical Weapons Convention[72] would include United Nations operations. These law enforcement operations are defined as actions within the scope of a nation's jurisdiction to enforce its national laws and as authorized by the United Nations. In respect of actions that are "taken in the context of law enforcement or riot control functions under the authority of the United Nation, they must be specifically authorized by that organization. No act is one of 'law enforcement' if it otherwise would be prohibited as a 'method of warfare'. . . ."[73]

Similarly, another analysis has concluded "peacekeeping operations authorized by the receiving state, including peacekeeping operations pursuant to Chapter VI of the UN Charter; and . . . peacekeeping operations where force is authorized by the UN Security Council under Chapter VII of the UN Charter. . . ." are operations falling within the context of "law enforcement."[74] This very broad concept of law enforcement increases the likelihood of an awkward interface between the two normative regimes governing the use of chemical agents.

Operating in the "Gray Zone"

Having established the increasing overlap and sometimes unclear interface between normative regimes, the question remains as to how the different norms governing the use of riot control agents and "expanding" bullets are applied in practice. The answer in part can be found in the reality that operating in an operational "gray zone" has long been a part of military operations.

However, it should be noted that the problem of viewing armed conflict as being limited to inter-State conflict is not unique to the legal community. Military forces themselves often look at "war" primarily through the lens of conventional combat between the armed forces of nation States. Preference for "traditional" armed conflict impacts on doctrine, equipment acquisition, training, and, ultimately, the capabilities of the armed forces. Generally, less time is spent on "low intensity conflict" and the range of operations which require consideration of law enforcement activities.

However, "warfare" has always included a range of conflict significantly broader than battles between the armed forces of a State. Such conflict has been termed, somewhat inaccurately, as "small wars" since they are not necessarily "small" in scope.[75] As Max Boot has stated "[t]hese days social scientists and soldiers usually call them either 'low intensity conflicts' or—a related category—'military operations other than war.'"[76] In 19th-century terms, they were identified as "campaigns undertaken to suppress rebellions and guerrilla warfare in all parts of the world where organized armies are struggling against opponents who will not meet them in the open field."[77] In those campaigns, beating a hostile army is not necessarily the main object. They may involve the subjugation of insurrection, the repression of lawlessness, or the pacification of territory. These operations "involve[d] struggles against guerrillas and banditti."[78] While 19th-century warfare was not necessarily sensitive to issues of "law," it is clear that governance and "law enforcement" type activities have been an integral part of operations at this end of the conflict spectrum.

Military involvement in law enforcement includes operations in times of occupation, non-international armed conflict and the campaign against terrorism. Further, a broad range of peace support operations can be added to this list. Such operations may not be dependent upon traditional sources of authorization such as a United Nations Security Council resolution, but could also involve a request from the governing authority of the territory involved. Military involvement can arise in a number of ways. The absence of police and other security forces in failed and failing States, or the responsibility to govern occupied territory, can result in the military performing a law enforcement role.[79] Even where local security forces exist, operations may be conducted in support of those forces in order to mentor or augment their capability. Such operations are evident in Afghanistan and Iraq.[80] In addition, law enforcement and military forces may conduct joint operations when the threat is one like global terrorism which contains elements of both criminal activity and armed conflict.[81]

The new complex operational environment is perhaps best articulated in the United States Marine Corps doctrine of the "three block war."[82] This doctrine has been integrated into Canada's 2005 International Policy Statement and has been described as "[o]ur military could be engaged in combat against well-armed militia in one city block, stabilization operations in the next block, and humanitarian relief and reconstruction two blocks over."[83] The doctrine recognizes the significant potential for military forces to be engaged in combat with armed groups while at the same time potentially being confronted with interfacing and controlling civilian populations. The latter responsibility can quickly take on the attributes of a policing function. Finally, military involvement in law enforcement is not restricted to international operations. Many nations regularly use military forces in a domestic law enforcement role including participation in hostage rescue.[84]

The interface with law enforcement means that military forces may themselves be conducting law enforcement operations, or may be conducting operations with security forces performing that function. This could mean participation in joint patrols with local security forces in a policing role under circumstances where the military and police forces both become involved in an engagement with organized insurgents.[85] The question immediately arises as to whether those security forces should be barred from carrying riot control or other chemical agents because of the potential to be engaged in armed conflict with insurgents. In this regard, it has been suggested the use of such agents would be permissible as part of law enforcement operations of an occupying power or in "non-traditional military operations such as peacekeeping operations, recognized as legitimate under international law."[86] It has also been acknowledged that "non-traditional military operations" may also apply to non-combatant evacuation and rescue missions.[87]

The question of whether riot control agents or "expanding" bullets should be applied in military operations is not limited to operations normally associated with law enforcement. For example, cramped, confined spaces on merchant vessels and the crewing of those vessels by diverse multi-national crews provide ample practical reasons to seek out less-lethal means to detain or act in self-defense while conducting visit and search or maritime interdiction operations.[88] The latter operations are normally authorized pursuant to a Security Council resolution. However, a strong argument can also be made that less-lethal law enforcement tools should be equally applicable to law of armed conflict-based visit and search operations when it is not anticipated there would be a confrontation with enemy forces.

Similarly, "expanding" bullets are the ammunition of choice for hostage rescue units in many States. At the same time, kidnapping, both criminal and insurgent based, appears common in many failed or re-building States.[89] It raises interesting moral issues to suggest the civilians of a State such as Afghanistan or Iraq should be exposed to greater risk of injury in a law enforcement operation because there also happens to be an armed conflict occurring in parts of the nation with insurgent forces. All of this points to a broader use of riot control agents and potentially "expanding" bullets than the concept of law enforcement might ordinarily imply.

State Practice

While many States and their legal advisors acknowledge the delineation of conflict into the various traditional categories, there is at some point a requirement to set out the legal framework to be used for operations in the "gray zone." The solution to this challenge is reflected in the approaches already referred to in the Canadian manual and the United Nations Secretary-General's Bulletin. The law of armed conflict is applied as a matter of policy in situations where it technically may not apply as a matter of law. The United States approach is articulated as all heads of Department of Defense Components who are required to "[e]nsure that the members of their DoD Components comply with the law of war during all armed conflicts, however such conflicts are characterized, and with the principles and spirit of the law of war during all other operations."[90]

In practical terms, States approach the use of law enforcement tools such as chemical agents and "expanding" bullets in different ways. The United States permits the use of riot control agents in a variety of circumstances, both during armed conflict and lower intensity peace support operations. That policy is set out in Executive Order 11850 which "allows their use in defensive military modes to save lives. Since riot control agents in this capacity are not being used against combatants, they are not being used as a 'method of warfare.'"[91] Authorized use includes the following situations: controlling riots in areas under United States military control; the rioting of prisoners of war; escaping prisoners of war in remotely controlled areas; dispersing civilians when they are used to mask an attack; rescue missions for downed pilots; and for police actions in rear areas.[92] The United States military has used both rubber bullets and tear gas in dealing with violent detainee disturbances in Iraq.[93] The US Navy's *Annotated Supplement to The Commander's Handbook on the Law of Naval Operations* notes that the United States prohibits the use of riot control agents as a form of warfare in both international and internal armed conflicts; however, it goes on to state "that it does not apply in normal peacekeeping operations, law enforcement operations, humanitarian and disaster relief operations, counter-terrorist and hostage rescue operations, and non-combatant rescue operations conducted outside of such conflicts."[94]

Australian Air Force doctrine outlines a non-exhaustive list where riot control agents can be used. These situations include: rioting prisoners of war; rescue missions involving downed aircrew or escaped prisoners of war; the protection of supply depots, military convoys and rear echelon areas from civil disturbances and terrorist activities; civil disturbance when acting in aid to the civil power; and during humanitarian evacuations involving Australian or foreign nations.[95] Under Canadian doctrine, "the use of CS gas or pepper spray is lawful and may be used for crowd control purposes, but their use as a means of warfare is illegal."[96] The United Kingdom, at least in respect of operations in Iraq, appears to have placed a total ban on the use of riot control agents in armed conflict. Defence Minister Hoon was reported to have stated that riot control agents "would not be used by the United Kingdom in any military operations or on any battlefield."[97] However, riot control agents appear to be permitted for riot control.[98]

The use of riot control agents in situations involving civilians used to mask or screen attacks; for rescue missions of downed aircrew; and to capture escaping prisoners of war has been criticized.[99] However, there has also been an acknowledgment that an "argument can be made that use of a RCA against an escaping prisoner of war in an isolated area might be legitimate. . . ."[100] This concession would not be extended to the use of chemical agents against enemy combatants seeking to capture a downed pilot because such use "more resembles a method of warfare than a law enforcement purpose."[101]

However, this viewpoint appears to assume such use would only be directed towards "enemy combatants." Regarding the rescue of downed aircrew it does not take into account the use of riot control agents to ensure local civilians do not attempt to attack the aircrew. If civilians were to attempt to capture and kill that aircrew those civilians might be considered to be taking a direct part in hostilities and therefore be liable to attack.[102] In any event, civilians capturing and causing the death or injury of downed aircrew would be the commission of a criminal act.[103]

Denying the ability to use riot control agents in such circumstances could be seen as an overly formalistic approach to a difficult moral situation. It would indeed be incongruous to end up with a "humanitarian" interpretation that those threatening to attack downed aircrew would have to be subjected to deadly force when military personnel would prefer to use riot control agents to spare the civilians.

Similarly, contemplating the use of riot control agents in situations where civilians are being used as human shields places military personnel in an extremely difficult moral and legal situation. Such chemical agents are not to be used as a "method of warfare," but they may offer the only viable alternative to killing innocent women and children. Interestingly, it has been suggested that riot control agents might be appropriate in some crowd situations during ongoing armed conflict. During an incident in Fallujah, Iraq on April 30, 2003, US military personnel fired on a crowd of demonstrators from which they believed insurgents were engaging them. This incident attracted the criticism of Human Rights Watch.[104] That non-governmental organization noted that the troops "had no teargas or other forms of non-lethal crowd control"[105] and among the recommendations was that "U.S. troops in Iraq be equipped with adequate crowd control devices to avoid a resort to lethal force."[106]

A recommendation that law enforcement means be used against rioting civilians is an appropriate one in most circumstances. However, the challenge is applying it during an armed conflict with an ongoing insurgency when armed members of armed opposition groups may be in the crowd. In that circumstance "the separation between a law enforcement role and operations in armed conflict may not lend itself to being neatly drawn as the occupying power struggles to bring order out of chaos."[107] However, to the extent the use of riot control means provides a viable alternative in situations like those presented in Fallujah, it becomes difficult to argue they should also not be applied to limit casualties to human shields being set up by similar armed groups.

Similar challenges arise in respect of military operations in failed or failing States where it may not be possible to easily separate the civilians from the opposing forces, or those forces from ordinary criminals. Here it may be helpful to consider the reason why the ban on the use of riot control agents as a means of warfare was imposed, namely, to avoid a misunderstanding as to whether a Party to the conflict is being attacked by chemical weapons.[108] If, however, that rationale does not apply to the operational situation and the use of riot control agents involving civilians more closely approximates situations of domestic law enforcement, it would be much more difficult to suggest that the use of riot control agents does not provide an appropriate response. Further, the opportunity for misunderstanding could be reduced by the use of an information operations campaign explaining the circumstances under which such chemical agents are going to be used for riot control or other forms of law enforcement. Of course, many of these situations will be fact dependant. However, the challenge is to ensure rules are not applied overly formally at the expense of employing more humane options.

Regarding the use of "expanding" bullets, there appears to have been less overt reference to State practice. Identifying a consistent interpretation of the test for what constitutes "unnecessary suffering" and "superfluous injury" is itself problematic. One approach has been to see the terms as synonymous,[109] while others have viewed the expression to cover "both measurable—objective (mostly physical) injury and subjective—psychological suffering and pain."[110] In addition, as Yoram Dinstein has noted "[s]ome scholars speak about proportionality between injury or suffering and the military advantage anticipated" although he is not in agreement with that approach.[111] This lack of consensus nearly 140 years after the development of the 1868 St. Petersburg Declaration[112] highlights the challenges in applying this area of law.

The Study does indicate that the prohibition on the use of "expanding" bullets is set forth in numerous military manuals and states that "no State has asserted that it would be lawful to use such ammunition."[113] However, it also indicates the United States has taken an "ambiguous" position regarding the use of "expanding" ammunition if there is "a clear showing of military necessity for its use."[114] The Study reaches a similar conclusion regarding non-international armed conflict.[115] However, the Study deals only tentatively with the question of the use of "expanding" bullets for law enforcement and relies heavily on references to domestic law enforcement. It is here that the issue of State practice needs to be further explored. It is likely more than the "several states" alluded to in the Study permit the use of "expanding" bullets for law enforcement purposes. It is a common practice in North America.

The Study describes the two most common reasons for using such ammunition in a domestic law enforcement context: avoiding over-penetration and the stopping power of such ammunition. Then, in a somewhat ambiguous fashion of its own, the Study notes "expanding bullets commonly used by police in situations other than armed conflict are fired from a pistol and therefore deposit much less energy than a normal rifle bullet, or a rifle bullet which expands or flattens easily."[116] It could be argued that this statement is problematic for those supporting a complete ban on hollow point ammunition. If the effect of hollow point or "expanding" bullets fired by a pistol has a less damaging effect than a normal rifle bullet, an argument might be made that the ammunition causes neither unnecessary suffering nor superfluous injury. If that is the case, then it would be difficult to see why it should not be permitted in armed conflict situations as well. However, it is not apparent this was the intention of the authors of the Study.

A more fundamental question is why ammunition that is viewed as causing unacceptable injury and suffering under international law is viewed as lawful under a human rights-based law enforcement regime governing domestic law enforcement. This issue becomes even more complex when the humanitarian factor of limiting collateral damage to uninvolved civilians, including those of the opposing State, through the use of "hollow point" ammunition is considered. For example, in the same way that "law enforcement" has been interpreted to permit the use of riot control agents during many international operations, a convincing argument can be made that "expanding" ammunition would also be permitted under that exception.[117]

Conclusion

In respect of the use of chemical agents and "expanding" bullets, the increasing influence that human rights norms are having on both military operations and the law of armed conflict may very well require a re-assessment of long held beliefs regarding the use of law enforcement means during armed conflict. In many respects, the spotlight turned on the "law enforcement" role performed by States in complex security environments is already having that effect, although it is a role that has long been performed by military forces on international operations.

On a practical level, many military lawyers advising commanders are placed in an awkward situation of explaining why riot control agents or "expanding" bullets can be used domestically (i.e., against your own citizens) and even internationally in a law enforcement role, but cannot be used against an enemy. This is a discussion that becomes even more challenging as military forces are forced to confront the reality of conducting operations in "three block wars" or performing law enforcement duties in failed or failing States.

It is not suggested that the long held and important prohibitions under the law of armed conflict with respect to the use of riot control agents as a "method of warfare," or using "expanding" bullets, be removed. However, there is considerable merit to the argument that the underlying rationale for these prohibitions, created more than a century ago, be critically analyzed. The interpretation of how the customary law of armed conflict rules apply to complex security situations requires careful consideration of the more flexible application of law traditionally applied by many States. The law of armed conflict has not been rigidly or formally applied to those situations, but rather the "spirit and principles" of those laws have been followed. Given the continuing complexity of 21st-century conflict, the need to be flexible and to search out humane approaches to applying force, remains an important goal.

The extension of law of armed conflict norms to internal conflicts highlights this need for a flexible approach. As Lindsay Moir has noted, many States that would be "happy to see an increase in the level of humanitarian protection and regulation for internal conflicts are unlikely to agree to the wholesale adoption in such cases of the rules for international armed conflicts." There remains a broad acceptance throughout the international community that internal and international armed conflicts are fundamentally different in character."[118] A similar challenge arises in attempting to apply law of armed conflict rules to other complex security situations such as occupation and the war on terror.

In the words of Thomas Franck:

> There has always been a large measure of agreement that terrorism poses a new challenge to the rule of law. Now that it seems clear that the rule of law—in both its domestic and its international configurations—still applies, the next task is to make it more responsive to the onerous new circumstances in which it must operate.[119]

This ultimately will require all the parties who have an interest in the law of armed conflict, or international humanitarian law, however it is termed, to rethink some long held views on the conduct of operations, particularly when military forces are required to also perform law enforcement functions. Included among the areas for analysis should be the use of less-lethal means such as chemical agents and "expanding" bullets in order to ensure the protection for uninvolved civilians and other non-combatants is not unduly handcuffed by rules designed for large scale inter-State conflict.

Notes

1. For example, *see* Toni Pfanner, *Asymmetrical Warfare from the Perspective of Humanitarian Law and Humanitarian Action*, 87 INTERNATIONAL REVIEW OF THE RED CROSS 149 (2005); Gabor Rona, *Interesting Times for International Humanitarian Law: Challenges from the "War on Terror,"* 27 THE FLETCHER FORUM OF WORLD AFFAIRS 55 (2003), *available at* http://www.icrc.org/Web/eng/siteeng0.nsf/htmlall/5PWELF/$File/Rona_terror.pdf; and Noelle Quenivet, *The Applicability of International Humanitarian Law to Situations of a (Counter-)Terrorist Nature, in* INTERNATIONAL HUMANITARIAN LAW AND THE 21ST CENTURY'S CONFLICTS 25 (Roberta Arnold & Pierre-Antoine Hildbrand eds., 2005). *Also see generally* Kenneth Watkin, *Controlling the Use of Force: A Role for Human Rights Norms in Contemporary Armed Conflict*, 98 AMERICAN JOURNAL OF INTERNATIONAL LAW 1, 2–6 (2004).

2. CARL VON CLAUSEWITZ, ON WAR 86 (Michael Howard & Peter Paret trans. & eds., 1986) (1832). (Although most of his work is dedicated to removing external factors when considering the application of force Clausewitz also indicates that in his view wars between "civilized nations are far less cruel and destructive than war between savages.")

3. The terms "law of armed conflict," "law of war" and "international humanitarian law" are often used synonymously. However, the fact that military writers exhibit a preference for the more martial connection to armed conflict or war, while humanitarian organizations (such as the International Committee of the Red Cross (ICRC)) and human rights non-government organizations (NGOs), such as Human Rights Watch and Amnesty International, prefer to use "humanitarian" law, graphically demonstrates a fundamental tension in this area of the law, i.e., the balancing of military necessity and humanity.

4. Protocol Additional to the Geneva Conventions of 12 August 1949, and Relating to the Protection of Victims of International Armed Conflicts, Dec. 12, 1977, 1125 UNTS 3 [hereinafter Additional Protocol I]. *See* Michael J. Matheson, *The United States Position on the Relation of Customary International Law to the 1977 Protocols Additional to the 1949 Geneva Conventions*, 2 AMERICAN UNIVERSITY JOURNAL OF INTERNATIONAL LAW AND POLICY 415 (1987); Christopher Greenwood, *Customary Law Status of the 1977 Geneva Protocols, in*

HUMANITARIAN LAW OF ARMED CONFLICT: CHALLENGES AHEAD 93 (Astrid J. M. Delissen & Gerard J. Tanja eds., 1991); and George S. Prugh, *American Issues and Friendly Reservations Regarding Protocol I, Additional to the Geneva Conventions*, 31 MILITARY LAW AND LAW OF WAR REVIEW 224 (1992). *See also* JEAN-MARIE HENCKAERTS & LOUISE DOSWALD-BECK, CUSTOMARY INTERNATIONAL HUMANITARIAN LAW *xxvii–xlv* (2005) [hereinafter CUSTOMARY LAW STUDY].

5. Jefferson D. Reynolds, *Collateral Damage on the 21st Century Battlefield: Enemy Exploitation of the Law of Armed Conflict, and the Struggle for a Moral High Ground*, 56 AIR FORCE LAW REVIEW 1, 23–24 (2005) ("[Additional Protocol I] is thoroughly represented in U.S. military doctrine, practice and rules of engagement").

6. *See* Kenneth Watkin, *Warriors, Obedience and the Rule of Law*, 3/4 THE ARMY DOCTRINE AND TRAINING BULLETIN 24, 28 (Winter 2000, Spring 2001) *available at* http://armyapp.forces.gc.ca/ael/adtb/vol_3/No_4/vol3_no_4_E.pdf.

7. *See* Pfanner, *supra* note 1.

8. *Id.* at 158.

9. CUSTOMARY LAW STUDY, *supra* note 4.

10. *See, e.g.*, Prosecutor v. Tadic (Appeal on Jurisdiction) paras. 65–142 (Oct 2, 1995) *available at* http://www.un.org/icty/tadic/appeal/decision-e/51002.htm [hereinafter Tadic], and Lindsay Moir, *Towards the Unification of International Humanitarian Law?*, *in* INTERNATIONAL CONFLICT AND SECURITY LAW: ESSAYS IN MEMORY OF HILAIRE MCCOUBREY 108 (Richard Burchill, Nigel D. White & Justin Morris eds., 2005).

11. Hague Declaration 2 Concerning Asphyxiating Gases, July 29, 1899, UKTS 32 (1907), *reprinted in* DOCUMENTS ON THE LAWS OF WAR 59 (Adam Roberts & Richard Guelff eds., 3d. ed. 2000).

12. Protocol for the Prohibition of the Use in War of Asphyxiating, Poisonous or Other Gases, and of Bacteriological Methods of Warfare, June 17, 1925, UKTS 24 (1930), *reprinted in* DOCUMENTS ON THE LAWS OF WAR, *supra* note 11, at 155.

13. Convention on the Prohibition of the Development, Production, Stockpiling and Use of Chemical Weapons and on their Destruction, Jan. 13, 1993, *reprinted in* THE LAWS OF ARMED CONFLICTS 239 (Dietrich Schindler & Jiri Toman eds., 4th ed. 2004). There are 174 States parties to the Chemical Weapons Convention. *See* States Parties to Main Treaties *available at* www.icrc.org.

14. Rome Statute of the International Criminal Court, July 17, 1998, *reprinted in* THE LAWS OF ARMED CONFLICTS, *supra* note 13, at 1309 [hereinafter ICC Statute].

15. CUSTOMARY LAW STUDY, *supra* note 4, at 259.

16. *Id.* at 260.

17. David Kaye & Steven A. Solomon, *The Second Review Conference of the 1980 Convention on Certain Conventional Weapons*, 96 AMERICAN JOURNAL OF INTERNATIONAL LAW 922, 922 (2002).

18. *See* Hiwa Osman, *Iraqi Kurds Recall Chemical Attack*, BBC NEWS (Mar. 17, 2002), *available at* http://news.bbc.co.uk/1/hi/world/middle_east/1877161.stm.

19. *See* Tadic, ICTY Appeal Chamber (1995), *supra* note 10, at para. 124 ("It is therefore clear that, whether or not Iraq really used chemical weapons against its own Kurdish nationals—a matter on which this Chamber obviously cannot and does not express any opinion—here undisputedly emerged a general consensus in the international community on the principle that the use of those weapons is also prohibited in internal armed conflicts."). *See also* CUSTOMARY LAW STUDY, *supra* note 4, at 263; Antonio Cassesse, *The Statute of the International Criminal Court: Some Preliminary Reflections*, 10 EUROPEAN JOURNAL OF INTERNATIONAL LAW 144, 152–153 (1999) ("That Appeals Chamber rightly [found] . . . that the prohibition of weapons causing

unnecessary suffering, as well as the specific ban on chemical weapons, also applies to internal armed conflicts.").

20. Convention on the Prohibition of the Development, Production, Stockpiling and Use of Chemical Weapons and on Their Destruction, art. II, para. 1, Jan. 13, 1993, 32 INTERNATIONAL LEGAL MATERIALS 800, *reprinted in* THE LAWS OF ARMED CONFLICTS, *supra* note 13, at 239, 242.

21. *Id.*, art. II, para. 9(c), at 243.

22. *Id.*, art. I, para. 5, at 242.

23. *Id.*, art. II, para. 9(d), at 244.

24. See CUSTOMARY LAW STUDY, *supra* note 4, at 265 quoting in part the military manual of the Netherlands.

25. *See* FM 8-9 Nato Handbook On The Medical Aspects Of NBC Defensive Operations Amedp-6(B) Chap. 7, Riot Control Agents para. 701 (1996), *available at* http://www.fas.org/nuke/guide/usa/doctrine/dod/fm8-9/toc.htm ("Riot control agents are irritants characterised by a very low toxicity (chronic or acute) and a short duration of action. Little or no latent period occurs after exposure. Orthochlorobenzylidene malononitrile (CS) is the most commonly used irritant for riot control purposes. Chloracetophenone (CN) is also used in some countries for this purpose in spite of its higher toxicity. A newer agent is dibenzoxazepine (CR) with which there is little experience. Arsenical smokes (sternutators) have in the past been used on the battlefield. Apart from their lachrymatory action they also provoke other effects, e.g., bronchoconstriction and emesis and are some times referred to as vomiting agents.").

26. CUSTOMARY LAW STUDY, *supra* note 4, at 263–264 (The noted exceptions are Australia, Portugal and the United Kingdom).

27. *Id.* For a detailed outline of the US position regarding the 1925 Gas Protocol, see ANNOTATED SUPPLEMENT TO THE COMMANDER'S HANDBOOK ON THE LAW OF NAVAL OPERATIONS 467–471 (A.R. Thomas & James C. Duncan eds., 1999) (Vol. 73, US Naval War College International Law Studies) [hereinafter ANNOTATED SUPPLEMENT].

28. David Carlton & Nicholas Sims, *The CS Gas Controversy*, SURVIVAL 333, 333 (1971) quoting Hansard (Commons) vol. 795, c. 17–18. Written answers: February 1970. (The authors suggest "it may well be the British Government in 1969–1970 came to share [the US delegate's] opinion either as a result of the use of CS gas in Northern Ireland or as a result of contemplating how best to assist President Nixon . . . in seeking to persuade Congress to approve . . . the Geneva Protocol.") *Id.* at 336–337.

29. *See* David P. Fidler, *Law Enforcement Under the Chemical Weapons Convention*, FAS Working Group on Biological and Chemical Weapons for the Open Forum on Challenges to the Chemical Weapons Ban 5 (May 1, 2002), *available at* http://www.armscontrolcenter.org/cbw/papers/wg/wg_2002_law_enforcement.pdf ("application of international law on treaty interpretation indicates that the definition of a RCA in Article 11.9(d) [of the 1993 Chemical Weapons Convention] does not limit the range of toxic chemicals that can be used for law enforcement purposes.").

30. *See* CNN.com./World, Protesters Battle Police at Summit of Americas, http://archives.cnn.com/2001/WORLD/americas/04/20/summit.americas.02/ ("Riot police with helmets, batons and shields stood shoulder-to-shoulder trying to maintain their perimeter while demonstrators lobbed rocks, bottles and parts of the fence at the officers. Police answered with tear gas. Protesters picked up some of the tear gas canisters and tossed them back at police. The air soon grew hazy with the gas.").

31. *See* The Effectiveness and Safety of Pepper Spray, US Department of Justice, Office of Justice Programs, National Institute of Justice 1, 1 (April 2003) *available at* www.ncjrs.org/pdffiles1/nij/195739.pdf ("Pepper spray, or oleoresin capsicum (OC), is used by law enforcement and

corrections agencies across the United States to help subdue and arrest dangerous, combative, violent, or uncooperative subjects in a wide variety of scenarios.").

32. *See* Squadron Leader C.R. Coles, *Air-delivered Non-lethal Weapons and the RAAF Weapons Inventory,* Geddes Papers, Australian Command and Staff College 70, 78 (2003) ("Commonly referred to as 'stink bombs' malodorants are derived from living organisms or toxins and produce a powerful smell which humans find repugnant. When applied can be used to disperse a crowd or deny an area to an adversary and quite clearly have potential application in all forms of military action including peacekeeping. The effects of exposure to malodorants can range from mild displeasure to gagging and vomiting.").

33. *Id.* ("Calmatives act much like sedatives—they depress the central nervous system having a psychological effect in altering moods as well as a physiological effect by depressing the respiratory system. Calmatives have obvious applications against large bodies of people or against individuals who are either unmanageable or are dispersed among a group of civilians.") However, *see* Sarah V. Hart, *Less-Than-Lethal Weapons*, Statement Before the Subcommittee on Aviation Committee on Transportation and Infrastructure, U.S. House Of Representatives (May 2, 2002) *available at* http://www.ojp.usdoj.gov/nij/speeches/aviation.htm (outlining the challenges of using calmatives in an aircraft hijacking situation.).

34. See Quenivet, *supra* note 1, at 31.

35. *See* CUSTOMARY LAW STUDY, *supra* note 4, at 268 ("Rule 77. The use of bullets which expand or flatten easily in the human body is prohibited.").

36. The "expanding" bullets prohibition is contained in Hague Declaration (IV, 3) Concerning Expanding Bullets, July 29, 1899, UKTS 32 (1907), *reprinted in* DOCUMENTS ON THE LAWS OF WAR, *supra* note 11, at 64.

37. *Supra* note 4.

38. *Supra* note 14, art. 8(2)(b)(xix).

39. HENCKAERTS & DOSWALD-BECK, *supra* note 4, at 270.

40. *Id.*

41. CANADIAN FORCES DOCTRINE MANUAL: THE LAW OF ARMED CONFLICT AT THE OPERATIONAL AND TACTICAL LEVEL, B-GJ-005-104/FP-021,¶ 510, at 5-2 (Aug. 13, 2001), *available at* http://www.forces.gc.ca/jag/training/publications/loac_man_e.asp [hereinafter OPERATIONAL AND TACTICAL LEVEL MANUAL] ("bullets that expand or flatten easily in the human body, such as bullets with a hard envelope that does not entirely cover the core or is pierced with incisions (that is, hollow point or 'dum-dum' bullets)").

42. Article 3, common to the Geneva Conventions of 1949, e.g., Convention for the Amelioration of the Condition of the Wounded and Sick in Armed Forces in the Field, Aug. 12, 1949, 75 U.N.T.S. 31 [Geneva Convention I]; Convention for the Amelioration of the Condition of the Wounded, Sick and Shipwrecked Members of Armed Forces at Sea, Aug. 12, 1949, 75 U.N.T.S. 85 [Geneva Convention II]; Convention Relative to the Treatment of Prisoners of War, Aug. 12, 1949, 75 U.N.T.S. 135 [Geneva Convention III]; Convention Relative to the Protection of Civilian Persons in Time of War, Aug. 12, 1949, 75 U.N.T.S. 287 [Geneva Convention IV]; all *reprinted in* DOCUMENTS ON THE LAWS OF WAR, *supra* note 11, at 197, 222, 244 and 301, respectively.

43. Protocol Additional to the Geneva Conventions of 12 August 1949, and Relating to the Protect of Victims of Non-International Armed Conflicts, June 8, 1977, 1125 U.N.T.S. 609, *reprinted in* DOCUMENTS ON THE LAWS OF WAR, *supra* note 11, at 483 [hereinafter Additional Protocol II].

44. *See* OPERATIONAL AND TACTICAL LEVEL MANUAL, *supra* note 41, at 17-1 para. 1702. *See also* the CODE OF CONDUCT FOR CF PERSONNEL, B-GG-005-027/AF-023, 1–2, para. 10 [hereinafter

CODE OF CONDUCT], *available at* http://www.forces.gc.ca/jag/training/publications/code_of_conduct/Code_of_Conduct_e.pdf ("The Law of Armed Conflict applies when Canada is a party to any armed conflict. During peace support operations the spirit and principles of the Law of Armed Conflict apply. The CF will apply, as a minimum, the spirit and principles of the Law of Armed Conflict in all Canadian military operations other than Canadian domestic operations.").

45. *See* Tadic (Appeals Chamber) (1995), *supra* note 10, at para. 126.

46. *See* ICC Statute, *supra* note 14, art. 8(2)(d). See also Cassesse, *supra* note 19, at 152 ("The prohibited use of weapons in internal armed conflicts is not regarded as a war crime under the ICC statute.").

47. HENCKAERTS & DOSWALD-BECK, *supra* note 4, at 270.

48. *See Rules of War and Arms Control, in* A Short History of SALW International and Domestic Constraints 3 n.32 (Foreign Affairs Canada), *available at* http://www.dfait-maeci.gc.ca/arms/Trends/section09-en.asp. *See also* David Cracknell et al., *The Web of Terror*, THE SUNDAY TIMES (July 17, 2005), at 12 (where it is indicated that the special Scotland Yard police unit, S019, tasked with stopping suicide bombers "use 'frangible' ammunition that releases all its energy in the targets body, instead of passing through it and endangering nearby civilians."). *See supra* note 88.

49. MICHAEL WALZER, JUST AND UNJUST WARS xviii–xix, (1977).

50. *See* Additional Protocol II, *supra* note 43, art. 1(2).

51. LESLIE GREEN, THE CONTEMPORARY LAW OF ARMED CONFLICT 55–56 (2d ed. 1996) (where it is noted that "to some extent certain non-international conflicts have come under the aegis of international law since 1977 with the adoption of Article 1(4) of Protocol I and Protocol II additional to the 1949 Geneva Conventions . . . .").

52. This can occur either because of the limited application of Additional Protocol I to movements seeking "self-determination" or because of an inability of the national liberation movements to apply the provisions of the Protocol. For a discussion of the limitations of the application of Additional Protocol I, see Theodor Meron, *The Time Has Come for the United States to Ratify Geneva Protocol I*, 88 AMERICAN JOURNAL OF INTERNATIONAL LAW 678, 682–685 (1994) and George H. Aldrich, *Prospects for United States Ratification of Additional Protocol I to the 1949 Geneva Conventions*, 85 AMERICAN JOURNAL OF INTERNATIONAL LAW 1, 4–7 (1991). The responsibility of non-State actors to apply the law are discussed in Hans-Peter Gasser, *Acts of Terror, "Terrorism" and International Humanitarian Law*, 84 INTERNATIONAL REVIEW OF THE RED CROSS 547, 563 (2002). *See also* KEITH SUTER, AN INTERNATIONAL LAW OF GUERRILLA WARFARE: THE GLOBAL POLITICS OF LAW-MAKING 167 (1984) ("Guerrillas, by contrast, would find it much harder if not impossible, to implement these provisions.").

53. Legality of the Threat or Use of Nuclear Weapons, Advisory Opinion, 1996 I.C.J. 226 (July 8).

54. Legal Consequences Of The Construction Of A Wall In The Occupied Palestinian Territory, Advisory Opinion (I.C.J. 41–42 (July 9, 2004), 43 INTERNATIONAL LEGAL MATERIALS 1009, 1038–1039, *available at* http://www.icj-cij.org/icjwww/idocket/imwp/imwpframe.htm ("there are thus three possible situations: some rights may be exclusively matters of international humanitarian law; others may be exclusively matters of human rights law; yet others may be matters of both these branches of international law.").

55. Michael J. Dennis, *Application of Human Rights Treaties Extraterritorially in Times of Armed Conflict and Military Occupation*, 99 AMERICAN JOURNAL OF INTERNATIONAL LAW 119, 141 (2005).

56. *Supra* note 42.

57. *Supra* note 43.

58. *Id.*, art. 1(2).
59. *Id.* (For example, Additional Protocol II does not apply to "situations of internal disturbances and tensions, such as riots, isolated and sporadic acts of violence and other acts of a similar nature.")
60. *See* Waldemar A. Solf, *The Status of Combatants in Non-International Armed Conflicts Under Domestic Law and Transnational Practice*, 33 AMERICAN UNIVERSITY LAW REVIEW 53, 58–59 (1983) and Robert K. Goldman & Brian D. Tittemore, *Unprivileged Combatants and the Hostilities in Afghanistan: Their Status and Rights Under International Humanitarian and Human Rights Law*, The American Society of International Law Task Force on Terrorism 5–6 (Dec. 2002), *at* http://www.asil.org/taskforce/goldman.pdf (last visited Nov. 5, 2005).
61. In Case 11.137, Juan Carlos Abella v. Argentina, 1997 INTER-AMERICAN YEAR BOOK ON HUMAN RIGHTS 602, 681–84, at paras. 152–53, (Commission report) (the line separating an especially violent incident of internal disturbances from the application of international humanitarian law principles "may sometimes be blurred and, thus, not easily determined.").
62. *Id.*
63. Tadic, *supra* note 10, at paras. 96–127.
64. *Id.* at para. 97 ("A State-sovereignty-oriented approach has been gradually supplanted by a human-being-oriented approach. Gradually the maxim of Roman law *hominum causa omne jus constitutum est* (all law is created for the benefit of human beings) has gained a firm foothold in the international community as well. It follows that in the area of armed conflict the distinction between interstate wars and civil wars is losing its value as far as human beings are concerned.").
65. Watkin, *supra* note 1, at 3–4.
66. *See* Rona, *supra* note 1, at 58 and Pfanner, *supra* note 1, at 154–156.
67. Anthony Dworkin, *Revising the Law of War to Account for Terrorism: The Case Against Updating the Geneva Conventions, On the Ground That Changes Are Likely Only to Damage Human Rights*, Findlaw's Writ: Commentary (Feb. 4, 2003), *at* http://writ.news.findlaw.com/commentary/20030204_dworkin.html (last visited Nov. 5, 2005) and Leila Nadya Sadat, *Terrorism and the Rule of Law*, 3 WASHINGTON UNIVERSITY GLOBAL STUDIES LAW REVIEW 135, 136 (2004).
68. *See* Watkin, *supra* note 1, at 5.
69. *Reprinted in* 38 INTERNATIONAL LEGAL MATERIALS 1656 (1999).
70. *Id.* at section 1.
71. *"Law Enforcement" and the CWC*, 58 THE CBW CONVENTIONS BULLETIN, Dec. 2002, at 1.
72. *Supra* note 13.
73. *Supra* note 71, at 1 (quoting a March 1997 issue of the Bulletin).
74. *See* Fidler, *supra* note 29, at 14–15. *See also* Barbara Hatch Rosenberg, *Riot Control Agents and the Chemical Weapons Convention*, FAS Working Group on Biological and Chemical Weapons for the Open Forum on Challenges to the Chemical Weapons Ban 3 (May 1, 2003) *available at* http://www.armscontrolcenter.org/cbw/papers/wg/wg_2003_riot_control_agents.pdf (last visited Nov. 2, 2005).
75. MAX BOOT, THE SAVAGE WARS OF PEACE: SMALL WARS AND THE RISE OF AMERICAN POWER xvi (2002). Boot categorizes the Vietnam Conflict as a "small" war because of the tactics used rather than the scale of the conflict. *See also* United States Marine Corps, SMALL WARS MANUAL (1940), which provides, in part, that:

> Small wars vary in degrees from simple demonstrative operations to military intervention in the fullest sense, short of war. They are not limited in their size, in the extent of their theater of operations nor their cost in property, money, or lives. The essence of a small war is its purpose and the circumstances surrounding its inception

and conduct, the character of either one or all of the opposing forces, and the nature of the operations themselves. . . . The ordinary expedition of the Marine Corps which does not involve a major effort in regular warfare against a 'first-rate power' may be termed a small war.

76. *See* BOOT, *supra* note 75, at *xiv*.
77. *See* C.E. CALDWELL, SMALL WARS: THEIR PRINCIPLES AND PRACTICE 21 (3d ed. 1996) (1906).
78. *Id.* at 42.
79. As is set out in the 1907 Hague Regulations, an occupying power has the responsibility to "take all measures in his power to restore, and ensure, as far as possible, public order and safety, while respecting, unless absolutely prevented, the laws in force in the country." Regulations Respecting the Laws and Customs of War on Land, Hague Convention IV Respecting the Laws and Customs of War on Land (and annexed Regulations), art. 43, Oct. 18, 1907, UKTS 9 (1910), *reprinted in* DOCUMENTS ON THE LAWS OF WAR, *supra* note 11, at 69. See also Geneva Convention IV, *supra* note 42, art. 64, regarding the obligation of an occupying power "to maintain the orderly government of the territory."
80. As is set out in United Nations Security Council Resolution 1386 (2001), the mandate for the International Security Assistance Forces (ISAF) broadly involves providing assistance to Afghan security forces in the maintenance of security:

The establishment for 6 months of an International Security Assistance Force to assist the Afghan Interim Authority in the maintenance of security in Kabul and its surrounding areas, so that the Afghan Interim Authority as well as the personnel of the United Nations can operate in a secure environment.

Such a mandate can entail assisting police forces, training security forces and potentially participating in armed conflict with armed groups such as the Taliban and Al Qaeda threatening the Afghan governing authority.

81. *See* Gerald L. Neuman, *Comment, Counter-terrorist Operations and the Rule of Law*, 15 EUROPEAN JOURNAL OF INTERNATIONAL LAW 1019, 1019–1020 (2004).
82. General Charles C. Krulak, *The Strategic Corporal: Leadership in the Three Block War*, MARINES, Jan. 1999, at 26, *available at* http://www.usmc.mil/marinesmagazine/pdf.nsf/8e8afdade19e000c852565e700807312/ba6c7b077948be1b852566e800538752/$FILE/jan99.pdf (last visited Nov. 5, 2005).
83. A ROLE OF PRIDE AND INFLUENCE IN THE WORLD 11 (Apr. 2005), *available at* http://www.dfait-maeci.gc.ca/cip-pic/IPS/IPS-Overview.pdf.
84. *See* Watkin, *supra* note 1, at 14.
85. *See* Kenneth Watkin, *Warriors Without Rights? Combatants, Unprivileged Belligerents, And The Struggle Over Legitimacy* 2 HPCR OCCASIONAL PAPER SERIES 66 (Winter 2005), *available at* http://www.hpcr.org/pdfs/OccasionalPaper2.pdf ("Both military forces and their traditional law enforcement counterparts may be confronted with threats that range from violence associated with normal criminal activity to military type attacks under circumstances where it could be difficult to distinguish initially the nature or scope of the threat. In each of these situations, internal order may be maintained by a combination of military and police forces engaged primarily, but not exclusively, in law enforcement against 'criminal' activity.").
86. *See* Fidler, *supra* note 29, at 14. *See also* Rosenberg, *supra* note 74, at 3.
87. *See* Fidler, *supra* note 29, at 14 n.7.
88. *See* Global Security.org, Frangible Ammunition, http://www.globalsecurity.org/military/systems/munitions/frangible.htm (last visited Nov. 5, 2005) ("Concerns with over penetration/ricochet hazards aboard aircraft, ships and (e.g.) nuclear power plants that might release

hazardous materials have led to efforts to provide small caliber ammunition with reduced ricochet, limited penetration (RRLP) for use by SOF to reduce risk to friendly forces and innocent persons. There are three general levels of frangible: Training [may be used for training only]; reduced ricochet, limited penetration [RRLP, designed for purposes stated]; and general purpose frangible [though no military requirement has been established for a general purpose round for use by conventional forces]. Specific ammunition must undergo wound ballistics testing/legal review once developed. It can be used for: Close Quarter Battle (CQB); Military Operations in Urban Terrain (MOUT); Visit Board Search and Seizure; and Counter-Narcotics (CN) Operations.").

89. For example, see Guardian Unlimited, Associated Press, Militants Extend Afghanistan Hostages Deadline, http://www.guardian.co.uk/afghanistan/story/0,1284,1340957,00.html and new.amnesty.com, Iraq: Violence Must Stop - Rule Of Law Must Prevail, http://news.amnesty.org/pages/iraq_press ("Amnesty International condemns the use of civilians as bargaining chips in the continuing political instability in Iraq. . . . Armed groups must set free all hostages they are detaining and refrain from kidnapping people or attacking civilians.") (both last visited Aug. 28, 2005).

90. *See* Deputy Secretary of Defense, DoD Law of War Program, Department of Defense Directive 5100.77 4, para. 5.3.1 (Dec. 9, 1998) *available at* http://www.dtic.mil/whs/directives/corres/pdf/d510077_120998/d510077p.pdf (last visited Aug. 28, 2005).

91. *See* Center for Law and Military Operations, Legal Lessons Learned From Afghanistan and Iraq: Vol. I Major Combat Operations (11 September 2001 to 1 May 2003), Appendix A-6, at 297 (Aug. 1, 2004) *available at* https://www.jagcnet.army.mil/JAGCNETIntranet/Databases/Operational+Law/CLAMO.nsf/(JAGCNetDocID)/399A488BDCB4F6BB85256F3C0065B445/$FILE/OEF%20OIF%20Volume%20I.pdf (last visited Nov. 5, 2005) [hereinafter Lessons Learned]. *See also* ANNOTATED SUPPLEMENT, *supra* note 27, at 10-17 n.39 (where it is indicated that the United States Senate Resolution of Ratification for the 1993 Chemical Weapons Convention required that "[t]he President shall take no measure, and prescribe no rule or regulation, which would alter or eliminate Executive Order 11,850 of April 8, 1975.").

92. *See* Lessons Learned, *supra* note 91, at 297–98.

93. *See* Steve Fainaru and Anthony Shadid, *In Iraq Jail, Resistance Goes Underground*, WASHINGTON POST FOREIGN SERVICE, Aug. 24, 2005, at A01. ("The Americans fired back with rubber bullets and tear gas but failed to slow the projectiles cascading from the courtyard.").

94. *See* ANNOTATED SUPPLEMENT, *supra* note 27, at 10-15 to 10-16.

95. *See* ROYAL AUSTRALIAN AIR FORCE, FUNDAMENTALS OF AUSTRALIAN AIRPOWER 76–77 (4th ed. 2002), *available at* http://www.raaf.gov.au/airpower/publications/doctrine/aap1003/highres/Ch_9.pdf (last visited Nov. 5, 2005).

96. CODE OF CONDUCT, *supra* note 44, at 2-4, para. 9.

97. *See* Lessons Learned, *supra* note 91, at 116 n.31.

98. *See* Rosenberg, *supra* note 74, at 3 ("The UK Ministry of Defence recently encapsulated a clear understanding of the CWC regarding the use of RCA, as follows: RCA 'are permitted for dealing with riot control,' but the CWC precludes the use of chemicals, including RCA, in [other] 'military operations or on any battlefield' (G. Hoon, Press Conference, Mar. 27, 2003)."

99. *See* Fidler, *supra* note 29, at 15–16.

100. *Id.* at 15.

101. *Id.*

102. Additional Protocol I, *supra* note 4, art. 50(3).

103. *See* Yoram Dinstein, *The Distinction Between Unlawful Combatants and War Criminals*, *in* INTERNATIONAL LAW AT A TIME OF PERPLEXITY 111 (Yoram Dinstein & Mala Tabory eds., 1989).

104. HUMAN RIGHTS WATCH, VIOLENT RESPONSE: THE U.S. ARMY IN AL-FALLUJA (June 2003), *available at* http://www.hrw.org/reports/2003/iraqfalluja/ (last visited Nov. 5, 2005).
105. *Id.* at 1.
106. *Id.* at 3. See also Fidler, *supra* note 26 at 13–14 (where an interpretation of "law enforcement" is provided that supports some of the circumstances in which the United States has indicated riot control agents could be used: "in rear echelon areas outside the zone of immediate combat to secure convoys from civil disturbances.").
107. Watkin, *supra* note 1, at 32.
108. *See* HENCKAERTS & DOSWALD-BECK, *supra* note 4, at 265
109. Sniper Use of Open-Tip Ammunition, Memorandum for Commander, United States Army Special Operations Command 3, at para. 3 (Oct. 12, 1990) ("In some law of war treatises, the term 'unnecessary suffering' is used rather than 'superfluous injury.' The terms are regarded as synonymous.") (On file with the author).
110. *See* YORAM DINSTEIN, THE CONDUCT OF HOSTILITIES UNDER THE LAW OF INTERNATIONAL ARMED CONFLICT 59 (2004).
111. *Id.*
112. Declaration Renouncing the Use, in time of War, of Explosive Projectiles Under 400 Grammes Weight, Dec. 11, 1868, *reprinted in* DOCUMENTS ON THE LAWS OF WAR, *supra* note 11, at 54–55.
113. *See* HENCKAERTS & DOSWALD-BECK, *supra* note 4, at 269.
114. *Id.*
115. *Id.* at 270.
116. *Id.*
117. See ANNOTATED SUPPLEMENT, *supra* note 27, at 9-3 n.7, where it is noted the US practice is to apply hollow-point ammunition in peacetime counter terrorist and special security missions.
118. Moir, *supra* note 10, at 128.
119. Thomas M. Franck, *Criminals, Combatants, or What? An Examination of the Role of Law in Responding to the Threat of Terror*, 98 AMERICAN JOURNAL INTERNATIONAL LAW 686, 688 (2004).

PART V

COALITION WARFARE

X

Legal Issues in Coalition Warfare: A US Perspective

Charles Dunlap*

With increasing frequency, a growing number of nations find themselves engaged in operations with US forces. I hope to give you some perspective on how the United States views the legal obligations and challenges of operations within coalitions.

A nation's participation as a member of a coalition is more than just a synchronization of military plans and objectives; it is also a synchronization of legal issues. Interpreting and applying the law are rarely easy tasks with coalitions comprised of nations with widely differing political, cultural, and historical influences on their legal systems. The precise legal context is becoming increasingly technical, yet vitally important—and hardly intuitive. Indeed, legal issues and the differing approaches amongst coalition partners make the legal aspects of conflict a strategic issue that must be addressed. As General James L. Jones observes:

> It used to be a simple thing to fight a battle. . . . In a perfect world, a general would get up and say, "Follow me, men," and everybody would say, "Aye, sir" and run off. But that's not the world anymore. . . . [Now] you have to have a lawyer or a dozen. It's become very legalistic and very complex.[1]

---

* Brigadier General, US Air Force. The views and opinions expressed by the author are his alone and do not necessarily reflect those of the US Government or any of its components.

Of course, even when lawyers are there to advise, a variety of legal challenges will still affect coalition operations. Each one will be discussed in more detail, but here are the big issues: interpreting and applying international law in coalition warfare; domestic law and policy limitations on the different coalition partners (including the United States); and how coalition partners provide legal support within the operational area. I will close with a challenge that faces military forces of every democratic nation: the enemy's abuse of law as a tool of asymmetrical warfare.

With all of these issues, often the biggest question is "which law governs?" On one hand, national commanders in the field and leaders back at home ask, "How does my nation's interpretation and application of law affect my ability to conduct operations with coalition partners?" On the other hand, the coalition commander must overcome these same legal issues to effectively employ national forces in coalition operations.

International Law: The Challenge of Applying the Law of Armed Conflict in Coalition Warfare

International law in coalition operations may appear, at first glance, to be a matter of interpreting and applying established rules to the coalition as a whole. Much of international law related to coalition operations is fairly settled, for example, law of the sea and diplomatic relations law. However, difficulties arise as to whether a particular international law is recognized by each nation participating in the coalition and as to widely different interpretations of seemingly fundamental rules. In the end, a nation's domestic law and policy will shape its application of international law.

The law of armed conflict (LOAC) is international law that everyone agrees covers coalition warfare.[2] Yet, the interpretation and application of armed conflict laws differ, sometimes significantly, between coalition partners. Which law governs? To illustrate this thorny question from a US point of view, we'll look at examples from customary international law and international agreements.

Some LOAC is based in customary international law. These are rules that nations have historically followed because of a sense of legal obligation to do so. However, how each nation views them can vary widely. For example, depleted uranium (DU) is a common element used in making armor piercing rounds for a variety of ammunition, including the A-10's 30 mm cannon.[3] The United States views DU as a legal weapon that can be used. However, some other nations consider it unlawful because of the potential dangers of exposure from the resulting debris.[4]

International agreements, or treaties, are arguably more robust international law than customary law because nations agree to be bound by the terms of treaties to which they are parties. The bulk of LOAC has been established and defined by widely accepted international agreements.[5] Treaties that most individuals associate with LOAC are the Geneva Conventions and its Protocols.[6] However, not all coalition partners are parties to the same treaties. For instance, the United States has not ratified Protocol I, yet it still follows the principles as part of customary law.[7] Another example is the Ottawa Convention on anti-personnel mines.[8] The United States is not a party to this while most coalition partners are.

Even if coalition partners are all parties to the same treaties, various domestic implementation laws affect how and when each nation follows the treaties. This can be seen in the different interpretation and application of the Geneva Conventions in the war on terror by long-time allies and coalition partners.

One area that created a legal debate and a flurry of press coverage is the International Criminal Court (ICC).[9] Although the United States was an original signer of the treaty that created the ICC, it was never ratified by the Senate. Thus, the United States is not a party to the treaty. Among other things, the US government has concerns about politicized prosecutions by individuals or entities who seek to use the process not to redress legitimately made allegations, but merely to disrupt US operations. In fact, the United States routinely asks other nations to sign "Article 98" agreements[10] which would operate to protect US service members from being sent to the ICC for trial. This has not stopped other individuals from filing suit in other nations' courts alleging that US leaders were committing war crimes.[11] In any event, as a matter of policy the United States prefers to handle allegations of misconduct in American courts, and seeks to avoid subjecting its military personnel to the jurisdiction of foreign courts.

Even when nations agree on the law, the application to individual cases can vary widely. For example, radio and television stations are seen by the United States as potential military targets. During the Kosovo operations, US aircraft participating in a NATO operation bombed a Serb radio and television facility. Many considered this an unlawful attack on a civilian target, despite the military use of the airwaves.[12] This also very nearly became an issue during Operation Iraqi Freedom (OIF) when the United States, as part of coalition operations, considered attacking Iraqi television and radio stations. In this case, the Iraqis themselves made it clear that these were valid military targets under LOAC. Even though the television is traditionally thought of as a civilian medium, the Iraqis used it to rally troops and provide military direction. The news reports were even read by individuals wearing uniforms of the Iraqi army. Nevertheless, this is an area where there will be controversy in future conflicts. Coalition commanders will have to address this on a case-by-case basis.

Domestic Law, Policy, and Regulation: Limits on National Commanders

As we have seen, international law affecting coalition warfare is viewed through the lenses of nations taking part in a coalition. Domestic law further shapes, and often limits, nations' ability to work as coalition partners. National commanders and their forces must comply with their domestic laws, policies, and regulations, further complicating the legal aspects of coalition operations.

US domestic law, policies, and regulations have the potential to significantly impact US forces' conduct in coalitions. For US forces, domestic law is another aspect of LOAC. Our policy is to apply LOAC principles to any conflict, no matter how characterized.[13] Going even further, US forces normally operate within rules of engagement (ROE) for a particular operation. Using LOAC as a foundation, civilian and military leadership develops ROE based on domestic law and policy considerations, in addition to LOAC. Common ROE for coalition forces is highly desirable. However, even ROE for coalition forces can be different as a result of each partner's own domestic laws and policy. The United States works with coalition partners to develop and abide by common ROE in coalition operations; however, US forces always retain the right to "use necessary and proportional force for unit and individual self-defense."[14]

As with other aspects of law, ROE are not immune from differing interpretations. US ROE typically permit units and individuals to use force in self-defense in situations where someone or some group displays hostile intent and capability. This is the "threat of imminent use of force against . . . US forces" or the use of the threat of force to "impede the mission and/or duties of US forces."[15] Each coalition partner defines hostile intent differently and may even limit the ability of their forces to engage in self-defense in these types of situations. This becomes an even more interesting determination when dealing with air operations. What represents "hostile intent" to an aircraft?

Domestic law can create challenges for US commanders in areas other than LOAC. Commanders must abide by those international agreements to which the United States is a party, which may limit their authority. Furthermore, under US law American commanders usually cannot provide logistic support to coalition partners without some type of government-to-government agreement covering the exchange of goods and services—and often having a reimbursement requirement.[16]

Command and control issues are also very important. The US Constitution and domestic law place limits on the ability of US forces to serve under foreign command. Typically, operational control or tactical control is not a problem as long as there is ultimately a US commander who exercises actual command.

Discipline is at the core of every successful military operation, including coalition operations. Historically, each coalition partner is responsible for disciplining its troops in accordance with domestic military and criminal law. This authority does not rest with the coalition commander, but with the national commanders of the coalition partners. However, every coalition commander has a strong interest in unit welfare and discipline, and should make sure that discipline is carried out to avoid adverse operational effects. As General Sanchez learned during the Abu Ghraib abuse scandal, a failure of discipline can be just as bad as a defeat on the battlefield.[17]

Applying domestic law to disciplinary matters creates challenges for all coalition commanders, especially with respect to situations that arise during specific operations. Since Operation Desert Shield in 1990, US forces deployed for a contingency operation generally operate with some form of "General Order #1" applicable to all components of the American contingent.[18] Such orders are typically issued at the beginning of an operation and may limit the actions of troops for policy reasons. They limit, for example, the ability of troops to consume alcohol in certain locations. While US troops often are prohibited from drinking alcohol, other troops may be free to do so. A US soldier is likely to be punished for drinking, while her British friend might not. It is just another area where coalition partners may differ and may present complications for US commanders.

The US illustrations, above, highlight some of the international and domestic law challenges faced by coalition commanders and their legal teams when tackling the question of "which law governs?" We now move to the individuals who can assist commanders to effectively accomplish the coalition mission within the compass of the law.

Legal Support to Commanders: The Role of Lawyers in the Coalition

The types of legal support commanders receive vary greatly between the coalition members. Although General Jones would not go to war without a dozen or so lawyers, many coalition partners do not have judge advocates (JAG)[19] or do not train them on the various aspects of operational law. In many cases, their legal advisors are not even deployed forward with the troops they service. For operations law, many coalition partners have to rely on civilian attorneys back in their nation's capital for advice on complex and ever-changing operational issues. However, when coalition JAGs do deploy together, great things can happen.

Bright Star 99/00—a biannual exercise held in Egypt[20]—was a perfect example of coalition JAGs working together. The 1999/2000 exercise brought together military lawyers from the United States and Britain into a coalition warfare setting. The coalition JAGs bring their knowledge of their nations' domestic law and policy to the table and help educate other JAGs on why they cannot engage in certain operations or use certain weapons. This is a reason we like to see robust, international JAG participation in coalition operations.

In the United States, and for coalition partners as well, JAGs must have more and more knowledge about areas beside the law. JAGs need to know the weapon systems that are being used, how they are being used, and the overall strategy for a particular operation. They also need to understand the complex and intricate command and control environment in which they operate.

How do US JAGs cope with the issues they face in operations, especially serving in Coalition Air Operations Centers (CAOC)? All JAGs that deploy to CAOC positions are required to attend a six-week-long training program on the computer systems and methodologies used to run a CAOC. This is not a JAG-specific course, but one attended by all specialties who serve in the CAOC. It enables them to learn how things are done and what attributes each career field brings to the fight.

In contrast to the increased training and resources available for US JAGs, many coalition partners do not have the access to high-tech systems found in the CAOC to enable them to provide effective oversight to operations. Nor do all coalition lawyers receive training in the complex and fast-paced conduct of modern warfare. Unfortunately, this may be leading to a tech and training gap between US JAGs and our coalition partners that will need to be addressed.

What about friendly fire cases? As the United States saw with the Tarnak Farms "friendly fire" case, this can cause both political and operational problems. Tarnak Farms was an incident in Afghanistan where US aircraft mistakenly bombed Canadian ground forces. Canadian and US military lawyers were deeply involved in investigating and advising commanders after this unfortunate incident. Legal issues ranged from LOAC to discipline to release of information. These are difficult questions that still need more thoughtful study.

Another challenge facing the United States is how to respond to allegations of LOAC violations. Unfortunately, in conflicts innocent civilians will be harmed. The United States must maintain a transparent approach to its targeting especially in the media-intense world. US targeting philosophies and the lengths we go to in order to avoid unnecessary casualties need to be highlighted and available to the media. When incidents occur, reports should be made available for the media and the general public so nothing is hidden. In addition to being an integral part of the targeting process, JAGs must be prepared to advise commanders and military spokespersons on alleged LOAC violations.

What roles to JAGs play in modern conflict? Michael Sirak in *Jane's Defence Weekly* suggests that JAGs are the ones who determine what weapons are built, the bombs, and their targets.[21] The reality for US forces is that JAGs are *advisors—commanders* make the decisions about weapons and targets.[22] Effective legal support to coalition forces is critical in this age of complex legal challenges, but lawyers should not and cannot displace commanders as decision-makers.

Lawfare: An Asymmetrical Threat to Coalitions

Besides being a foundation for how we operate, the law is being used as a weapon by our adversaries. As Rivken and Casey said in 2001, "international law may become one of the most potent weapons ever deployed against the United States."[23] Our enemies, as William Eckhardt said, are now attacking our military plans as being illegal and immoral. Our laws have become a new Clausewitzean "center of gravity."[24]

This is a new form of asymmetrical warfare I call "lawfare."[25] As more and more adversaries learn they cannot go up against our coalition forces on the battlefield, they have moved to attack us through the law to achieve their operational objectives. However, not all lawfare is "bad" and the United States applies it when necessary, like controlling the cameras on commercial satellites with coverage areas over Operation Iraqi Freedom/Operation Enduring Freedom bases. Such control is achieved through the use of law, not the use of force. Lawfare, as I use this term, is an operational methodology that can be used for "good" or "bad" purposes.

Our adversaries often employ an abusive form of lawfare aimed at undermining the kind of public support democracies need to conduct military operations. It very much has a Clausewitzean basis. When we talk about Clausewitz, we are talking about the "remarkable trinity" that coalesces to create warfighting potential: the government, the people, and the military. America's typical approach to conflict is to focus its energy and effort against the military capability of the enemy. Using lawfare, adversaries are not trying to defeat the United States militarily; they seek to separate the people from the trinity and erode their will for the conflict. How do they erode the will of the people?

One way is to use actual or perceived LOAC violations. By repeatedly characterizing military actions as illegal and immoral, for example declaring LOAC violations, the enemy's objective is to cause the people to grow weary of war and begin to question the military and government's conduct. Increasingly, organizations and forums are facilitating these messages so the enemy has a variety of ways to spread the word. As technology continues to develop in the 21st century, so too do new means of spreading information. Our adversaries have been quick to utilize the Internet and the power of the globalized media to spread their message.

Another strategy that we have seen is actually goading coalition forces into committing LOAC incidents that would have strategic impact on our operations. For example, bin Laden has attempted to exploit the fact that women and children were victims of collateral damage in an effort to ensnare the United States into a larger East-West conflict, further inflaming Muslim opinion against the United States and other friendly nations, including those in the Persian Gulf.[26] Our enemies know that the secret to any democratic society is to get their message to the people and the people will respond.

We have also seen Iraqi forces that feigned surrender and then turned to attack.[27] These incidents occurred frequently, causing coalition and civilian casualties. The enemy's perfidy created an environment in which US troops have been known to shoot first and ask questions later when they encounter surrendering individuals. However, the television-viewing public sees only the US conduct. The more we see incidents like this, the more people believe the war is being wrongly fought. Professors W. Michael Reisman and Chris T. Antoniou explain:

> In modern popular democracies, even a limited armed conflict requires a substantial base of public support. That support can erode or even reverse itself rapidly, no matter how worthy the political objective, if people *believe* that the war is being conducted in an unfair, inhumane, or iniquitous way. [28]

However, this does not mean that democracies are at a disadvantage in future wars. In fact, history proves that those nations that comply with the accepted norms of behavior in warfare are more successful than those nations that wage war against civilians.

Coalitions must develop strategies to counter lawfare; just as they must be prepared to fight any asymmetrical attack. Foremost, every coalition partner must be committed to complying with the law. Participating nations should strive to harmonize their interpretation and application of LOAC, despite the legal and political challenges of doing so. Many of these issues are for the civilian leadership to tackle. Yet, commanders, with their lawyers, can emphasize common ground among coalition forces and be ready to respond to lawfare through transparency and prompt public response.

Coalition Warfare: A Synchronization of Legal Issues

Nations with a stunningly broad range of operational capabilities and legal systems have joined the United States in a number of military operations. Integrating these diverse forces into an effective coalition requires more than coordination of military plans, objectives, and logistics. It requires orchestration of each nation's interpretation and application of law.

I have tried to present a US perspective on some of the legal challenges faced by modern coalitions. Far from being secondary, domestic law and policy are at the heart of different legal perspectives, from LOAC to the legal services provided by a nation to its commanders. The United States views its legal obligations and challenges through this lens, which neither discounts nor minimizes the importance of international law. In addition to confronting legal issues between coalition partners, the coalition must be prepared to counter the enemy's lawfare. In the highly complex environment of coalition warfare, synchronization of legal issues is critical to operational success.

Notes

1. Lyric Wallwork Winik, *A Marine's Toughest Mission (Gen. James L. Jones)*, PARADE MAGAZINE, Jan. 19, 2003. General Jones is the Supreme Allied Commander, Europe.
2. Compliance with the Law of Armed Conflict, Air Force Policy Directive 51-4 (Apr. 26, 1993). Paragraph 6.4, defines LOAC as "All international law which concerns the conduct of hostilities during armed conflict and is binding on the United States or US citizens. It includes international treaties and agreements to which the United States is a party as well as customary international law. These treaties include the 1949 Geneva Conventions and the 1907 Hague Conventions and Regulations, among others."
3. For information about the A-10 aircraft, see http://www.af.mil/factsheets/factsheet.asp?fsID=70.
4. *See generally*, Depleted Uranium Education Project, http://www.iacenter.org/depleted/du.htm (last visited July 14, 2006); *contra, see* Jim Garamone, *Study Finds Little Risk From Depleted-Uranium Particles*, Armed Forces Information Service, Oct. 19, 2004, *available at* http://www.defenselink.mil/news/Oct2004/n10192004_2004101903.html (last visited July 14, 2006).
5. At least 15 significant LOAC treaties have come into force since 1948. *See* DOCUMENTS ON THE LAWS OF WAR (Adam Roberts & Richard Guelff eds., 3d ed. 2000).
6. The four Geneva Conventions of August 12, 1949, are the Geneva Convention for the Amelioration of the Condition of the Wounded and Sick in Armed Forces in the Field (Geneva Convention I), 75 U.N.T.S. 31; Geneva Convention for the Amelioration of the Condition of Wounded, Sick and Shipwrecked Members of Armed Forces at Sea (Geneva Convention II), 75 U.N.T.S. 85; Geneva Convention Relative to the Treatment of Prisoners of War (Geneva Convention III), 75 U.N.T.S. 135; and Geneva Convention Relative to the Protection of Civilian Persons in Time of War (Geneva Convention IV), 75 U.N.T.S. 287. All *reprinted in* DOCUMENTS ON THE LAWS OF WAR, *supra* note 5, at 197, 222, 244 and 301, respectively. The two Protocols Additional to the Geneva Conventions of 1949 are the 1977 Additional Protocol to the Geneva Conventions of 1949, and Relating to the Protection of Victims of International Armed Conflicts (Additional Protocol I), June 8, 1977, 1125 U.N.T.S. 3, *reprinted in id.* at 422; and the 1977 Additional Protocol to the Geneva Conventions of 1949, and Relating to the Protection of Victims of Non-International Armed Conflicts (Additional Protocol II), June 8, 1977, 1125 U.N.T.S. 609, *reprinted in id.* at 483.

7. The United States is not a party to the Additional Protocols; however, to the extent that certain provisions of the Protocols reflect customary international law or existing law under the Geneva Conventions of 1949, the United States adheres to those provisions. For a discussion on the US views concerning the Additional Protocols, see Michael J. Matheson, *The United States Position on the Relation of Customary International Law to the 1977 Protocols Additional to the 1949 Geneva Conventions*, 2 AMERICAN UNIVERSITY JOURNAL OF INTERNATIONAL LAW & POLICY 419 (1987).

8. The technical title of the Ottawa Convention is the Convention on the Prohibition of the Use, Stockpiling, Production and Transfer of Anti-personnel Mines and on their Destruction, Sept. 18, 1997, 36 INTERNATIONAL LEGAL MATERIALS 1507, *reprinted in* DOCUMENTS ON THE LAWS OF WAR, *supra* note 5, at 648, *available at* http://www.icrc.org/ihl (last visited Mar. 1, 2006).

9. For information about the ICC, see http://www.icc-cpi.int/about.html (last visited Mar. 1, 2006).

10. For information about Article 98, see http://www.state.gov/t/pm/art98/ (last visited July 14, 2006).

11. *See e.g., Rumsfeld Sued for War Crimes in Germany*, DEUTSCHE WELLE, Nov. 30, 2004, *available at* http://www.globalresearch.ca/index.php?context=viewArticle&code=20041130&articleId=269 (last visited Mar. 1, 2006).

12. Human Rights Watch, Civilian Deaths in the NATO Air Campaign (Feb. 2000), *available at* http://www.hrw.org/reports/2000/nato/index.htm#TopOfPage (last visited Jul. 5, 2006).

13. Office of the General Counsel, Department of Defense, DoD Law of War Program, DoD Directive 5100.77 (Dec. 9, 1998). Paragraph 4.1 states "The law of war obligations of the United States are observed and enforced by the DoD Components."

14. Chairman of the Joint Chiefs of Staff Instruction 3121.01A, Standing Rules of Engagement for U.S. Forces, Encl. A, para. 1.c(1) at A-1 (Jan. 15, 2000), *available at* http://www.fas.org/man/dod-101/dod/docs/cjcs_sroe.pdf (last visited July 14, 2006).

15. *Id.*, para. 5.h, at A-5.

16. For a brief discussion of sale, disposal, and transfer of defense articles and services, see US Air Force Judge Advocate General's Department, Air Force Operations & the Law: A Guide for Air & Space Forces, Ch. 48 (2002), *available at* http://www.au.af.mil/au/cpd/jagschool/press/iodb/index.htm (last visited July 14, 2006).

17. Tom Brokaw, National Broadcasting Corporation Nightly News, June 30, 2004, *available at* http://www.msnbc.msn.com/id/5333895 (last visited March 3, 2006).

18. For an example of a General Order #1, see US Central Command, General Order Number 1A, Prohibited Activities for U.S. Department of Defense Personnel Present Within the United States Central Command (USCENTCOM) AOR, December 19, 2000, *available at* http://www.mnf-iraq.com/archive/regulations/go1a.pdf (last visited July 14, 2006).

19. In US usage, the term "judge advocate" refers to a legal advisor on the staff of a military commander. The United States designates the senior uniformed lawyer of each military Service as "Judge Advocate General," thus the common use of "JAG" to identify military lawyers. *See* BLACK'S LAW DICTIONARY 976 (4th ed. 1968).

20. *See* US Department of Defense, Memorandum for Correspondents, No. 143-M, Sept. 14, 1999, *available at* http://www.defenselink.mil/news/Sep1999/m09141999_m143-99.html (last visited July 14, 2006).

21. Michael Sirak, Fighting by the Rules: Debating the Laws of War on the Unconventional Battlefield, JANE'S DEFENCE WEEKLY, Jan. 14, 2004.

22. This has been codified in Chairman of the Joint Chiefs of Staff Instruction 5810.1B, Implementation of the DOD Law of War Program (Mar. 22, 2002), *available at* http://www.dtic.mil/cjcs_directives/cdata/unlimit/5810_01.pdf, which mandates that JAGs provide advice to commanders at all operational levels.
23. David Rivkin & Lee Casey, *The Rocky Shoals of International Law*, THE NATIONAL INTEREST, Winter 2000/2001, at 35, extract *available at* http://ontology.buffalo.edu/smith//courses01/rrtw/Rivkin.htm (last visited July 14, 2006).
24. William G. Eckhardt, *Lawyering for Uncle Sam When He Draws His Sword*, 4 CHICAGO JOURNAL OF INTERNATIONAL LAW 431 (2003).
25. *See* Charles J. Dunlap, Jr., *Law and Military Interventions*, Working Papers, Carr Center for Human Rights Policy, Harvard University, Nov. 29, 2001 *available at* http://www.ksg.harvard.edu/cchrp/Web%20Working%20Papers/Use%20of%20Force/Dunlap2001.pdf (last visited July 14, 2006).
26. Lisa Beyer, *Osama's Endgame; His aims are clear—to expel the U.S. from the Islamic world and unite Muslims in one empire*, TIME, Oct. 15, 2001, at 17.
27. Ron Harris, *Surprise attacks by Iraqis who "surrendered" turn military's mood mean*, ST. LOUIS POST-DISPATCH (Missouri), Mar. 25, 2003, at A1.
28. W. MICHAEL REISMAN & CHRIS T. ANTONIOU, THE LAWS OF WAR xxiv (1994) (emphasis added).

XI

"England Does Not Love Coalitions" Does Anything Change?

Charles Garraway*

My title comes from a quote from Benjamin Disraeli, speaking in the House of Commons on December 16, 1852.[1] In 1852, Victoria was on the throne of England and Abbott Lawrence was the United States Ambassador to the Court of St. James. Lawrence was born at Groton, Massachusetts, not too far from the Naval War College, and is the founder of Lawrence, Massachusetts and of the Lawrence Scientific School at Harvard. The British Empire was at its height in 1852 and on it the sun never set. Livingstone was setting out on his journeys into the African hinterland. This was two years before the start of the Crimean War; British forces were fighting in Burma; the Punjab had just been annexed and gold had been discovered in a remote prison colony called Australia. Disraeli was not yet Prime Minister—that was yet to come. He was Chancellor of the Exchequer—Treasury Secretary in US terms.

But what did Disraeli mean by "coalition"? I have not been able to find an 1852 English dictionary and I therefore take my definition from my old copy of the *Concise Oxford Dictionary* (which still bears my school particulars in the front cover!). This reads: "Coalition, n. Union, fusion; (Pol.) temporary combination for special ends between parties that retain distinctive principles."[2]

* Visiting Professor at King's College, London and an Associate Fellow of Chatham House.

Why, therefore, did England not love coalitions? I would suggest that the problem is similar to that facing the United States today. Britain at that time did not need coalitions—except, as it soon found out in the Crimea, in Europe. In the rest of the world, it was supreme and could act as it liked. A coalition, by my definition, is a "temporary combination for special ends between parties that retain distinctive principles." The problem is not so much in the "temporary combination" as in the "distinctive principles." For a coalition to work, those "distinctive principles" must be at least similar. If there is no "coalescing" there, there can be no "coalition." In Europe, coalitions came and went as principles coalesced in certain fields and then parted again. The Crimean War itself was a classic example where British and French interests in stopping Russian expansion led to a temporary coalition between countries that less than half a century before had been locked in bloody conflict.

Modern history is full of talk of coalitions. The most relevant here is that of the "United Nations"—not the modern entity, but the group of countries that came together in the 1940s to stand up to tyranny and fascism. That metamorphosed into the North Atlantic Treaty Organization (NATO) alliance where the need to hold the Communist bear in check outweighed the "distinctive principles" of the different countries involved. The collapse of the Soviet Union and the end of the Cold War has led to the balance shifting and more emphasis now being on the "distinctive principles" rather than the common purpose. It is the new World Superpower that now states that it has no love for coalitions. Joseph Fitchett of the International Herald Tribune writing in 2002 in European Affairs, talks of "[t]he dismissive attitudes that have recently seemed to prevail in Washington toward NATO, ranging from benign neglect during the Afghan campaign to forthright dislike for coalition warfare in the comments of some Pentagon officials."[3]

Yet, as the British found less than two years after Disraeli's dismissive comment, coalitions are a necessary evil when the interests of the differing parties combine sufficiently to outweigh the differences in the principles. But does that mean that the differences are removed or set aside? No. The distinctiveness of each coalition partner remains and ways are found of working around the differences without prejudicing the position of any of the partners. That is difficult and requires compromise on all sides. It is that need for compromise that superpowers—whether Great Britain in the mid-19th century or the United States in the 21st century—find so difficult.

What I would like to examine is the way that we have reached the current state of affairs and then look at two specific areas of apparent disagreement between the United States and some of its major Allies. I will also try to see whether these "distinctive principles" are in fact distinctive and, if so, whether they can be worked around. Those two specific areas are the impact of Additional Protocol I[4] and of human rights law.

Ambassador James B. Cunningham, United States Deputy Permanent Representative to the United Nations, speaking in the Security Council on September 24, 2003 on Justice and the Rule of Law in International Affairs, stated:

> The United States of America is a nation founded, not upon ethnicity or cultural custom or territory, but upon law enshrined in our Constitution. As a consequence, establishing and maintaining the rule of law has been an enduring theme of American foreign policy for over two centuries. Notably, the U.S. Constitution specifically provides that treaties shall be the supreme law of the land. We therefore do not enter into treaties lightly because we believe the importance of the rule of law to a successful system of peace cannot be overstated. Democracy, justice, economic prosperity, human rights, combating terrorism, and lasting peace all depend on the rule of law. The rule of law is essential to fulfill the ideas behind the UN Charter we are all pledged to support.[5]

I make this point right at the start because it is often overlooked. The United States is a country founded on and believing in the rule of law. The very fact that debate today in political circles often centers on that phrase is an illustration of how fundamental it is to the American psyche. The United States does not only recognize the validity of the rule of law in the domestic sphere but also in the international sphere as Ambassador Cunningham makes plain. It is therefore of vital importance to those who work with and alongside the United States to understand where, in the opinion of the United States, that law exists and what it is. However, what is good for the goose is also good for the gander and it is just as vital that the United States understands the laws that govern the activities of their Allies. It would not be appropriate for the United States to demand that their Allies act outside the law that binds them, even if that law is not binding on the United States. Such a demand would make a mockery of the rule of law as a concept.

This was recognized by the United States in the early 1990s, and in particular in Operation Desert Storm. Although Additional Protocol I did not apply as a matter of treaty law because Iraq was not a party (nor at the time were the United States, the United Kingdom or France), it was recognized by the United States that many of the provisions of that Protocol were seen as binding law by some of the Coalition forces. Indeed, the Final Report to Congress on the Conduct of the Persian Gulf War of April 1992, in Appendix O, The Role of the Law of War, discusses Additional Protocol I at some length, confirming that parts are "generally regarded as a codification of the customary practice of nations, and therefore binding on all."[6] However, the Report also confirms the US view that parts of the Protocol are not such a codification and seeks to identify specific "deficiencies" therein.[7]

There are frequent approving references to specific articles of Additional Protocol I throughout Annex O and, under "Observations," the remark is made that

"Adherence to the law of war impeded neither Coalition planning nor execution; Iraqi violations of the law provided Iraq no advantage."[8]

This very practical approach mirrored that taken by President Reagan in his Letter of Transmittal of Additional Protocol II (Non-International Armed Conflict) to the Senate on January 29, 1987,[9] when he announced that he would not seek Senate advice and consent to Additional Protocol I, describing it as "fundamentally and irreconcilably flawed."[10] However, he referred to the Protocol as containing "certain sound elements" and to "the positive provisions of Protocol I that could be of real humanitarian benefit if generally observed by parties to international armed conflicts." He went on to state:

> We are therefore in the process of consulting with our allies to develop appropriate methods for incorporating these positive provisions into the rules that govern our military operations, and as customary international law. I will advise the Senate of the results of this initiative as soon as it is possible to do so.[11]

In fact, that initiative had been under way since the adoption of the Protocols, with a NATO working group looking at possible agreed reservations which would enable the Alliance to adopt a united front. Unfortunately, that process seemed to go on for too long for some European States, who broke ranks and ratified Protocol I while negotiations were still continuing, adopting some—but not all—of the NATO working group reservations. For example, and I am not seeking to isolate any particular State, Belgium, who ratified in 1986, prior to the Reagan transmittal, made "interpretative declarations" on Article 44 and Article 1(4), the two areas of particular concern identified by the United States. While the former was in accordance with the NATO formula, that on Article 1(4) was in less stringent terms.[12] The statements made by the United Kingdom on its ratification in 1998 probably bear the closest resemblance to the almost-agreed NATO position.[13]

Unfortunately, the failure of the NATO initiative seemed to bring an end to negotiation on a formal level though there was continuous contact among military lawyers, particularly those tasked with the drafting of military manuals. There were a series of meetings in various countries at which such issues were discussed and attempts were made to strike a common balance. In addition, Michael Matheson, then the Deputy Legal Adviser at the US Department of State, in a presentation made in 1987 at the Washington College of Law,[14] provided a comparatively detailed analysis of Protocol I indicating those areas which the United States found acceptable and those that it did not.

Although, as we have seen, Additional Protocol I was considered and tested during Desert Storm, the tide in the United States was already beginning to turn against the treaty. There had always been a strong element within the United States that opposed any compromise, illustrated by Douglas Feith's writing in 1985.[15] On the other hand, the military, who actually had to work in the field, were seeking to adopt the Reagan approach and to develop "appropriate methods for incorporating these positive provisions into the rules that govern our military operations." The problem that the military faced was in identifying those "positive provisions" in the absence of any clear government position. The military inevitably turned to the only guidance that they could find, namely the Matheson article, and this found its way into military manuals of all the Services. There are frequent references to parts of Additional Protocol I, such as in the *Annotated Supplement to The Commander's Handbook on the Law of Naval Operations* (NWP 1-14M),[16] usually citing Matheson as the authority. For example, in referring to Article 54(1) of Additional Protocol I creating a new prohibition on the starvation of civilians as a method of warfare, NWP 1-14M states that this is a prohibition that "the United States believes should be observed and in due course recognized as customary law," citing Matheson.[17] The *Operational Law Handbook* of the Army Judge Advocate General's Corps[18] went further, publishing in detail a list of the articles which "the U.S. views . . . as either legally binding as customary international law or acceptable practice though not legally binding."[19] This type of detail appeared in the *Handbook* from 2000 to 2003 but was omitted in 2004. It reappeared in 2005,[20] only to be overtaken by an Errata note stating that the entry should be "disregarded." This note went on to state that "Information was taken from an Article written by Michael Matheson in 1986. It takes an overly broad view of the U.S. position and as a result may cause some confusion as to U.S. Policy."[21] This followed an article by Hays Parks in 2003 in which in a footnote he had stated that Michael Matheson had expressed "his personal opinion that 'certain provisions of Protocol I reflect customary international law or are positive new developments which should... become part of that law'."[22] In fact, the full text of that paragraph of Matheson's article reads:

> The executive branch is well aware of the need to make decisions and to take action on these issues. We know from our conversations with our allies that there is a shared perception, particularly among North Atlantic Treaty Organization (NATO) countries, of a strong military need for common rules to govern allied operations and a political need for common principles to demonstrate our mutual commitment to humanitarian values. We recognize that certain provisions of Protocol I reflect customary international law or are positive new developments which should in time become part of that law.[23]

This should be read together with his opening statement that: "I appreciate the opportunity to offer this distinguished group a presentation on the United States position concerning the relationship of customary international law to the 1977

Protocols Additional to the 1949 Geneva Conventions."[24] It is hard to see this as reflecting a personal statement. The Royal "we" went out in American English at the time of George III!

So where are we now? It appears that the Matheson analysis is no longer considered "authoritative." It is interesting in reading the so-called "Torture Memos,"[25] to find the almost complete lack of reference to Additional Protocol I. It is as if it has been wiped out of the memory bank. It is no longer even clear whether the United States accepts such key provisions as Article 75 on Fundamental Guarantees, of which Matheson had said: "We support in particular the fundamental guarantees contained in article 75. . . ."[26]

This lack of legal clarity causes acute problems for Allies seeking to work alongside the United States. Quite apart from the issues arising from targeting decisions—what is the US definition of a military objective?—serious issues arise over detainee handling. If the United States is not prepared even to accept the fundamental guarantees of Article 75, it is hard to see how allies can hand over detainees to the custody of the United States. This is before one takes into account the presidential decision that Common Article 3 to the Geneva Conventions does not apply outside non-international armed conflict.[27] While this may be correct as a matter of treaty law, it is now generally accepted that, in the words of the International Court of Justice, "there is no doubt that, in the event of international armed conflicts, these rules [Common Article 3] also constitute a minimum yardstick. . . ."[28]

My point here is not to criticize the United States decision not to ratify Additional Protocol I. That is an acceptable position. However, the existence of the Protocol cannot be ignored, nor the fact that the majority of the United States' traditional allies are parties to it, including the United Kingdom, Japan and Australia.[29] You will note that I have omitted other parts of "Old Europe" such as France and Germany[30] though in fact almost all the NATO States are indeed parties.[31] We need to know what the United States position is and uncertainty simply undermines the trust that is vital for coalition operations. I appreciate that the role of customary international law—and even its very existence—is sometimes questioned within the US government.[32] However, it should still be possible for the Administration to publish in an authoritative form its stance on the provisions of Additional Protocol I which at least will allow a baseline from which others can work. It is to be hoped that the planned law of war manual under preparation in the Office of General Counsel of the US Department of Defense will in fact do exactly that and for that reason, if for no other, I would urge its early completion. As Michael Matheson noted, "The United States [must] give some alternative clear indication of which rules they consider binding or otherwise propose to observe."[33] Indeed he went on to put it even more clearly: "It is important for both the United States government and the United States scholarly community to devote attention to determining which elements in Protocol I deserve recognition as customary international law, either now or in the future."[34] That was true in 1987 and remains true today. If Matheson saw his effort as "work in progress," it needs to be completed.

My second point is the increasing role of human rights law. Again there is a growing divide between the United States and, in particular, Europe—and not just "Old Europe." The European Convention for the Protection of Human Rights[35] has probably the most effective enforcement mechanism of any human rights organization in the world. The European Court of Human Rights passes binding judgments and presents a progressive interpretation of human rights law. Whether one agrees with that approach or not, it is a fact.

The Convention requires parties to "secure to everyone within their jurisdiction the rights and freedoms" contained in the Convention.[36] Jurisdiction has been interpreted widely and it has been ruled that although the application of the Convention is primarily territorial, extraterritorial jurisdiction is not ruled out, *inter alia,* "when the respondent State, through the effective control of the relevant territory and its inhabitants abroad as a consequence of military occupation or through the consent, invitation or acquiescence of the Government of that territory, exercises all or some of the public powers normally to be exercised by that Government."[37] The United Kingdom courts have interpreted that as allowing the application of the Convention to some activities in Iraq.[38]

There is a difference here from the wording of the International Covenant on Civil and Political Rights which requires States to grant rights to "all individuals within its territory and subject to its jurisdiction."[39] This clearly seems to lay down a two-part test which is lacking in the text of the European Convention where jurisdiction alone is the standard. However, this has been interpreted as "those within its territory and those otherwise subject to its jurisdiction."[40] This interpretation was confirmed by the United Nations Human Rights Committee in General Comment 31, adopted March 29, 2004, when it stated, "A State Party must respect and ensure the rights laid down in the Covenant to anyone within the power or effective control of that State Party, even if not situated within the territory of the State Party."[41]

The United States position, however, appears to be to adopt the literal reading of the text and to limit the application of the Covenant to United States territory. This position is confirmed by the Working Group Report on Detainee Interrogations in the Global War on Terrorism which stated, "The United States has maintained consistently that the Covenant does not apply outside the United States or its special maritime and territorial jurisdiction, and that it does not apply to operations of the military during an international armed conflict."[42]

It is interesting to note that the American Convention on Human Rights, signed but not ratified by the United States, in Article 1, also refers to the obligation to ensure rights "to all persons subject to their jurisdiction," thus equating to the language of the European Convention.[43]

Thus the first divergence of opinion is to the territorial applicability of human rights law. The United States considers that it is not bound in law to grant rights to persons within its jurisdiction if they do not meet the territoriality test. The Europeans—and many others—consider that, while territoriality is a key factor, it is not the sole governing factor and that they are therefore obliged as a matter of law to extend certain rights outside their own territory.

But the quote from the Working Party also reveals another divergence. The United States view appears to be that in time of international armed conflict, human rights law is inapplicable and is replaced by the law of armed conflict. This was indeed an accepted view among many in the past and seemed to reflect the classic divide between the law of peace and the law of war. But in the same way that the boundary between peace and war itself has become blurred, so an analysis of the treaties themselves no longer supports the purist view. Article 4 of the International Covenant deals with derogations and provides for such "in time of public emergency which threatens the life of the nation and the existence of which is officially proclaimed." Even then, there are certain rights that are non-derogable.

The European Convention is even more specific referring in Article 15 to "in time of war or other public emergency threatening the life of the nation." In Article 15(2), it specifically states: "No derogation from Article 2 [the right to life], except in respect of deaths resulting from lawful acts of war . . . shall be made under this provision." It is clearly not open to the European States to argue that the Convention does not apply in time of war as it specifically caters for that eventuality. It is therefore necessary for them to examine how the two bodies of law mesh together in time of conflict.

For purposes of completeness, the American Convention refers, in its derogation clause, to "war, public danger, or other emergency that threatens the independence or security of a State Party."[44]

The International Court of Justice has addressed this issue in a number of cases including the *Nuclear Weapons* case[45] and, most recently, the "*Barrier*" case involving the so-called "Wall in the Occupied Palestinian Territory."[46]

In the *Nuclear Weapons* case, the Court observed:

> [T]hat the protection of the International Covenant of Civil and Political Rights does not cease in times of war, except by operation of Article 4 of the Covenant whereby certain provisions may be derogated from in a time of national emergency. Respect for the right to life is not, however, such a provision. In principle, the right not arbitrarily to be

> deprived of one's life applies also in hostilities. The test of what is an arbitrary deprivation of life, however, then falls to be determined by the applicable *lex specialis*, namely, the law applicable in armed conflict which is designed to regulate the conduct of hostilities. Thus whether a particular loss of life, through the use of a certain weapon in warfare, is to be considered an arbitrary deprivation of life contrary to Article 6 of the Covenant can only be decided by reference to the law applicable in armed conflict and not deduced from the terms of the Covenant itself.[47]

In the "*Barrier*" case, the Court quoted from the *Nuclear Weapons* case and continued:

> More generally, the Court considers that the protection offered by human rights conventions does not cease in case of armed conflict, save through the effect of provisions for derogation of the kind to be found in Article 4 of the International Covenant on Civil and Political Rights. As regards the relationship between international humanitarian law and human rights law, there are thus three possible situations: some rights may be exclusively matters of international humanitarian law; others may be exclusively matters of human rights law; yet others may be matters of both these branches of international law. In order to answer the question put to it, the Court will have to take into consideration both these branches of international law, namely human rights law and, as *lex specialis*, international humanitarian law.[48]

Lawyers operating with Allied countries have no choice but to wrestle with this complex interaction and find it difficult to understand the United States objections, particularly if they lead to presidential statements such as, "Of course, our values as a Nation, values that we share with many nations in the world, call for us to treat detainees humanely, *including those who are not legally entitled to such treatment.*"[49] (Emphasis added.)

Is the president seriously suggesting that there are people who are not legally entitled to "humane treatment"? Indeed, this sits oddly with the words of the same president on his second inauguration when he said: "From the day of our Founding, we have proclaimed that every man and woman on this earth has rights, and dignity, and matchless value."[50] I agree with these words and the president is right, not least because this is indeed the exact opposite of the doctrine preached by our terrorist opponents. The United States has stood as a bastion for human rights since its founding. It was the United States that led the human rights movement in the early days and the Universal Declaration of Human Rights[51] itself had Eleanor Roosevelt as its guiding force. It was the United States who during the Cold War stood as a beacon of light offering a different vision to oppressed people. It is therefore unfortunate that the view being given to the world now is that only Americans have rights—the rest of the world has them only at the will of the United States! That is not the message of the

Founding Fathers, nor is it the message of the president but "[i]f the trumpet give an uncertain sound, who shall prepare himself to the battle?"[52]

In the same way as there is confusion about the status of Additional Protocol I in the United States, so there is confusion on the applicability of human rights law to military operations. Whether we like it or not, the world is moving on and the United States is part—a big part—of that world. However, it is not so big that it can ignore what is going on in the rest of the world. Those of us who are wrestling with these knotty legal problems need the help and expertise that the United States can bring. Furthermore, if the United States wants to shape the legal landscape, it can only do so by a position of active involvement. There are many who are concerned with the manner in which human rights law is being used to reinterpret accepted principles of the law of armed conflict. The law of armed conflict reflects the realities of war in a way that human rights law does not—and was never designed to do.

I come back to my definition of coalition: "temporary combination for special ends between parties that retain distinctive principles."

The United States has distinctive principles but so do all its friends and allies. If a coalition is to work, all parties need to retain those distinctive principles. The fact that they exist—and are distinctive—cannot be ignored. If the United States wishes to impose its own distinctive principles on others, that is not a "coalition." Nor can we—or should we—, as allies, impose our own principles on the United States. However, in recognizing that we do have differences, we need to work together to find ways of channeling those distinctive principles so that we move forward together. Our purpose is the same.

Notes

1. Hansard, Dec. 16, 1852, at Col.1666.
2. THE CONCISE OXFORD DICTIONARY OF CURRENT ENGLISH (Henry W. Fowler & Francis G. Fowler eds., 4th ed. 1960) (1911).
3. Joseph Fitchett, *New NATO Force Could Help, Not Hinder Europe*, 3 EUROPEAN AFFAIRS, (Fall 2002), *available at* http://www.ciaonet.org/olj/ea/2002_fall/2002_fall_34.html.
4. Protocol Additional (I) to the Geneva Conventions of 12 August 1949, and Relating to the Protection of Victims of International Armed Conflicts, Jun. 8, 1977, 1125 U.N.T.S. 3, *reprinted in* DOCUMENTS ON THE LAW OF WAR 422 (Adam Roberts & Richard Guelff eds., 3d. ed. 2000).
5. United States Mission to the United Nations Press Release #147, Sep. 24, 2003, *available at* http://www.un.int/usa/03_147.htm.
6. US Department of Defense, Conduct of the Persian Gulf War, Final Report to Congress, Appendix O at O-13 (Apr. 1992).
7. *Id.* at O-15.
8. *Id.* at O-36.
9. *Reprinted in Agora: The U.S. Decision not to Ratify Protocol I to the Geneva Conventions on the Protection of War Victims*, 81 AMERICAN JOURNAL OF INTERNATIONAL LAW 910 (1987).

10. *Id.* at 911.
11. *Id.* at 911–912.
12. These can be found in DOCUMENTS ON THE LAW OF WAR, *supra* note 4, at 501.
13. *Id.* at 510.
14. *See* Michael J. Matheson, *The United States Position on the Relation of Customary International Law to the 1977 Protocols Additional to the 1949 Geneva Conventions*, 2 AMERICAN UNIVERSITY JOURNAL OF INTERNATIONAL LAW AND POLICY 415, 418 (1987).
15. Douglas J. Feith, *Law in the Service of Terror—The Strange Case of the Additional Protocol*, THE NATIONAL INTEREST, Fall 1985, at 36.
16. ANNOTATED SUPPLEMENT TO THE COMMANDER'S HANDBOOK ON THE LAW OF NAVAL OPERATIONS (A. R. Thomas & James Duncan eds., 1999) (Vol. 73, US Naval War College International Law Studies).
17. *Id.*, para. 8.1.2.1 n.17, at 404.
18. International and Operational Law Department, The Judge Advocate General's Legal Center & School, Operational Law Handbook.
19. *Id.*, 2001 version, at 10.
20. *Id.*, 2005 version, at 15.
21. Errata Sheet dated Sep. 27, 2004, *in id.*, 2005 version.
22. Hays Parks, *Special Forces' Wear of Non-Standard Uniforms,* 4 CHICAGO JOURNAL OF INTERNATIONAL LAW 519 n.55 (2003).
23. Matheson, *supra* note 14, at 421.
24. *Id.* at 419.
25. These have been compiled in THE TORTURE PAPERS—THE ROAD TO ABU GHRAIB (Karen Greenberg & Joshua Dratel eds., 2005).
26. Matheson, *supra* note 14, at 427.
27. White House Memo, Humane Treatment of Al Qaeda and Taliban Detainees, Feb. 7, 2002, *reprinted in* TORTURE PAPERS, *supra* note 25, at 134.
28. Military and Paramilitary Activities (Nicar. v. U.S.), 1986 I.C.J. 14, para. 218 at 104 (June 27).
29. The United Kingdom ratified Additional Protocol I on January 28, 1998, Japan on August 31, 2004, and Australia on June 21, 1991.
30. France ratified Additional Protocol I on April 11, 2001. Germany did so on February 14, 1991.
31. Turkey is a notable exception.
32. *See e.g.*, US Department of Justice Office of Legal Counsel Memorandum for Alberto Gonzales, Counsel to the President, and William J. Haynes Jr., General Counsel of the Department of Defense, Application of Treaties and Laws to al Qaeda and Taliban Detainees, Jan. 22, 2002, *reprinted in* TORTURE PAPERS, *supra* note 25, at 81, 111–116.
33. Matheson, *supra* note 14, at 420.
34. *Id.* at 421.
35. European Convention for the Protection of Human Rights and Fundamental Freedoms, Nov. 4, 1950, 213 U.N.T.S. 222, *reprinted in* BASIC DOCUMENTS IN INTERNATIONAL LAW 244 (Ian Brownlie ed., 5th ed. 2002).
36. *Id.*, art. 1.
37. Banković v. Belgium and Others, Case No. 52207/99, 123 INTERNATIONAL LAW REPORTS 94, para. 71 at 113 (2001).
38. R (Al-Skeini and others) v. Secretary of State for Defence, Divisional Court, 2005 2 WEEKLY LAW REPORTS 1401 and Appeal Court, 2005 ALL ENGLAND REPORTS (D) 337 (December).

39. International Covenant on Civil and Political Rights art. 2(1), G.A. Res. 2200, at 52, U.N. GAOR, 21st Sess., Supp. No. 16, U.N. Doc. A/6316 (1966), *reprinted in* BASIC DOCUMENTS IN INTERNATIONAL LAW, *supra* note 35, at 205, 206.
40. *See* Thomas Buergenthal, *To Respect and to Ensure: State Obligations and Permissible Derogations, in* THE INTERNATIONAL BILL OF RIGHTS: THE COVENANT ON CIVIL AND POLITICAL RIGHTS 73–75 (Louis Henkin ed., 1981).
41. Human Rights Committee, General Comment 31, Nature of the General Legal Obligation on States Parties to the Covenant, Mar. 29, 2004, U.N.Doc.CCPR/C/21/Rev.1/Add.13 (2004).
42. Working Group report on Detainee Interrogations in the Global War on Terrorism: Assessment of Legal, Historical, Policy and Operational Considerations, 6 Mar. 6, 2003, *reprinted in* TORTURE PAPERS, *supra* note 25, at 241, 243.
43. American Convention on Human Rights art. 1, Nov. 22, 1969, 1144 U.N.T.S. 123, *reprinted in* HUMAN RIGHTS: DOCUMENTARY SUPPLEMENT 374 (Louis Henkin et al. eds., 2001).
44. *Id.*, art. 27.
45. Legality of the Threat or Use of Nuclear Weapons, Advisory Opinion, 1996 I.C.J. 226 (July 8).
46. Legal Consequences of the Construction of a Wall in the Occupied Palestinian Territory, Advisory Opinion, 2004 I.C.J. ___ (9 July), *available at* http://www.icj-cij.org/icjwww/idocket/imwp/imwpframe.htm.
47. Nuclear Weapons, *supra* note 45, para. 25 at 240.
48. Legal Consequences of the Construction of a Wall in the Occupied Palestinian Territory, *supra* note 46, at para. 106.
49. White House Memo, *supra* note 25, at 134.
50. Inauguration speech of President George W. Bush, Jan. 20, 2005, *available at* http://www.whitehouse.gov/news/releases/2005/01/20050120-1.html.
51. Universal Declaration of Human Rights, G.A. Res. 217A, at 71, U.N. GAOR, 3d Sess., 1st plen. mtg., U.N. Doc A/810 (Dec. 10, 1948), *reprinted in* BASIC DOCUMENTS IN INTERNATIONAL LAW, *supra* note 35, at 192.
52. *1 Corinthians* 14:8 (King James).

XII

Coalition Warfare: Challenges and Opportunities

Dale G. Stephens*

When planning for coalition warfare, the military lawyer is concerned with achieving effective interoperability under applicable international and domestic law. In the modern context of "coalitions of the willing," this essentially means achieving a harmonization of rules of engagement (ROE) with the lead nation, having regard to the specific taskings and missions the coalition partners have assumed. Usually (but not always) the lead nation in conducting serious global operations in the contemporary environment is the United States. As is well known, the United States has asserted formally that it is not prepared to sign and ratify a number of treaties applicable in the context of armed conflict[1] and has been consistently critical of the "progressive" nature of a number of assertive statements of customary law heralded by some.[2] Therein lays the obvious, but "ostensible" challenge, for coalition military partners in trying to ensure operational effectiveness when operating under potentially divergent legal regimes. The word "ostensible" is emphasized, because at the working officer level of coalition warfare, there is much

---

* Commander, Royal Australian Navy. The views expressed in this article are those of the author alone and do not necessarily represent the views of the Australian Government, the Australian Defence Force, or the Royal Australian Navy. This article was first published in volume 36 of the *Israel Yearbook on Human Rights* (2006) and is reprinted with permission.

more commonality of approach than what one might expect notwithstanding the stridency of statements sometimes made as to national divergence under the law.

It is a theme of this article that coalition operations are frequently successful due to the pragmatic approach taken to interpreting the law by coalition partners. This is not to suggest any subversion of the law, but rather reflects choices made by coalition partners to intelligently accommodate differing legal approaches among them for the common good. This success is also due to the nature of the law itself, which is generally cast in terms of "standards" as opposed to "bright line" rules and thus is more usually predicated upon the invocation of "values" by the military decision-maker. Within this interdependent world, such values are more convergent and synonymous with those of society at large than what many outside of the military may think.

Modes of Analysis—Formalism

There are, of course, a number of ways in which to assess the issue of coalition interoperability under the law. At the immediate or formalist level, one can merely compare treaties ratified by coalition partners and statements of customary law made by such partners to determine who is able to do what in the course of a campaign and to orchestrate missions accordingly. Of course, this assumes the absence of a single consensus standard to which all will comply, which in terms of coalitions of the willing, is a relatively safe assumption.[3]

From this formalist position, we are faced with some obvious direct inconsistency issues under international law. The Ottawa Land Mines Convention[4] is the classic example of such inconsistency, especially Article 1(c) which provides that "Each State Party undertakes never under any circumstances: to assist, encourage or induce, in any way, anyone to engage in any activity prohibited to a State Party under this Convention."[5] US allies such as Australia, Canada, Germany, Japan, New Zealand and the United Kingdom[6] have all signed and ratified this treaty. Having regard to the literal wording of the obligations imposed, mission taskings by such signatories could not, for example, contemplate the tactical level carriage of US forces or refueling of US assets where such forces or assets are carrying and/or contemplate the use of anti-personnel landmines.[7] Additionally, a number of US allies have assumed obligations under the International Criminal Court Statute[8] and under the 1980 Conventional Weapons Convention and its five Protocols.[9] The United States is not a party to the International Criminal Court treaty nor to two of the five Conventional Weapons Convention Protocols.[10] Again, these disparities have their own dynamics regarding tactical level mission taskings.

Such dissonance is also found in differing interpretations of customary international law. The potential dichotomy between the definitions "war sustaining" under the US Commander's Handbook on the Law of Naval Operations[11] and "effective contribution to direct military action" under the San Remo Manual on International Law Applicable to Armed Conflicts at Sea[12] is one such obvious area.

Similarly, those who have ratified Additional Protocol I[13] are bound by a number of provisions that the United States is not. For example, Article 56 with its prohibition on attacking dams, dikes and nuclear electrical generating stations is one where the United States has stressed its opposition as a ground for non-ratification.[14] Similarly divisive is the issue of belligerent reprisal. Article 51(6) of Additional Protocol I expressly prohibits attacks on civilians. Such a constraint does not, however, apply to US forces under US formulations as to the residual scope of this right pursuant to customary international law.[15] Such differences in obligation are real and are necessarily reflected in default statements of national ROE and "red card" directives to coalition commanders.[16]

Under the formalist paradigm, all of this would seem to render the chance of effective interoperability very difficult, if not impossible. But of course this has not been the case. In recent years, coalition forces have participated with the United States in numerous operations without any serious compromise to mission effectiveness. Coalition operations during Operations Desert Shield and Desert Storm, during operations in Somalia, in East Timor, in Afghanistan and during Operation Iraqi Freedom are, in fact, a testament to coalition effectiveness under the law. Why is this so? The answer to this question lies not in a formalist paradigm of the law, but rather resides in a realist critique of formalism.

Realist Critique

The theme of this essay is that effective legal interoperability is possible, indeed very common, despite the impression of grave differences of view. This is not a unique observation. Colonel David Graham, JAGC, US Army (Ret.) has previously addressed this theme[17] and has put forward a number of explanations for why this may be so. Firstly, he offered the proposition that while US allies had ratified these treaties, they had submitted a number of agreed-upon reservations or declarations that effectively achieved a common understanding of application.[18] Secondly, Colonel Graham highlighted the extensive consultation and sharing of military law manuals that has happened in more recent times, which have prompted a greater socialization of concepts.[19] Finally, he stressed the operational significance of multilateral ROE development on operations occurring since 1977, which has driven a convergence of legal principle.[20]

The insightful observations of Colonel Graham are fully supported in this article. It is the third ground in particular which, it is submitted, has been decisive in forging successful legal compatibility. The investigation of this phenomenon is the principal focus of this article. Firstly, however, it is useful to examine the initial ground proffered by Colonel Graham, namely the issue of collective reservations/declarations. There is no doubt that the language used in such reservations/declarations by many nations when ratifying Additional Protocol I is very similar, if not identical. A cursory review of the tenor of declarations made to operative provisions of the Protocol does evidence a certain symmetry of language and intent with respect to issues like the definition of military advantage concerning attacks to be assessed as a "whole,"[21] to the incorporation of the lives of one's own military members in the proportionality equation,[22] and to the definition of "deployment" for ascertaining combatant status.[23] This necessarily allows for a common understanding and confidence when applying potentially ambiguous operative provisions in the specific contexts contemplated in the course of combined/coalition operations.

The second ground put forward relates to the increasing declassification and sharing of military manuals, such publication having had the effect of engendering a convergence of thinking. There is ample normative evidence that official publications which distill national interpretations of the law do have significant impact upon international thinking. The US Commanders Handbook on The Law of Naval Operations[24] and public release of Standing ROE for US Forces in the mid-1990s,[25] have had a tremendous proselytizing effect on the development of manuals and ROE doctrine in other countries. Partly because of the simple availability of such resources, and partly because of the accomplished line of reasoning employed, the tenor and substance of the positions reached in these sources has consciously and subconsciously influenced the operational legal thinking of others. Indeed, the very phrases of the US ROE are repeated in numerous iterations of coalition ROE that have been relied upon and have even found their way into the UN Model ROE for Peacekeeping Forces.[26]

Finally, it is in the last category of Colonel Graham's three grounds, the question of ROE development through multilateral operations, where the most effective tool for convergence of legal principle is found.

The Psychology of Mission Accomplishment

The psychology of coalition ROE development in active, combined operations is something that is little explored in the literature.[27] As a normative experience, it is evident that this process is one that engenders an irresistible quality of intellectual facilitation. The methodology of coalition ROE harmonization appeals to the pragmatic, mission accomplishment goals of the military psyche. The process of intense consultation between military partners generates a compulsive mindset and fosters cooperative and creative legal engagement to achieve nationally agreed-upon strategic outcomes. Obvious legal prohibitions, such as those contained in the Ottawa Convention concerning anti-personnel land mines for example, plainly constitute "show stoppers," but the law is not commonly that stark. The modern law of armed conflict is generally more concerned with attaining specific standards, than imposing bright line rules. Thus, the perennial issues of deciding upon questions of "military advantage"[28] and quantifying "proportionality"[29] anticipate a calibrated discretion, which in turn allows for realistic acuity between coalition force ROE.

The issue of "law choice" theory is not new. Answering international relations school critics of international law's alleged "legalistic-moralistic" inertia in the early 1950s, the well known international lawyer, Myres McDougal, emphasized the dynamic nature of international law and spoke of a choice between "effective and ineffective" law.[30] He observed that:

> The process of decision-making is indeed, as every lawyer knows, one of continual redefinition of doctrine in its application to ever-changing facts and claims. A conception of law which focuses upon doctrine to the exclusion of the pattern of practices by which it is given meaning and made effective, is therefore, not the most conducive to understanding.[31]

McDougal concluded that "A realistic conception of law, must, accordingly, conjoin formal authority and effective control and include not only doctrine but also the pattern of practices of both formal and effective decision makers."[32] This thesis of "effective law" shares much with the subsequent Hammerskjold approach to innovative and pragmatic legal resolution[33] and is anchored very heavily within a defined societal value set.

This thinking also draws on the concept of the law of armed conflict as "soft power," a process articulated masterfully by Professor Schmitt.[34] Professor Schmitt examined the decision-making calculus resident within US attitudes concerning treaty ratification and offered a number of hypotheses concerning law as a policy choice. Professor Schmitt sought to identify the causative impact of American decision making, both with respect to those treaties that are ratified, and more intriguingly, those that are not. Hence, he made the significant point that:

> Law can even shape war for those not party to a particular normative standard. For instance, Additional Protocol I, which the United States has not ratified, prohibits most attacks on dams, dikes, and nuclear electrical generating stations. Despite U.S. opposition to this particular provision, there have been no U.S. attacks on any of these

> target sets since the Vietnam War; should it conduct such an attack it would be condemned. . . . Apprehension over condemnation certainly influences the policy choice of whether to engage in such strikes. . . . [I]t would be hard to imagine . . . U.S. forces in a coalition intentionally conducting an operation that would violate Protocol I . . . if any significant coalition partners were parties to the treaty. The realities of coalition-building and maintenance would simply not allow it.[35]

The point artfully made by Professor Schmitt discloses two underlying precepts. The first is that US views on the scope of action legally available as a consequence of not ratifying Additional Protocol I is often contextualized in an operational environment in a manner that accommodates coalition harmony. Just because the United States retains the full legal capacity to attack the types of objects prohibited by the Protocol to others does not mean that it will necessarily undertake such attacks. Policy imperatives regarding coalition cohesion plainly inform decisions concerning attack profiles.

Secondly, the assessment made by Professor Schmitt acknowledges the role of "values" when assessing the relative cost exchange for attacking particular targets or deciding upon requisite levels of collateral damage or incidental injury. The law of armed conflict requires that a military commander exercise his/her judgment as to whether the significance of attacking a particular military objective is worth the "cost." There is actually a wide level of discretion available to the commander under the law provided that such judgments are "reasonable and made in good faith." In the modern context of volunteer military and naval forces, it is likely that military commanders will reflect the very values of the population at large when assessing amorphous standards like "concrete and direct military advantage anticipated." One is often struck with how civilian audiences will go through a target evaluation process and arrive at strikingly similar legal solutions concerning the proportionality equation as would a seasoned military audience. Indeed, the political ramifications of such methodologies tend to be more prescient within military decision-making evolutions than that found within civilian thinking.

It is also evident that within professional military audiences of different nations there tends to be a broad consensus as to the values placed upon the military significance of certain targets and the costs deemed acceptable in terms of incidental civilian injury and collateral damage to property when attacking (or not) those targets. This has been a product of the increasing frequency of multilateral coalition operations over recent years, in conjunction with the dramatic increase of UN peace operations that have operated under common sets of ROE. Similarly, it is also the product of the increasing socialization process brought about by international professional military education. Venues such as the US Naval War College have been hosting officers from around the world for almost

50 years and have been inculcating the teaching program with the promotion of democratic liberal values. These values find precise expression in the targeting decisions made by senior commanders who are driven by both the goals of mission achievement under extant ROE and the increasingly homogenous cultural imperatives of modern societies.

Challenges to Coalition Warfare

While there is much greater commonality to ROE development than what one may imagine, that isn't to deny the very real challenges that pervade this process. At the tactical level, it is self-evidently difficult to frame appropriate ROE in circumstances where government policy as to the existing law is either unarticulated or has been subject to several reversals. While governments may prefer the policy flexibility of leaving their options open as to what they perceive to be customary international law, this has an obviously deleterious consequence for planning for both the subject nation and coalition partners.

The other challenge to coalition interoperability is overt political intervention in the ROE process by governments. Although to be fair, unlike the Vietnam era, the contemporary practice of governments has been to allow the military full reign for the execution of the campaign under the law and to interject political involvement once calculations concerning compliance with the law have been undertaken. Hence, approval may be required for an attack even though it fulfills the proportionality test, but nonetheless anticipates a significant loss of life. Such "intervention" is plainly appropriate and reflects the realities of the political dimension of undertaking modern armed conflict.[36]

Ironically, the greatest potential challenge to coalition operations may come from the application of domestic law to the ROE process. It is somewhat of a paradox that military lawyers of different countries can speak easily about applicable legal concepts and yet when those same lawyers speak to national legal colleagues of other government departments who may have a stake in ROE development, such conversations are at cross-purposes.

The Rome Statute of the International Criminal Court[37] has also brought into focus the challenge of aligning criminal law standards reflected in that treaty with more traditional standards contained within domestic law. Issues such as "intent" and "recklessness" and their translation into an operational context are obvious points of potential difficulty. Similarly, the use of lethal force to protect mission essential property and the application of domestic law self-defense criteria to operations against deadly enemies in the jungles and deserts of the world where military forces operate in the twilight zone between war and peace are two other areas where there is potential for dichotomous answers.

The issue of dealing with domestic legal conundrums when striving for coalition interoperability is not unique. It may be time to revisit the concept of "transnational law" that was originally championed by those such as Professor Jessup in the 1920s as a more reliable way to advance international law's reforming promise.[38] It is a theme that, in a modified way, has been picked up more recently by Anne-Marie Slaughter and her liberalist, international relations critique of the modern legal method and may well be a profitable avenue of focus for those of us keen to reconcile public international law rights and responsibilities with domestic law.[39] Professor Slaughter advocates a recasting of international law to assimilate public and private law, across and between territorial boundaries of liberal States, to conceive of a more effective body of resulting law that is defined not by "subject or source but rather in terms of purpose and effect."[40]

Conclusion

Professor Louis Henkin famously observed that "Almost all nations observe almost all principles of international law and almost all of their obligations almost all of the time."[41] It remains a trite but powerfully correct statement. Despite some clear differences of opinion on some aspects of the law of armed conflict, and despite some very real challenges under both domestic and international law, the process of ensuring legal interoperability for ROE development and mission fulfillment between coalition partners is not as grave as one might imagine. It is incumbent upon professional military lawyers to continue to use their best creative endeavors to seek solutions to otherwise intractable legal problems. This is essential not only to ensure the success of the mission, which is always the paramount obligation, but to also instill greater strength into the intricate mosaic that is international law.

Notes

1. At the time of this writing the United States had not ratified the Protocol Additional to the Geneva Conventions of 12 August 1949, and Relating to the Protection of Victims of International Armed Conflicts [Protocol I], June 8, 1977, 1125 U.N.T.S. 3, *reprinted in* DOCUMENTS ON THE LAWS OF WAR 422 (Adam Roberts & Richard Guelff eds., 3d ed. 2000); the Rome Statute of the International Criminal Court, July 17, 1998, 37 INTERNATIONAL LEGAL MATERIALS 999; nor the Convention on the Prohibition of the Use, Stockpiling, Production and Transfer of Anti-Personnel Mines and on their Destruction, Sept. 18, 1997, 36 INTERNATIONAL LEGAL MATERIALS 1507.

2. See generally critical commentary on the International Committee of the Red Cross (ICRC) customary law study by David Rivkin and Lee Casey, *Rule of Law: Friend or Foe*, THE WALL STREET JOURNAL, Apr. 11, 2005, *available at* http://www.defenddemocracy.org/research_topics/.
3. This conundrum may even apply in the circumstances of a standing alliance such as NATO. *See* Michael Kelly, *Legal Factors in Military Planning for Coalition Warfare and Military Interoperability*, 2 AUSTRALIAN ARMY JOURNAL 161, 162–3 (2005).
4. *Supra* note 1.
5. *Id.*
6. Australia ratified the Ottawa Convention on January 14, 1999; Canada on December 3, 1997; Germany on July 23, 1998; Japan on September 30, 1998; New Zealand on January 27, 1999; and the United Kingdom on July 31, 1998.
7. Kelly, *supra* note 3, at 169.
8. *Supra* note 1.
9. Convention on Prohibitions or Restrictions on the Use of Certain Conventional Weapons which may be deemed to be Excessively Injurious or to have Indiscriminate Effects, and Protocol I on Non-Detectable Fragments; Protocol II on Prohibitions or Restrictions on the Use of Mines, Booby Traps and other Devices; Protocol III on Prohibitions or Restrictions on the Use of Incendiary Weapons, Oct. 10, 1980, 1342 U.N.T.S. 137; Protocol IV on Blinding Laser Weapons, Oct. 13, 1995, 35 INTERNATIONAL LAW MATERIALS 1218; and Protocol V on Explosive Remnants of War, Nov. 28, 2003, (not yet in force).
10. The United States has not ratified Protocol IV (Blinding Laser Weapons) nor Protocol V (Explosive Remnants of War).
11. *See* ANNOTATED SUPPLEMENT TO THE COMMANDER'S HANDBOOK ON THE LAW OF NAVAL OPERATIONS ¶ 7.4 n.88 (A. R. Thomas and James Duncan eds., 1999) (Vol. 73, US Naval War College International Law Studies) [hereinafter ANNOTATED SUPPLEMENT], which states:

> Although war-sustaining commerce is not subject to precise definition, commerce that indirectly but effectively supports and sustains the belligerent's war-fighting capability properly falls within the scope of the term. . . . Examples of war-sustaining commerce include *imports* of raw materials used for the production of armaments and *exports* of products the proceeds of which are used by the belligerent to purchase arms and armaments. (Emphasis added.)

12. SAN REMO MANUAL ON INTERNATIONAL LAW APPLICABLE TO ARMED CONFLICTS AT SEA ¶ 60.11 (Louise Doswald-Beck ed., 1995) where, after discussing the US formulation of "war-fighting/war-sustaining" outlined above, states:

> [T]he Round Table accepted the view that the descriptive phrase "integration into the enemy's war-fighting/war-sustaining effort" was too broad to use for the residual category. The phrase chosen to describe the residual category of merchant vessels which were legitimate military objectives was merchant vessels which make an effective contribution to military action by, for example, carrying military materials.

13. *Supra* note 1.
14. Michael N. Schmitt, *The Law of Armed Conflict as Soft Power: Optimizing Strategic Choice*, *in* INTERNATIONAL LAW ACROSS THE SPECTRUM OF CONFLICT: ESSAYS IN HONOUR OF PROFESSOR L.C. GREEN ON THE OCCASION OF HIS EIGHTIETH BIRTHDAY 455, 459 (Michael N. Schmitt ed., 2000) (Vol. 75, US Naval War College International Law Studies).
15. See ANNOTATED SUPPLEMENT, *supra* note 11, ¶ 6.2.3, n.36, which provides that:

> Reprisals may lawfully be taken against enemy individuals who have not yet fallen into the hands of the forces making the reprisals. Under customary international law,

members of the enemy civilian population are legitimate objects of reprisals. The United States nonetheless considers reprisal actions against civilians not otherwise legitimate objects of attack to be inappropriate in most circumstances. For nations party to [Additional Protocol I], enemy civilians and the enemy civilian population are prohibited objects of reprisal. The United States has found this new prohibition to be militarily unacceptable. . . .

16. Kelly, *supra* note 3, at 165.
17. David E. Graham, *Coalition Operations – Commentary, in* LEGAL AND ETHICAL LESSONS OF NATO'S KOSOVO CAMPAIGN 377 (Andru E. Wall ed., 2002) (Vol. 78, US Naval War College International Law Studies).
18. *Id.* at 378.
19. *Id.*
20. *Id.* at 378–9.
21. Australia:

> In relation to paragraph 5(b) of Article 51 and to paragraph 2(a)(iii) of Article 57, it is the understanding of Australia that references to the "military advantage" are intended to mean the advantage anticipated from the military attack considered as a whole and not only from isolated or particular parts of that attack.

United Kingdom:

> In relation to paragraph 5(b) of Article 51 and paragraph (2)(a)(iii) of Article 57, that the military advantage anticipated from an attack is intended to refer to the advantage anticipated from the attack considered as a whole and not only from isolated or particular parts of the attack.

Canada:

> It is the understanding of the Government of Canada in relation to sub-paragraphs 5(b) of Article 51, paragraph 2 of Article 52, and clause 2(a)(iii) of Article 57 that the military advantage anticipated from an attack is intended to refer to the advantage anticipated from the attack considered as a whole and not from isolated or particular parts of the attack.

Italy:

> In relation to paragraph 5(b) of Article 51 and paragraph 2(a)(iii) of Article 57, the Italian Government understands that the military advantage anticipated from an attack is intended to refer to the advantage anticipated from the attack considered as a whole and not only from isolated or particular parts of the attack.

Germany:

> In applying the rule of proportionality in Article 51 and Article 57, "military advantage" is understood to refer to the advantage anticipated from the attack considered as a whole and not only from isolated or particular parts of the attack.

The complete text of all reservations and declarations is available at http://www.icrc.org/ihl.nsf/WebSign?ReadForm&id=470&ps=P#res.

22. For example, New Zealand declared: "In relation to paragraph 5(b) of Article 51 and to paragraph 2(a)(iii) of Article 57 . . . the term "military advantage" involves a variety of considerations, including the security of attacking forces." A similar declaration was made by Australia. While not a party to Additional Protocol I, the United States has included in The Commander's Handbook on the Law of Naval Operations (*supra* note 11, ¶ 8.1.1) the following

commentary: "Military advantage may involve a variety of considerations, including the security of the attacking force."

23. Australia:

> It is the understanding of Australia that in relation to Article 44, the situation described in the second sentence of paragraph 3 can exist only in occupied territory or in armed conflicts covered by paragraph 4 of Article 1. Australia will interpret the word "deployment" in paragraph 3(b) of the Article as meaning any movement towards a place from which an attack is to be launched. It will interpret the words "visible to the adversary" in the same paragraph as including visible with the aid of binoculars, or by infra-red or image intensification devices.

United Kingdom:

> In relation to Article 44, that the situation described in the second sentence of paragraph 3 of the Article can exist only in occupied territory or in armed conflicts covered by paragraph 4 of Article 1, and that the Government of the United Kingdom will interpret the word "deployment" in paragraph 3(b) of the Article as meaning "any movement towards a place from which an attack is to be launched."

Canada:

> It is the understanding of the Government of Canada that:
>
> a. the situation described in the second sentence of paragraph 3 of Article 44 can exist only in occupied territory or in armed conflicts covered by paragraph 4 of Article 1; and
>
> b. the word "deployment" in paragraph 3 of Article 44 includes any movement towards a place from which an attack is to be launched.

Germany:

> The criteria contained in the second sentence of Article 44, paragraph 3, of Additional Protocol I for distinction between combatants and the civilian population are understood by the Federal Republic of Germany to apply only in occupied territories and in the other armed conflicts described in Article 1, paragraph 4. The term "military deployment" is interpreted to mean any movements towards the place from which an attack is to be launched.

Ireland:

> It is the understanding of Ireland that:
>
> a. The situation described in the second sentence of paragraph 3 of Article 44 can exist only in occupied territory or in armed conflicts covered by paragraph 4 of Article 1: and
>
> b. The word "deployment" in paragraph 3 of Article 44 includes any movement towards a place from which an attack is to be launched.

Spain:

> It is understood that the criteria mentioned in sub-paragraph b of Article 44(3) on the distinction between combatants and civilians can be applied only in occupied territories. The Spanish Government also interprets the expression "military deployment" to mean any movement towards a place from which or against which an attack is going to be launched.

The complete text of all reservations and declarations is available at http://www.icrc.org/ihl.nsf/WebSign?ReadForm&id=470&ps=P#res.

24. *Supra* note 11.

25. Chairman, Joint Chiefs of Staff, Standing Rules of Engagement for U.S. Forces, CJCS Inst. 3121.01 (series).
26. Department of Peacekeeping Operations, Guidelines for the Development of Rules of Engagement (ROE) for United Nations Peacekeeping Operations, May 2002.
27. In the broader context of national security decision making, an insightful analysis of the psychological foundation for such thinking can be found in YEHADA BEN-MEIR, NATIONAL SECURITY DECISIONMAKING: THE ISRAELI CASE (1986).
28. See, e.g., ANNOTATED SUPPLEMENT, *supra* note 11, ¶ 8.1.1, where, in describing "military advantage" in the context of determining the efficacy of an attack, it is stated:

> Only military objectives may be attacked. Military objectives are combatants and those objects which, by their nature, location, purpose, or use, effectively contribute to the enemy's war-fighting or war-sustaining capability and whose total or partial destruction, capture, or neutralization would constitute a definite military advantage to the attacker under the circumstances at the time of the attack. Military advantage may involve a variety of considerations, including the security of the attacking force.

29. See *id.* ¶ 8.1.2.1, where proportionality is described as follows: "It is not unlawful to cause incidental injury to civilians, or collateral damage to civilian objects, during an attack upon a legitimate military objective. Incidental injury or collateral damage must not, however, be excessive in light of the military advantage anticipated by the attack."
30. Myers S. McDougal, *Law and Power*, 46 AMERICAN JOURNAL OF INTERNATIONAL LAW 102, 113 (1952).
31. *Id.* at 110.
32. *Id.*
33. Oscar Schachter, *Dag Hammarskjold and the Relation of Law to Politics*, 56 AMERICAN JOURNAL OF INTERNATIONAL LAW 1 (1962).
34. *See* Schmitt, *supra* note 14.
35. *Id.* at 459.
36. See DAVID KENNEDY, THE DARK SIDES OF VIRTUE: REASSESSING INTERNATIONAL HUMANITARIANISM 117 (2004), who comments upon the "CNN effect" and consequential political significance of proportionality determinations.
37. *Supra* note 1.
38. Phillip C. Jessup, *The Functional Approach as Applied to International Law, in* PROCEEDINGS OF THE THIRD CONFERENCE OF TEACHERS OF INTERNATIONAL LAW 134, 137 (1928).
39. *See* Anne-Marie Slaughter, *International Law in a World of Liberal States*, 6 EUROPEAN JOURNAL OF INTERNATIONAL LAW 503 (1995).
40. *Id.* at 516.
41. LOUIS HENKIN, HOW NATIONS BEHAVE 47 (2d ed. 1979).

PART VI

FUTURE NAVIES

XIII

Toward 2015, Challenges for a Medium Navy: An Australian Perspective

Raydon Gates*

The purpose of this article is to provide an operator's assessment of future challenges for a medium sized Navy from an Australian perspective. I am going to range quite widely across warfighting and organizational issues and suggest a few areas where I might be able to generate some work for our judge advocate colleagues. I will conclude with a short scenario that I hope will set people thinking about the legal issues associated with future combat operations, enabled by network centric warfare in a coalition setting.

Let me begin by addressing what I see as the most important future warfighting trends. I am sure that they will not be a surprise to most of you. The Royal Australian Navy's (RAN) job is to protect the sovereignty of Australia, Australia's interests and Australian citizens. Australia's interests are global, our national security strategy is maritime in nature and our government's approach to global security issues reflects these facts. Therefore, the first enduring trend is a requirement for our Navy to be able to project maritime power at home and offshore, wherever Australia's interests may lie. This trend is accompanied by a requirement to deliver combat power across the spectrum of conflict, whether that be in support of coalition

---

* Rear Admiral, Royal Australian Navy. The views expressed in this article are those of the author alone and do not necessarily represent the views of the Australian Government, the Australian Defence Force, or the Royal Australian Navy.

combat operations in the war on terror, providing a secure environment in a failed State or delivering humanitarian support to regional neighbors. That being said, the Australian Defence Force (ADF) acquires capabilities in support of combat operations and adapts those capabilities, along with our tactics, techniques and procedures, to deliver options to the Government across the remainder of the mission space. We do not, as a general rule, acquire major capabilities that only have applications in operations other than combat. We simply can't afford it.

Earlier, I perhaps over-emphasized that the RAN is in the business of looking after Australia's national interest to make a point. Often in the coalition context we hear about the notion of common national interests. I would argue that this notion is generally a fallacy. In coalitions, compatible national interests are and certainly must be present, but compatible interests are not necessarily common interests. Even in the tightest of alliances or coalitions we will see divergences in the handling of certain issues. The fact that coalition partners are signatories, or not signatories, to a range of international treaties is a direct reflection of political divergence. Noting the observations of Clausewitz—that war is a continuance of the political discourse by other means—it follows that within the coalition force we immediately have the potential for a number of different military objectives, reflecting differing national political objectives. A tension is thus created within coalition structures; in my view that tension is an enduring feature of coalitions and therefore of the future war fighting landscape. It is up to military commanders to account for and manage national divergences so that unity of effort is maintained, within national constraints and in accordance with national priorities.

Military lawyers play a large part in harmonizing, where practicable, national rules of engagement (ROE) and establishing procedures within coalitions to account for political divergences. I would offer that these issues need to be addressed very early in the planning process as they have the potential to affect the very essence of an operation; from targeting to operating areas, from rules of engagement to task group disposition. Before I leave this subject I would not want to leave you with the impression that political divergence always offers problems, in fact it often offers opportunities. It may be possible for a coalition commander to use the forces of another nation to undertake a task with more freedom of maneuver than would be available to their own forces. For example, I experienced this in the Red Sea in 1992/93 where Australian ROE gave our units greater freedom of action, in certain areas, when conducting maritime interception operations with coalition partners. This was an advantage to the US commander, who subsequently employed RAN units closest to the Straits of Tiran at the mouth of the Gulf of Aqaba to intercept "inspection runners" when required.

A trend in all Western armed services is that warfighting is being undertaken via the application of joint effects. In Australia, we are a relatively small defense force and enjoy a close relationship between the Services. Yet we have still learned lessons about operating as a joint force in recent times. The joint application of combat power will be an enduring feature of the future warfighting landscape. Even simple issues such as terminology can mean different things to people from different Services from the same nation. Maritime forces are also increasingly being required to provide support to the joint force ashore. I will have more to say on this issue a little later on.

In the Australian context, we are also seeing responses to security issues increasingly being approached from a whole-of-government perspective. The military must work with other government, and importantly non-government, agencies to achieve the mission at hand. In some circumstances, perhaps most, it could be argued that the activities of other, non-military government agencies are the war winners. In these circumstances, the military's role becomes one of providing a secure environment so they can get on with their job; this is probably now the case in Iraq.

Australia's recent lead role in the Regional Assistance Mission to the Solomon Islands is another example. This was a Department of Foreign Affairs and Trade led mission in close partnership with the Australian Federal Police, the ADF and others. The ADF contributed its weight and presence to the equation, creating a secure environment so police and other government agencies could assist the Solomon Island authorities to regain control of their community and system of government. As a result of this whole-of-government trend, we are seeing increased numbers of non-military personnel legitimately in combat zones. This has advantages and challenges. Obviously, some adversaries often fail to make any distinction between a combatant and a noncombatant in this regard; they simply fight by a different set of rules or lack thereof. This poses interesting force protection and ROE quandaries for the modern day and future commander.

The future maritime warfighting environment is characterized by lethality no matter what mission you are conducting, whether it is peace operations, assisting with law enforcement in territorial waters or delivering humanitarian aid. The asymmetric threat of non-State players, including disaffected people and elements of transnational crime, enabled by the proliferation of weapon technologies and unrestrained by an obligation to comply with the law of armed conflict, has diminished warning time for a potential engagement and has further blurred the distinction between combatants and noncombatants. Lethal effects can be delivered by individuals or small groups on an increasingly devastating scale. A humanitarian aid mission in an area frequented by terrorist groups can be as lethal as combat operations in a State-on-State scenario. It is only the duration, magnitude and potential warning time of the lethal engagement that varies, not whether lethality is present or not.

As a result of the global trend of urbanization, particularly in coastal regions, and the importance of the sea for global trade, I think it is fair to say that the majority of the world's future security issues will have an element either on, or within influence of, the sea. Accordingly, we conclude that future maritime force operations will be dominated by the littoral; a parallel development to the increasing importance of urban terrain to the land force. Littoral environments mean an increase in the density of noncombatants, complications from terrain and the environment, and the increased presence of sea mine and land-based threats. Combine this with asymmetric tactics, the blurring of combatants and non-combatants, reduced warning times and increased lethality and we have significant ROE, target identification, threat response time and force protection challenges.

Another trend from recent conflicts that we see continuing is the problem of access, basing and overflight rights. In Australia's region, this is particularly relevant. From my observations, it is not the culture of Asian nations to get involved in what they consider each other's internal business—a fair enough stance. The recent Southeast Asian regional non-aggression pact proposal is probably a reflection of this position. Combine this trend with the littoral emphasis of future operations and the response is to develop sea basing concepts. The RAN's Future Maritime Operating Concept also looks to leverage the freedoms and maneuver space of the sea. Those freedoms are embedded in the United Nations Convention on Law of the Sea (1982 LOS Convention).[1] Australia has signed and ratified this treaty. Archipelagic sea lanes, international straits and complex maritime boundary interpretations abound in Australia's potential mission space. Our lines of communication lay across and through all of these maritime areas. The 1982 LOS Convention remains a key convention in a globalized world where seaborne trade accounts for the vast majority of global commerce and is crucial to energy flows. Freedom of the sea is obviously key to the freedom of maneuver of coalition navies.

On the technology side of warfare, we are seeing the increased use of unmanned vehicles for surveillance and for offensive and defensive purposes. With the future development and confluence of miniaturization, propulsion technologies and fuel cells, nanotechnology, communications and computing technologies we will see the capabilities and presence of unmanned platforms increase in all warfighting domains. Potential legal issues abound here.

Missile technologies are proliferating at an accelerated rate; their speed and in particular their ranges are rapidly increasing. These missiles are now fire-and-forget, but I am sure we will see increasing levels of artificial intelligence in missiles. For example, on arrival at a target area a missile may reassign itself if the target appears to have moved or seems absent. How does this sit with ROE and identification criteria? There is also the potential for land forces to reassign the missile in flight should a target be destroyed while the missile is inbound. Again, take the situation of forces from one nation reassigning a missile from another with the firing unit having little say in the process. Vexing legal problems arise that must be overcome so that warfighters can leverage advances in technology. Sea mines are in the inventories of many maritime nations and it would be reasonable to expect that non-State actors could acquire these technologies without too much trouble, should they so desire. Of course, submarines are entering service with many nations, particularly in Australia's area of interest. They are a great weapon if you are trying to leverage an asymmetric advantage or are simply outgunned on or above the surface of the ocean.

To top it all off, the future maritime battlespace will be wrapped in a network, linking sensors to shooters and, in theory, facilitating a pervasive situational awareness that will synchronize forces and provide subordinate commanders with the information they need to act independently to implement the senior commander's intent. Decision cycles will be compressed and fires delivered faster to deal with elusive and mobile targets. Network enabled operations will be a feature of the future.

As you are well aware, the United States leads the world in military technology in most areas and in particular in implementing a network centric approach. The cost of technology is generally very high and for some, possibly our own Navy, the full implementation of network centric warfare (NCW) may simply be unaffordable. Australia uses technology to generate a fighting edge. Importantly, this also includes the smarter application of technology as proliferation of modern weapons and sensors narrows the gap between others and ourselves. Let me say at this juncture, there is no quandary in the mind of Australia's military leaders when we examine where we might need to be technologically; we use interoperability with the United States as a benchmark. However, we must strike a balance that ensures we remain interoperable with both technically advanced allies and those not as technically advanced, but no less important, regional and coalition partners. Australia successfully led the UN effort in East Timor because it had the ability to flex its command and control systems, technology, tactics, techniques and procedures in both directions to accommodate coalition partners across a range of technological capabilities. We must continue to achieve this balance within a tight budget. This will challenge our ingenuity and, I suspect at times, our patience!

Let me move on to organizational challenges. Recently, my Chief of Navy released his strategic guidance for the Future Navy known as Plan Blue. This document examined the future Navy we need to be and the challenges that will face us. I would like to touch on but a few of those issues.

I think it is fair to say that our two largest concerns will be people and budgets. Western populations are aging and stagnating, yet our economies continue to grow. This places an enormous strain on our all volunteer Navy's traditional recruiting base. Competition with industry for the right people will sharpen markedly over the coming decades. Engineering and technical skills will be in particular demand. In our view, the RAN will probably become incrementally smaller with time, yet it must deliver the same—if not a greater—warfighting punch. Careful management and preservation of our most precious resource, people, will be required to manage workloads, ensure the Service is an attractive career option and, once people are part of our Service, ensure we retain them. As you are all well aware, uniformed people are a rare and very expensive asset in which the armed services make a substantial investment. Regardless of technological prowess, war is a clash of wills, it is a human endeavor and, at the end of the day, the fighting effectiveness of militaries is all about the quality of their people.

An aging population and infrastructure reinvestment requirements will generate increasing fiscal demand within the budgetary structure of a decreasing personal tax base. By our Government's own analysis, post-2017 Australia will not be able to fund its governance without incurring budget deficits. Obviously, structural changes to taxation and spending patterns will be required to address this challenge. I think the impact on a medium navy is obvious; an expectation of real funding increases in the longer term, while possible, is not likely, barring a major discontinuity in the world's security situation. So it is a pretty simple problem to articulate; do our business better with fewer people and fewer resources.

These two critical factors, along with the warfighting trends addressed above, will generate a range of other future issues. I will touch on but a few. Within our ships we will see increasing automation to decrease the requirement for people and help manage the workload of smaller ships' companies. There will be an increasing number of human-machine interfaces and eventually machine-machine interfaces. Decision support systems may be required to implement decisions programmed into them without a human in the loop. Ships will have to stay at sea longer in order to maximize greater reliability and availability, but somehow we must balance workloads and retain our people. In the future, our ships will continue to have to comply with international treaties to which our governments may be party. Environmental law and occupational health and safety will play an increasing role in ship design, maintenance and operation. As some will be aware, the RAN has recently purchased the double hulled merchant tanker *Delos*, soon to be commissioned as *HMAS Sirius*, so that we comply with the International Maritime

Organization's (IMO) pollution from ships requirements for the transportation of fuels at sea,[2] just as an example.

The eternal drive for fiscal efficiency will see the greater use of contracted support both on and off board our ships. Contractors will have to be integrated into the way we do our business rather than being seen as simply delivering services. We may find that the armed services and defense industry effectively share people as the workforce skill base decreases in proportion to demand. The legal aspect of contracted support to deployed operations is an area we could talk about for hours. Are contractors in providing direct support to the force combatants or noncombatants, and from whose perspective? In this case are they under military command or are they not? Are they subject to the Defence Force Discipline Act (or the Uniform Code of Military Justice (UCMJ) for the United States)? What if a contractor refuses to deliver services into a combat zone despite the usual fiscal enticements and contractual requirements? Can we compel a contractor to put civilians in harm's way and subject to the constant presence of lethal force? The status of contractors vis-à-vis host nations who provide logistic support also raises issues as, for example, in the application of local health, safety and insurance laws and regulations. With regard to the protection of host nation contractors, do they become designated persons under our rules of engagement or not? Not to mention status of forces agreements or arrangements or memorandums of understanding, or whatever the flavor of the month happens to be. These are issues that we have had to address during recent operations and must continue to address in the future.

There are numerous other issues to consider, such as the competition for maritime practice areas with commercial interests and environmental concerns. The issue of whales and sonar has recently been of contention both in the United States and in Australia. Increasing commercial traffic and access to ports, security of warships in ports and the application of security zones around warships are but a few of the contentious issues with which we must wrestle.

Let me conclude with a very brief scenario that encapsulates some interesting contemporary and future warfighting and international law issues.

The year is 2015 and His Majesty's Australian Ship *Adelaide* lays 20 miles offshore on the boundary of the new territorial sea limit. It would be better if she were in at 12 miles like the old days. The combat system is up, the decision support software filters information, delivering only, as the system has been programmed, assessments that a person can consume. A hypersonic, autonomous, fire-and-forget missile is on the rails. The ship is waiting for the call for fire. There are boats everywhere; whether friend or foe it is hard to tell. Are they hostile intelligence collectors or fishermen? They are all traveling fast and can't all be stopped, boarded and checked out. They seem to be avoiding the 500-meter warship exclusion zone though. (Legal or not, the zone seems to be having its desired effect and that's all that counts.)

Ashore Purpleland special forces have identified the target. The E-message streaks through the ether to the Orangeland commanded coalition headquarters. This is a time sensitive target. Just one shot, no time to mess around. The E-message is permitted to auto-progress from the sensor network to the shooter grid for fires allocation. Onboard *Adelaide* the missile launcher bell sounds and almost immediately the familiar sound of a missile streaking landward breaks the silence. The Combat Information Center (CIC) duty officer watches on his heads up, virtual 3D display. He sees the target position and terrain, observes the correct protocols and thinks nothing more of it. There are plenty of time sensitive targets that arise in these war on terror operations. No need to tell the Captain, she was on the bridge and saw the bird go. *Adelaide* sets off for a port visit, a job well done.

Upon arrival, a defense contractor climbs the mast to replace an aerial; he is from the contractor support unit based in the Fleet Forward Operating base. A Captain's worst nightmare unfolds; a sniper has just shot the contractor, and one of her sailors has shot a local who he believes was the assailant. The sailor had no time to think, he had to make a decision. One moment the assailant was bunkering the ship from the wharf, the next minute he was a sniper. No time to ask permission. The ROE talked about this situation, but he never fully understood what he was really meant to do.

The Captain's day is not going to get any better. She has been advised that the missile *Adelaide* fired struck its target. She has also been advised that the target was a local politician. He was visiting a community center; 50 people have been killed. How could this happen? That politician wasn't a combatant within the Australian ROE. His targeting was not consistent with our international obligations! A community center is not an approved target for Australian units and the death of 50 noncombatants is outside national collateral damage/incidental injury limits. The NCW system was meant to be programmed, there were meant to be safeguards in place. What could she have done from sea with the system in automatic? There was no time to confirm the target in any event. It was time sensitive.

Purpleland and Orangeland commanders seem to be notably absent; all the locals know is that the round that killed the apparent sniper came from an Australian ship, as did the missile that hit the community center. In both cases Australia applied the lethal force. These are Australian problems. The Captain sits down and decides to have a drink; you can do that on Australian ships. Common versus compatible national interests, divergent international legal obligations, status of forces agreements, it's all networked, it's all automated and it's all too much for a simple warrior. She decides to call a lawyer . . . after she finishes her drink!

Notes

1. United Nations Convention on the Law of the Sea, Dec. 10, 1982, 1833 U.N.T.S. 3, *reprinted in* 21 INTERNATIONAL LEGAL MATERIALS 1261, *available at* www.un.org/Depts/los/convention_agreements/texts/unclos/closindex.htm.
2. International Convention for the Prevention of Pollution from Ships, Nov. 2, 1973, *reprinted in* 12 INTERNATIONAL LEGAL MATERIALS 1319 (with Protocol of Feb. 17, 1978) [hereinafter MARPOL 73/78]. Regulation 13f to Annex I of MARPOL 73/78 requires that all new tanker vessels built after a designated date be equipped with double hulls, a mid-deck design or the equivalent.

XIV

The Current State of The Law of Naval Warfare: A Fresh Look at the *San Remo Manual*

Wolff Heintschel von Heinegg*

Introduction

The 1994 *San Remo Manual*[1] has met widespread approval as a contemporary restatement of the principles and rules of international law applicable to armed conflicts at sea. In view of the fact that many of its provisions are but a compromise between the differing views within the group of international lawyers and naval experts who drafted it, some of its provisions may be far from perfection. Still, this has not prevented a considerable number of States from adopting most of the San Remo rules in their respective manuals or instructions for their naval armed forces.[2] Against that background it is somewhat surprising that there are an increasing number of both operators and lawyers criticizing parts of the *San Remo Manual* as outdated and as an unreasonable obstacle to the success of their operational or strategic goals. They, *inter alia*, refer to the provisions on measures short of attack and on methods and means of naval warfare, especially on blockade and operational zones. In their view, those provisions meet neither the necessities of modern operations, e.g., maritime interception operations (MIO) nor non-military enforcement measures decided upon by the UN Security Council, nor do they offer operable solutions to the naval commander.[3]

---

* Professor of International Law at Europe-University in Frankfurt (Oder), Germany. This article was first published in volume 36 of the *Israel Yearbook on Human Rights* (2006) and is reprinted with permission.

Of course, the *San Remo Manual* does not prioritize military or operational necessity. Rather it imposes legal restrictions on naval commanders that may prove inconvenient in view of the means available and in view of the task of the respective mission. The said criticism, however, goes beyond such general complaints about legal rules. It is based upon the belief that whenever it comes to other States' shipping, interference would be permissible only if it is in accordance with the law of naval warfare, i.e., with the provisions of the *San Remo Manual.* If so, it would be difficult, indeed, to maintain that certain missions, e.g., MIO, conducted within the framework of the Global War on Terror are legal. It would be similarly difficult to explain the legality of measures enforcing an embargo if they had to be judged in the light of the law of blockade alone.

However, the said criticism is based upon an erroneous understanding of the law of naval warfare, of its scope of applicability and, thus, of the *San Remo Manual.* Maritime interception operations aimed at combating transnational terrorism[4] or the proliferation of weapons of mass destruction[5] and related components do have a legal basis that is independent from the law of naval warfare. The same holds true with regard to enforcing an embargo—either with or without the authorization of the UN Security Council.[6] Therefore, neither the law of naval warfare nor the *San Remo Manual* as its most recent restatement pose an insurmountable obstacle to such operations. The *San Remo Manual*'s provisions apply exclusively to situations of international armed conflicts.[7] MIO and other maritime operations have to be based upon that body of law only if they occur in the course of an armed conflict between two or more States.

However, the said criticism does not seem to be absolutely unjustified insofar as the *San Remo Manual* may indeed no longer properly reflect contemporary State practice or meet the realities of modern maritime and naval operations. Moreover, some of its provisions seem to be quite ambiguous and, thus, may be misinterpreted. This lack of legal clarity could ultimately render obsolete the great progress achieved by the *San Remo Manual.*

Therefore, it is time to take a fresh look at the *San Remo Manual.* The task this author has been entrusted with is to identify those provisions that ought to be reconsidered or modified[8] and to evaluate the persuasiveness of some of the critical arguments that have been put forward.

Definitions

At first glance, the list of definitions in paragraph 13 of the *Manual* seems to be comprehensive and reflective of customary law. The latter is certainly true in principle.[9] Still, this does not necessarily mean that all the definitions continue to reflect contemporary State practice.

Civilian Mariners and Private Contractors on Board Warships

There is a tendency in contemporary State practice to crew warships with civilians or at least to make use of civilian contractors who work on board warships.[10] In many cases, the contribution of civilian contractors is essential for the operation of the ship or of its weapons systems. Hence, the question arises whether the presence of civilian mariners or civilian contractors affects the legal status of the ship concerned. The ability to exercise belligerent rights remains reserved for warships.[11] Warships are authorized to engage in offensive military activities, including visit and search, blockade, interdiction and convoy escort operations. Auxiliary vessels are expressly prohibited from exercising belligerent rights.[12] There are convincing arguments according to which civilians on board warships should perform neither crew functions nor other functions related to the operation of the ship and its weapons or electronic systems. Such activities should indeed remain reserved for the armed forces personnel who have traditionally performed them.

It should be noted, however, that the definition of warships in paragraph 13 (g) and in customary international law does not necessarily rule out the use of civilian mariners and of civilian contractors. According to that definition the warships must be manned by "*a* crew that is under regular armed forces discipline." In contrast, the 1907 Hague Convention VII Relating to the Conversion of Merchant Ships into Warships,[13] in Article 4, provides that "*the* crew" of a converted merchant ship "must be subject to military discipline." While the use of the definite article in Hague Convention VII rules out the (further) use of civilian mariners, the indefinite article in the definition of warships justifies the conclusion that not necessarily all crew members must be under regular armed forces discipline. Leaving aside the ensuing question of the permissible proportion of civilian mariners (or private contractors) in comparison to sailors and officers proper, it, thus, becomes clear that the manning of warships with civilian mariners does not affect the legal status of the ship as long as the other criteria are met and as long as a certain portion of the crew remains under regular armed forces discipline. Of course, these findings are without prejudice to the legal status of civilian mariners and of civilian contractors. If captured they could, with good reasons, be considered unlawful combatants and prosecuted for direct participation in hostilities. The latter problem could be solved by conferring a special legal status on civilian mariners and private contractors. Still, it would certainly contribute to legal clarity if paragraph 13 (g) were supplemented by an explanatory statement with regard to the presence of civilians on board warships.

Unmanned Vehicles

Paragraph 13 lacks a definition of unmanned—aerial or underwater—vehicles.[14] This issue is raised here because their legal status may well be of importance with regard to the rights and duties of neutral States. An unmanned vehicle is either an integral part of a warship's weapons systems or otherwise controlled from a military platform. If that military platform is a warship or a military aircraft, the unmanned aerial vehicle (UAV), unmanned combat air vehicle (UCAV), or unmanned underwater vehicle (UUV), according to the position taken here, necessarily shares the legal status of that platform and it, thus, enjoys sovereign immunity as long as it is operated in high seas areas or in international airspace. Accordingly, neutral States would under no circumstances be allowed to interfere with them.

Regions of Operations

The provisions of the *San Remo Manual* on the Regions of Operations are evidently influenced by the 1982 UN Convention on the Law of the Sea.[15] The adaptation of the rules on the regions of operations to the contemporary law of the sea is by all means a realistic, and the only operable, approach to reconcile the interests of belligerent and neutral States. Of course, this delicate compromise is continuously challenged by excessive maritime claims.[16] Creeping jurisdiction may unsettle that compromise and may, ultimately, render obsolete that part of the *San Remo Manual*. Therefore, States should take all necessary measures to preserve the achievements of both the Law of the Sea Convention and of the *San Remo Manual*.[17] Still, the provisions of the *San Remo Manual* on the regions of operations are far from perfect.

Those provisions reflect the approach underlying the Law of the Sea Convention not only with regard to the determination of "neutral waters,"[18] but also with regard to the obligations of belligerents at sea to pay due regard to the legitimate rights of coastal States, when operating within their EEZ, and of third States, when operating in high seas areas.[19] The author is aware that during the drafting process of the *San Remo Manual* there was a controversy about the exact meaning of the due regard principle and that its inclusion in the manual was a compromise decision.[20] Nevertheless, there should be a little further guidance as to its exact meaning. Unless specified, the due regard principle will only be paid lip service or, even worse, it will be abused by coastal States in order to camouflage acts of unneutral service.

The same holds true with regard to paragraph 15 of the *Manual* which states that "within and over neutral waters . . . hostile actions by belligerent forces are forbidden." Paragraph 16 contains a non-exhaustive list of activities that are covered by the term "hostile actions." This enumeration predominantly refers to traditional naval operations during armed conflict. Of course, the term "hostile action," as well as one of the activities listed—"use as a base of operations"—would be broad enough to also cover other activities, e.g., the use of means for electronic warfare (EW), target acquisition, or reconnaissance purposes. Such an interpretation would, it is maintained here, certainly be in accordance with customary international law. However, the examples following that term could cast doubt on whether such activities would also be covered by the prohibition of using neutral waters and neutral airspace as a base of operations. One way of avoiding such cases of doubt would be the deletion of all examples. In order to contribute to legal clarity, however, it seems preferable to add to the examples listed a formulation similar to that of Article 47 of the 1923 Hague Rules[21] which provides:

> A neutral state is bound to take such steps as the means at its disposal permit to prevent within its jurisdiction aerial observations of the movements, operations or defenses of one belligerent, with the intention of informing the other belligerent.
>
> This provision applies equally to a belligerent military aircraft on board a vessel of war.

Such a clarification also seems appropriate with regard to combat rescue operations in neutral territory. Such rescue operations are not specially protected under the law of armed conflict. Rather, they are to be considered military operations that would also fall into the category of "hostile action."

The Aerial Element—Underestimated

Modern naval operations are no longer conducted in a purely maritime environment. Naval battles proper, as traditionally envisioned, belong more or less to the past. Today naval forces operate jointly with other forces, especially with air forces.[22] As an integral part of these joint operations, naval forces can no longer be considered bound by only one set of rules specifically and exclusively designed for them. Moreover, even if naval operations were confined to the maritime environment, they would always imply the use of aircraft and of missiles because these assets are among the most effective weapons against enemy naval forces.

Of course, the *San Remo Manual* does not follow the limited approach of the treaties of 1907[23] or of 1936.[24] Its provisions are not limited to naval platforms, but also relate to military aircraft, civil aircraft, and to missiles.[25] Thus, the *Manual* has broadened—or at least clarified—the scope of the term "law of naval warfare" to cover not only ship-to-ship, but also ship-to-air and air-to-ship operations, including the use of missiles; as well as "prize measures," and the protection of vessels, aircraft, objects and persons at sea, on land, and in the air.

While the *San Remo Manual* addresses many of the issues arising from the interaction of naval and air warfare, its provisions sometimes give reason to assume that naval warfare still has been regarded in isolation. At least one cannot entirely escape the impression that the aerial element of maritime operations, as well as the possible impact of aircraft on naval operations, has been dealt with only marginally.

With paragraph 45 stating that "surface ships, submarines and aircraft are bound by the same principles and rules," the *San Remo Manual* starts from the premise that when it comes to methods and means of naval warfare there is no need to distinguish between the vehicles or platforms employed. Since the basic principles of the law of armed conflict apply to all methods and means of warfare, this approach seems to be logical and cogent. Still, the question remains whether this approach will lead to operable and viable provisions for the conduct of modern maritime operations. For example, the *Manual*'s rules on mine warfare and on blockade do not seem to meet that test. The same holds true with regard to those rules dealing with enemy and neutral aircraft.

Aerial Threats

Aircraft have always posed, and continue to pose, a considerable threat—a threat not limited only to naval platforms. Accordingly, particularly the conditions that render civil aircraft legitimate military objectives need to be reconsidered. An aircraft approaching naval surface forces can inflict damage to a warship by the use of comparatively inexpensive and non-sophisticated means. Moreover, it may gain and transmit information that is vital to the success of the military operation in question. The drafters of the 1923 Hague Rules[26] understood this and, accordingly, agreed upon Articles 33, 34, and 35[27] that would have enabled belligerents to deal with those threats adequately.

Spaight, who is hesitant to accept the 1923 Hague Rules relating to the treatment of civil aircraft as suitable for adoption,[28] doubts whether Article 34 would prove operable in practice for the following reasons:[29]

> Item (1) of the Article contemplates a contingency which is improbable; enemy non-military aircraft are hardly likely to venture into the jaws of the enemy's jurisdiction. The term 'operations' in item (3) of the same Article is unduly restricted. If a belligerent warship saw an enemy private aircraft suddenly approaching at high speed, surely it would be entitled to repel the aircraft by gunfire even if no operations were in progress in the locality? The reference to the 'immediate vicinity' of a 'jurisdiction'—a new test in international law—may lead to difficulties in interpretation; it will not be an easy test for the officers concerned to apply in practice.

> The framing of both Articles in a positive, instead of the usual prohibitory, sense leads to lack of precision. The quite unchallengeable right of a belligerent to fire upon a non-military aircraft which disobeys his signal or order to stand off or change its course does not seem to be safeguarded, at any rate in the open sea when 'operations' are not in progress.

Spaight therefore suggests replacing Articles 30, 33, and 34 with the following formulation:[30]

> A non-military aircraft may not be fired upon in flight, unless
>
> (1) It disobeys a belligerent's signals or orders; or
>
> (2) It enters an area notified by him as one of military activity in which aircraft circulate at their peril and are liable to be fired upon without warning.

Spaight's criticism is not necessarily valid today. On the one hand, it is not improbable that civil aircraft continue to fly within the jurisdiction of the respective enemy. On the other hand, the term "immediate vicinity of operations" has obviously gained some support and, moreover, has to be distinguished from self-defense situations obviously (also) envisaged by Spaight. While we will return to these concepts, it needs to be emphasized here that Spaight, despite his criticism, agrees that aircraft—enemy or neutral—pose a considerable risk and that the belligerents are entitled to counter that risk if necessary by the use of armed force.

Unlike Spaight and the 1923 Hague Rules,[31] the *San Remo Manual* obviously underestimates that threat and imposes upon belligerents obligations of abstention that will hardly meet the test of reality. Accordingly, therefore paragraph 63 (f) is too restricted. Pursuant to that provision, an enemy civil aircraft is a legitimate military objective if it, *inter alia*, is "armed with air-to-air or air-to-surface weapons." This excludes, as emphasized in the explanations, "light individual weapons for defence of the crew, and equipment that deflects an attacking weapon or warns of an attack."[32] But it remains an open question of what weapons can be qualified as coming within the categories of paragraph 63 (f). Moreover, this formulation leaves out of consideration the possibility that the aircraft itself is used as a weapon. The way modern warships are constructed would not enable them to sustain a hit by an aircraft. In this context, one should not think of "Kamikaze" aircraft used as a pattern of an unsuccessful military tactic or strategy. What needs to be considered are scenarios similar to that of the *USS Cole* incident.[33]

Mine Warfare

One consequence of equating warships and aircraft is that the latter would also be obliged to "record the locations where they have laid mines."[34] States possessing advanced military equipment may be in a position to comply with that obligation, e.g., by equipping air delivered mines with a system that would transmit their location without the enemy belligerent profiting from the signals. The majority of States will, however, hardly be in a position to acquire such systems. As the practice of World War II demonstrated, the recording of minefields laid by aircraft is a most difficult undertaking[35] and an obligation to do so does not seem to reflect customary international law.[36] Closely related is the problem—at least for a considerable number of States—of how to provide "safe alternative routes for shipping of neutral States"[37] in case the mining is executed by military aircraft. The minelaying belligerent will, in many cases, only be in a position to identify the mine area as such but not routes through the minefield that would be sufficiently safe. No considerable difficulties arise with regard to the obligation laid down in paragraph 85 of the *San Remo Manual*.[38] For example, the United States, when mining Haiphong harbor, made it possible for merchant vessels lying there to leave the harbor by daylight. The mines delivered by aircraft were activated three days after their delivery.[39]

Blockade

It is true that in the past blockades were a method of economic warfare at sea; however, today a blockade will regularly be an integral part of a genuinely military operation. Therefore, the lack of a definition of the concept of blockade in the *San Remo Manual* could give rise to some unnecessary misunderstandings.[40] Such a definition could read as follows: "Blockade is a method of naval warfare by which a belligerent prevents vessels and/or aircraft of all nations from entering or exiting specified ports, airfields, or coastal areas belonging to, occupied by, or under the control of an enemy nation."

The purpose of establishing a blockade is to deny the enemy the use of enemy and neutral vessels or aircraft to transport personnel and goods to or from enemy territory. It should be emphasized that a blockade is the only method of naval warfare by which belligerents may interfere with enemy exports.

But even if exclusively directed against the enemy's economy, there will always be a strategic element because the enemy's capabilities of resistance will necessarily be weakened.[41] Regardless of the distinction between economic and strategic blockades there is today general agreement that a blockade need not be enforced exclusively against seagoing vessels but that it may also be enforced against aircraft.[42] Moreover, and in view of the importance of aerial reconnaissance, a blockade may be maintained and enforced "by a combination of legitimate methods and means of warfare,"[43] including military aircraft.[44]

The *San Remo Manual*'s provisions on blockade, however, lack any express reference to aircraft. Of course, an interpretation of paragraphs 96[45] and 97[46] justifies the conclusion that a blockade may also be enforced and maintained by military aircraft. In most cases, these aircraft will operate from a warship that serves as their base.[47] It is also possible, however, that the aircraft entrusted with the enforcement of a blockade are deployed on airfields on land. Still, while there seems to be general agreement on the lawfulness of the enforcement of a blockade by military aircraft, two questions remain unanswered. (1) Is the presence of a warship or its operational control of the military aircraft necessary for a blockade to be lawful or may a blockade be enforced by aircraft (and mines) alone? (2) What criteria have to be met in order for the blockade to be effective if it is maintained and enforced by aircraft?

In most cases, the aircraft entrusted with the enforcement of a blockade need not be dependent upon a warship, i.e., they are not necessarily under the operational control of a warship. However, the answer to the first question becomes a little complicated if one takes into consideration the following scenario: A merchant vessel or a neutral warship may be damaged or in another distress situation. Therefore, it will have to access the blockaded coast or port but the blockade is maintained by mines and aircraft only. How will the blockading power be able to comply with its obligation to allow ships in distress entry into the blockaded coastline if no warship is in the near vicinity?[48] Accordingly, there is at least one argument against the legality of a blockade that is enforced and maintained without a surface warship present in, or in the vicinity of, the blockaded area.

As regards the second question, one may be inclined to point to the well-established rule according to which the "question whether a blockade is effective is a question of fact."[49] While it is clear that "effectiveness" can no longer be judged in the light of the state of technology of the 19th century[50] and, while the view is widely held that effectiveness continues to be a constitutive element of a legal blockade,[51] it must be recognized that there are no criteria that would make possible an abstract determination of the effectiveness of all blockades. In this context, Castrén postulates:

> Aircraft in the blockaded area may leave the area when there are other aircraft on patrol duty so that the blockade remains in force the whole time. The activities of aircraft even in connexion with a naval blockade are effective only to the extent that they do in fact dominate the air.[52]

It is maintained here that this position is correct. In any event, aircraft will be used for the enforcement of a blockade only if the respective belligerent has gained air superiority. Otherwise, the use of aircraft would be too dangerous.

A further aspect regarding blockade, as dealt with in the *San Remo Manual*, is whether this method of naval warfare is necessarily restricted to vessels or whether it may also be enforced vis-à-vis aircraft. Again, the provisions of the *San Remo Manual* are silent on this issue. The "explanations" reveal that the legal and naval experts, in the context of the effectiveness of a blockade, considered that question only indirectly.[53] While it may be correct that a (purely) naval blockade may not be considered to have lost its effectiveness for the sole reason that a considerable small number of aircraft continue to land within the blockaded area, this is but one aspect. Although traditionally blockades have been viewed as a method of naval warfare proper, there is no reason why it may not be extended (or even restricted) to aircraft.[54] In this context, the argument that "transport by air only constitutes a very small percentage of bulk traffic"[55] is not absolutely convincing. The blockaded belligerent State, either alone or together with its allies, may have a considerable air fleet at its disposal. As the example of the "blockade of Berlin" shows—although the cargoes only served humanitarian purposes—a considerable percentage of bulk traffic can be transported by air over a considerable period of time.

Methods and Means of Naval Warfare

Despite the lack of a definition and despite the disregard of the aerial elements, the provisions of the *San Remo Manual* on blockade certainly reflect customary international law.[56] Whether this also holds true with regard to the provisions on zones[57] is far from settled. Of course, it seems that, in principle, zones have become a recognized method of naval warfare[58]—and it is quite probable that the *Manual* has contributed to that development. Still, as already stated elsewhere,[59] the *San Remo Manual*'s provisions on zones remain rather obscure, particularly with regard to the purpose such zones may serve. This, however, is not the only criticism of the *Manual*'s provisions on methods and means of naval warfare.

Precautions in Attack

The *Manual*'s rules on precautions in attack are directly taken from the 1977 Additional Protocol I.[60] In principle, this does not necessarily pose problems—even though Additional Protocol I is far from being recognized by all States of the world. It would be futile to reopen the famous dispute between Meyrowitz[61] and Rauch[62] on whether and to what extent the provisions of Additional Protocol I apply to naval warfare at all. It is maintained here that, according to Article 49(3) of the

Protocol I, a special body of rules applies to ship-to-ship, ship-to-air, and to air-to-ship attacks as long as such attacks do not affect civilians or civilian objects on land. That is also clear from a reading of Article 49(4).[63] Accordingly, Articles 58 and 59 of Additional Protocol I are inapplicable to naval warfare as treaty law. Whether and to what extent they are customary in character is not quite settled.[64] Moreover, it is far from clear whether paragraph 46 of the *San Remo Manual* offers operable solutions for the conduct of hostilities at sea. The use of the concept of "feasibility" certainly mitigates some of the difficulties. Still, if naval operations are conducted in sea areas with dense maritime traffic, like in the Persian Gulf, it could become nearly impossible to determine "whether or not objects which are not military objectives are present in an area of attack."[65] The *USS Vincennes* incident may be indicative of the difficulties involved.[66] Legal rules that are merely paid lip service will certainly not pass the test of practice.

Naval Bombardment

Attacks against targets on land (naval bombardment) are not dealt with explicitly in the *San Remo Manual*. This is partly due to the fact that the participants regarded this subject as already covered by the respective provisions of Additional Protocol I.[67] It should be kept in mind, however, that not all States are bound by the Protocol. Then the question arises whether the provisions of the 1907 Hague Convention IX[68] constitute customary international law.

Even if that question is answered in the affirmative,[69] it remains unsettled how to deal with aircraft launched from warships attacking targets on land. According to Article XLI of the 1923 Hague Rules "aircraft on board vessels of war, including aircraft-carriers, shall be regarded as part of such vessels." This could imply that the rules applicable to warships engaged in naval bombardment also apply to aircraft launched from them. Then, however, such aircraft would be allowed to attack military objectives in non-defended localities.[70] While Additional Protocol I, Article 59, paragraph 1, prohibits attacks on such localities "by any means whatsoever," i.e., including aircraft, such attacks would not be prohibited under Articles 1 and 2 of Hague Convention IX. Castrén takes the position that Hague Convention IX "must probably be understood to concern warships only, and not aircraft even when collaborating with them."[71] If, however, Article XLI of the 1923 Hague Rules is a correct statement of customary law, warships and military aircraft launched from warships would be bound by the same rules.

Apart from the wording of these provisions, a further argument in favor of the view that land attacks by aircraft operating from warships should be governed by Additional Protocol I is the ability of modern aircraft to discriminate and to conduct surgical strikes by means of high-precision ammunition.

Still, it must be remembered that for a locality to be entitled to protection against attacks, Article 59(2) of Additional Protocol I, and the probably corresponding rule of customary law, provides that four conditions must be met:

(a) all combatants, as well as mobile weapons and mobile military equipment must have been evacuated;

(b) no hostile use shall be made of fixed military installations or establishments;

(c) no acts of hostility shall be committed by the authorities or by the population; and

(d) no activities in support of military operations shall be undertaken.

Accordingly, even if fixed military installations or establishments remain in the respective port or town this would not justify an attack "by any means whatsoever" if no hostile use is made of them. Then, regardless of the binding force of Additional Protocol I, an attack would probably be contrary to the law of armed conflict because the object in question would not make an effective contribution to military action and its neutralization would not offer a definite military advantage. Be that as it may, a clarification of the rules applicable to naval bombardment, including the use of aircraft and missiles launched from warships, should be taken into consideration.

Deception (and Surrender)

The *San Remo Manual*'s rules on deception are too vague and, thus, do not provide the necessary guidance for naval commanders. On the one hand, it is rather difficult to distinguish "active simulation"[72] from "passive simulation." The capabilities of modern technologies could open a vast grey area and, consequently, could render the provision obsolete. On the other hand, there should be a definition of legitimate ruses amended by a non-exhaustive list of permitted ruses that should be drafted with a view to modern technologies. The traditional examples given for permissible ruses of naval—especially *Count Luckner* and the Cruiser *Emden*—have a romantic charm but they certainly are too remote from the realities of modern naval operations.[73]

In a highly electronic environment and with over-the-horizon or beyond-visual-range capabilities, the hoisting of the true flag prior to an attack no longer seems to make much sense. However, ruses remain an important pattern of modern naval warfare. Therefore, there is a growing need for specific rules enabling naval commanders to distinguish between permissible ruses and prohibited acts of perfidy. While perfidy has been clarified in the *San Remo Manual*, ruses are not adequately addressed. It needs to be emphasized in this context that it is not always sufficient to draw the necessary conclusions from the prohibition of perfidy. For example, actively feigning the status of a protected vessel is prohibited by paragraph 110 of the *Manual* and the corresponding customary law.[74] This rule, however, is without prejudice to a decision to feign neutral status by the use of civilian radars or other electronic equipment. According to the position taken here, the use of civilian navigational radars (thus taking advantage of the respective emissions) is to be considered a permissible ruse of naval warfare if the radar is switched off immediately prior to the launching of an attack. It may well be, however, that this position is not shared by all. It should be recalled that, in 1983, the World Administrative Conference for the Mobile Services adopted Resolution No. 18[75] on the identification of vessels and aircraft of States not participating in an international armed conflict, recommending the use of adequate transponders and that:

> The frequencies specified in No. 3021 of the Radio Regulations may be used by ships and aircraft of States not parties to an armed conflict for self-identification and establishing communications. The transmission will consist of the urgency or safety signals, as appropriate, described in Article 40 followed by the addition of the single group 'NNN' in radiotelegraphy and by the addition of the single word 'NEUTRAL' pronounced as in French 'neutral' in radiotelephony. As soon as practicable, communications shall be transferred to an appropriate working frequency. . . .

It would, of course, be a considerable progress if the protection of neutral vessels were enhanced. However, that proposal is not suited for achieving that aim. As Fenrick has rightly pointed out, the resolution:

> appears to have been issued by a forum unfamiliar with law of armed conflict issues and without consultation with national officials responsible for such matters. Ships and aircraft using such procedures may assume they are entitled to protection when in fact they are not. The fact that a ship or aircraft is registered in a state not party to the conflict does not, in and of itself, mean that it is not a legitimate military objective.[76]

Therefore, it would certainly add to legal clarity and legal certainty if the rules on permissible ruses were amended by a non-exhaustive list of examples.

A problem closely related, but not limited, to ruses and perfidy is the surrender of warships and military aircraft. The provision of the *San Remo Manual* referring to the surrender of warships[77] certainly reflects customary international law.[78] Still, in a modern battlefield environment, visual identification is rather the exception than the rule. Therefore, an effort should be undertaken to specify the different possibilities of how warships and military aircraft can surrender at all. The more so since the *San Remo Manual* lacks a provision on enemy aircraft exempt from attack which have surrendered. It may, indeed, be difficult to verify whether a military aircraft has surrendered.[79] If, however, surrender has been offered *bona fide*, an attack on it would be contrary to basic rules of the law of armed conflict.

Maritime Neutrality

Probably, the law of neutrality is one of the most disputed aspects of public international law. The diversity of views on the subject makes it almost impossible to establish the continuing validity of that body of law, its scope of applicability, and its content. The drafters of the *San Remo Manual* have been heavily criticized for having adopted a rather traditional approach to the law of maritime neutrality.[80] It is maintained here, however, that this criticism is unfounded.

Obsolete by Desuetude or Irrelevant under the *Jus ad Bellum*?

Although the said uncertainties persist, there is general agreement that there is a need to protect States not taking part in an international armed conflict, as well as their nationals, the vessels flying their flags and the aircraft bearing their markings.[81] Moreover, there is similar agreement on the need for there to be obligations on neutral States, their nationals and their merchant shipping and civil aviation with a view to effectively prevent the escalation of an ongoing international armed conflict.[82] However, there is no consensus on how these objectives ought to be pursued.

According to a widely held view, the traditional law of neutrality is incompatible with the *jus ad bellum*.[83] The proponents of that view claim that the traditional rules have been extensively modified by the UN Charter. Therefore, they maintain, States not parties to an ongoing international armed conflict are entitled to take a position of "benevolent" neutrality if one party to the conflict has violated the *jus ad bellum*.[84] Indeed, under the right of collective self-defense, States are entitled to participate in an international armed conflict on the side of the victim of aggression. If they may assist the victim militarily then, *a fortiori*, they must be entitled to discriminate against the aggressor and to assist the victim State by any means short of war. In theory, this is certainly correct. However, the concept of benevolent neutrality is operable only if the Security Council has authoritatively determined the aggressor. This is expressly recognized in paragraphs 7 and 8 of the *San Remo Manual*.[85] If, however, the Security Council is unable or unwilling to act under Chapter VII, the benevolent neutral's right will compete with the right of the aggrieved belligerent to take appropriate counter measures in order to induce the neutral State to comply with the traditional rules. The better view is, therefore, to apply the laws of neutrality to such situations because only by so doing can the object and purpose agreed upon—protection of neutrals and prevention of an escalation of the armed conflict—be achieved.

Moreover, the concept of benevolent neutrality has no foundation in State practice. The proponents of that view ignore the fact that, since 1945, third States assisting one belligerent to the disadvantage of the other never referred to the right of collective self-defense.[86] Rather, they either advanced contractual obligations, or they claimed that their assistance did not cover military ("lethal") items,[87] or they simply acted clandestinely.[88] Hence, State practice since 1945 is not apt "for proving that a new legal status of non-belligerency has emerged as a concept of law. It would be all too easy to avoid duties of neutrality by just declaring a different status."[89] The fact that in many instances "non-belligerents" endeavored to conceal their assistance indicates, if not proves, that they had not based their conduct on a corresponding *opinio juris*.

Hence, State practice, as well as military manuals[90] and the International Law Association's Helsinki Principles,[91] support the view that the traditional rules of the law of maritime neutrality as codified in the 1907 Hague Convention XIII[92] have neither become obsolete nor have they been extensively modified. Therefore, the provisions of the *San Remo Manual* continue to reflect customary international law.

Continuing Value of the Laws of Maritime Neutrality

The main reason why most States continue to pledge allegiance to the laws of maritime neutrality is the intrinsic value of its principles and rules. On the one hand, this body of law serves the interests of neutral States by protecting them, their nationals, their merchant shipping and their aviation against the harmful effects of ongoing hostilities.[93] On the other hand, it guarantees that legitimate belligerent interests are not jeopardized by neutral States, their nationals, their merchant shipping and aviation unduly interfering in the warfighting and war-sustaining effort.[94]

It should be remembered, however, that the applicability of that law in its entirety is not triggered automatically as soon as an international armed conflict is in existence. This only holds true with regard to those rules of the law of maritime neutrality that are essential for safeguarding its object and purpose (*essentialia neutralitatis*). There is widespread agreement that the following rules of the law of maritime neutrality become applicable to every armed conflict at sea, irrespective of a declaration of war or of a declaration of neutrality: protection of neutral waters,[95] the obligation of neutral States to terminate violations of their neutral status,[96] and the prohibition of unneutral service.[97]

It needs to be emphasized that, despite allegations to the contrary,[98] the 24-hour rule[99] also belongs to those *essentialia neutralitatis*. If a neutral State does not, on a non-discriminatory basis, prohibit access to its territorial sea and its internal waters by belligerent warships,[100] a passage or sojourn exceeding 24 hours (unless unavoidable on account of damage or stress of weather) would amount to the use of neutral waters as a sanctuary. If the neutral State does not terminate that violation of its neutral status, the aggrieved belligerent will be entitled to take appropriate countermeasures.[101] The ensuing potentialities for escalation are obvious. The fact that the international armed conflict takes place in areas remote from the neutral waters in question is irrelevant. While the aggrieved belligerent may not be in a position to enforce the neutral State's obligations by directly interfering with its warships or military aircraft, it would certainly be entitled to take other measures in response to that violation of international law. Even if the aggrieved belligerent does not react at all, this does mean that there has not been a violation unless the aggrieved belligerent's conduct amounts to acquiescence.

Of course, the 24-hour rule implies some inconveniences for belligerent warships and auxiliaries, especially if their visit in a neutral port is unrelated to the ongoing international armed conflict. However, the object and purpose of the 24-hour rule is not limited to the protection of the belligerents, it also contributes to the protection of neutral States. If neutral States wish to remain under the protection of the law of maritime neutrality they are under an obligation to apply and to enforce the 24-hour rule. It should not be forgotten that the rule may prove a most valuable tool in pursuing belligerent goals as the case of the *Graf Spee* clearly demonstrates.[102]

Measures Short of War

A final criticism of the *San Remo Manual* relates to its section on "measures short of attack," i.e., prize law. The United Kingdom in particular has long taken the view that this part of the law of naval warfare and neutrality at sea has been considerably modified by the *jus ad bellum*. This approach must be rejected. The provisions of the *San Remo Manual* on prize measures certainly reflect customary international law. There are, however, two aspects that should be reconsidered.

Prize Law—Modified by the Jus ad Bellum?

The *San Remo Manual*—as well as the military manuals of some navies—starts from the premise that the *jus ad bellum* and the *ius in bello* are two distinct parts of international law.[103] In view of the basic principle of the equal application of the *ius in bello*,[104] the *San Remo Manual* does not distinguish between the aggressor and the victim of aggression, unless the UN Security Council has acted under Chapter VII of the Charter of the United Nations.[105] Accordingly, it allows all parties to an international armed conflict at sea to make use of the full spectrum of methods and means of naval warfare, including measures short of attack.[106]

According to the UK Manual, however, "the conduct of armed conflict at sea is subject to the limitations imposed by the UN Charter on all use of force." Therefore, in "a conflict of limited scope . . . a belligerent state is constrained, to a greater extent than the rules set out in the present chapter might suggest, in the action that it may lawfully take against the shipping or aircraft of states not involved in the conflict."[107]

This position is far from new. The UK government has maintained it since the 1980s—and has been heavily criticized for it. According to the position taken here, this criticism is well-founded. The British position would, if adopted by other States, lead to a most unfortunate lack of legal clarity and it would enable some malevolent States to arbitrarily deny the legality of measures taken by a belligerent against the shipping and aviation of States not parties to an ongoing international armed conflict.

This position is not shared by the UK's allies who are unwilling to limit the spectrum of methods and means provided by the law of naval warfare.[108] Obviously, those allies maintain that it will be up to them to decide whether and to what extent they will interfere with neutral shipping and aviation when engaged in an international armed conflict. And indeed the question arises as to who other than the belligerent State is competent to decide what is "necessary and proportionate to the achievement of the goal for which force may be used."

Of course, in case of an authoritative decision by the UN Security Council based upon Chapter VII of the UN Charter, a belligerent may be prevented from making use of the full spectrum provided by the law of naval warfare. However, if there is no such decision by the Security Council, it is generally recognized that the belligerent States alone are entitled to decide whether they will interfere with neutral shipping and aviation. The affected neutral States will be limited to a legal evaluation of the concrete measures taken, i.e., they may judge their legality in the light of the law of naval warfare and the law of maritime neutrality.[109] The right to judge, in a legally binding manner, the legality of the initial decision to resort to actions such as visit and search has been conferred upon the UN Security Council. Therefore, statements by neutral States on the legality of measures short of attack based upon rules other than those of the *ius in bello* (including the law of maritime neutrality) are to be considered merely political in character.

Another concern with the UK position is that it may lead to an arbitrary application of the law of naval warfare. In this respect, the British conduct during the

Falklands War (1982) and during the Iran-Iraq War (1980-1988) may serve as an example.[110]

As is well known, during the Falklands War the British government, on April 28, 1982, announced a Total Exclusion Zone (TEZ).[111] According to the wording of that proclamation the UK was prepared to attack every ship encountered within the limits of the TEZ. In the light of the jurisprudence of the Nuremberg Tribunal and of customary international law the legality of the TEZ, or of attacks performed therein, would have been more than doubtful.[112] It may well be that the proclamation was intended to deter rather than to serve as a legal basis for attacks on neutral shipping. It may well be that it was, after all, nothing but a—permissible—ruse of war. Taken at face value, however, and in view of the fact that the British government tried to justify the TEZ by referring to the right of self-defense, the British conduct during the Falklands War could also justify the following conclusion: if the British Government considers it necessary for its self-defense, it may decide to go beyond what is provided for by the law of naval warfare by establishing and enforcing a "free-fire zone."

During the Iran-Iraq War, the British Government chose the same approach. That time, however, it did not lead to a widening but rather to a restriction of the spectrum of measures provided by the law of naval warfare. After Iranian forces had stopped the British merchant vessel *Barber Perseus*, the Foreign Office, on January 28, 1986, declared:

> [U]nder Article 51 of the United Nations Charter a State such as Iran, actively engaged in an armed conflict, is entitled in exercise of its inherent right of self-defence, to stop and search a foreign merchant ship on the high seas if there is reasonable ground for suspecting that the ship is taking arms to the other side for use in the conflict. . . ."[113]

Thus, the British Government claimed the right to judge the legality of belligerent measures not in the light of the law of naval warfare alone, but also in the light of Article 51 of the UN Charter.

In other words, if party to an international armed conflict, the British Government, by referring to its inherent right of self-defense, considers itself entitled to enlarge the spectrum of methods and means under the law of naval warfare. If not party to an international armed conflict, the British government denies that very right to the belligerents but claims to be entitled to judge and declare what is necessary and proportionate for the belligerents' self-defense.

Hence, the British position will not lead to operable and practicable solutions. Of course, in theory it is always possible to identify a breach of the *jus ad bellum*. However, it must be emphasized that the prohibition of the use of force is an integral part of the UN system of collective security.[114] If the Security Council is not in a position to authoritatively determine the limits of the right of self-defense in a given case, it remains with the parties to the conflict to determine and decide which measures are necessary. The only operable legal yardstick providing practical solutions will then be the *jus in bello*. Moreover, the British position is irreconcilable with the principle of the equal application of the *ius in bello*. The continuing validity of that principle is confirmed by State practice since 1945 and by the Preamble to the 1977 Additional Protocol I. Accordingly, there is an overwhelming international consensus that the *jus in bello* does not discriminate between the alleged aggressor and the alleged victim of aggression. Moreover, that position may prove counterproductive for British interests in case the United Kingdom is party to an international armed conflict at sea. The use of prize measures by the Royal Navy, as provided for in the UK Manual,[115] could be qualified as illegal by other States that may refer to this very statement.

Prize Measures and the Necessity of Prize Courts

In view of the fact that, under customary international law, belligerents, by resorting to prize measures, are entitled to interfere with enemy and neutral merchant shipping and aviation,[116] it is indispensable to provide for the establishment of prize courts. There is no evidence in State practice or in legal writings that the traditional maxim "*Toute prise doit être jugée*" has become obsolete by desuetude.[117] Rather, pre- and post-World War II practice and scholarly statements give ample proof that the maxim remains in force.[118]

Aspects to Be Reconsidered

It has been shown in the foregoing that the provisions of the *San Remo Manual* on prize measures indeed restate the customary rules and principles on the subject matter. Still, the question remains whether those rules sufficiently take into account practical requirements.

On the one hand, there seems to be an unjustified discrimination between warships and military aircraft. As regards the rules applicable to military aircraft conducting visit and search operations, the *San Remo Manual* unnecessarily denies military aircraft the same rights as warships. While paragraphs 139 and 151 allow, "as an exceptional measure," the destruction of enemy and of neutral merchant vessels, there is no such exception for enemy or neutral civil aircraft. It should be kept in mind that, according to Articles 57 to 59 of the 1923 Hague Rules,[119] the destruction of such aircraft would be permissible if certain conditions are met beforehand.[120]

Moreover, the *San Remo Manual*, in paragraph 128, obliges belligerents "to adhere to safe procedures for intercepting civil aircraft as issued by the competent international organization," i.e., to the International Civil Aviation Organization's (ICAO) Manual concerning Interception of Civil Aircraft.[121] While it is true that "the ICAO manual contains detailed procedures for interception,"[122] those provisions are designed for interception operations in times of peace. It is, therefore, far from settled whether and to what extent the detailed procedures laid down in the ICAO manual are operable in times of armed conflict.

On the other hand, a further alternative to visit and search should be considered. Modern armed forces possess multi-sensors enabling them to identify certain cargoes, like chemicals or explosives.[123] Therefore, as an alternative to visit and search conducted in the traditional way, a belligerent may very well be satisfied with verifying the innocent character of cargo on board neutral merchant vessels and civil aircraft by merely "scanning" the vessels or aircraft with such sensors. Of course, whether the use of sensors is practicable and sufficient will depend upon the circumstances of each case.

Conclusion

The 1994 *San Remo Manual* has contributed in an invaluable manner to a clarification of the law applicable to naval warfare and maritime neutrality. The vast majority of its provisions are a contemporary restatement of customary international law. Since those provisions almost perfectly balance the interests of belligerents and of neutrals alike everything feasible should be undertaken to safeguard its tremendous achievement in restating a body of law that had not been comprehensively addressed since the adoption of the *Oxford Manual*[124] in 1913.

We do, however, live in a time of rapid technological development that certainly has a deep impact upon military doctrine and on the conduct of hostilities. Disregarding that development and the way modern armed conflicts are fought would marginalize the *San Remo Manual* and could even make it obsolete. While thanks to Yoram Dinstein considerable efforts are being undertaken to fill the *Manual*'s gaps with regard to the aerial issues involved, the other issues addressed here should be thoroughly scrutinized and ultimately solved. The best way of adapting the *San Remo Manual* to the said developments would be to reconvene, under the auspices of the International Institute of International Humanitarian Law and of the International Committee of the Red Cross, a group of experts with a view to adopt an informal declaration that would not substitute for but merely amend or clarify parts of the *San Remo Manual*.

Notes

1. INTERNATIONAL INSTITUTE OF HUMANITARIAN LAW, SAN REMO MANUAL ON INTERNATIONAL LAW APPLICABLE TO ARMED CONFLICTS AT SEA (1994), *available at* http://www.icrc.org/Web/eng/siteeng0.nsf/iwpList74/966627225C719EDCC1256B6600598E01 [hereinafter SAN REMO MANUAL]. An accompanying explanation is written in the form of a commentary and indicates the sources used by the drafters for each of the provisions of the Manual, and the discussion which led to their adoption. *See* EXPLANATION: SAN REMO MANUAL ON INTERNATIONAL LAW APPLICABLE TO ARMED CONFLICTS AT SEA (Louise Doswald-Beck ed., 1995) [hereinafter EXPLANATION].

2. US Navy: The Commander's Handbook on the Law of Naval Operations, NWP 1-14M/MCWP 5-2.1./COMDTPUB P5800.1 (1997) [hereinafter NWP 1-14]; Royal Navy: UK Ministry of Defence, The Manual of the Law of Armed Conflict, chap. 13 (2004) [hereinafter UK Manual]; German Navy: Commander's Handbook (Kommandanten-Handbuch) (2002) [hereinafter GN Manual].

3. *See*, *inter alia*, the papers presented by Steven Haines and by Jane Dalton in 36 ISRAEL YEARBOOK ON HUMAN RIGHTS (forthcoming 2006).

4. See Wolff Heintschel von Heinegg, *Current Legal Issues in Maritime Operations: Maritime Interception Operations in the Global War on Terrorism, Exclusion Zones, Hospital Ships and Maritime Neutrality*, 34 ISRAEL YEARBOOK ON HUMAN RIGHTS 151 (2004).

5. *See* Wolff Heintschel von Heinegg, *The Proliferation Security Initiative – Security vs. Freedom of Navigation?*, 35 ISRAEL YEARBOOK ON HUMAN RIGHTS 181 (2005).

6. In that case, the legal basis is the Security Council's decision based on Chapter VII of the Charter. While some navies, in their rules of engagement, also refer to rules and principles of the law of naval warfare, this is due to the fact that there exists no specific rules on the conduct of enforcement measures authorized by the Security Council. Therefore, they rely on the law of naval warfare as a general guidance only. This practice does not give evidence of an *opinio juris* that the respective States consider the law of naval warfare to be applicable in a formal sense.

7. *See* SAN REMO MANUAL, *supra* note 1, para. 1. Note, however, that this provision does not correctly reflect customary international law as rightly pointed out by Steven Haines, *supra* note 3.

8. The issues of arming hospital ships and of the use of secure communications on board hospital ships is dealt with in the article by Jane Dalton, *supra* note 3, and by Heintschel von Heinegg, *supra* note 4.

9. For corresponding definitions, see UK Manual, *supra* note 2, para. 13.5; NWP 1-14M, *supra* note 2, paras. 2.1.1, 2.1.3, 2.2.1; GN Manual, *supra* note 2, paras. 83 *et seq.*

10. For a long time, the Royal Navy has used civilian personnel to provide ship's services including food service, cleaning, and laundry. The US Navy also experimented with the concept of augmenting warship crews with civilian mariners supplied by the Military Sealift Command (MSC). Three years ago, MSC identified fleet command and control ships as platforms that can be transferred to MSC and staffed with civilian mariners. The *USS Coronado* had been chosen as the "pilot program" for this initiative. In addition, there is very often a considerable number of private contractors on board warships who maintain and/or operate electronic and weapons systems.

11. NWP 1-14M, *supra* note 2, paras. 2.1 and 7.6.1; UK Manual, *supra* note 2, paras. 13.5 and 13.91; GN Manual, *supra* note 2, paras. 200 *et seq.* and 280. *See also* Federal Ministry of Defence, Humanitarian Law in Armed Conflicts – Manual, paras. 1002 and 1015 (1992) (hereafter German Manual).

12. *See, e.g.*, German Manual, *supra* note 11, para. 1016.

13. Convention (VII) Relating to the Conversion of Merchants Ships into Warships, Oct. 18, 1907, *reprinted in* DOCUMENTS ON THE LAWS OF WAR 97 (Adam Roberts & Richard Guelff eds., 3d ed. 2000).
14. While there is a growing use of unmanned aerial vehicles (UAVs) for reconnaissance and for combat operations (UCAVs), there are but a few scholarly works on the legal questions involved in their use. Unmanned submarine or underwater vehicles (UUVs) that are used for purposes other than counter mine operations have not been dealt with at all by legal writers because most of the information on such vehicles is still classified.
15. United Nations Convention on the Law of the Sea, Dec. 10, 1982, 1833 U.N.T.S. 3, *reprinted in* 21 INTERNATIONAL LEGAL MATERIALS 1261, *available at* www.un.org/Depts/los/convention_agreements/texts/unclos/closindex.htm.
16. For an overview, see J. ASHLEY ROACH & ROBERT W. SMITH, UNITED STATES RESPONSES TO EXCESSIVE MARITIME CLAIMS (2d ed. 1996). A regular update is provided in the Maritime Claims Reference Manual, http://www.dtic.mil/whs/directives/corres/html/20051m.htm (last visited Jan. 15, 2006).
17. For example, the US Freedom of Navigation Program, established in 1979, continues as an active tenet of national policy. Probably the biggest success of the program, from the perspective of public international law, was the Joint Statement by the United States of America and the Union of Soviet Socialist Republics on the Uniform Interpretation of Rules of International Law Governing Innocent Passage (Sept 23., 1989) (the Jackson Hole Agreement), *reprinted in* ANNOTATED SUPPLEMENT TO THE COMMANDER'S HANDBOOK ON THE LAW OF NAVAL OPERATIONS 161 (A.R. Thomas & James C. Duncan eds., 1999) (Vol. 73, US Naval War College International Law Studies) which followed the so called "bumping incident" in the Black Sea.
18. SAN REMO MANUAL, *supra* note 1, para. 14.
19. *Id.*, paras. 34 and 35.
20. *See* EXPLANATIONS, *supra* note 1, para. 12.2, at 84.
21. The 1923 Hague Rules of Aerial Warfare, *reprinted in* DOCUMENTS ON THE LAWS OF WAR, *supra* note 13, at 141, were never adopted in legally binding form and are generally referred to as the "1923 Hague Draft Rules of Aerial Warfare."
22. Naval air components contribute to and enhance (sea) power projection. Before and during armed conflict their tasks include the establishment and maintenance of air superiority and the conduct of a variety of air interdiction operations. This, however, only in a very generic way describes the missions assigned to naval aircraft, fixed or rotary wing, in the course of an armed conflict. For regularly updated fact sheets on US Navy weaponry, see http://www.chinfo.navy.mil (last visited Jan. 18, 2006).
23. Hague Conventions of October 18, 1907: No. VI Relating to the Status of Enemy Merchant Ships at the Outbreak of Hostilities; No. VII Relating to the Conversion of Merchant Ships into War-Ships; No. VIII Relative to the Laying of Automatic Submarine Contact Mines; No. IX Concerning Bombardment by Naval Forces in Time of War; No. XI Relative to Certain Restrictions with Regard to the Exercise of the Right of Capture in Naval War; No. XIII Concerning the Rights and Duties of Neutral Powers in Naval War; all *reprinted in* THE LAWS OF ARMED CONFLICT (Dietrich Schindler & Jiri Toman eds., 4th ed. 2004) at 1059, 1065, 1071, 1079, 1087, and 1407, respectively.
24. Procés-verbal relating to the Rules of Submarine Warfare Set Forth in Part IV of the Treaty of London of April 22, 1930, Nov. 6, 1936, *reprinted in* DOCUMENTS ON THE LAWS OF WAR, *supra* note 13, at 171. For a short analysis, see Edwin I. Nwogugu, *Submarine Warfare – Commentary, in* THE LAW OF NAVAL WARFARE 353 (Natalino Ronzitti ed., 1988).

25. SAN REMO MANUAL, *supra* note 1, paras. 13, 18, 23–30, 45, 53–58, 62–66, 70–78, 106, 108–109, 112, 115–117, 125–134, 141–145, 161, 163, 165–166, 174–183.
26. *Supra* note 21.
27. Article 33: "Belligerent non-military aircraft, whether public or private, flying within the jurisdiction of their own state, are liable to be fired upon unless they make the nearest available landing on the approach of enemy military aircraft." Article 34: "Belligerent non-military aircraft, whether public or private, are liable to be fired upon, if they fly (1) within the jurisdiction of the enemy, or (2) in the immediate vicinity thereof and outside the jurisdiction of their own state or (3) in the immediate vicinity of the military operations of the enemy by land or sea." Article 35: "Neutral aircraft flying within the jurisdiction of a belligerent, and warned of the approach of military aircraft of the opposing belligerent, must make the nearest available landing. Failure to do so exposes them to the risk of being fired upon."
28. JAMES M. SPAIGHT, AIR POWER AND WAR RIGHTS 409 *et seq.* (3d ed. 1947), concludes: "For the present, little seems to be gained by an attempt to analyze them. They were, and are, rather long shots or dips into a distant future."
29. *Id.* at 402.
30. *Id.*
31. For a discussion of these provisions, see also II OPPENHEIM'S INTERNATIONAL LAW 530 (Hersch Lauterpacht ed., 7th ed. 1963).
32. EXPLANATIONS, *supra* note 1, para. 63.6, at 153.
33. For the details of the *Cole* incident, see the DoD USS Cole Commission Report (Jan. 9, 2001), *available at* http://www.defenselink.mil/pubs/cole20010109.html (last visited Jan. 17, 2006). *See also* CRS Report for Congress, Terrorist Attack on USS Cole: Background and Issues for Congress (Jan. 30, 2001), *available at* http://news.findlaw.com/cnn/docs/crs/coleterrattck13001.pdf (last visited Jan. 17, 2006).
34. SAN REMO MANUAL, *supra* note 1, para. 84.
35. *See, inter alia,* REINHARD OSTERTAG, DEUTSCHE MINENSUCHER: 80 JAHRE SEEMINENABWEHR 128 (1986).
36. SPAIGHT, *supra* note 28, at 494 *et seq.*
37. SAN REMO MANUAL, *supra* note 1, para. 88.
38. "Mining operations in the internal waters, territorial sea or archipelagic waters of a belligerent State should provide, when the mining is first executed, for free exit of shipping of neutral States."
39. *See* Howard S. Levie, Mine Warfare at Sea 117 et seq., 147 (1992).
40. Therefore, this author is in disagreement with Steven Haines article (*supra* note 3) insofar as he maintains that blockade is to be considered a pattern of *guerre de course.*
41. For the differences between economic and strategic blockades, see OPPENHEIM'S, *supra* note 31, at 769 *et seq.*
42. See, *inter alia,* NWP 1-14, *supra* note 2, para. 7.7.1; OPPENHEIM'S, *supra* note 31, at 781; ERIC CASTRÉN, THE PRESENT LAW OF WAR AND NEUTRALITY 301 (1954). *See also* ROBERT W. TUCKER, THE LAW OF WAR AND NEUTRALITY AT SEA 283 n.1 (1957): "The extension of blockades to include the air space over the high seas remains a development for the future. It is next to impossible to declare with any degree of assurance what procedures may govern blockade by air. Certainly, there are grave difficulties in assuming that the practices of naval blockade can be applied readily, by analogy, to aerial blockade." Note, however, that Tucker does not doubt the legality of a blockade if applied and enforced against air traffic.
43. SAN REMO MANUAL, *supra* note 1, para. 97.
44. OPPENHEIM'S, *supra* note 31, at 780 f.; CASTRÉN, *supra* note 42, at 300 *et seq.*

45. "The force maintaining the blockade may be stationed at a distance determined by military requirements." The term "force" is broad enough to also cover military aircraft.
46. *Supra*, text accompanying note 42.
47. *See* CASTRÉN, *supra* note 42, at 409 *et seq.*
48. *See also* EXPLANATIONS, *supra* note 1, para. 97.1, at 178.
49. SAN REMO MANUAL, *supra* note 1, para. 95.
50. Frits Kalshoven, *Commentary on the 1909 London Declaration, in* THE LAW OF NAVAL WARFARE, *supra* note 24, at 274 maintains: "[D]evelopments in the techniques of naval and aerial warfare have turned the establishment and maintenance of a naval blockade in the traditional sense into a virtual impossibility. It would seem, therefore, that the rules in the Declaration on blockade in time of war are now mainly of historical interest." This position is certainly not shared by those States having published manuals for their respective navies or by other authors. See JULIUS STONE, LEGAL CONTROLS OF INTERNATIONAL CONFLICT 508 (1954): "The realities of the present century require the British long distance blockade to be viewed as a long term transformation of the traditional law of blockade, rather than as mere reprisals, or mere breach of the traditional law." *See also* OPPENHEIM'S, *supra* note 31, at 796 *et seq.*
51. *See* NWP 1-14 M, *supra* note 2, para. 7.7.2.3; UK Manual, *supra* note 2, para. 13.67; GN Manual, *supra* note 2, para. 293 *et seq.*
52. CASTRÉN, *supra* note 42, at 409.
53. EXPLANATIONS, *supra* note 1, para. 95.2, at 177: "The Round Table considered whether the fact that aircraft could still land within the territory of the blockaded belligerent would affect the effectiveness of a sea blockade. This was found not to be the case, as, on the one hand, transport of cargo by air only constitutes a very small percentage of bulk traffic and, on the other hand, the fact that transport over land could take place without affecting this criterion."
54. See *supra* text accompanying notes 42 *et seq.*
55. EXPLANATIONS, *supra* note 1, para. 95.2, at 177.
56. Those rules were codified in the Paris Declaration Respecting Maritime Law, Mar. 13, 1856, *reprinted in* DOCUMENTS ON THE LAWS OF WAR, *supra* note 13, at 48. Moreover, they have been incorporated into military manuals. See NWP 1-14M, *supra* note 2, para. 7.7; UK Manual, *supra* note 2, para. 13.65 *et seq.*; GN Manual, *supra* note 2, para. 291 *et seq.* Moreover, they have been recognized by the International Law Association in paragraph 5.2.10 of the Helsinki Principles on the Law of Maritime Neutrality. *See* International Law Association Committee on Maritime Neutrality, Final Report: Helsinki Principles on Maritime Neutrality, in International Law Association, Report of the Sixty-Eighth Conference 496 (1998), reprinted in THE LAWS OF ARMED CONFLICTS, *supra* note 23, at 1425, 1430 (less Commentaries) [hereinafter Helsinki Principles]. While it is true that in post–WW II State practice blockades have only played a minor role, it is untenable to maintain that the law of blockade has been rendered obsolete by desuetude.
57. SAN REMO MANUAL, *supra* note 1, paras. 105 *et seq.*
58. UK Manual, *supra* note 2, para. 13.77 *et seq.*; NWP 1-14M, *supra* note 2, para. 7.9; GN Manual, *supra* note 2, para. 302 *et seq.*
59. *See* Heintschel von Heinegg, *supra* note 4.
60. Protocol Additional to the Geneva Convention of 12 August 1949, and Relating to the Protection of Victims of International Armed Conflicts (Protocol I), Dec. 12, 1977, 1125 U.N.T.S. 3, *reprinted in* DOCUMENTS ON THE LAWS OF WAR, *supra* note 13, at 422.
61. Henri Meyrowitz, *Le protocole additionel I aux conventions de Genève de 1949 et le droit de la guerre maritime*, 89 REVUE GÉNÉRALE DE DROIT INTERNATIONAL PUBLIC 245, 254 *et seq.* (1985): "Cette différence, répétons-le, est fondamentale et absolue. *Fondamentale*, en ce qu'elle découle

de l'éssence respective du droit de la guerre terrestre et du droit de la guerre maritime, cette différence découlant elle-même de la différence entre les données de la guerre sur terre et celles de la guerre maritime. *Absolue*, parce qu'elle interdit de transposer les règles de l'une à l'autre."

62. Rauch maintains that the provisions of Part IV, Section I, Additional Protocol I apply to all measures of naval warfare directed against merchant vessels. ELMAR RAUCH, THE PROTOCOL ADDITIONAL TO THE GENEVA CONVENTIONS FOR THE PROTECTION OF VICTIMS OF INTERNATIONAL ARMED CONFLICTS AND THE UNITED NATIONS CONVENTION ON THE LAW OF THE SEA: REPERCUSSIONS ON THE LAW OF NAVAL WARFARE 57 *et seq.* (1984); *see also* Elmar Rauch, *Le droit contemporain de la guerre maritime*, 89 REVUE GÉNÉRALE DE DROIT INTERNATIONAL PUBLIC 958 (1985).

63. See, *inter alia*, Michael Bothe, *Commentary on the 1977 Geneva Protocol I, in* THE LAW OF NAVAL WARFARE, *supra* note 23, at 761; Sally V. Mallison & W. Thomas Mallison, *Naval Targeting: Lawful Objects of Attack, in* THE LAW OF NAVAL OPERATIONS 259 *et seq.* (Horace B. Robertson, Jr. ed., 1991) (Vol. 64, US Naval War College International Law Studies).

64. GN Manual, *supra* note 2, para. 321, and UK Manual, *supra* note 2, para. 13.32, both repeat the wording of paragraph 46 of the *San Remo Manual.* However, in NWP 1-14M, *supra* note 2, there is no express reference to precautions in attack.

65. SAN REMO MANUAL, *supra* note 1, para. 46 (a).

66. For the details, see David Evans, *Vincennes – A Case Study*, 119 U.S. NAVAL INSTITUTE PROCEEDINGS 49 (Aug. 1993); Norman Friedman, *The Vincennes Incident*, 115 U.S. NAVAL INSTITUTE PROCEEDINGS 74 (May 1989).

67. While this view is shared by most writers, O'Connell seems to take the position that naval bombardment is governed by both Hague Convention IX and Additional Protocol I. *See* II DANIEL P. O'CONNELL, THE INTERNATIONAL LAW OF THE SEA 1130 *et seq.*, 1139, (Ivan A. Shearer ed., 1984).

68. *Supra* note 23.

69. *See, inter alia*, EBERHARD SPETZLER, LUFTKRIEG UND MENSCHLICHKEIT [AIR WARFARE AND HUMANITY] 127 *et seq.* (1956).

70. Obviously, this is the position taken by SPAIGHT, *supra* note 28, at 221 *et seq.* For an early criticism, see MORTON W. ROYSE, AERIAL BOMBARDMENT 162 *et seq.* (1928).

71. CASTRÉN, *supra* note 42, at 402.

72. SAN REMO MANUAL, *supra* note 1, para. 110.

73. *See* Mary T. Hall, *False Colors and Dummy Ships: The Use of Ruse in Naval Warfare*, 40 NAVAL WAR COLLEGE REVIEW 52 (1989). See also TUCKER, *supra* note 42, at 139, who, in 1957, still believed that flying a false flag was of most practical importance.

74. UK Manual, *supra* note 2, para. 13.83; NWP 1-14M, *supra* note 2, para. 12.1; GN Manual, *supra* note 2, para. 406 *et seq.*

75. *Reprinted in* 238 INTERNATIONAL REVIEW OF THE RED CROSS 58 *et seq.* (Jan.–Feb. 1984).

76. William J. Fenrick, *Introductory Report: Military Objectives in the Law of Naval Warfare, in* THE MILITARY OBJECTIVE AND THE PRINCIPLE OF DISTINCTION IN NAVAL WARFARE 40 (Wolff Heintschel von Heinegg ed., 1991).

77. SAN REMO MANUAL, *supra* note 1, para. 47 (i).

78. UK Manual, *supra* note 2, para. 13.33; GN Manual, *supra* note 2, para. 324 *et seq.*; NWP 1-14M, *supra* note 2, para. 8.2.1.

79. In NWP 1-14M, *supra* note 2, para. 8.2.1, it is emphasized: "Disabled enemy aircraft in air combat are frequently pursued to destruction because of the impossibility of verifying their true status and inability to enforce surrender. Although disabled, the aircraft may or may not have lost its means of combat. Moreover, it still may represent a valuable military asset. Accordingly,

surrender in air combat is not generally offered. However, if surrender is offered in good faith so that circumstances do not preclude enforcement, it must be respected."

80. E.g., by Steven Haines, *supra* note 3.

81. CASTRÉN, *supra* note 42, at 500 *et seq.*; TUCKER, *supra* note 42, at 206 *et seq.*; OPPENHEIM'S, *supra* note 31, at 675 *et seq.*; Yoram Dinstein, *Neutrality in Sea Warfare*, *in* III ENCYCLOPEDIA OF PUBLIC INTERNATIONAL LAW 558 *et seq.* (Rudolf Bernhardt ed., 1997).

82. *Supra* note 81. *See also* STEFAN OETER, NEUTRALITÄT UND WAFFENHANDEL 129 *et seq.* (1992); Dietrich Schindler, *Aspects contemporains de la neutralité*, 121 RECEUIL DE COURS 263 (1967); Michael Bothe, *Neutrality at Sea*, *in* THE GULF WAR 1980–1988, at 205 *et seq* (Ige F. Dekker & Harry H.G. Post eds., 1992).

83. Schindler, *supra* note 82, at 261 *et seq.*; Krzysztof Skubiszewski, *Use of Force by States. Collective Security: Law of War and Neutrality*, *in* MANUAL OF PUBLIC INTERNATIONAL LAW 840 *et seq.* (Max Sorensen ed., 1968); Philip C. Jessup, *Should International Law Recognize an Intermediate Status Between War and Peace?*, 48 AMERICAN JOURNAL OF INTERNATIONAL LAW 98 *et seq* (1954); Quincy Wright, *Rights and Duties Under International Law*, 34 AMERICAN JOURNAL OF INTERNATIONAL LAW 238 *et seq.* (1940); Frederick R. Coudert, *Non-Belligerency in International Law*, 29 VIRGINIA LAW REVIEW 143 (1942); Andrea Gioia, *Neutrality and Non-Belligerency*, *in* INTERNATIONAL ECONOMIC LAW AND ARMED CONFLICT 51 *et seq.* (Harry H.G. Post ed., 1994); Ove Bring, *Comments*, *in* THE GULF WAR 1980–1988, *supra* note 82, at 244.

84. *Supra* note 83; *see also* OPPENHEIM'S, *supra* note 31, at 651.

85. Paragraph 7: "Notwithstanding any rule in this document or elsewhere on the law of neutrality, where the Security Council, acting in accordance with its powers under Chapter VII of the Charter of the United Nations, has identified one or more parties to an armed conflict as responsible for resorting to force in violation of international law, neutral States: (a) are bound not to lend assistance other than humanitarian assistance to that State; and (b) may lend assistance to any State which has been the victim of a breach of the peace or an act of aggression by that State." Paragraph 8: "Where, in the course of an international armed conflict, the Security Council has taken preventive or enforcement action involving the application of economic measures under Chapter VII of the Charter, Member States of the United Nations may not rely upon the law of neutrality to justify conduct which would be incompatible with their obligations under the Charter or under decisions of the Security Council."

86. *See* OETER, *supra* note 82, at 136.

87. For example, the British Government, during the Iran-Iraq War (1980–1988), stated that it would not deliver "lethal equipment" to Iraq, but added that it would nevertheless "attempt to fulfill existing contracts and obligations." *See* 56 BRITISH YEARBOOK OF INTERNATIONAL LAW 534 (1985).

88. It suffices here to mention the Iran-Contras affair. *See* Alan T. Leonhard, *Introduction*, *in* NEUTRALITY – CHANGING CONCEPTS AND PRACTICES 4 (Alan T. Leonhard ed., 1988).

89. Bothe, *supra* note 82, at 207.

90. NWP 1-14M, *supra* note 2, chap. 7; GN Manual, *supra* note 2, chap. 3; UK Manual, *supra* note 2, para. 13.9 (note that para. 13.9 has been supplemented by para. 13.9 A to E).

91. *Supra* note 56.

92. *Supra* note 23.

93. See the references, *supra* note 81 *et seq.*

94. *Id.*

95. Hague Convention XIII, *supra* note 23, arts. 1, 2, and 5; UK Manual, *supra* note 2, para. 13.8 *et seq.*; NWP 1-14M, *supra* note 2, paras. 7.3.2, 7.3.4; GN Manual, *supra* note 2, para. 236, 243;

SAN REMO MANUAL, *supra* note 1, paras. 15–17; Helsinki Principles, *supra* note 56, paras. 1.4, 2.1.

96. Hague Convention XIII, *supra* note 23, art. 8; UK Manual, *supra* note 2, para. 13.9E; NWP 1-14M, *supra* note 2, paras. 7.3 and 7.3.4.1; GN Manual, *supra* note 2, para. 232; SAN REMO MANUAL, *supra* note 1, para. 22.

97. The term "unneutral service" refers to a conduct of neutral merchant vessels which is in support of the enemy belligerent, e.g. the carriage of contraband. *See* Dinstein, *supra* note 81, at 564 *et seq.* With regard to the prohibition of unneutral service, see Declaration Concerning the Laws of War arts. 45, 46, Feb. 26, 1909, *reprinted in* THE LAWS OF ARMED CONFLICTS, *supra* note 23, at 1113; NWP 1-14M, *supra* note 2, para.7.4; UK Manual, *supra* note 2, para. 13.84 *et seq.*; GN Manual, *supra* note 2, para. 258 *et seq.*; SAN REMO MANUAL, *supra* note 1, paras. 112 *et seq.*; Helsinki Principles, *supra* note 56, paras. 5.2.1 *et seq.*

98. See UK Manual, *supra* note 2, para. 13.4: "[T]he United Kingdom takes the view that the old rule which prohibited belligerent warships from remaining in neutral ports for more than 24 hours except in unusual circumstances, is no longer applicable in view of modern state practice."

99. The 24-hour rule is expressly recognized in Hague Convention XIII, *supra* note 23, art. 12; NWP 1-14M, *supra* note 2, para. 7.3.2.1; GN Manual, *supra* note 2, para. 236 *et seq.*; SAN REMO MANUAL, *supra* note 1, para. 21; Helsinki Principles, *supra* note 56, para. 2.2. *See also* Dinstein, *supra* note 81, at 559 *et seq.*; Paul Parfond, *Le statut juridique des navires de guerre belligérants dans les ports neutres*, REVUE MARITIME 867 (1952).

100. Hague Convention XIII, *supra* note 23, art. 9; NWP 1-14M, *supra* note 2, paras. 7.3.2 and 7.3.4; UK Manual, *supra* note 2, para. 113.9B; GN Manual, *supra* note 2, para. 245. *See also* Tucker, *supra* note 42, at 240; OPPENHEIM'S, *supra* note 31, at 727 *et seq.*; CASTRÉN, *supra* note 42, at 519 *et seq.*

101. See the references *supra* note 96.

102. For an in-depth analysis of the *Graf Spee* incident, see DANIEL P. O'CONNELL, THE INFLUENCE OF LAW ON SEA POWER 27 *et seq.* (1975).

103. *See* SAN REMO MANUAL, *supra* note 1, paras. 3 *et seq.* *See also* NWP 1-14M, *supra* note 2, para. 5.1; GN Manual, *supra* note 2, para. 218.

104. For a detailed analysis of this principle, see HENRI MEYROWITZ, LE PRINCIPE DE L'ÉGALITÉ DES BELLIGÉRANTS DEVANT LA DROIT DE LA GUERRE (1970). See also YORAM DINSTEIN, THE CONDUCT OF HOSTILITIES UNDER THE LAW OF INTERNATIONAL ARMED CONFLICT 4 (2004).

105. SAN REMO MANUAL, *supra* note 1, paras. 6 *et seq.*

106. The same approach underlies NWP 1-14M, *supra* note 2, and the GN Manual, *supra* note 2.

107. UK Manual, *supra* note 2, para. 13.3.

108. *Supra* note 106.

109. Evidence can be found in the practice of States during the Iran-Iraq War. The attacks on neutral merchant vessels were condemned by the UN Security Council (SC Res. 552, June 1, 1984) and by the member States of the European Community. *See* Bulletin of the European Communities, Commission, No. 9, at 7 (1980); European Political Cooperation Documentation Bulletin, Vol. 3, No. 2, at 93 (1987) and Vol. 4, No. 1, at 173 *et seq.* (1988).

110. For a detailed analysis of that practice, see William J. Fenrick, *The Exclusion Zone Device in the Law of Naval Warfare*, 24 CANADIAN YEARBOOK OF INTERNATIONAL LAW 91 (1986). *See also* Ronald P. Barston & Patricia Birnie, *The Falkland Islands/Islas Malvinas Conflict – A Question of Zones*, 7 MARINE POLICY 14 (1983); A. Vaughan Lowe, *Commentary*, in THE IRAN-IRAQ WAR (1980–1988) AND THE LAW OF NAVAL WARFARE 241 *et seq.* (Andrea de Guttry & Natalino Ronzitti eds., 1993).

111. "[T]he exclusion zone will apply not only to Argentine warships and naval auxiliaries but also to any other ship, whether naval or merchant vessel, which is operating in support of the illegal occupation of the Falkland Islands by Argentine forces. The zone will also apply to any

aircraft, whether military or civil, which is operating in support of the Argentine occupation. Any ship and any aircraft, whether military or civil, which is found within the zone without authority from the Ministry of Defence in London will be regarded as operating in support of the illegal occupation and will therefore be regarded as hostile and will be liable to be attacked by British forces." TIMES (London), Apr. 29, 1982, *reprinted in* 53 THE BRITISH YEARBOOK OF INTERNATIONAL LAW 542 (1982).

112. However, Fenrick, *supra* note 110, at 112 *et seq.*, maintains that the British TEZ was legal in view of the fact that in was established in a remote sea area and that neutral ships were not attacked.

113. Statement by the Minister of State, Foreign and Commonwealth Office, Jan. 28, 1986, House of Commons Debates, Vol. 90, col. 426, *reprinted in* 57 THE BRITISH YEARBOOK OF INTERNATIONAL LAW 583 (1986).

114. *See* YORAM DINSTEIN, WAR, AGGRESSION AND SELF-DEFENCE 80 *et seq.* (3d ed. 2001).

115. UK Manual, *supra* note 2, para. 13.84 *et seq.*

116. NWP 1-14M, *supra* note 2, para. 7.4; GN Manual, *supra* note 2, para. 258 *et seq.*; Helsinki Principles, *supra* note 56, paras. 5.2.1 *et seq. See also* Wolff Heintschel von Heinegg, *Visit, Search, Diversion and Capture in Naval Warfare: Part I, The Traditional Law*, 29 CANADIAN YEARBOOK OF INTERNATIONAL LAW 283 *et seq.* (1991); *Part II, Developments since 1945*, 30 Canadian Yearbook of International Law 89 *et seq.* (1992).

117. Paul Reuter, ETUDE DE LA RÈGLE: 'TOUTE PRISE DOIT ÊTRE JUGÉE' (1933).

118. See the references *supra* note 116. *See also* Dinstein, *supra* note 81, at 566.

119. *Supra* note 21.

120. As already mentioned, these conditions are similar to those laid down in the San Remo Manual on the destruction of "prizes." Note that SPAIGHT, *supra* note 28, at 394 *et seq.* and 409 *et seq.*, doubts whether the 1923 Hague Rules would be operable.

121. *See also* Convention on International Civil Aviation, Annex 2, Dec. 7, 1944, 61 Stat. 1180, 15 U.N.T.S. 295.

122. EXPLANATIONS, *supra* note 1, para. 128.1.

123. For a most recent description of the capabilities of such sensors, see JANE'S DEFENCE WEEKLY, Apr. 14, 2004, at 23 *et seq.*

124. INSTITUTE OF INTERNATIONAL LAW, THE LAWS OF NAVAL WAR GOVERNING THE RELATIONS BETWEEN BELLIGERENTS (1913), *reprinted in* THE LAWS OF ARMED CONFLICT, *supra* note 23, at 1123.

XV

Future Navies—Present Issues

Jane G. Dalton*

The US Navy is transforming to deal with a wider range of missions than the traditional blue-water, major combat operations which it has traditionally been equipped to handle.[1] That emerging transformation has resulted in a number of new programs, technologies, and strategies that raise interesting, and sometimes complex, legal issues. Lawyers advising the Navy's leadership through this transformational process are analyzing these legal issues now, in the present, to ensure that the future US Navy is properly, and legally, organized, trained and equipped. This article will address five topics of interest for naval planners and legal advisors who are building the Navy of tomorrow.

Civilian Mariners and Sea Basing

The US Navy currently maintains a force of approximately 550,000 full-time personnel, about 35% of whom are civilians. At any given time, 130-plus of the Navy's 283 ships are underway. That constitutes about 45% of the total ship inventory.[2] In 2004, former Chief of Naval Operations (CNO) Admiral Vern Clark directed the

* Charles H. Stockton Professor of International Law at the United States Naval War College. The views expressed in this article are those of Professor Dalton and are not necessarily those of the Naval War College, the United States Navy, or the Department of Defense. This article was previously published in the *Naval War College Review*, Volume 59, No. 1 (Winter 2006) at page 79.

Navy to maximize capabilities, minimize payroll, improve productivity and eliminate unnecessary billets.[3] One way to meet those goals is to remove sailors from billets that have little to do with warfighting, and replace them with civilians. At sea, sailors cut hair, serve meals, maintain the engineering plant, chip paint—all tasks that civilians are equally capable of performing, and do perform, at commands ashore. Placing civilians on warships to perform those tasks is a logical extension of the CNO's guidance and would free sailors to engage in combat-related activities.

The Navy's answer to the CNO's challenge is an experimental program to place federal civil service mariners onboard warships. These civilian mariners perform tasks sailors have traditionally performed onboard warships, but that civilian mariners have performed onboard auxiliary vessels for decades and onboard merchant vessels for centuries—navigation, engineering, and deck seamanship. For example, in early 2005, *USS Mount Whitney* (*LCC/JCC-20*) deployed to the European theater as the new US Sixth Fleet and North Atlantic Treaty Organization (NATO) command ship—one of the most sophisticated Command, Control, Communications, Computer, and Intelligence (C4I) ships ever commissioned.[4] *Mount Whitney* is manned by a hybrid crew consisting of 157 US Navy sailors and 143 civilian mariners employed by the Military Sealift Command. These 300 personnel represent a reduction of 276 people from the previous all active-duty Navy crew. "By supplementing the crew with civilian mariners," the Sixth Fleet Public Affairs Office reports, "the Navy is operating the command ship at a reduced cost and employing captured uniformed personnel billets on forward combatant vessels."[5] *Mount Whitney* will be engaged in NATO exercises and Standing Naval Forces Mediterranean maritime operations and will be available as a command and control ship for future combat operations if required.

In addition to placing civilian mariners on warships performing functions active-duty sailors have performed in the past, the Navy is simultaneously pursuing the concept of "sea basing" as a transformational initiative. Sea basing is the Navy's answer to the concern that access to bases in foreign territory will be less predictable and more *ad hoc* than in the past. This concern is not an idle or speculative one, as evidenced by Turkey's refusal during Operation Iraqi Freedom to permit the 4th Infantry Division to cross Turkish territory into Northern Iraq.

The sea base is envisioned as a system of systems—a flotilla of ships that serves as a staging and sustainment area for ground forces to launch attacks ashore in a non-permissive environment—sometimes referred to as "forcible entry operations." Though no one knows exactly what the sea base will look like in any detail, it will probably consist of a "network of ships providing offshore artillery fire, air support, supplies and a secure home for troops fighting on land."[6] The primary components of the sea base could include the Maritime Prepositioning Force Future

(MPF-F) cargo ship, the next generation destroyer (DDX), the Littoral Combat Ship (LCS) and the Amphibious Assault Ship (LHA-R) in conjunction with existing guided-missile cruisers and destroyers, aircraft carriers, and submarines.[7]

Of particular interest for this discussion is the role of the MPF-F cargo ship in sea basing operations. The MPF-F is designed as the replacement for today's prepositioning force cargo ships and would serve as a floating logistics center. One report notes that it would be "nearly as large as an aircraft carrier" and would "accommodate heavy-lift helicopters and perhaps cargo planes as large as the Air Force's C-130. It would be able to move supplies and equipment to those aircraft and other ships while at sea."[8] Another report, however, depicts a role directly involved in combat operations. It refers to the MPF-F as a replacement for the big-deck *Tarawa*-class ships and describes it as a "fighting logistics ship with a flight deck big enough to send hundreds of Marines ashore in rotorcraft and launch Joint Strike Fighters."[9]

If the MPF-F ship is manned similar to existing prepositioning ships, the crew will consist entirely of civilian mariners. There is no legal prohibition against manning naval auxiliaries such as oilers, ammunition ships, supply ships, and prepositioning ships with civilian mariners. In fact, these mariners have a recognized status under the Geneva Conventions as "civilians accompanying the force" and are entitled to prisoner of war status if captured.[10] Issues arise, however, if the MPF-F is indeed to become part of the "assault echelon"—if Marines or soldiers actually launch from the ship into combat operations ashore. Similar issues arise if *Mount Whitney*, with a hybrid crew of active-duty sailors and civilian mariners, is employed as a C4I ship in a future armed conflict.

The issues that arise are twofold: First, under conventional and customary international law, a warship is manned by a crew under regular armed forces discipline. Second, civilians who assist in operating and maintaining a warship engaged in international armed conflict could be viewed as participating actively or directly in hostilities, and thus as having lost their protected status as civilians accompanying the force. These two issues will be addressed in turn.

Article 29 of the 1982 United Nations Convention on the Law of the Sea[11] and Article 8 of the 1958 Convention on the High Seas[12] identify warships by four characteristics: they belong to the armed forces of a State; they bear external marks distinguishing warships of their nationality; they are commanded by officers duly commissioned by the government of the State and whose names appear in the appropriate service lists or equivalents; and they are manned by crews under regular armed forces discipline. These characteristics originated in the 1856 Declaration of Paris[13] which abolished privateering, and the 1907 Hague Convention VII[14] which established the conditions for converting merchant ships into warships. The rules served to distinguish bona fide warships from privateers, which operated from motives of personal gain, by clearly establishing that the warships operated on behalf of a State. They also furthered the requirement in Hague VII that warships are to observe the laws and customs of war. These four characteristics are so universally identified with warships throughout the world that they may be said to have attained the status of customary international law.

Left undefined, however, is what the phrase "manned by a crew" actually means in practice. Many US Navy warships today have civilians onboard performing a variety of functions—technical representatives, science advisors, contractors. Under customary practice, warships have carried civilians onboard. In the War of 1812, for example, Commodore Stephen Decatur's ship, the frigate *United States*, embarked female contract nurses to care for the sick and wounded.[15] The mere presence of small numbers of civilians clearly does not deprive a warship of its status as a warship. But the issue takes on greater meaning if one-third or one-half of a warship's complement is composed of civilians who, though subject to a civilian disciplinary system, are not subject to the Uniform Code of Military Justice.[16] Though there is no "bright line" rule that determines what percentage of a warship's crew should be active-duty sailors, it is fair to say that the greater the percentage of civilians onboard performing functions traditionally accomplished by sailors, the less likely the warship will be able to maintain swift and effective discipline over its entire manning complement. The inability to effectively discipline a crew thus calls into question the ship's ability to "observe the laws and customs of war" as required by Hague VII.

The first issue concerning civilian mariners, as just discussed, implicates the warship's ability to meet its international obligation to observe the laws and customs of war and to meet the criteria established for warships in conventional and customary law. The second issue is related to the civilian mariners themselves and to their status if they are captured during an international armed conflict. One of the basic principles of the law of armed conflict is that of "distinction"—combatants and noncombatants must be distinguished so as to spare noncombatants as much as possible from the exigencies of war.[17] A corollary of the basic principle is that noncombatants (civilians) enjoy protections under the law of armed conflict unless and until they take a direct or active part in hostilities.[18] Civilians accompanying the force certainly assume the risk of becoming casualties of war due to their proximity to military operations. For example, civilian mariners manning oilers replenishing warships at sea are aware that the platforms on which they serve are legitimate military objectives. The mariners themselves, however, retain their status as "persons who accompany the armed forces without actually being members thereof." They carry identification cards reflecting their authority to accompany the force, and are entitled to prisoner of war status if captured.[19]

If the civilian mariners are employed onboard a warship engaged in combat operations, however, it is possible that questions could be raised as to their status. Unfortunately, there is no authoritative definition of "direct" or "active" participation in hostilities.[20] Purely collateral duties such as cutting hair, running the ship's store and performing housekeeping functions may contribute to the quality of life onboard the warship, but are not necessary to its combat effectiveness. On the other end of the spectrum, firing weapons, maintaining the weapons systems or serving as members of belligerent boarding parties are more akin to actual participation. Running the engineering plant, navigating the ship and operating the small boats and cranes could be considered collateral functions or could be considered actual participation.

A sailor who needs a haircut can nevertheless man the weapons systems or serve on a boarding party. A ship that is not within its assigned Tomahawk Land Attack Missile (T-LAM) launch basket or is not properly heading into the wind for the launch of fighter aircraft cannot perform its combat function. Further, the warship itself is a weapons system and the full crew complement is required for the weapons system to be effective. Civilian engineers running the propulsion plant, navigators plotting ship's movement, and technicians working on the missile system all contribute to the war fighting effectiveness of the ship. It is difficult to argue that any of these personnel are not actively and directly contributing to the combat functions of the ship. It is conceivable that an opposing belligerent could perceive civilian mariners serving onboard a warship engaged in international armed conflict, particularly those engaged in engineering, navigation and deck seamanship, as having taken an active and direct part in hostilities. That same enemy belligerent would also be unlikely to grant the civilian mariners combatant immunity for such acts and could prosecute them for murder, arson and other violations of the belligerent's domestic law.

The above discussion posits the most extreme examples. To date, the only warships manned with civilian mariners have been those warships designated as command and control platforms such as *Mount Whitney*. The MPF-F ships are still in the planning stages and it is not determined exactly how they will be employed in the sea basing construct. As the Navy continues its transformational efforts, however, there will no doubt be continued pressure to contract out or seek civilian substitution for more and more administrative and support functions in order to free active-duty sailors for actual combat duties.

To address both issues raised by the potential "civilianization" of warship crews, the Navy has proposed legislation[21] that would create a 5-year pilot program to require civilian mariners employed by the Navy to affiliate with a special Navy Reserve component. If the legislation is enacted, the mariners will remain civilian federal employees unless the ship is ordered into combat operations in international armed conflict, at which time the mariners will be ordered to active duty. In their active duty status, the mariners will be subject to the Uniform Code of Military Justice, thus ensuring that the entire crew is subject to armed forces discipline. Further, if captured, they will be members of the active duty force entitled not only to prisoner of war status, but also to combatant immunity for any belligerent acts in which the warship engaged. Though there may be other ways to approach the international law concerns raised by placing hybrid crews on warships, the proposed legislation is attractive in that it resolves both issues satisfactorily and provides the civilian mariners with the highest degree of protection under international law in the event they are captured during belligerent operations.

Unmanned Aerial and Underwater Systems[22]

In April 2005, General John Jumper reported that there were over 750 unmanned aerial vehicles operating in Iraq.[23] At about the same time, the US Navy deployed its first operational unmanned undersea vehicle, a Remote Minehunting System (RMS), to identify and chart suspicious objects in Khwar Abd Allah channel at the Iraqi port of Umm Qasr.[24] Most readers are surely familiar with the use of the Predator as a precision weapon in Iraq, Afghanistan and Yemen.[25] There is even talk of a future unmanned aerial system which would track and engage targets without a "man in the loop."[26] The relatively low cost, ease of transport, technological sophistication, and lack of manned crew combine to make unmanned systems the surveillance platform and armed weapon of choice for the foreseeable future,[27] even to the point of replacing F-16 and KC-135 aircraft in the current US Air Force inventory.[28]

The use of these unmanned systems, however, raises a primary legal issue: Should they be treated under international law like their manned counterparts—airplanes and submarines? For example, do the regimes of innocent passage, straits transit passage and archipelagic sea lanes passage apply? Are they required to comply with the International Regulations for the Prevention of Collisions at Sea (COLREGs)? Do they enjoy sovereign immunity? What is the legal framework for attacking an unmanned system? Unfortunately, developing a complete answer to most of these questions is beyond the scope of this article, and each could be the topic of a scholarly legal treatise. Some of the answers, however, are relatively intuitive and will be addressed below.

Take, for example, a carrier strike group transiting the Strait of Hormuz and employing an unmanned Scan Eagle intelligence, surveillance and reconnaissance vehicle[29] for a "channel sweep" mission. The Strait of Hormuz, as an international strait connecting the Arabian Gulf with the Gulf of Oman and the Arabian Sea, is subject to the regime of straits transit passage throughout the strait and its approaches.[30] Under that regime, all states enjoy the right of unimpeded navigation and overflight solely for the purpose of continuous and expeditious transit of the strait.[31] While exercising the right of transit passage, ships and aircraft "shall refrain from any activities other than those incident to their normal modes of continuous and expeditious transit."[32]

Accordingly, in analyzing whether a carrier strike group may employ a reconnaissance vehicle during straits transit passage, the question is not whether the vehicle is manned or unmanned,[33] but whether it is consistent with the strike group's "continuous and expeditious transit" in its "normal mode" of operation. *The Commander's Handbook on the Law of Naval Operations* provides that the normal mode of operation for surface ships includes "transit in a manner consistent with sound navigational practices and the security of the force, including formation steaming and the launching and recovery of aircraft."[34] The *San Remo Manual* addresses straits transit passage during armed conflict and concludes that belligerents "are permitted to take defensive measures consistent with their security, including launching and recovery of aircraft, screen formation steaming, and acoustic and electronic surveillance."[35]

The Scan Eagle's "channel sweep" mission is a surveillance mission designed for force protection and navigational safety—normal operational concerns for all Navy vessels wherever they are transiting and whether the transit is in peacetime, in a period of heightened tensions, or during an armed conflict. The need for defensive, force protection measures is particularly acute when transiting in relatively close proximity to land, in high traffic areas such as the straits, where an asymmetric enemy such as a terrorist could strike without warning.[36] Accordingly, employment of the Scan Eagle in a force protection and safety of navigation surveillance and reconnaissance mode is completely consistent with the regime of straits transit passage. It may be launched from the aircraft carrier or other surface platform. If it were an unmanned undersea vehicle, it could operate submerged, if that is consistent with its normal mode of operation. The same would apply if the strike group were operating in archipelagic sea lanes transit through an archipelagic nation.

It must be noted, however, that the Scan Eagle is also an intelligence-gathering platform. The rules concerning straits transit passage provide that passage must be "solely for the purpose of continuous and expeditious transit of the strait,"[37] and States are to "refrain from any activities other than those incident to their normal modes of continuous and expeditious transit unless rendered necessary by *force majeure* or by distress."[38] States are also to refrain from "the threat or use of force against the sovereignty, territorial integrity or political independence of States bordering the strait, or in any other manner in violation of the principles of international law embodied in the Charter of the United Nations."[39] Importantly, unlike the rules governing innocent passage through territorial seas, intelligence-gathering is not identified as inconsistent with straits transit passage. Indeed, some amount of photographic or electronic intelligence-gathering may inevitably occur incidental to the "channel sweep" mission. Such intelligence-gathering would not be inconsistent with the regime of transit passage since the "channel sweep" mission is related to safety of navigation and security of the force.[40]

Compare the transit passage regime with that of innocent passage through territorial seas. When engaged in innocent passage, submarines are required to operate on the surface, ships may not launch or recover aircraft or any military device, and any act aimed at collecting information to the prejudice of the defense or security of the coastal State is considered inconsistent with the innocent passage regime.[41] Accordingly, a carrier strike group engaged in innocent passage could not launch or recover the Scan Eagle or the RMS underwater vehicle. Since there is no right of innocent passage through a nation's territorial airspace, an unmanned aircraft launched outside the territorial sea would not be entitled to innocent passage over the territorial sea.

Consider, though, whether an unmanned *undersea* vehicle launched prior to entry into the territorial sea is entitled to innocent passage on the surface as other submarines are. The 1982 LOS Convention provides that "ships of all States . . . enjoy the right of innocent passage through the territorial sea."[42] The Convention does not define "ship," but it does define "warship" as "a ship belonging to the armed forces of a State bearing the external marks distinguishing such ships of its nationality, under the command of an officer duly commissioned by the government of the State and whose name appears in the appropriate service list or its equivalent, and manned by a crew which is under regular armed forces discipline."[43] Arguably, the RMS vehicle fits this definition if one considers that the commanding officer of the ship from which it is launched is in "command" of the RMS and the crew operating it is "manning" the vehicle. In any event, the RMS does not have to be a warship to be entitled to innocent passage, since the right applies to "ships" of all States. Webster's dictionary distinguishes between ships, rather large vessels adapted for deep-water navigation, and boats, rather small, usually open, craft.[44] But Webster's also notes that for legal purposes, a ship is "a vessel intended for marine transportation, without regard to form, rig or means of propulsion."[45] Arguably, then, an unmanned undersea vehicle, if it is considered a ship, could engage in continuous, expeditious innocent passage, provided it transited on the surface, showed its flag, and did not engage in intelligence collection to the prejudice of the defense or security of the coastal state.

A related issue is whether unmanned systems like the RMS are "vessels" which must comply with the Regulations for the Prevention of Collisions at Sea (COLREGs). The COLREGs apply to "all vessels on the high seas," and define a vessel to include "every description of watercraft, including non-displacement craft and seaplanes, used or capable of being used as a means of transportation on water."[46] The COLREGs definition is also found in US statutes[47] and is the generally accepted definition in admiralty law. The US Supreme Court has ruled on this subject, and continues to expand the type of watercraft encompassed by the term "vessel."[48] Though the RMS system is incapable of transporting people, it does carry a payload of sensors, other instrumentation and equipment, has its own propulsion system of up to 16 knots, and is able to operate as far as 14 nautical miles from the launch platform.[49] If the RMS and similar systems are "vessels," they must meet a number of design and operational requirements, such as being equipped with lookouts, sound, lighting, and dayshapes.[50]

Regardless whether the RMS is required to comply with the COLREGs requirements, those in command of the launching platform and the unmanned system have a duty to act with due regard for the safety of others on the high seas—a duty imposed by both the COLREGs[51] and the Law of the Sea.[52] The RMS system is currently equipped with a mast-mounted camera that allows the operator to safely avoid surface objects; forward-looking sonar to alert the operator to submerged objects; and a mast-mounted strobe light to advise nearby vessels of its presence. A radar reflector may also be mounted on the mast.[53] Given the unsettled state of the law on the status of unmanned undersea systems,[54] the prudent course of action for the US Navy is to ensure these systems comply with all applicable COLREGs requirements or obtain appropriate exemptions.

Hospital Ships

Military hospital ships are granted extraordinary protection under the Second Geneva Convention. Current technology and the threat of global terrorism, however, are posing two vexing problems for navies of the future.

Military hospital ships are those ships built and equipped solely to assist, treat and transport the wounded, sick and shipwrecked.[55] They may "in no circumstances" be attacked or captured, but shall "at all times be respected and protected," provided that the parties to the conflict are notified of their names and descriptions ten days before the ships are employed.[56] Hospital ships are entitled to the aforementioned protections "unless they are used to commit . . . acts harmful to the enemy."[57] The presence on board hospital ships of "apparatus exclusively intended to facilitate navigation or communication" does not deprive the ships of the protections due them.[58] Somewhat in contradiction, however, it is expressly forbidden for hospital ships to "possess or use a secret code for their wireless or other means of communication."[59] It is this prohibition that proves difficult to implement in this day and age.

Professor Richard Grunawalt has conducted an in-depth analysis of the origins of this prohibition,[60] which derived from a desire to conclusively prevent any further instances of hospital ships being used to signal and provide non-medical services to combatants, as occurred during the Russo-Japanese War of 1904–1905[61] and again during World War I.[62] Even as the Second Geneva Convention was being negotiated, it was recognized that a prohibition on the use of secret codes by hospital ships would be difficult to implement in practice. So the Diplomatic Conference recommended that the High Contracting Parties draw up an international code providing regulations for the use of "modern means of communication" between hospital ships and warships and military aircraft.[63] Unfortunately, that code never came into being, and the High Contracting Parties are left with the prohibition as it was drafted in 1949.

Interestingly, the equally authentic French text of the Convention contains a prohibition only on the use of a secret code to transmit[64] traffic, not to receive it. In addition, Article 28(2) of Additional Protocol I of 1977, concerning medical aircraft provides that such aircraft "shall not be used to collect or transmit intelligence data and shall not carry any equipment intended for such purposes," but does not prohibit the use of a secret code or encrypted communications to further the humanitarian mission of the aircraft.[65] Additional Protocol I clearly takes a more realistic approach that recognizes the developments in communications technology since 1949. The French text of the 1949 Geneva Convention also appears to recognize the necessity for hospital ships to receive encrypted communications, at a minimum.

Professor Grunawalt's article provides ample discussion of the problems inherent in the use of unencrypted communications by hospital ships, not the least of which is that US federal privacy standards require that patient medical information be transmitted over secure circuits if it is reasonable and appropriate to do so.[66] There are also practical security issues with transmitting patient information, such as social security numbers, in the clear. With identity theft an ever-growing concern, it would be unfortunate if wounded and injured personnel were exposed to yet an additional risk as a consequence of being treated onboard a hospital ship. Further, it has been reported that when *USNS Mercy (T-AH 19)* deployed in support of Operation Iraqi Freedom in January 2003, it in fact was equipped with encrypted communications systems.[67] There is no need in this article to further belabor the point that the prohibition on use of a "secret code" by hospital ships is anachronistic, unrealistic, and unworkable in today's high technology environment where satellite communications are both routinely encrypted and routinely employed by military systems. Accordingly, this author joins with Professor Grunawalt[68] in recommending that the US Navy formally abandon adherence to this requirement, while reaffirming adherence to the underlying mandate that hospital ships may not be used for military purposes harmful to an adversary.

The second vexation facing hospital ships is the need to arm them for force protection against *USS Cole*-type attacks. Again, the Second Geneva Convention provides the baseline legal requirement—and in this instance the basic rule is far more realistic than the one just discussed prohibiting the use of a secret code. Article 35(1) provides that arming the crews of hospital ships for the maintenance of order, or for their own defense or the defense of the sick and wounded, does not deprive the ships of their protected status.[69] In this author's opinion, that should end all debate, and the Navy should not hesitate to man its hospital ships with security teams armed with crew-served weapons—such as machine guns and grenade launchers for close-in defense against attacks by terrorists or others who do not comply with the law of armed conflict. Professor Grunawalt, however, aptly points out the very legitimate reasons one should be cautious about deploying hospital ships bristling with defensive armaments.[70] And on this topic, the *San Remo Manual* has taken a decidedly anachronistic viewpoint by opining that hospital ships may be armed "only" with "deflective" means of defense (such as chaff and flares) and "not with means that could be used in offensive fashion, such as anti-aircraft guns."[71]

Not only are chaff and flares ineffective against a determined suicide attack like that launched against *Cole*, but the requirement as stated in the *San Remo Manual* is nowhere found in the Geneva Conventions and is an unnecessary and untimely restriction of the plain letter of the law. Accordingly, this author concurs with Professor Grunawalt that in addition to crew-served weapons like .50 caliber machine guns, hospital ships should be equipped with the Phalanx Close-In Weapons System or other state-of-the art defensive anti-air and anti-surface weapons systems.[72] While the Royal Navy concurs that encryption equipment may be fitted in hospital ships "to assist with the humanitarian mission," they are not as supportive on the arming issue. A Royal Navy official told *Jane's Defence Weekly* that any armaments beyond small sidearms "would compromise the protected status of the vessels" under current international law.[73] The Royal Navy approach at present, apparently due to budgetary rather than legal considerations[74]—to develop more versatile platforms that can accomplish other missions in addition to caring for the wounded and sick—may be more in line with the US Navy's plans for sea basing.

As Dr. Arthur M. Smith pointed out in a recent edition of the *Naval War College Review*, "plans for afloat casualty care and strategic evacuation may be dramatically altered" under the Navy's sea basing concept.[75] He suggests that commercially chartered cruise ships or Military Sealift Command logistics ships might deliver troops and equipment to the sea base, and then be converted to casualty care. Further, given the terrorist threat worldwide, aeromedical evacuation could provide a more practical method to care for and evacuate the wounded than evacuation by hospital ships. Given that potential terrorists could view white ships with large red crosses as attractive targets rather than as specially protected vessels, force protection considerations alone could dictate developing flexible, multi-mission platforms as substitutes for traditional white-hulled hospital ships. As Dr. Smith points out, combatant commanders will define their casualty care and evacuation requirements in the future, and those requirements might not include ships like *USNS Comfort* and *USNS Mercy*.[76]

The Law of the Sea Convention and the Future of Naval Warfare

As the Navy looks to sea basing and the future, some have questioned whether Navy leadership's long-standing support for United States accession to the Law of the Sea Convention continues to be in the best interests of the Navy and the United States. Some have asked whether the Convention helps or hinders the Navy's vision of sea basing. Throughout his term as Chief of Naval Operations, Admiral Clark never wavered from his strong position in favor of the Convention. He testified before Senate committees on more than one occasion that the Convention supports sea basing and "provides the stable and predictable legal regime with which to conduct our operations today and in the future. Joining the Convention will support ongoing U.S. military operations, including continued prosecution of the Global War on Terrorism."[77] Likewise, the current Chief of Naval Operations, Admiral Michael Mullen, follows a long line of distinguished predecessors in his support of United States accession to the Convention.[78] It is this author's opinion that the Law of the Sea Convention preserves our ability to fully leverage use of the world's oceans by providing a body of widely accepted and recognized law that protects navigational freedoms and our ability to operate on the high seas.

First, the Convention does not impair or inhibit the inherent right of self-defense. The Convention was negotiated under the auspices of the United Nations and the precepts of the Charter, Article 51 of which clearly recognizes and reflects the inherent right of self-defense. Second, the stipulation in the Convention that "The high seas shall be reserved for peaceful purposes"[79] must be read in light of Article 58, which specifically reserves freedom of navigation and overflight and "other internationally lawful uses of the sea related to these freedoms" to be enjoyed by all States.[80] State practice over hundreds of years, by which the navies of the world have operated and trained in waters seaward of other nations' territorial seas—including what is now recognized as their contiguous and exclusive economic zones—confirms that military uses of the seas that do not violate Article 2(4) of the United Nations Charter[81] are lawful under customary international law.

The Law of the Sea Convention reaffirms this position by limiting military activities in only a few narrow circumstances, such as Article 19 regarding innocent passage through the territorial sea. Moreover, the Resolution of Advice and Consent to Ratification approved by the Senate Foreign Relations Committee specifically provides that "The advice and consent of the Senate . . . is subject to the following . . . understandings: (1) The United States understands that nothing in the Convention, including any provisions referring to 'peaceful uses' or 'peaceful purposes' impairs the inherent right of individual or collective self-defense or rights during armed conflict."[82] The "peaceful purposes" provision of the Law of the Sea Convention creates no new rights or obligations and imposes no restraints on military operations or traditional uses of the seas any more than does the equivalent provision in the Outer Space Treaty, which provides that the moon and other celestial bodies shall be used "exclusively for peaceful purposes."[83] It has long been the position of the United States that "peaceful purposes" means "nonaggressive" purposes. Consequently, military activity not constituting the use of armed force against the sovereignty, territorial integrity or political independence of another nation, and not otherwise inconsistent with the United Nations Charter, is permissible.[84]

Third, a word about innocent passage. Some have argued that the Law of the Sea Convention would negatively impact national security because the innocent passage regime "prohibits" or makes "illegal" intelligence gathering or submerged submarine operations within a coastal nation's 12 nautical mile territorial sea. What the critics do not recognize or acknowledge is that the United States has been complying with the navigational provisions of the Convention since 1983. In his Ocean Policy Statement of March 10, 1983, President Reagan announced that the Law of the Sea Convention "contains provisions with respect to traditional uses of the oceans which generally confirm existing maritime law and practice and fairly balance the interests of all States," and that the United States would "accept and act" in accordance with those provisions.[85] Further, the United States is a party to the 1958 Convention on the Territorial Sea and Contiguous Zone, which contains innocent passage provisions similar to those in the Law of the Sea Convention, including that submarines in innocent passage are "required to navigate on the surface and to show their flag."[86]

Like the Territorial Sea Convention, the Law of the Sea Convention requires that submarines engaged in innocent passage navigate on the surface and show their flag.[87] The Law of the Sea Convention, however, is an improvement over the Territorial Sea Convention, in that it specifically delineates those activities that may be considered prejudicial to the peace, good order, or security of the coastal State—thus shielding the United States and other sea-going nations from efforts by coastal States to regulate other types of conduct in the territorial sea. It denotes "any act aimed at collecting information to the prejudice of the defence or security of the coastal State" as inconsistent with innocent passage and prejudicial to the peace, good order or security of the coastal State.[88] Such activities are not deemed "illegal," nor are they forbidden. The coastal State may have national laws prohibiting such activities, may take necessary steps to prevent passage which is not innocent,[89] and may require a warship to leave the territorial sea "immediately" if the warship disregards requests by the coastal State to comply with its national laws and regulations concerning passage through the territorial sea.[90] These provisions reflect the carefully crafted balance the United States sought to protect its own interests as both a coastal State and a flag State. Thus, if a warship or submarine transits through the territorial sea in innocent passage, it must comply with the requirements for innocent passage. If it does not do so, the coastal State that becomes aware of such non-innocent passage may require the warship to depart the territorial sea immediately, and may then address the matter through diplomatic channels.

Fourth, accession to the Law of the Sea Convention would in no way negatively affect the President's Proliferation Security Initiative (PSI). The PSI is a global effort to stop trafficking of weapons of mass destruction (WMD) and their delivery systems to and from States of proliferation concern. It is not a treaty or a formal organization. It is a cooperative effort to apply all the tools at the disposal of the PSI partner nations—intelligence, diplomacy, law enforcement, military, customs authorities, financial—to prevent transfers of WMD-related items at sea, in the air, and on land. More than 60 countries around the world have indicated their support for PSI—most, if not all, of which are parties to the Law of the Sea Convention. While the goal is "to create a more dynamic, creative, and proactive approach" to preventing proliferation, "actions taken in support of the PSI will be consistent with national legal authorities and relevant international law and frameworks."[91] Certainly the goal is to strengthen existing authorities where they are weak or inefficient, but only within the bounds of national and international law, which includes the Law of the Sea Convention. Numerous multilateral exercises have taken place, and the initiative had one publicly announced success, in the fall of

2003, when four nations (the United States, the United Kingdom, Italy and Germany) cooperated to interdict and prevent a shipment of centrifuge parts to Libya.[92]

Conflict Resolution in the Exclusive Economic Zone

There is no doubt that the Navy's plans for sea basing could give pause to allies and potential competitors alike. After all, it is based on the notion that "America will never seek a permission slip to defend the security of our country."[93] Lieutenant General James Mattis, head of the Marine Corps Combat Development Command, says the idea is to minimize the need for the United States military to rely on allies to supply territory from which United States forces can operate abroad.[94] One hears phrases like "using the sea as maneuver space," exploiting the United States' "control of the seas," and, from a large display in the Pentagon in June 2005, the "command of the commons."[95] Carried to its logical conclusion, it will inevitably involve the staging of large, floating military bases off the coasts of other nations, probably in their contiguous or exclusive economic zones, from which joint forces and weapons could be projected ashore in a future conflict. Sea basing also has a more benign side. Former Naval Sea System Commander Vice Admiral Phillip Balisle pointed to the Navy's tsunami relief efforts in Indonesia as an example of sea basing in action. Relief efforts were launched and directed from a collection of ships stationed off-shore. "We have always had a sea base, or at least for many years. What we're talking about now is the shaping of that sea base for [a] 21st-century environment."[96]

Will the sea base impact the sovereignty of other nations, threaten their security or convert the oceans to "non-peaceful" purposes? The answer is no. Each sea base will be established consistent with principles of law applicable to the operation in question—whether it be humanitarian relief operations, international armed conflict, or United Nations sanctions enforcement. Is it possible that other nations may disagree with the United States over the applicable legal principles? Of course. Conflicts and disagreements will arise in the future, as they have in the past. One has only to recall the P-3 incident off Hainan Island in the People's Republic of China and the difference of opinion between the United States and China over the propriety of military activities conducted in a coastal State's exclusive economic zone to realize that there will often be differing interpretations of the applicable law.[97]

Because of these differing interpretations, particularly as between the United States and the People's Republic of China, one might ask whether it would be advisable for the United States to attempt to negotiate an agreement with China similar to the 1972 Incidents at Sea Agreement[98] or the 1989 Dangerous Military Activities Agreement[99] with the former Soviet Union. At the time of those agreements, both the United States and the former Soviet Union had substantial blue-water navies. Several dangerous incidents had occurred between units of the two nations and the potential for unpredictable future confrontations existed around the world.

With China, the potential for confrontation exists primarily within China's exclusive economic zone due to China's objections to US military activities there such as surveillance and military surveys. An existing mechanism, the Military Maritime Consultative Agreement,[100] is available and is probably sufficient, given the limited area and scope of potential confrontations, to address these issues concerning military activities in areas where high seas freedoms apply. In fact, it was presumably under the auspices of this agreement that Ambassador Prueher proposed a meeting to discuss the EP-3 incident, and suggested that the agenda include a "discussion of causes of the accident and possible recommendations whereby such collisions could be avoided in the future."[101] However, this author would not rule out the value of a more comprehensive agreement, embodying special signals like those in the Incidents at Sea Agreement, for indicating one's intentions and operations, if the consultative mechanism proves unsuccessful in preventing future dangerous encounters.

It is certainly appropriate that the United States continue to communicate with our allies and potential competitors alike concerning plans for the Navy of the future. Concerning all five of the issues discussed in this article, it would be advisable to inform other nations of United States intentions and engage in a dialogue with them concerning the legal bases for our actions. A cooperative, consultative approach would be useful in obtaining the support and understanding of potential coalition partners, as well as alleviating the concerns of potential competitors. In a recent speech to the US Naval War College, Chief of Naval Operations Admiral Mullen stressed how important coalition partners will be to future naval operations.[102] And while President Bush has made it clear that the United States will not jeopardize its national security by acquiescing to "the objections of the few,"[103] the preferred *modus operandi* is to seek international support and international partnerships. The Proliferation Security Initiative, for example, is evidence that the President wants to work with multi-national partners to the maximum extent possible. The issues discussed in this article provide ample opportunities for collaboration and cooperation on the international level.

Notes

1. *See, e.g.*, Jason Sherman, *Changing Vision*, SEA POWER (Mar. 2005), *available at* http://www.navyleague.org/sea_power/mar_05_10.php, quoting former Chief of Naval Operations Admiral Vern Clark that the Navy is not "correctly balanced and optimized for the future we're

facing. . . . The Navy that we possess today must be reshaped to deal with the challenges that we [will] have in the future."

2. *Status of the Navy*, Sept. 2, 2005, *available at* http://www.navy.mil.

3. Admiral Vern Clark, Chief of Naval Operations Guidance 2004, Guidance for Leaders: Manpower, Jan. 4, 2004 (on file with author).

4. Commander, Naval Forces Europe/Commander, U.S. 6th Fleet Public Affairs, USS Mount Whitney Underway for NATO's Allied Action, Chinfo News Clips, May 18, 2005, *available at* www.navy.mil.

5. *Id.* These savings are accomplished in a number of ways: some civilian mariner billets onboard ship are manned (and paid) only when the ship is underway, while sailors fill their billets both at sea and in port; sailors frequently have collateral duties, training requirements and temporary additional duty assignments that civilian mariners are not required to perform, thus civilian billets are matched only to the at-sea requirement while there must be sufficient active-duty billets to account for the absence/unavailability of a percentage of the crew at all times; and civilian mariners are trained to do one job proficiently—a mariner may serve as a deck seaman for 30 years—whereas active duty sailors are in an "up-or-out" system; as each sailor moves up in the ranks a new sailor must be trained to take his or her place.

6. Dale Eisman, *Sea Base: The Navy's New Way to Fight*, THE VIRGINIAN-PILOT, Mar. 8, 2005, *available at* http://home.hamptonroads.com/stories/print.cfm?story=101429&ran=138749.

7. *Id.* For additional information on sea basing, *see* Sherman, *supra* note 1; Dale Eisman, *The Navy's Changing Tide: Service Floats "Sea Base" Concept*, THE VIRGINIAN-PILOT, Mar. 8, 2005, *available at* http://home.hamptonroads.com/stories/story.cfm?story=101390&ran=75707; US Congress, Congressional Budget Office, The Future of the Navy's Amphibious and Maritime Prepositioning Forces, ix–xiii (Nov. 2004).

8. Eisman, *supra* note 6.

9. Sherman, *supra* note 1; Congressional Budget Office, *supra* note 7, at xiii (follow-on assault echelons would assemble and deploy on the ships comprising the sea base, of which the MPF-F is the "linchpin").

10. Geneva Convention (III) Relative to the Treatment of Prisoners of War, Aug. 12, 1949, art.4.A.(4), 75 U.N.T.S. 135, *reprinted in* DOCUMENTS ON THE LAWS OF WAR 243, 246 (Adam Roberts & Richard Guelff eds., 3d ed. 2000), "Prisoners of war . . . are persons belonging to one of the following categories, who have fallen into the power of the enemy: (4) Persons who accompany the armed forces without actually being members thereof . . . ."

11. United Nations Convention on the Law of the Sea, Dec. 10, 1982, 1833 U.N.T.S. 3 [hereinafter 1982 LOS Convention].

12. Convention on the High Seas, Apr. 29, 1958, 13 U.S.T. 2312, 450 U.N.T.S. 82, *reprinted in* NATIONAL SECURITY DOCUMENTS 570, 571 (John Norton Moore, Guy B. Roberts, & Robert F. Turner eds., 1995).

13. Declaration Respecting Maritime Law, Apr. 16, 1856, *reprinted in* DOCUMENTS ON THE LAWS OF WAR, *supra* note 10, at 48.

14. Convention (VII) Relating to the Conversion of Merchant Ships into Warships, Oct. 18, 1907, arts. 1–4, *reprinted in* NATIONAL SECURITY DOCUMENTS, *supra* note 12, at 95, 97.

15. Women in Military Service for America Memorial, Highlights of Women in the Military, *available at* curators@womensmemorial.org; The United States Navy, Women in the Navy (on file with author).

16. Some might suggest that the most obvious solution to this dilemma is simply to subject the civilian mariners to the Uniform Code of Military Justice (UCMJ). As currently written, the Code only provides for jurisdiction over persons serving with or accompanying armed forces in

the field "in time of war." 10 U.S.C. 802(a)(10) (2003). Courts have held that the phrase "in time of war" should be construed narrowly and only includes declared wars. United States v. Averette, 41 C.M.R. 363 (U.S.C.M.A. 1970). Although it is possible the law could be amended, that solution would address only one of the two issues related to civilian mariners onboard warships. The second issue, whether the civilian mariners would be afforded status as prisoners of war if they were to be captured, would be unaffected by an amendment to the UCMJ.

17. ANNOTATED SUPPLEMENT TO THE COMMANDER'S HANDBOOK ON THE LAW OF NAVAL OPERATIONS para. 8.1, at 401 (A. R. Thomas & James C. Duncan eds., 1999) (Vol. 73, US Naval War College International Law Studies) [hereinafter ANNOTATED SUPPLEMENT].

18. *See, e.g.*, Articles 50 and 51, Protocol Additional to the Geneva Conventions of 12 August 1949, and Relating to the Protection of Victims of International Armed Conflicts (Additional Protocol I), June 8, 1977, 1125 U.N.T.S. 3, *reprinted in* DOCUMENTS ON THE LAWS OF WAR, *supra* note 10, at 419, 448. The United States is not a party to Additional Protocol I.

19. *Supra* note 10.

20. *See* THE HANDBOOK OF HUMANITARIAN LAW IN ARMED CONFLICTS 232 (Dieter Fleck ed., 1995) ("[A]ctivities . . . must be . . . directly related to hostilities or, in other words, to represent a direct threat to the enemy"). The International Committee of the Red Cross (ICRC) has embarked on a project to further define the phrase, but to date has not proposed a comprehensive description.

21. Pilot Program for the Employment, Use, and Status of Reserve Civilian Mariners, (on file with author). The legislation was proposed for the Fiscal Year 2006 National Defense Authorization Act, but was not included in the Act considered by Congress. It is anticipated the proposal will be submitted in future years.

22. A recent news article announced that the Pentagon has begun informally referring to unmanned aircraft as "unmanned aerial systems" rather than "unmanned aerial vehicles"—and that the change may soon become official. The reason for the shift in terminology is to connote that the aircraft are only one part of a "complex network of systems" rather than independently operated units. Vince Crawley, *Pentagon: Don't Call Them UAVs Anymore*, www.DefenseNews .com, Aug. 17, 2005.

23. Nathan Hodge, *Jumper: Military Must Reorganize UAV Efforts*, DEFENSE DAILY, at 7, Apr. 29, 2005.

24. Rowan Scarborough, *Special Report – Unmanned Warfare*, WASHINGTON TIMES, May 8, 2005, at A01.

25. *Id.*; Eric Schmitt, *U.S. Drones Crowding The Skies To Help Fight Insurgents In Iraq*, NEW YORK TIMES, Apr. 5, 2005, at A9. For a description of the synergy developed between manned and unmanned aircraft and between coalition partners to destroy a surface-to-air missile site during Operation Iraqi Freedom, see Ministry of Defence, Operations in Iraq: Lessons for the Future 33 (Dec. 2003) 33, *available at* http://www.mod.uk/DefenceInternet/AboutDefence/CorporatePublications/Reports/ReportsForResearchers/OperationsInIraqLessonsForTheFuture.htm.

26. Peter A. Buxbaum, *Shedding Ships and Sailors*, ARMED FORCES JOURNAL, Apr. 2005, at 20, 22 (citing Rear Admiral (select) William Rodriguez, Space and Naval Warfare Systems Command, San Diego, who predicts that unmanned aerial vehicles may soon have the "cognitive ability" to detect hostile platforms and vector weapons against them, apparently without relying on commands from a human being controlling the unmanned system. This capability, of course, raises significant legal issues that are beyond the scope of this article.)

27. Katie Fairbank, *Unmanned Aircraft are Wowing Defense Industry*, DALLAS MORNING NEWS, June 14, 2005; Scarborough, *supra*, note 24.

28. *Air Force to Add Spy Plane Squadron*, LAS VEGAS REVIEW-JOURNAL, June 4, 2005, at 1B.
29. Scan Eagle was developed by Boeing and The Insitu Group as an affordable, runway-independent, long endurance, autonomous, unmanned vehicle and is designed to provide real-time intelligence, surveillance and reconnaissance. Scan Eagle carries either an inertially stabilized electro-optical or infrared camera. It is 4 feet long with a wingspan of 10 feet. Scan Eagle can remain on station for more than 15 hours and is capable of providing intelligence from high (above 16,000 feet) or low altitude. *See* US Air Force, Innovative Solutions for the Warfighter, Scan Eagle, *available at* http://www.nellis.af.mil/UAVB/uavbspotlight.asp; Boeing Integrated Defense Systems, Unmanned Systems, ScanEagle UAV, *available at* http://www.boeing.com/defense-space/military/unmanned/scaneagle.html.
30. Article 37 of the 1982 LOS Convention provides that the transit passage regime applies to "straits which are used for international navigation between one part of the high seas or an exclusive economic zone and another part of the high seas or an exclusive economic zone." 1982 LOS Convention, *supra* note 11. The United States is not a party to the Convention. President Reagan announced, however, that the Convention "contains provisions with respect to traditional uses of the oceans which generally confirm existing maritime law and practice" and declared that the United States would act "in accordance with the balance of interests relating to traditional uses of the oceans—such as navigation and overflight." White House Press Release, Statement of the President (on the 1982 LOS Convention), Mar. 10, 1983, *reprinted in* NATIONAL SECURITY DOCUMENTS, *supra* note 12, at 591.
31. 1982 LOS Convention, *supra* note 11, art 39.
32. *Id.*
33. Most definitions of ships and aircraft assume, if they do not explicitly state, that the vehicles are "manned by a crew," the assumption being that the crew is actually located within the vehicle. *See, e.g.*, ANNOTATED SUPPLEMENT, *supra*, note 17, para. 2.1.1, at 109 (". . . a warship [is] . . . manned by a crew which is under regular armed forces discipline") and para. 2.2.1, at 114 (". . . military aircraft . . . include . . . aircraft . . . manned by a crew subject to regular armed forces discipline"). That the existence and employment of unmanned systems may not have been fully appreciated or contemplated when these definitions were developed does not prevent the incorporation of such systems into existing legal regimes. The definitions may, however, need to be updated to reflect current technology.
34. ANNOTATED SUPPLEMENT, *supra* note 17, para. 2.3.3.1, at 125.
35. SAN REMO MANUAL ON INTERNATIONAL LAW APPLICABLE TO ARMED CONFLICTS AT SEA para. 30, at 106 (Louise Doswald-Beck ed., 1995). The *San Remo Manual* was prepared by a group of international legal and naval experts participating in their personal capacity in a series of Round Tables convened by the International Institute of Humanitarian Law. The Manual was intended to provide a contemporary restatement of international law applicable to armed conflicts at sea. As such, it is a useful document for analyzing general legal principles on various issues, though it is not dispositive as to the law on any particular subject.
36. International and Operational Law Division, Office of the Judge Advocate General of the Navy, Point Paper on the Use of Unmanned Aerial Vehicles (UAVs) while Transiting the Strait of Hormuz, Apr. 15, 2000 (on file with author).
37. 1982 LOS Convention, *supra* note 11, art. 38.
38. *Id.*, art. 39.
39. *Id.*
40. A recent note in DEFENSETECH reported that the Central Intelligence Agency was operating unmanned aerial vehicles—the IGnat and Predator—in Iranian airspace searching for dispersed nuclear weapons development sites. *Available at* http://www.defensetech.org/archives of March

1, 2005. If the article is correct, the legal rationale for such activity would have to be that, while "spying" may be a violation of the domestic law of the over-flown State, intelligence gathering is not forbidden by international law and has long been an accepted State practice. The cited article was rather cryptic and does not provide enough information to conduct a complete legal analysis.
41. 1982 LOS Convention, *supra* note 11, art. 19.
42. *Id.*, art. 17.
43. *Id.*, art. 29.
44. WEBSTER'S II NEW RIVERSIDE UNIVERSITY DICTIONARY 1075, 186 (2d ed. 1988).
45. *Id.* at 1075.
46. US Department of Transportation, US Coast Guard, "Navigation Rules, International – Inland," COMMANDANT INSTRUCTION M16672.2D, Mar. 25, 1999 (containing the International Regulations for Prevention of Collision at Sea, 1972, also known as COLREGs 72), Rules 1a and Rule 3a.
47. 1 U.S.C. 3 (2005) ("The word "vessel" includes every description of watercraft or other artificial contrivance used, or capable of being used, as a means of transportation on water.").
48. Stewart v. Dutra Construction Co., 543 U.S. 481 (2005), holding that a dredge is a "vessel" under the Longshore and Harbor Workers Compensation Act.
49. International and Operational Law Division, Office of the Judge Advocate General of the Navy, Legal Review of the Remote Minehunting System AN/WLD-1(V), June 10, 2005 (on file with author).
50. Given the characteristics of the system, the COLREGs requirements might not be onerous. For example, it is possible the light requirements could be satisfied by the presence of a white all-round light with visibility of 3 nautical miles as required by Rule 22(d) for inconspicuous, partly submerged vessels. It is also possible, under Rule 1(e), to obtain a US Navy certificate of alternative compliance for some or all of the requirements under special circumstances where strict compliance is impossible.
51. COLREGs, *supra* note 46, Rule 2.
52. 1982 LOS Convention, *supra* note 11, art. 87.
53. Legal Review, *supra* note 49.
54. *See, e.g.*, Stephanie Showalter, *The Legal Status of Autonomous Underwater Vehicles*, 38 MARINE TECHNOLOGY SOCIETY JOURNAL, Spring 2004, at 80, 81 (". . . it is unclear whether [autonomous underwater vehicles] are subject to the maritime regulations for vessels . . . .); Michael R. Benjamin & Joseph A. Curcio, *COLREGs-Based Navigation of Autonomous Marine Vehicles*, Proceedings of the Institute of Electrical and Electronics Engineers (IEEE) Conference on Autonomous Unmanned Vehicles 2004, at 32, 34 (on file with author), (concluding that autonomous marine vehicles "very likely" qualify as vessels and are subject to the COLREGs rules, though this conclusion has not been "clearly determined" through the judicial process).
55. Geneva Convention (II) for the Amelioration of the Condition of Wounded, Sick and Shipwrecked Members of Armed Forces at Sea, art. 22, Aug. 12, 1949, 75 U.N.T.S. 85, *reprinted in* DOCUMENTS ON THE LAWS OF WAR, *supra* note 10, 221, 230 (hereinafter Geneva II).
56. *Id.*
57. *Id.*, art. 34, at 233.
58. *Id.*, art. 35(2), at 233.
59. *Id.*, art. 34, at 233.
60. Richard J. Grunawalt, *Hospital Ships in the War on Terror – Sanctuaries or Targets?*, 58 NAVAL WAR COLLEGE REVIEW, Winter 2005, at 89.

61. In 1905, the Russian hospital ship *Orel* was captured and condemned by a Japanese prize court for "signaling" to the Russian fleet "in ways that amounted to use for military purposes." *Id.* at 91.

62. In 1914, the German hospital ship *Ophelia* was captured and condemned by a British prize court for being "adapted and used as a signaling ship for military purposes." *Id.* at 93.

63. *Id.* at 98.

64. The French text reads, "En particulier, les navires-hopitaux ne pourrant posseder ni utiliser de code secret pour leurs emissions par T.S.F. [wireless] ou par tout autre moyen de communication." *Available at* www.icrc.org/dih.nsf.

65. Additional Protocol I, *supra* note 18, at 436.

66. Health Insurance Portability and Accountability Act of 1996, Public Law 104-191, implementing regulations "Health Insurance Reform, Security Standards – Final Rule," published in Federal Register, Vol. 68, No. 34, Feb. 20, 2003, sec. 164.312. Granted, treaties to which the United States is a party are part of the supreme law of the land. Domestic law cannot serve to invalidate or override treaty obligations. Nonetheless, domestic law that is inconsistent with international treaty obligations presents problems of compliance that are not easy to resolve in practice. In this case, the implementing regulations permit the use of equivalent alternative measures if it is not "reasonable and appropriate" to encrypt medical information.

67. Michael Sirak, *U.S. Navy Seeks to Revise Laws of War on Hospital Ships*, JANE'S DEFENCE WEEKLY, Aug. 27, 2003, at 29.

68. Grunawalt, *supra* note 60, at 109. It should be noted that the drafters of the *San Remo Manual* also concluded that the prohibition in Article 34 is unworkable, and recommended that hospital ships "should be permitted to use cryptographic equipment." SAN REMO MANUAL, *supra* note 35, para. 171, at 236–237.

69. Geneva II, *supra* note 55, at 233.

70. Grunawalt, *supra* note 60, at 109–111 (discussing the traditional view that hospital ships found "safety in vulnerability").

71. SAN REMO MANUAL, *supra* note 35, para. 170.3, at 235.

72. Grunawalt, *supra* note 60, at 112.

73. Sirak, *supra* note 67.

74. Richard Scott, *UK casualty ship project faces major surgery,* JANE'S DEFENCE WEEKLY, May 11, 2005, at 14. ("[B]udget pressures have forced the [Minister of Defence] to reconsider the scope of its current requirement and look instead at a cheaper option" which involves equipping a medical facility onboard an auxiliary vessel with additional combat-related missions.)

75. Arthur M. Smith, *Has the Red Cross-Adorned Hospital Ship Become Obsolete?* 58 NAVAL WAR COLLEGE REVIEW, Summer 2005, at 120, 130 ("Hospital ships, as we have come to know them, may no longer play a role in a military structured for rapid flexible response in asymmetric warfare").

76. *Id.* at 131. A recent news article reported that non-governmental organizations are operating white-hulled "Mercy Ships" which operate in the waters off developing countries providing medical care to those in need. The ships do not bear red crosses, but in other respects appear similar to military medical ships. *Mercy Mission,* WALL STREET JOURNAL, Aug. 26, 2005, at W2. Professor George K. Walker has raised a number of very good questions concerning how those vessels should be treated in the event of an international armed conflict. George K. Walker, e-mail to Naval War College, Aug. 29, 2005 (on file with author). The Second Geneva Convention and Additional Protocol I actually foresee and make provisions for hospital ships owned or operated by neutral States, private citizens, officially recognized relief societies, and impartial international humanitarian organizations. Geneva II, *supra* note 55, arts. 24–25, at

231, and Additional Protocol I, *supra* note 18, art. 22(2), at 434. One of the primary conditions for such ships to receive the same protections as military hospital ships is that they have to be made available to or under the control of a State party to the conflict. The presence of hospital ships not under the control of a party to the conflict would certainly complicate the targeting solution if they operate in waters near belligerent activities.

77. Admiral Vern Clark, Posture Statement, Testimony Before the Defense Subcommittee of the Senate Appropriations Committee 4–5 (Mar. 16, 2005), *available at* www.navy.mil.

78. *See, e.g.*, "Advance Questions for Admiral Michael G. Mullen, USN, Nominee for the Position of Chief of Naval Operations," 10–11, *available at* www.navytimes.com/content/editorial, (the Convention "codifies fundamental benefits important to our operating forces as they train and fight . . . *codifies essential navigational freedoms . . . supports the operational maneuver space . . . enhances our own maritime interests*").

79. 1982 LOS Convention, *supra* note 11, art. 88.

80. *Id.*, art. 58.

81. Charter of the United Nations, *reprinted in* NATIONAL SECURITY DOCUMENTS, *supra* note 12, at 89, 90. (Article 2(4) provides that "All Members shall refrain in their international relations from the threat or use of force against the territorial integrity or political independence of any State, or in any other manner inconsistent with the Purposes of the United Nations.")

82. S. EXEC. RPT. NO. 108-10, at 17–18 (2004).

83. Treaty on Principles Governing the Activities of States in the Exploration and Use of Outer Space, Including the Moon and Other Celestial Bodies, art. IV, Jan. 27, 1967, 18 U.S.T. 2410, 610 U.N.T.S 205, *reprinted in* NATIONAL SECURITY DOCUMENTS, *supra* note 12, at 332, 333. By specific terms of the treaty other than the "peaceful purposes" provision, the United States agreed not to establish military installations, test weapons, or conduct military maneuvers on celestial bodies and not to station in outer space or place in orbit nuclear weapons or other weapons of mass destruction (Article IV). Importantly, these sorts of prohibitions do not appear in the Law of the Sea Convention.

84. COMMANDER'S HANDBOOK, *supra* note 17, at 149 n.114. *See also*, SAN REMO MANUAL, *supra* note 35, at 82. ("With respect to the high seas, the Round Table wished to emphasize that it did not accept the interpretations of some publicists that the LOS Convention's Articles 88 and 301, reserving the high seas for peaceful purposes, prohibit naval warfare on the high seas.")

85. Statement of the President, *supra* note 30.

86. Convention on the Territorial Sea and the Contiguous Zone, art. 14, Oct. 31, 1958, 15 U.S.T. 1606, *reprinted in* NATIONAL SECURITY DOCUMENTS, *supra* note 12, at 565.

87. 1982 LOS Convention, *supra* note 11, art. 20.

88. *Id.*, art. 19.

89. *Id.*, art. 25.

90. *Id.*, art. 30.

91. US Department of State, The Proliferation Security Initiative (PSI) (May 26, 2005), *available at* http://www.state.gov/t/np/rls/other/46858.html.

92. Andrew C. Winner, *The Proliferation Security Initiative: The New Face of Interdiction*, THE WASHINGTON QUARTERLY, Spring 2005, at 129.

93. President George W. Bush, State of the Union Address, Jan. 20, 2004, *available at* www.whitehouse.gov.

94. *Naval Officials Focus on Broader Missions, Seabasing and Sea Shield*, Inside the Navy, INSIDE WASHINGTON PUBLISHERS, Jan. 17, 2005, *available at* InsideDefense.com.

95. *See also*, Barry R. Posen, *Command of the Commons*, 28 INTERNATIONAL SECURITY, Summer 2003, at 5 (arguing that the United States enjoys command of the commons—that is,

command of the sea, space and air—which is a key military enabler of the US global power position).

96. John T. Bennett, *Notes from the Surface Navy Association's 2005 Annual Symposium*, Inside the Pentagon, INSIDE WASHINGTON PUBLISHERS, Jan. 20, 2005, *available at* InsideDefense.com.

97. On April 1, 2001, a United States EP-3 was conducting routine surveillance 80 nautical miles southeast of Hainan Island in the South China Sea. A Chinese fighter intercepted the EP-3, maneuvered close aboard and impacted the EP-3. The fighter broke up and ditched into the ocean; the pilot was not recovered. The EP-3's nose cone was sheared off, but the EP-3 pilot managed to land the aircraft safely at Langhui Airport. The Chinese held the 24-person American crew in "protective custody" for 11 days before releasing them. The United States position was that the EP-3 was operating in international airspace in full accordance with all laws and regulations and did nothing to cause the accident. The Chinese claimed the EP-3 (which was flying on autopilot) "veered" into the Chinese fighter. The Chinese also took the position that surveillance is a threat or use of force against the coastal State and that the exclusive economic zone is sovereign air and sea space. This position is entirely inconsistent with Article 58 of the 1982 LOS Convention, which reserves to all States the freedom of overflight above the exclusive economic zone. 1982 LOS Convention, *supra* note 11. For additional information on the incident, *see generally*, USCINCPAC Virtual Information Center, Special Press Summary: China–US EP3 and J-8 Mid-Air Collision, Apr. 12, 2001, *available at* www.vic-info.org; and Margaret K. Lewis, Note: *An Analysis of State Responsibility for the Chinese-American Airplane Collision Incident*, 77 NEW YORK UNIVERSITY LAW REVIEW 1404 (2002).

98. Agreement Between the Government of the United States of America and the Union of Soviet Socialist Republics on the Prevention of Incidents On and Over the High Seas, May 25, 1972, *reprinted in* 11 INTERNATIONAL LEGAL MATERIALS 778.

99. Agreement Between the Government of the United States of America and the Government of the Union of Soviet Socialist Republics on the Prevention of Dangerous Military Activities, Sept. 23, 1989, *reprinted in* 28 INTERNATIONAL LEGAL MATERIALS 877.

100. Agreement on Establishing a Consultative Mechanism to Strengthen Military Maritime Safety Between the Department of Defense of the United States and the Ministry of National Defense of the People's Republic of China, Jan. 1998. *See generally*, William S. Cohen, Working Together is Best Avenue for U.S. and China, 13 DEFENSE ISSUES, No. 12, Jan. 19, 1998.

101. Letter from Ambassador Prueher to Chinese Minister of Foreign Affairs Tang, Apr. 11, 2001, *available at* www.whitehouse.gov.

102. Admiral Michael Mullen, Remarks at the US Naval War College, Newport, R.I. Aug. 31, 2005, *available at* http://www.navy.mil ("Our vision is and ought to be to extend the peace through an inter-connected community of maritime nations working together. The enemy goes global. So should we.").

103. State of the Union Address, *supra* note 93. "From the beginning, America has sought international support for our operations in Afghanistan and Iraq, and we have gained much support. There is a difference, however, between leading a coalition of many nations, and submitting to the objections of a few."

APPENDIX

CONTRIBUTORS

Contributors

Editor's Note: In order to most accurately portray the events of the conference, the biographical data in this appendix reflects the position in which the authors were serving at the time of the conference, as set forth in the conference brochures and materials.

Ms. Lucy Brown is Senior Advisor, International Humanitarian Law for the American Red Cross. Her responsibilities within the International Policy and Relations unit include building cooperative relationships with external organizations and working closely with partners in the International Red Cross and Red Crescent Movement. As a senior level advisor on issues relating to international humanitarian law application, policy and training, she serves as the primary liaison on these matters between the American Red Cross and nongovernmental organizations working in international relief and development. Ms. Brown has been actively involved in the American Red Cross international humanitarian law dissemination program since the early 1990s as a technical advisor and trainer of trainers.

Captain Jane Dalton, JAGC, US Navy, is the Assistant Judge Advocate General (Civil Law), Office of the Judge Advocate General and Commanding Officer, Naval Civil Law Support Activity. Her previous major duty assignments include Legal Counsel to the Chairman of the Joint Chiefs of Staff, Washington, D.C.; Commanding Officer, Naval Legal Service Office North Central, Washington, D.C.; Deputy Legal Counsel to the Chairman of the Joint Chiefs of Staff, Washington, D.C.; and Staff Judge Advocate, Commander Third Fleet, San Diego, California. Captain Dalton has a Juris Doctor (J.D.) degree from Georgetown University Law Center and a Master of Laws (LL.M.) degree from the University of Virginia School of Law.

Professor Yoram Dinstein is the Yanowicz Professor of Human Rights at Tel Aviv University (Israel), where he is the immediate past President. Professor Dinstein served two appointments (1999/2000, 2002/2003) as the Charles H. Stockton Professor of International Law at the US Naval War College. He was also a Humboldt Fellow at the Max Planck Institute for International Law at Heidelberg (Germany), 2000/2001. Professor Dinstein is a Member of the Institute of International Law. He has written extensively on subjects relating to international law, human rights and the law of armed conflict. He is the founder and Editor of the *Israel Yearbook* on *Human Rights*. He is the author of *War, Aggression and Self-Defence*, now in its 4th edition. His latest book is *The Conduct of Hostilities under the Law of International Armed Conflict*.

Brigadier General Charles J. Dunlap Jr., JAGC, US Air Force, is the Staff Judge Advocate, Headquarters Air Combat Command, Langley Air Force Base, Virginia. General Dunlap entered the Air Force in 1972 as a graduate of the Air Force ROTC program at St. Joseph's University, Philadelphia, Pennsylvania. He has deployed to support various operations in the Middle East and Africa, to include Operations Provide Relief, Restore Hope, Vigilant Warrior, Desert Fox, Bright Star and Enduring Freedom. He has led military-to-military delegations to Uruguay, the Czech Republic, South Africa and Colombia. General Dunlap speaks widely on legal and national security issues, and is published in *Aerospace Power Journal*, *Peacekeeping & International Relations*, *Parameters*, *Proceedings*, the *Fletcher Forum of World Affairs*, the *Air Force Times*, the *Wake Forest Law Review*, the *Air Force Law Review*, the *Tennessee Law Review* and the *Strategic Review*, among others.

Colonel Charles H. B. Garraway, CBE, is the Charles H. Stockton Professor of International Law at the US Naval War College. Colonel Garraway's tours of active duty with the British Army have included assignments in Cyprus, Germany, Belgium (SHAPE) and Hong Kong, and various tours in the United Kingdom. He is a former Visiting Fellow at the Research Centre for International Law, Cambridge University (now the Lauterpacht Centre) and a Member of the International Institute of Humanitarian Law at San Remo. Colonel Garraway is also a member of the Board of Directors of the International Society for Military Law and the Law of War and was one of the General Rapporteurs for the 2003 Congress in Rome and served as Chairman of the General Affairs Committee. He has represented the United Kingdom at various international conferences, including the Preparatory Committee for Amended Protocol II to the Conventional Weapons Convention, the Diplomatic Conference on the Second Protocol to the Hague Cultural Property Convention and negotiations on the establishment of an International Criminal Court. During the 1990–91 Gulf War, he served as senior Army Legal Services Officer where he was involved, in particular, with prisoner of war handling. In December of 2002, Colonel Garraway was appointed a Commander of the Most Excellent Order of the British Empire by Her Majesty The Queen.

Rear Admiral Raydon Gates, Royal Australian Navy, is the Head, Australian Defence Staff (Washington) and Australian Defense Attaché. He graduated from the Royal Australian Naval College in 1974. His early career was spent mainly at sea serving in over 15 ships. His sea service culminated with the command of the guided missile frigates *HMAS Canberra* from 1991–93 and *HMAS Adelaide* from 1995–97. Admiral Gates' shore postings have included operational and personnel positions in Sydney and Canberra in various headquarters. He was promoted to Rear Admiral in January 2001 and appointed the inaugural Commander of the Australian Defence College in Canberra responsible for joint staff training for officers from O-1 to the O-6 rank levels. He was Maritime Commander Australia, July 2002 to June 2004, responsible for the entire Australian Fleet. He commanded the Fleet during the Iraq War and the continuing Global War on Terror. Admiral Gates has been awarded a Master Degree in Business Administration, a Graduate Diploma in Strategic Studies, and a Diploma of Company Directorship.

Professor Wolff Heintschel Von Heinegg is a Professor of International Law at the University of Frankfurt-Oder and the University of Augsburg, Germany, having returned to that position following a year-long appointment as the Charles H. Stockton Chair of International Law at the US Naval War College. He was the Rapporteur of the International Law Association Committee on Maritime Neutrality and is currently the Vice-President of the German Society of Military Law and the Law of War. Professor Heintschel von Heinegg was among a group of international lawyers and naval experts who produced the *San Remo Manual on International Law Applicable to Armed Conflicts at Sea*. He is a widely published author of articles and books on the law of sea and naval warfare.

Mr. Jean-Marie Henckaerts is a legal adviser in the Legal Division of the International Committee of the Red Cross (ICRC). Mr. Henckaerts coauthored the ICRC's two-volume *Customary International Humanitarian Law* study. He was a member of the ICRC delegation to the 1999 Diplomatic Conference on a Second Protocol to the 1954 Hague Convention for the Protection of Cultural Property in the Event of Armed Conflict (The Hague, 1999). Mr. Henckaerts has a Bachelor of Laws (LL.B.) degree from the University of Brussels, a Master of Laws (LL.M.) degree from the University of Georgia School of Law and a Doctor of Juridical Science (S.J.D.) degree from The George Washington University Law School. Mr. Henckaerts is a member of the International Law Association, European Society of International Law, American Society of International Law, Academic Council of the United Nations System and the United Nations Association. He has published four books and numerous articles on international law, international humanitarian law and human rights law.

Doctor Marie Jacobsson is the Principal Legal Adviser on International Law to the Swedish Ministry for Foreign Affairs. Doctor Jacobsson holds a Doctor of Law degree from the University of Lund, Sweden. She has participated as a representative of the Swedish Ministry for Foreign Affairs in numerous international negotiations, conferences and meetings on issues relating to the laws of warfare. She is a member of the Swedish Government's Delegation for International Humanitarian Law Monitoring of Arms and the Swedish Humanitarian Law Delegation. Doctor Jacobsson is a frequent lecturer at Swedish and foreign universities. Her publications can be found primarily in the areas of international law and security policy, the laws of warfare and law of the sea.

Professor David Kennedy is the Manley O. Hudson Professor of Law at Harvard Law School and Director of the European Law Research Center. He teaches international law, international economic policy, European law, American legal theory, and law and development. Professor Kennedy holds a Doctor of Philosophy (Ph.D.) degree in international affairs from the Fletcher School at Tufts University and a Juris Doctor (J.D.) degree from Harvard Law School. He has practiced law with various international institutions, including the United Nations High Commissioner for Refugees and the Commission of the European Union, and with the private firm of Cleary, Gottlieb, Steen and Hamilton in Brussels. He has worked as a special consultant for the United Nations, as a legal advisor in the Legal Services of the Commission of the European Communities, and consulted for a range of projects involving European and international law. Professor Kennedy has lectured at numerous universities and institutes, and has been a Visiting Professor at New York University, at the University of Paris – Nanterre, at the University of Toronto and at the University of Paris (II). He was a Visiting Scholar at the School of Oriental and African Studies, University of London. He is the author of various articles and books on international law and legal theory, and founder of the New Approaches to International Law project. He is the author of the recently published *Of War and Law*.

Professor Tim McCormack is on the faculty of the University of Melbourne Law School where he serves as the Foundation Australian Red Cross Professor of International Humanitarian Law and also the Foundation Director of the Asia-Pacific Centre for Military Law, a collaborative training and research venture between the Law School and the Australian Defence Force Legal Service. Professor McCormack acted as *amicus curiae* on international law matters to the judges of Trial Chamber III at the International Criminal Tribunal for the former Yugoslavia in The Hague for the trial of Slobodan Milosevic. He was a Vice-President of the Australian Red

Cross and chaired the Australian Red Cross National Advisory Committee on International Humanitarian Law until 2002. Professor McCormack has a Bachelor of Laws (LL.B.) degree from the University of Tasmania (LL.B.) and a Doctor of Philosophy (Ph.D.) degree from Monash University. He has special research interests in the fields of international humanitarian law, international criminal law, arms control and disarmament, and the law of international institutions.

Lieutenant Colonel David Lloyd Roberts, MBE, is a retired officer of the British Army. He graduated from the Royal Military Academy, Sandhurst in 1966 and was commissioned into the Parachute Regiment. Lieutenant Colonel Roberts' army career took him to various conflict zones, including the Former Yugoslavia, the Persian Gulf, Lebanon, Northern Ireland and South Arabia. On leaving the Army in 1993, he joined the International Committee of the Red Cross (ICRC) as its operational security adviser and two years later moved to the department responsible for dissemination of international humanitarian law to armed forces. He has conducted ICRC missions to nearly 30 countries. He holds a Master of Laws (LL.M.) degree in International Human Rights Law from the University of Essex. His humanitarian work includes a consultancy mission for the Office of the United Nations High Commissioner for Human Rights to investigate allegations of mass killings in Northern and Central Afghanistan in 1997–98. He retired from the ICRC in 2003 and is now a consultant and lecturer on international humanitarian law, human rights and security issues. His published works include *The Law of Armed Conflict*, a training manual for armed and security forces that were published by the ICRC and is now translated into six languages.

Professor Michael N. Schmitt is Professor of International Law at the George C. Marshall European Center for Security Studies in Garmisch-Partenkirchen, Germany and also serves as Director of the Program in Advanced Security Studies. Professor Schmitt served in the United States Air Force for 20 years before joining the Marshall Center faculty. During his military career, he specialized in operational and international law and was senior legal adviser to multiple Air Force units, including units conducting combat operations over Northern Iraq. Formerly on the faculties of the United States Air Force Academy and Naval War College, he also has been a Visiting Scholar at Yale Law School and lectures regularly at the International Institute of Humanitarian Law and the NATO School. The author of many scholarly articles on law and military affairs and contributing editor for multiple volumes of the US Naval War College's International Law Studies (the "Blue Book") series, his works have been published in Belgium, Chile, Germany, Israel, Peru, the United Kingdom and the United States. Professor

Schmitt is a member of the American Society of International Law and the International Law Association (British Branch). He serves on the Editorial Board of the International Review of the Red Cross, the Executive Committee of the American Society of International Law's Lieber Society, the Steering Committee for Harvard University's International Humanitarian Law Research Initiative, and Office of the High Commissioner for Human Right's Advisory Board on Human Rights Training for National Armed Forces.

Commander Dale Stephens, Royal Australian Navy (RAN), is on the faculty of the US Naval War College's International Law Department. He joined the faculty following a year in residence at Harvard University School of Law from which he received a Master of Laws (LL.M.) degree. His previous assignments have included Fleet Legal Officer, Maritime Headquarters Australia (Sydney); Deputy Director Operations Law, Strategic Operations Division (Canberra) and Chief Legal Officer, UN Transitional Administration in East Timor Peacekeeping Force Headquarters. Commander Stephens has served as a Legal Officer in the RAN since being admitted to practice in 1989 and has had considerable experience in matters of operational and international law, especially in the context of combined operations. He is the author of several articles dealing with, *inter alia*, the law of naval mine warfare, navigational rights under the 1982 United Nations Convention on the Law of the Sea and the intersection of the law of armed conflict and human rights.

Colonel Kenneth W. Watkin, Canadian Forces, is the Deputy Judge Advocate General/Operations where he is responsible for the provision of operational and international legal advice regarding deployments of the Canadian Forces. During his more than 20 years as a military legal officer, Colonel Watkin has served as the Special Assistant to the Judge Advocate General, the Assistant Judge Advocate General/Atlantic Region, and the Deputy Judge Advocate at a major army base in Petawawa, Ontario. Colonel Watkin has also been the Director of offices dealing with human rights and information law, operational law, claims and civil litigation, and training. His operational law experience has included service as a legal adviser to the Canadian Navy, advising Canadian commanders in Bosnia and as the Deputy Judge Advocate General/Operations at the time of the terrorist attacks on September 11, 2001. He was the legal advisor to a 1993 military/civilian Board of Inquiry that investigated the Canadian Airborne Regiment Battle Group in Somalia. Colonel Watkin has Bachelor of Laws (LL.B.) and Master of Laws (LL.M.) degrees from the Queen's University Law School, Kingston, Ontario. He is a widely published author on a variety of operational law topics, including the law of armed conflict.

Index

A

B

C

D

E

F

G

H

I

J

K

L

M

N

O

P

R

S

T

U

V

W

Z